W9-BPO-776

WITHDRAWN

Illinois Central College
Learning Resource Center

Productive Speaking
for
Business and the Professions

Productive Speaking
for
Business and the Professions

JAMES N. HOLM

Professor of Speech and
Chairman of Rhetoric and Public Address
Kent State University

Allyn and Bacon, Inc.   Boston

Dedicated to the Memory of
My Father,
Who Often Asked When This
Book Would Be in Print.

Preface

THIS BOOK PRESENTS THE ACT OF SPEECH COMMUNICATION BOTH AS an event in the continuing life process of a business, industrial, or professional organization, and as a part of the human interaction which takes place in that life process. Thus on the one hand it views its subject as one of the fundamental forces which create social organization, and on the other as an element in the total behavior of a human being.

At the same time the book deals directly with the main concern of the student, that of improving his own communicative skills. To do so, it recognizes four common forms of speech communication—person-to-person talk, interviewing, group interaction, and public speaking—and offers specific principles and methods by which a person can function effectively in each.

No book can escape expressing the author's experience, and so it is with this. For nearly thirty years I have been teaching courses in business and professional speaking, and for more than twenty I have served in business offices and industrial classrooms as teacher, consultant, and lecturer. Moreover, I have been involved as director or participant in more conventions and conferences than I care to count, wherein people were brought together from the academic and business worlds to consider their mutual communication problems. Consequently this book draws from both the theories of the scholar and the workaday needs and experiences of the manager or administrator. The philosophy it expresses can be summarized by the following principles:

1. Productive communication begins in the *person* of an individual who is both psychologically healthy and personally responsible, and who uses the principles and methods of speech as part of a way of life.

2. Speech is only an element in a larger process of communication in which the listener shares with the speaker equal responsibility for the communicative outcome.

3. Productive communication stems in part from an understanding of perception and motivation as fundamentals of interaction.

4. Business, industrial, and professional speech communication is unique, not in the principles and methods to be learned, but in their application to the life and structure of the economic world.

5. Business and professional organizations are an integral part of the American industrial free society, and with government and other social institutions, bear a responsibility for the well-being of that society.

The book is intended primarily for undergraduate students who are preparing for careers in business, industry, or the professions, and who will take one or more courses designed to develop their communicative skills. If my experience is any criterion, many of these students already have held at least one significant job, and some will be working full or part time while studying. And while the text is aimed at the undergraduate, much of the material has been tested with graduate students seeking a Master's degree in Business Administration, who have found the content both relevant and challenging. Therefore, I hope the book will be useful to other students or to those who may seek self-improvement.

I am grateful for the help of the uncounted writers and speakers whose ideas have become integral with my own, and whose influence cannot be individually recognized. Then there are the many students who have written useful commentaries on some chapters, and whose suggestions have strengthened the whole. More specifically, I am indebted to friends and co-workers for reading sections of the manuscript and offering constructive advice: Michael Dubetz, Charles R. Petrie, Jr., and Thomas McManus who shared offices with me, Martin Baron of the Psychology Department, Maurice Baum of the Philosophy Department, whose specialty is business ethics, and Robert E. Hill, former Dean of the College of Business Administration at Kent State University, now President of Chico State College. I was helped, too, by Clyde O. DeLong, former President of the B. F. Goodrich Industrial Products Corporation, and by my wife, Sarah, whose experience teaching university speech classes and speech courses for the American Savings and Loan Institute was perceptively useful. Finally, I would like to thank the many individuals and organizations who granted permission to quote from copyrighted materials.

Two observations on the content may be helpful. First, because learning seems better when a given principle is seen in several contexts, there has been little attempt to treat a principle only once. Rather, it is discussed wherever its application is pertinent to a given situation or form of speech. Second, although the majority of the cases used for illustration are based on actual instances or events, the names are invented and any similarity to the names of real persons is accidental.

JAMES N. HOLM
Kent, Ohio

Contents

CONTENTS

CONTENTS

Part One

THE CONTEXT

Chapter 1

Speech Communication
in Business and
Industry

The subject of communication is of vital interest not only to those especially devoted to employee relations, and to leaders in the industrial field, but also to men in widely divergent walks of life. Historians, psychologists, clergymen, teachers, politicians, anthropologists, and physicists, as well as industrialists, personnel administrators, and salesmen, have made substantial contributions to our understanding of the nature of the industrial society by emphasizing the importance of communication in their particular fields.[1]

RAYMOND W. PETERS
Esso Standard Oil Company

YOU ARE PREPARING FOR A CAREER IN OUR AMERICAN INDUSTRIALIZED democracy. Perhaps you have already entered upon that career, and are concerned with improving your competence in order to fit yourself for greater responsibility. In either event you have discovered —or you will discover before long—that whatever your vocation, you must work with and through people. And to do this you cannot escape communicating with them.

[1] R. W. Peters, *Communication Within Industry* (New York: Harper & Brothers, 1949), p. xiv.

3

Nils Johnson, a nationally-known architect, discovered he could not be a hermit. Says he, "I went into architecture because I had trouble talking with people, and the idea of working alone over a drawing board appealed to me. Now I have found that at least 50 percent of my time is taken in selling my architectural ideas to others. I couldn't escape talking."

Like Nils Johnson, thousands of people have sought careers which they thought did not demand serious or critical speaking contact with others. They have prepared to be bookkeepers, clerks, designers, dentists, or statisticians, hoping to minimize the amount of talking they would have to do. Part of them have repeated Nils Johnson's discovery—that in order to succeed on the job it was necessary for them to develop skill in speaking. Many have set about the task of improving their communication skills, while others are content to let the problem remain a barrier to more effective job performance.

But the fact that you are reading this book indicates that you are hoping for a career which will lead you into growing responsibility. You are concerned with your ability to meet the communicative demands of that career, and desirous of improving your skills. Let's examine some of the demands.

Effective speech communication must be developed

Studies have shown that of the total time people spend in communicating with others—reading, writing, listening, and speaking—approximately three quarters is used in speaking and listening. You can expect, then, to do much more talking and listening than you do reading or writing. Yet, while you have been carefully taught to read and write, you have had relatively little instruction in speaking and probably none in listening. You have exerted the least effort in increasing your skill in the communication activities which you will use most.

Many people seek refuge from these uncomfortable facts in the rationalization that they have been talking and listening since childhood, and have had no need to be taught. Unfortunately, most of them also assume that they speak and listen adequately. This is not necessarily true. Speaking is learned behavior, the same as reading; the first we begin to "pick up" in infancy, the second is taught from childhood. If people, in the course of growing up,

4

automatically developed effectiveness in speech communication, we should expect to find a wide-spread high level of competency. But such is not the case. Productive speech is much more than the uttering of words. It necessitates skill in thinking, the ability to understand people and to present ideas clearly and acceptably to them, a knowledge of listening as the reciprocal of speaking, and a host of other learned elements which we shall consider in later chapters. There is little reason to conclude that behavior which is "picked up" is skilled or well done.

As a matter of fact, common testimony is to the contrary, for the greatest demand for training in speech comes from those who have discovered that they must talk with people in the course of their work, and that they do so very ineffectively. Speaking at a convention of the National Association of Retail Druggists, James Cops, Executive Secretary, reported that only 50 percent of the graduates of a midwest pharmacy school had taken a course in speaking while in school, but that 99 percent of them after graduation said *they wished they had taken one.*

This book, then, is designed to help you develop the skills necessary to meet the speech demands of your career. It cannot replace persistent and supervised practice, but it can and will act as your guide to increasing effectiveness through understanding the basic forms and principles of speech communication as they apply to the world of business, industry, and the professions.

Communication is an integral part of any enterprise

Some two thousand years ago in the isles of Greece, Isocrates wrote, "Because there has been implanted in us the power to persuade each other and to make clear to each other whatever we desire, not only have we escaped the life of wild beasts, but we have come together and founded cities and made laws and invented arts; and, generally, there is no institution devised by man which the power of speech has not helped us to establish."[2]

If the power of speech made it possible for the Greeks to create enterprises and establish institutions, the full power of a more complete system of communication is even more necessary to estab-

---

[2] Quoted in Donald Lemen Clark, *Rhetoric in Greco-Roman Education* (New York: Columbia University Press, 1957), p. 53.

lish and maintain every enterprise and institution of modern America. The world has vastly changed since Isocrates wrote, and the change has made the skills and arts of communication even more important. Today architects design offices, factories, cathedrals, hospitals, and embassies to serve the communicative needs of the people who will use these buildings. It is literally true that nothing can be accomplished in our world without employing the power to communicate.

Why is this so? Not because of our modern mass communications, nor because of the way we can instantly transmit intelligence across vast distances. Telstar is only a dramatic symbol of technical triumphs. It is evidence that man invents to serve his needs. In this case his need lies in the fact that in our democratic industrialized society we must communicate or perish.

TODAY'S INDUSTRIAL SOCIETY COMPELS IMPROVED COMMUNICATION

The increasing need for better communication exists in the nature of our society and can be explained, at least in part, by three characteristics of our society. The first is the accelerating growth of knowledge. Learning at a constantly increasing tempo makes it difficult, if not impossible, for a business or professional person to keep abreast of developments in his field or affecting his field. "An engineer who was graduated 10 years ago," says a college dean, "is obsolete." Knowledge in chemistry is now doubling every eight years, while discoveries in physics outstrip publication space by at least one full year.

Outside the sciences, study, research, and change likewise affect every other field of endeavor, making the dissemination of new knowledge and of up-to-date thinking of vital importance. Physicians attend seminars and conventions to learn the latest developments. Potato growers listen to the reports of agricultural experts. Teachers take night courses or receive federal subsidies to attend special summer seminars. Production men are given on-the-job training to bring them up to the minute. H. E. Peiffer, former President of the Akron Council of Engineering and Scientific Societies writes, "Men of the scientific community are turning more and more to talk as a means of conveying ideas and distributing information in this age of high speed developments."[3] The same statement could be made of any business, industrial, or professional group. All agree that the accelerating rate of learning makes good communication a primary need.

A second characteristic of our society which contributes to the need for better communication is the high degree of specialization among skilled or professional people. Just as the specialists must communicate among themselves to maintain competency in their fields, so must they, because of the narrowness of their areas, work together in teams to accomplish major tasks. A given team may be made up of a variety of trained people, each contributing his skill and knowledge to an assignment for which all share responsibility. We have created a society in which teams and task forces make up significant units of work. A meeting of doctors, psychiatrists, and ministers is held to help each specialist in his counseling work. Members of the clergy meet with architects to consider the application of architectural skills to the needs of worship and fellowship. A federal public health official declares that problems of the aged will be solved only by teamwork that combines the efforts of government, voluntary agencies, the medical profession, and specialists in gerontology. Dr. Martin Andersen of the University of California writes:[4]

> More and more . . . engineers and scientists are called upon to work in "teams" on problems of development, production, and "trouble-shooting." Hence, not only are technical skills and knowledge needed, but they must have the ability to work with others in problem-solving situations. Thus, an ideal engineer, scientist, or technician is the one who is well trained in his capacity, knows the relationships of that specialty to other areas, (and) can communicate effectively.

In short, specialization breeds interdependence, interdependence necessitates team-work, and team-work makes good communication imperative.

The third characteristic of modern industrial democracy which creates the need for good communication is the growth in size of many of our enterprises and institutions. This growth is reflected in a clear tendency toward decentralization. As an enterprise spreads

---

[3] Personal letter, October 6, 1961. Used by permission.
[4] From a cover letter of a research survey. Used by permission.

out, administration and management tend to become autonomous within each unit. Each decentralized unit must then be staffed by persons capable of making decisions, often as part of management "teams," and frequently on the basis of information and evaluation supplied by other units. The decisions in turn must be transmitted to all who are affected by them. Communication must flow freely, not only within each unit, but among all units, and this may involve men located in fifty states and in foreign lands. Du Pont, for instance, has more than 90,000 people working in 69 plants in 25 states to produce 1200 basic products, with outlets in 76 nations and 39 colonies or dependencies. Its research is done by 2,100 technicians and scientists in 38 laboratories in 8 states. The communication flow in an enterprise like this staggers the imagination, yet it differs only in amount and complexity from that in a small company or a large school system. Much of the entire flow, of course, is in the form of written communication, yet commercial airlines and industrial aircraft fill the skies with men and women going from place to place for personal conferences.

Our accelerating accumulation of knowledge, our specialization and interdependence, and the growth and decentralization of enterprise, then, impose upon professional persons and upon executives and managers a vast burden to communicate and to do so effectively. Said Benjamin Wood, Executive Director of the American Rayon Institute, "A scientist in one of Du Pont's 38 laboratories, for example, must be personally articulate. His idea or development can only be extended to other technicians, can only reach the point of product application if he is personally articulate. He must be able to express and explain, not only to other technicians but to management, if his work is to be of real value."[5] For this reason good communication becomes indivisible from good management. It also becomes an integral part of the performance of any single professional person because he must also live and work in groups and among people.

[5] Speech to the College of Business Administration, University of Akron, May 12, 1956.

COMMUNICATION GENERATES ORGANIZATION

From the foregoing we can visualize any enterprise as a network of people among whom communication must flow. Some of the channels of communication may be understood by looking at the organizational chart of a typical enterprise, for messages will speed back and forth among the persons or offices identified on the chart. Other messages, of course, flow along channels not so officially identified, including the well-known "grapevine," which is a very real source of information in an enterprise even if it is not always entirely accurate.

Within this communicative network some of the messages will flow downward, from those of higher to those of lower authority or responsibility. Some of them will be sent upward, combining with the downward flow to make a system of vertical communication which links leaders and followers, managers and workers. At the same time other messages will be flowing horizontally, from one manager to another of equal rank or status, from one person to others of similar responsibility. Vertical and horizontal communication together make up the official internal communications of an enterprise—those which knit individuals and groups into a working whole of many parts.

Yet the enterprise also has an important set of external communications, for its people must be in touch with agents, suppliers, purchasers, stockholders, government agencies, donors, counterparts in other organizations, and a very important public of some sort. Professional and vocational affiliations must be maintained, an understanding public must be cultivated, business contacts must be kept fresh, and customers or patrons must be sought and satisfied. External communication becomes the vital counterpart of internal communication.

It is within such a network that you take your place as a communicative unit, a part of the nervous system of the enterprise. You will become, if you are not now, a vital link in receiving, originating, or transmitting messages, and upon you will fall some of the responsibility for the success or failure of the firm.

Yet we cannot consider communication as an end in itself. It is a means to an end, and is fully understandable only in terms of its function. Within the network and through you as a part of it, what messages are sent and received? For what purposes are these messages transmitted?

In the great complex of people who make up an enterprise, decisions must be made, and these decisions generally rest on an understanding of facts and relationships known to the decision-makers only as a result of some sort of communication. Rarely do decision-makers gather intelligence by personal inquiry and observation alone. Decisions once made must then be transmitted and often "sold" to those who will be affected. In the same managerial process, instructions, descriptions, and orders—information of all sorts—must be communicated or disseminated. Commands and orders must also frequently be "sold" so they will be carried out fully and effectively. Ideas must be explained and suggestions presented persuasively. Policy must be clarified, and people must frequently be exhorted to follow established policy. Attitudes of colleagues or cooperating personnel at various levels must be understood and sometimes must be developed or altered. Contracts and understandings must be negotiated. People must coordinate and harmonize their diverse activities. Knowledge must be shared; truth must displace rumor. Viable working relationships must be developed. Within the enterprise and with its external contacts an atmosphere conducive to understanding must be established through continual education and persuasion.

The constant flow of information among members of the organization reveal an enterprise in its true nature. It is a living, dynamic system, a process directing itself toward a goal, a being made up of parts which must work together if the organization is to succeed. Just as a nervous system is necessary for a human being to live and function, so a communicative system is necessary for the corporate existence of an enterprise.

Thus it is only through effective communication that an enterprise can function. From such an understanding we may arrive at a definition of communication as *a process whose purpose is the exchange of thoughts, ideas, opinions, and attitudes to establish understanding, guide behavior, create a common outlook, cultivate cooperation, and help provide the human satisfactions necessary to operating a successful enterprise.* It is an endless process of reading, listening, writing, and talking, never ceasing by day or night in

many an organization. It is integral to all functions of the enterprise.

Communication is part of every job

Through understanding and control of this process of communication, managers are able to manage, administrators to administer,
and every responsible officer to implement his responsibility. The
manager's job is to determine the content, the timing, the medium
or media, the audience, and the direction of each message, never
failing to keep in mind that because of rank, status, or position even
his slightest act, or utterance may have communicative significance
for others whose work behavior may be affected by the message.

Whether your job title is superintendent or admissions clerk,
whether your work is in accounting, production, development, engineering, finance, quality control or any other department of an
enterprise, communication will be an important part of your responsibility—perhaps its most important part. Communication is
involved in every relationship which exists between you and others
in your organization or those who may be concerned with it in some
way. Nor is this relationship shaped only by the specific messages
you send and receive—the letters, memoranda, consultations, interviews, or speeches—but by your every word and act from which
others will extract meaning whether you intend them to or not.
Since you must work with others, you cannot escape communicating
with them; this fact affects every other aspect of your job performance.

Poor communication is costly

Not long ago a department manager in one of the nation's largest
steel fabricators received a letter from a division of state government. The intent of the letter was not clear, and to get things
clarified the manager had to drive more than a hundred miles to the
state capital for an explanation. His company paid his time and
expenses as a hidden cost of poor communication.

Similarly, two hundred people taking part in a civic project
were released from work to hear the project leader explain the task
they were undertaking. The meeting lasted two hours, but the

11

leader's explanations were so confusing that another meeting had to be called for clarification. Four hundred man-hours of working time were lost because one person could not discharge his responsibility to speak clearly.

Whether written or spoken, poor communication unnecessarily increases the costs of doing business for thousands of enterprises each year, just as it did in these two cases. The costs of poor communication are not confined to wage and salary payments, however. They are sometimes to be found in production costs:[6]

> As an example of the need for closer integration of communication skills in industry, a few days ago the vice president of a large foundry was analyzing his monthly operating report. He discovered that an expected reduction in processing cost in a certain department was not in fact reflected in the cost accounting report. The Department Head was called in and each mechanical processing stage was examined in detail until the step which was to be changed was reached. The change had not been made even though the Staff had been given instructions for the change. The breakdown was in the human element. As the communication filtered down the lines of organization, the significance of the change was not understood. A loss in profit was the result. This experience is repeated too often in both business and industry.

Most business and professional people fully realize that if communication were eliminated for 24 hours, any enterprise would be frozen into immobility. Effective communication is a way of getting things done, and to the degree that it fails, to that degree things do not get done—or they are done grudgingly or poorly or incorrectly. Bad communication consumes time, money, and personal effort. It creates misunderstanding and sometimes friction and resentment. It results in faulty planning, bad decisions, erroneous operations, and administrative blunders.

Good communication is profitable

Conversely, good communication can be a method of reducing costs and creating profits. A non-profitmaking institution such as a hospi-

---

[6] Judd Perkins, "Staff and Line Communication in Business," *Central States Speech Journal*, VIII. (Fall, 1948), pp. 16–17.

tal is concerned with its communications to reduce costs and improve service. A profit-making institution such as the General Electric Company is concerned with communication as it may add to the profit side of the ledger. "Effective communication is a way to make money, not to spend it," explained C. J. Dover in discussing his work as a communication consultant with General Electric. The methods, channels, and content of communication, therefore, need to be considered in the light of their effect on the efficient or profitable administration of the enterprise.

Thus, alert managers in all types of firms and enterprises continue to seek ways of improving their communications and of solving problems to which profitable communication may provide some answer. Here is a list of problems discussed by business and professional people in recent conferences, illustrating some of the areas with which they are concerned:

How can we get the customers of our bank to feel the genuineness of our interest in them?

How can we get all foremen to understand the detailed terms of the new labor-management contract?

How can we keep employees appreciative of the health and hospitalization benefits provided in all employment contracts?

How can we keep our production people aware of the continuing need for safety precautions?

How can we get citizens of the town to take pride in the new plant we have located there?

How can we improve the foreman's sense of identification with management?

How can we combat the untrue rumors that the home office is going to be relocated?

How can we make our annual performance review of office personnel more productive?

How can we get distributors to fully understand the features of the new models?

How can we overcome the feeling some of the public has that our rates are too high?

What should we tell our employees about the coming changes in our operation?

How can we get our clients to see the virtues of the policy we propose in contrast to their own ideas?

How much should we tell our patients about the nature of their illnesses?

How can we reduce employee absenteeism?
How effective are our bulletin board notices?
How can we best maintain a high turnover of inventory?
How can we get the home office to appreciate our customers' need for quick delivery of special orders?
How can we get better cooperation in keeping people from leaving cars on the main streets in a blizzard?
How can we get employees to tell us more than just what they think we want to hear?
How can we reduce the cost of maintaining buildings and grounds?

Some of these problems are directly concerned with communication, and others are not. Yet the factor of communication exists in each and must be considered in arriving at an answer. Communication, for the people involved in the problems, becomes a part of the total operation, important in reducing costs and improving service and profits.

EFFECTIVE SPEECH IS VITAL TO THE TOTAL COMMUNICATION PATTERN OF AN ENTERPRISE

Within the communication flow of any enterprise there can be no real comparison of whether the written or spoken media is the more useful, necessary, or dependable. Both are indispensable, and each possesses qualities which make it preferable under given conditions. Frequently, maximum effect can be achieved only when both are combined to secure a needed result. You may find that your job demands an alternate use of your skill in both media.

The fact remains that on the job you will probably talk or listen more than you read or write. A recent study reported that the average production-line foreman may spend as much as half his working time in talking with others, while another investigation revealed that representative members of top management spend an equal amount of their time in conferences alone. Clearly then, any person who narrows his concept of communication to written or printed material fails to recognize the importance of oral communication in his daily role.

Talk is important in its consequences, too. A study made by Dr. Thomas L. Dahle, then at Purdue University, concluded that of five methods of transmitting information to employees (oral, written, combined oral and written, pictorial, and the grapevine), the most effective was the combined oral-written method. This was, however, only slightly more effective than the purely oral method. Similar results were obtained in three different types of enterprises.

In short, we recognize that speech is the most frequently used form of communication and that it is highly effective in getting results when used with skill. We know further that it is preferred to written messages, at least by an important percentage of employees.

What unique elements of oral communication help explain its effectiveness and desirability? It is reasonable to suppose that the fact of face-to-face confrontation (or a close approach to it via the telephone) gives oral an immediate benefit over written communication in many situations. The speaker has the vital advantage of deriving immediate feedback from the listener. He can observe or listen to the reactions of those to whom he speaks, and thus modify his communication to fit the demands of the situation. As a consequence he is granted an opportunity to overcome barriers which might distort his message if undetected. Beyond this he has the power to emphasize his intent by the resources of his speaking personality, by appropriate physical action such as gesture, or by vocal nuance.

The listener, in oral communication, has a feeling of "belonging" to the communication process which is missing in written or printed messages. No longer is he simply the target at which the message is aimed, but is, rather, a full participant in the development of mutual understanding. This is why Professor Harold Zelko of the Pennsylvania State University writes:[7]

> If the goal were only to keep people informed, this could be accomplished in most instances through the written medium. But you can't get people's reactions by having them read a printed page. You have to give them the opportunity to ask questions, to make comments, contribute judgments, and talk things over. There is no substitute for the oral face-to-face relationship in accomplishing these goals.

The results of oral communication, then, may be a greater depth of understanding of the message, a quicker willingness to see

[7] Harold P. Zelko, "How Effective Are Your Company Communications?" *Advanced Management*, XXI, No. 2 (Feb., 1956), p. 11.

and accept the point of the communicator, and greater certainty of full communication. In addition, oral communication can effect an exchange of meaning rather than only convey a message, creating heightened cooperation through mutual participation in the process.

In this chapter we have surveyed the context in which your speaking will take place. We have seen that communication is an integral part of any enterprise, that poor communication is costly while good communication is profitable, and that effective speech is a vital part of the entire communicative system of an organization. We have noted that a successful career can be expected to require ever-increasing effectiveness in speaking and listening as well as in reading and writing.

The balance of this book will be concerned with improving your abilities as a speech communicator. A very able man once observed, "Speakers are neither born nor made. They are born to be made." The same is true of listeners, and while your immediate interest may lie in improving your *speaking*, you will also have to work at improving your *listening* if you expect to function effectively on the job. Speaking and listening are complementary elements of the process of speech communication which we discuss in the next chapter.

Chapter 2

The Process of Com-
munication

*It is all too easy to succumb to the notion that there is a quick,
ready formula for establishing "right" communication patterns and
obtaining solutions applicable to all problems facing every human
being attempting to exchange ideas and information. . . . Effective
communication results only from an understanding of the situation
and a willingness to engage in an exchange. . . . All the techniques
are a means to an end, nothing more.*[1]

J. L. VAUGHAN
Chancellor for Community Colleges
The University of Virginia

IN CHAPTER I WE CONSIDERED THE PLACE OF COMMUNICATION IN
business and industry, and we defined the purpose of communication, but we did not describe the nature of communication nor examine the matrix in which it takes place.

What actually happens when human beings communicate with
one another? What effect does the environment in which they communicate have upon their talk?

As you began reading this book, you were undoubtedly concerned with but a single question: "How can I talk more effectively
with other people?" This concern is understandable, and even necessary, but there is more to speech communication than one's desire to

[1] J. L. Vaughan, "Communications for the Layman," *Business Topics*, IX,
No. 1 (Winter, 1961), p. 63.

speak effectively. As a matter of fact, you will be unable to do your best talking unless you see communication as a process in which your talk is only a part.

You will need to be impressed by the fact that communicating is not a simple act, and that to have talked does not at all mean that you have successfully communicated. You will need to understand that because an endless variety of *people* are involved there is therefore infinite opportunity for obstacles and breakdowns to distort what you intend to convey, or to prevent your message from getting through at all. You will need to see speaking as a form of behavior which takes place within a social or organizational setting and which is therefore conditioned by that setting. In the words of Weaver and Zelko,[2]

> [communication] appears simple because we readily think of the process as merely one person conveying thoughts and ideas to another. But as we stop to realize that this raises questions such as what kind of persons are involved, how much do they differ, what is their status, in what setting is the communication happening, and what is the degree of importance or complexity of the message, we have only scratched the surface in trying to understand what communication is.

Let us now go beyond the definition of communication in terms of its purposes which you found in Chapter I, and examine the nature of the process.

THE COMMUNICATION PROCESS IS A JOINT DYNAMIC INTERACTION OF FOUR ELEMENTS

In the previous chapter we noted that the purpose of communication was the exchange of messages among people. Many persons are content with this minimum understanding, and conclude that the process is therefore an uncomplicated one in which ideas are handed back and forth like so many loaves of bread. It is not that simple. As a matter of fact, the only thing which actually goes back and forth when people talk is a series of signals or symbols. Each party to the communicative process assigns his own meaning to the

---

[2] Robert G. Weaver and Harold P. Zelko, "Talking Things Over on the Job," *Supervision*, XX, No. 5 (May, 1958), p. 5. Copyright May, 1958.

signals, and everyone assumes or hopes that the meanings are common and that therefore the ideas are mutually understood. This desirable outcome is never perfectly accomplished, and sometimes the assigned meanings are so different that nothing whatever is shared except a commonality of signals.

Let's consider individually the four basic elements which comprise the communication process: sender, code, field, and receiver.

The sender intends a message

To initiate communication there must be a sender. Let's assume that this is you, finding yourself in a situation in which talking is necessary or desirable. To begin with, some *stimulus* sets off within you the complicated series of events we call speech. At times the stimulus may be external—something in the environment, such as a "conversation piece" in an office or living room, placed there for the purpose of stimulating conversation. Or the pressure of silence could drive you to speak, to break otherwise undesirable social tensions. Again, it could be your glimpse of an impending accident which stimulates you to cry a warning. At other times the stimulus may be internal, originating within yourself—perhaps an excited desire to share your recent triumph in golf, an urge to announce a piece of news, or a yearning to express sympathy in a moment of sadness. Regardless of its source, however, the stimulus initiates your speech behavior.

Beyond the stimulus, you must have some *motive* for speaking. Unless you sense that some benefit, some useful purpose, will be achieved, you are apt to remain silent. Indeed, you may have a counter motive urging you not to speak, and unless your motivation to communicate is stronger than its opposite, the stimulus will not impel you to talk.

The motive urging you to speak may be eagerness to fulfill an assigned task, a desire to enhance your prestige, the hope of promoting the solution of a vexing problem, the necessity of influencing the behavior of others, or some other incentive. If this incentive is stronger than your apprehension of undesirable consequences as a result of speaking, or of your uncertainty, tension, or insecurity, you organize yourself to talk.

You should not, however, confuse your motive for speaking with your *purpose*, which is the response you intend to produce, the

19

behavior you hope to induce in your receiver. Perhaps you want the listener or listeners to accept your idea, to think better of you, to understand the difficulties you have had to conquer in completing an assignment, or to perform a specified act or series of actions. Your motive should be understood as the personal benefit or satisfaction you expect to derive from speaking, your purpose as the response you wish to elicit from the listener.

As you were being stimulated and motivated, and as you were formulating your purpose for speaking, you were also perceiving the hearer and the circumstances of time and environment in which the talk would take place. In the light of these perceptions and from your background and experience, you now frame a message. You decide what it is you want to communicate, and you begin to choose words with which to express your message. You are ready to begin the process of communication.

As you speak, your entire being participates. Your memory of the past and your command of language are involved. Your hopes or expectations shape your expression, for what you say will be determined in high degree by your desire to influence future events or behavior. And your emotional state will be a part of your speaking, for you may communicate with grim determination, sharp anger, impassioned authority, or self-conscious diffidence. Your emotional condition includes not only your own awareness of feelings, but the physiological concomitants such as pulse rate, breathing, muscular tonicity, and the activity of the glandular system. Your entire nervous system is involved, including the brain and the central, the cerebrospinal, and the autonomic systems. You are a totality in speech, and it is the total person which sends a message, not your voice and language alone. The effective speaker is one whose whole being is an integrated unit dedicated to sending a forthright message.

The message is transmitted in code

The second element of the communication process is the *code of signals* which is used to *transmit* the intended message. As a telegraph message is sent in code along a wire in the form of electrical impulses, so your message is transmitted in code as light waves and sound waves through the atmosphere. It is these waves which your receiver intercepts and translates or decodes as he comprehends them.

The receiver is likely to be impressed first, and perhaps lastingly, by what he sees. Your posture, gestures and action, your facial expression, your muscular tonicity, the signs of emotion or lack of it, are carried on light waves and appear in the eye of the beholder as signals for interpretation. If you are well integrated as a speaker, the visual code will amplify and refine the verbal message. Significant and purposive physical action is always a vital part of good speaking.

Yet there may be times when your appearance, dress, or physical behavior may importantly modify or even counteract what you would like your words to convey. In a booklet for businessmen bound for Southeast Asia, the Federation of British Industries has recently advised, "Do not talk to a Chinese businessman (the most plentiful type in Southeast Asia) with hands on hips; he will take it for a sign of anger." And while our own code of visible signals may not be as highly formalized as that of the Chinese, we do know from surveys that in many speaking situations such things as failure to look another in the eye, signs of nervousness, or untidy personal appearance do have negative impacts. *What the receiver sees should be congruent with what he hears.*

Unlike the light waves, the sound waves carry two sets of signals. The receiver perceives distinct cues, first of all, from your voice and diction, adding such cues to his total impression of you and your message. He will not separate the sender from the message. A vibrant voice and clear diction stir up one kind of meaning in a listener, while a dull voice and garbled diction stir up another. As Thomas Carlyle once wrote to Ralph W. Emerson, "Many voices are not human, but more or less bovine, porcine, canine, and one's soul dies away in sorrow in the sound of them." Both vocal tone and articulation transmit something of the character and personality, the purpose, the background, and the intention of a speaker. They are a part of the code.

Sound, of course, transmits the language code, which is the most important set of signals in speech. This code is made up of the words you selected as you framed and uttered your intended message. Each word is a symbol which represents some part of your life experience and which in this way has meaning for you. You may be a baseball enthusiast, for instance, and so the word "run" symbolizes for you a successful circle of the bases by a uniformed player who thereby scores a tally for his side. This symbol brings to your mind a memory of the sights, sounds, and excitement of a myriad of games you have watched or played. On the other hand the symbol "Napoleon" may recall for you only the memory of a few pages in a history book read some time ago. Thus words as symbols vary in the richness and intensity of their meaning according to the experiences you are able to associate with them.

Each of the words you speak occurs within a context of other words which all together comprise the verbal element of your transmission. The receiver may assign meaning to any given word as it recalls significant experience to his mind, or he may find clues to your intention from the verbal context or from the visual and audible context. In effective communication the three codes combine in response to the speaker's integration of mind, body, and purpose, producing a single impression.

The surrounding field influences the communication process

The transmission of signals, the second element of the communication process, takes place within a specific set of circumstances made up of the time, place, and physical and social surroundings. These surrounding factors we may call the *field* in which communication occurs, and they make up the third element of the process.

Specific factors within the field, or the field as a whole, affect both the sender and the receiver of the message, and may at times affect the transmission. As a consequence the field can be a strong determinant of the degree of success of the communication.

Yet too frequently people seem unaware of the effect of the field on the success of their talk. They make sales calls on housewives at dinner time, they interrupt the chief when he's trying to concentrate on a problem, they call the teacher out of the classroom in the midst of an important demonstration, they announce a new policy only after rumors and gossip have been flying for days, they talk too long at a meeting already past adjournment time, or in a noisy shop they hold conversations which should be held in a quiet office.

In contrast, a skilled speaker will be sensitive to the impact of time, place, and surroundings on the success of his communication. He arranges interviews when both he and his respondent will be able to concentrate without competing pressures, he does not interrupt nor infringe on another's time, he resists speaking to an

audience under unfavorable circumstances, and avoids conversations when his colleagues seem concerned with other things. In
short, he knows that there is a time and place to speak and one to be
silent.

The field for a specific communicative situation may extend
beyond the limits of the immediate time, place, and surroundings,
for it may be a part of a larger *matrix* of communication. It may
involve the continuing personal, social, and institutional relationships of those who are talking.

The receiver decodes a message and reacts

The fourth element of the communication process is the *receiver*,
who intercepts the transmission of your message and decodes your
signals. Like you, the receiver must be motivated to participate in
the process by listening intently and by decoding in such a way as to
understand what he thinks you intend him to. He must sense that
listening and responding favorably will benefit him in some way.
Perhaps he may feel that the message itself will be of value to him,
that listening may enhance his status in the organization, or that he
will acquire some fresh insight to provide him the solution of a
professional problem. Or he may listen simply because of friendship
and respect for you. At any rate, if the receiver is motivated he will
pay close attention to the transmission, and will bend his full
abilities to the decoding. But if not motivated, his attention will
lapse and he may listen so carelessly that your words will be heard,
but not understood.

The reception of your message will be conditioned in part by
the way in which your listener perceives both you and the field, and
this will not necessarily be identical with the way you see them. In
fact, speaker and listener only infrequently perceive all elements in
the same way. You may see two youngsters fighting on a crowded
playground, and you approach to bring the disturbance to an end.
You perceive yourself as a friendly peacemaker who, before a group
of on-lookers, brings the wisdom of maturity to a children's quarrel.
But the young disputants see you as a meddlesome interloper who
will cause them to lose face in front of their friends and classmates.
Communication may fail if you do not take into consideration the
differences between what you think you see and what your listener
thinks he sees.

When you succeed in motivating your listener to give you fair and undivided attention and establish with him a common perception of the communicative situation, you must in addition make sure that your message is coded in terms of *his* background and experience. He will interpret your signals in terms of his own daily life, not yours. The word "run" which is rich with baseball significance for you may be decoded by another as a ravel in hosiery, a small creek in the hills, a series of successful shots in billiards, or a range for feeding sheep. Speaker and listener share the signals, but not necessarily the meaning; it is your responsibility to make your talk understandable in terms of your listener's experience.

If you are an able man, skilled in speaking, your listener will decode the message so that the meaning he determines will be similar to, but never identical with, the one you intended. From the total context, including visual and audible signals, language symbols, and the elements of the field, he will create a meaning consistent with his own experience and expectations, and if you are successful, his created meaning will be very similar to the one you intended. In spite of the variances between you and him, if he perceives you as a man of good will and just intent, he will decode as fairly as he can. You may then expect the response you desired. The listener will understand you. Perhaps he will be impressed. He will believe what you have told him. Or he will behave as you have instructed him.

This description of the four elements of the communicative process—*sender, code, field,* and *receiver*—oversimplifies a delicate and complicated dynamic interaction. We have been thinking of you as the speaker, but at any moment your listener may reply, and the entire direction of communication is reversed, with you becoming the receiver. In the interchange of normal conversation, the direction of talk may go back and forth like a tennis ball between players, except that as two or more people mutually stimulate one another, ideas and feelings can cumulate or fresh ones be created. In the middle of a conversation one of the parties may perceive the situation in a new and different light, altering the mood and direction of the talk. The flow is modified as one person's response triggers responding behavior in another. And always each speaker is listening to his own words, or at least is aware of them, and is influenced by his own evaluation of what he is saying and by the effect he estimates he is having on those who listen.

Communication as a process is more than the elements which

comprise it. It is a continuous, on-going and cyclical phenomenon, never static or at rest, and within it lie all the complexities which characterize the behavior of human beings, no two of whom are alike and all of whom are never fully predictable.

Because of the complexity of the process, and because of the infinite variation in human beings who take part in it, speech communication is hazardous. Its success is always uncertain, frequently incomplete, and subject to a host of factors which impede it. To achieve a uniformly more predictable and higher degree of success is not the result of chance, but of understanding and skill which begins by becoming acquainted with the common obstacles. To avoid them is to achieve some of the satisfaction of accomplishment in understanding and mutual cooperation.

OBSTACLES DEVELOPED IN THE COMMUNICATIVE PROCESS IMPEDE OR PREVENT MUTUAL UNDER- STANDING

During the process of communication one of three things may happen to garble the intended message. It may be so blocked that little or none of it gets through meaningfully, it may be so distorted that the message as decoded is only a caricature of the one intended, or it may be changed by addition or subtraction until the message as received is a substantial alteration of the one sent. The following are seven causes of misinterpreted communication.

Differences of viewpoint or background may exist between sender and receiver

When people have in common a strong identity of training, experience, and point of view, communication sometimes is a rapid and efficient process. A single word, a nod, or a glance, can become fraught with meaning which is completely shared by all concerned. Very little talk, for instance, is necessary in an operating room where a team of surgeons and nurses work as a highly disciplined group bent on saving life. Similarly, partners in a law firm, scientists on a research project, members of an athletic team, or players in an orchestra, can efficiently coordinate their efforts through a system of communication based on common experience, common training, and common purpose.

Outside of their professional or organizational competence, however, these same people may well have difficulty in communicating. Because the meaning each assigns to the code must be extracted from his own frame of reference, two people can rarely derive precisely identical understandings of a given transmission. And for this reason, not only is identity of understanding difficult, but often the differences created by diverse backgrounds can create barriers which to a tragic degree block understanding.

When backgrounds vary significantly, communication blockage may reach its maximum. Paul Pigors of the Massachusetts Institute of Technology gives us a sense of the variation in frames of reference which could make mutual understanding very difficult:[3]

> Certain kinds of communication naturally reach and are sent out from the company president. He is occupied with finance and control, is a Big Shot, presumably with a long and broad view; an intelligent individual with a logical mind.
>
> The union president, on the other hand, may be an hourly rated employee, a machinist. As such, he necessarily has a more limited view of company affairs. His understanding and way of talking are bound to be different from those of the company president, even though both are using the English language. When these two people need to talk together, can they do it effectively?

Mr. Pigors' concluding question could again be asked if a member of the City Planning Commission were to meet with a group of citizens to explain to them the necessity of tearing down the homes in which they live to make way for a new expressway. The speaker possesses a frame of reference dedicated to the long view of urban improvement, but the listeners see the proposition from the standpoint of having lived for years in a house and a neighborhood which to them mean home. Can communication be done effectively? In similar situations many a speaker has expressed his frustration in the words, "If I could only make them see it!" Differences in background and viewpoint have completely blocked understanding.

[3] Paul Pigors, *Effective Communication in Industry*. (New York: National Association of Manufacturers, 1949), pp. 17–18.

When you talk with others you can expect mutual understanding only when frames of reference are quite similar, or when differences of viewpoint are carefully considered and the talk is adapted to or understood in terms of the variance. The speaker for the City Planning Commission must see his proposal through the eyes of the home owners before he can make it understandable to them, while they will be better listeners if they are aware that he is a stranger to their outlook and therefore try to grasp the way he sees things.

One or both may have faulty perception of the respondent or field

Two people may have trouble understanding one another not only because their different points of view lead them to assign different meanings to the code, but also because they perceive themselves, each other, or the communicative field differently. Each responds to what he thinks he sees rather than to what he actually may see. Each communicates in terms of what he expects as well as in terms of how he sees himself.

Carl, for instance, is sixteen years old and proud that he now has his driver's license. After the family dinner he asks his father if he may have the car for an hour. Carl sees himself as a fully qualified driver, quite as competent as any other licensed driver. He sees himself as a peer among his friends, many of whom drive automobiles. He perceives his father as an equal, although conservative and a bit out of date. On the other hand, Carl's father sees himself as a benign parent, kindly and understanding, and possessed of the great responsibility of bringing up a son. How does he see Carl? After sixteen years of parenthood, he is still influenced by the two o'clock feedings of infancy, the doctor's bills of childhood, and the insurance policy he took out years ago to make sure of a college education for his boy. He doesn't perceive Carl as Carl perceives himself. To the father, Carl is almost the same lad who joined the Boy Scouts eight years ago. Full communication is hampered; neither is talking to the person he thinks is before him, and neither is quite the individual he believes himself to be.

Or again, consider a state highway patrolman in two different situations. In the first, he has halted a motorist for speeding, and approaches the car. In the second, he has stopped behind a stalled motorist whose lifted hood signals trouble. What does each driver perceive? Each *sees* exactly the same uniform approaching him. But the first *perceives* a threat or danger; the second perceives good will and assurance. The first situation is filled with insecurity; the second, with security. Each will talk to the patrolman *as he sees him*, and as he sees the entire field. And each situation is complicated by the way the patrolman sees himself. If perception is faulty, communication will be blocked.

Each of us projects our own standards and values on those we respect and admire. We perceive those people as similar to ourselves. We tend to project a different set of values and standards on those we dislike. We perceive them as unlike ourselves. We then talk to these people *as we perceive them*. This is one of the reasons why understanding is thwarted, why communication may be distorted. To talk successfully we must try to perceive people as they really are, and we must endeavor to make as objective as possible an assessment of ourselves.

People may vary in language usage

Two people, one speaking English and the other Gaelic, will obviously have difficulty in talking to one another. Yet the handicap is so marked that both are aware of the problem, and, if good will exists, anxious to overcome it. They join forces to achieve understanding. The really serious obstacle to communication happens when one or both assume that their language is common when it is not. Mr. A and Mr. B may both speak the English language, and therefore assume that no language barrier lies between them, failing to realize that there is little common meaning to the words they use.

Since words can mean many things to many people, meanings can become confused and communication distorted even in the most ordinary circumstances. A stranger in Pittsburgh, trying to find a certain street, pulled his car up beside a policeman and inquired directions. "Very simple," said the officer, "follow this street to the top of the bridge and turn left." *Top of the bridge?* Since the bridge was arched, did the officer mean to turn left in the middle where the arch was highest? This would be the middle of the river. Or did he mean to descend to the other side and turn? Common sense dictated the latter, but why use the word "top"?

During a study of the Kennedy-Nixon campaign debates at Purdue University, researchers discovered that subjects listening to selected passages of the debates derived as many as 15 or 16 different meanings from some of the passages. Only 23 per cent of the listeners could agree on the meaning of what was said in some paragraphs. Plainly, skilled speakers trying to make themselves clear and persuasive are misunderstood, even when using ordinary English.

And English is not a common language to many people when technical terms are involved. In our extremely specialized society, every vocation has its own vocabulary which acts as a barrier to communication with those outside the specialization. Most of us are aware of that fact, yet fail to realize the ease by which it traps us. A physician cheerfully reported to his hospitalized patient that her X-rays were "negative." The patient fainted. After reviving the victim, the doctor learned that his word "negative," which to the medical profession means that no organic trouble can be seen, was understood to mean "no hope." To the patient it seemed a death sentence, not reassurance.

Closely related to the confusing use of technical words is the jargon employed by a large fraction of would-be communicators. Jargon is the "secret" vocabulary of a profession or calling, often so secret that even its users aren't certain of the meaning of their language, giving critics the feeling that using jargon is a subtly defensive way of concealing true thought and feeling. Whether the opinion is valid or not, the fact remains that jargon is a barrier to effective communication, as evidenced by the following statement to parents of students in an Arizona high school. The statement supposedly outlined regulations for a student's getting on the honor roll.

A student whose average exhibited performance in all credited subjects in relation to the performance of all other students falls at a level which places him or her on the normal curve of probability at a point falling on the plus side of the mean and between the second and third standard deviations will have made the honor roll first class.

The foregoing example of jargon was written, but much jargon is spoken. Here is the complaint of the wife of a learned professional man :[4]

[4] Robert Gordon, "A Question of Style," *Bulletin of the American Association of University Professors*, XLIII, No. 1 (Spring, 1957), p. 24.

We had just sat down for breakfast and I had made some harmless remark about it being two months until Christmas and I wondered whether we should get our shopping done early this fall. Well, Tom looked at me with a fishy eye and said, "My, you have a strong tendency toward tradition-directed ethnocentrism this morning." My God, Bob . . . "tradition-directed ethnocentrism" before I'd even had my first cup of coffee! Of course, I know he said it just to be funny, but that's the only form his humor seems to take these days—and besides, he talks that way seriously sometimes. Can't you see what I'm up against?

When speakers use such terms as "dollarization," "highocracy," "satellited," or "ruggedize," all of which have appeared as Congressional jargon, they fail to generate a very clear understanding in others, thereby interrupting communication. Unless a speaker deliberately wishes not to be understood, he must be sure that his language is meaningful to his particular audience.

Motivation may block or distort communication

As we have already seen, if common meanings are to be established, both the sender and the receiver must want to communicate. If either lacks the desire to establish understanding, communication will be bad. Some persons, unfortunately, are not motivated for productive communication, and consequently their relations with others are likely to be fraught with misunderstanding. There are those who want to talk but not to listen, a desire which can become almost pathological in a few. These people talk compulsively and endlessly, but are insensitive or indifferent to what others have to say. (This condition has been known to exist in executives!) There are others who attend but don't listen, or who listen but are seldom motivated to speak.

An intense desire to communicate can even be self-defeating if an individual is insensitive to others. A speaker who feels that he is not being understood or accepted is apt to try repeating his message in a louder voice, apparently in the hope that sheer force will do the job. Or he repeats himself in simpler words, indicating in manner that he considers his respondent dull. In neither case does he stop to consider *why* he is not succeeding, or to listen carefully to the other. His very insistence establishes a blockage in the respondent.

A more frequent communication barrier is created by the tendency of people to listen selectively. As we will note again in Chapter 5, unconscious motivation acts as a screening device, admitting into the mind some parts of a message but effectively shutting out others. According to C. J. Dover in the *General Electric Review* :[5]

> If the subject being discussed arouses deep-set emotional reactions, the poor listener will often literally fail to hear anything the speaker says. This pitfall is especially obvious with a controversial subject when the speaker takes a position antithetical to the listener's. The poor listener will immediately adopt a defensive position mentally, and the complicated process of rejection that ensues usually includes a tuning-out of anything else the speaker says.

An individual's point of view becomes crystallized as a set of values which act as motives, influencing his communicative effectiveness, dictating the way a thing is said or the manner in which it is heard. The closed mind is a common human frailty. Even emotionally-toned words may trigger biases which form communication barriers, as indicated by Lester Tarnopol in *Personnel Journal* :[6]

> Let us look at top-management's attempts to communicate with employees through the language of logic and efficiency. They may use the technical jargon and cold discrimination of engineers and accountants. The workers in turn try to communicate with the "brass" through their own vernacular of social sentiments and feelings.
>
> Each hears the other's words and incorrectly assumes meanings based on what the words mean to him. Neither group really understands the other. To the rank-and-file the precise language of efficiency, instead of transmitting understanding, may convey feelings of dismay and insecurity. The workers, in turn, instead of transmitting successfully their fears of social dislocation, may convey emotional expressions of petty grievances and excessive demands to the top people.

[5] C. J. Dover, "Listening—The Missing Link in Communication," *General Electric Review*, LXI, No. 3 (May, 1958), p. 43.

[6] Lester Tarnopol, "Attitudes Block Communications," *Personnel Journal*, XXXVII, No. 9 (Feb., 1957), p. 328.

Words which have been shown to be emotion-laden for some people, and therefore which impede communication to them, include *sharecropper, automation, Red, Democrat, Republican, evolution,* and *union.* Every person may have his own unrecognized set of such words, and no two sets would be exactly alike. The fact remains that certain words do excite attitudes, biases, and emotions which motivate people not to hear and understand.

Emotional states such as fear, anger, jealousy, joy, and pride have for centuries been known to condition the way in which a person receives a message, or the manner in which he will send one. Experienced speakers may become proficient in arousing emotions which facilitate the response they want, or in allaying those which tend to check it. "When a man wants to talk to me and he's all hot under the collar," remarked a steel mill foreman, "I tell him to wait in my office until I finish an errand on the other side of the plant. Then I disappear for ten minutes. By the time I get back, he's cooled down enough so we can talk together. There's no sense in talking to a man when he's mad."

All in all, we must remember that while people must be motivated to communicate, many are actually motivated in a way which creates barriers to good communication. The effective speaker or listener arouses positive motivation in others as well as being positively motivated himself.

Lack of skill in communication

All the ability you have to understand other people or to make them understand you and act on your ideas, has been learned. Many tend to ignore this fact, and as a result they have made no systematic attempt to learn the basic skills and principles of effective speech communication. We can hardly wonder, then, that lack of skill in communication is one of the major barriers to understanding.

The want of communicative skill is evidenced in the experience of many men of business, professional, or industrial competence. Clarence B. Randall, former Chairman of the Board of Inland Steel Corporation, has asserted, "We are cut off from the public because we can neither write nor speak the English language with clarity and force." Hesket Kuhn, president of the Hardware and Supply Company of Akron, Ohio, told a convention of distributors, "Seventy-five per cent of our meetings should not be held. There is one of two reasons for their failure. Either the speaker does not know his subject, or if he does, he lacks the ability to put it over." And Dr. Arthur Nutt, vice president of Avco Lycoming, told a group of engineering students, "The average scientist or engineer can neither speak nor write . . . as he should. What good does it do to develop ideas and products if the results of these developments cannot be sold?"

Communication fails when a speaker has not taken time to clarify for himself the message he would like another to understand. It fails when he has not analyzed that message *in terms of the readiness and ability of the listener to grasp it.* It fails when the form in which the message is presented is not functionally adapted to the time, place, and people who are to receive it. It fails when the receiver has not recognized his responsibility as part of the communication process and marshalled his abilities as a listener. It fails when the speaker does not understand the psychology of attention involved in speaking to others, or when he does not avail himself of the means of getting and keeping attention. It fails when the speaker is vague or uncertain about his purpose—and for many other reasons, all of which involve the development of skills and abilities which can and must be learned. Newcomb and Sammons, industrial consultants, have written, "Many companies have learned, to their costly regret, that amateurism in communication doesn't pay. In the long run it's better to put a trained man or woman on the job."[7] Your study of this textbook indicates that you intend to be one of those trained men or women.

External factors

If you have ever tried to talk to someone over the hubbub of a busy foundry or the din of traffic on a crowded street, you know from experience that elements in the field surrounding the act of communication can create a very real barrier to understanding. So can interruptive telephone calls in an office, or the sudden outburst of a public address system piped through a school or store. In the jargon of some communicative experts, these things are called "noise" or "static," since they act on the transmission to reduce the amount of

[7] Robert Newcomb and Marg Sammons, "Employee Communications—First Order of Business," *Mill & Factory* LXVI, No. 1 (May, 1960), p. 14.

33

the message which gets through, either because the effective force of the transmission is reduced or because the attention of the speaker or listener is distracted.

External factors can have the same effect psychologically. For instance, pictures hanging on a wall have been known to interfere with communication in a room. Said the public relations director of a rubber company recently, "We used to burn scrap rubber every afternoon out behind one of the plants. The smoke and soot floated across town to the annoyance of every housekeeper. So long as we kept this up, it was utterly impossible to get across the idea that our company was a community good neighbor." Just as the smoke created unfavorable attitudes which made good community relations impossible, so do external factors in many speaking situations create psychological barriers to understanding.

Even a speaker's visual aids, employed to help communication, may at times actually become a barrier. A speaker with a great display of charts, pictures, or apparatus, may find his audience paying more attention to these than to what he is saying at any given moment. Just as he must learn to control and manipulate his visual aids to keep them from acting as "noise," so every speaker and listener must learn to be aware of the factors which surround the communicative process and which may tend to block or distort communication, either physically or psychologically. Being aware of such factors is the first step in avoiding or compensating for them.

Interpersonal difficulties

According to an ancient verse,

> I do not like thee, Dr. Fell,
> And why it is, I cannot tell.
> But this I know, and know full well—
> I do not like thee, Dr. Fell.

Like the writer of the verse, all of us are at times repelled or attracted by others without being able to explain the reason. Yet friendliness and respect are important conditioners of communication. As T. M. Higham, an English industrial psychologist, observed, "if a person dislikes or mistrusts us, he is not likely to be receptive to what we have to say, and his version of our words is likely to be distorted by his personal opinions of us, or his preconceived notions about our motives." The word *communication* itself, derived from the Latin *communis* which means *common*, suggests that full understanding can be achieved only between or among those who share a commonality of outlook and a mutuality of good will. Friction or discord between people establishes an emotional resistance which prevents or distorts communication.

Examples of this fact abound. Every salesman knows that many of those he calls on have an innate suspicion of salesmen in general, and are therefore difficult to talk with. Workers have trouble "getting through" to a surly associate in production. Office people tend not to relate themselves to a colleague who continually engages in horseplay. A manager with a dictatorial air cannot communicate fully with his subordinates, and a chronic troublemaker creates an impossible communicative situation wherever he goes.

There is nothing new in the principle that interpersonal relations have a major effect on communicative success, for Aristotle wrote, "There are three things which inspire confidence in the orator's own character. Good sense, good moral character, and good will. . . . Any one who is thought to have all three of these good qualities will inspire trust in his audience." And Dr. Jay M. Jackson, director of the Graduate Program in psychology of the University of Kansas, adds, "Communication flows along friendship channels. When trust exists, content is more freely communicated, and the recipient is more accurate in perceiving the sender's opinion."[8]

Interpersonal relationships characterized by friction, suspicion, or hostility, then, constitute barriers to communication. As we shall see in Chapter 6, good human relations open channels of understanding.

These seven most common causes of communication blockage are not mutually exclusive, of course, for at times they overlap, and in a specific situation several may operate at once. Yet if we understand each of the seven, we are better prepared for communicating successfully, either as speakers or as listeners.

In any event, when we talk with others we are more likely to do it within some kind of continuing organizational setting than to engage in an isolated and unrelated communicative act. We talk to people in our own organization or in related organizations more

[8] Jay M. Jackson, "The Organization and Its Communication Problems," *Advanced Management*, XXIV, No. 2 (Feb., 1959), p. 20.

often than we talk to utter strangers, and therefore most of our talking can be viewed as a kind of continuing dialogue. Today's talk stems from yesterday's, and is a prelude to what we will talk about tomorrow. Further, each party to the dialogue is more than an individual; he is a part of an organizational structure, a unit in a social order. We must see speech communication, then, as the continuing way in which people relate to one another within a social structure, for it is this living and dynamic structure which forms the setting for much of our talk, and which, in itself, is a creation of that talk.

THE COMMUNICATION PROCESS IS PART OF A SOCIAL MATRIX

It will be virtually impossible for you to escape becoming vocationally involved in the social order of some institution. Even if you are an independent proprietor of a small office or establishment, you will be professionally associated with others in similar situations, and you may have employees comprising your own organization. And if you become affiliated with a large store, station, office, or industry, you will accept membership in the society of the whole and become identified with one or more of its sub-groups. Inevitably you will become to some degree an "organization man."

During your life you will also be a member of many social groups only remotely connected, if at all, with your business or professional life. You may live in a neighborhood which has no observable structure, and yet which is held together by uncharted relationships. You may also be found among the members of the Boy Scouts, the country club, the P.T.A., some fraternal organization, a church, the Rotary or Lions Club, or one of the major political parties. It may be possible, in fact, to write your life story in terms of the groups with which you become affiliated, their purpose, organization, and membership, and of your relations with each group.

Inasmuch as a great deal of your talking will be done within these organizations, you can understand your speech communication better as you see it within its organizational setting. Our purpose in this part of the chapter is to examine briefly that setting, with emphasis on business or industrial organization.

An organization is a living organism made up of many parts

Let us begin with the fact suggested in Chapter 1, that an institution is a living social organism, made up of small, subordinate, overlapping, and interacting systems or groups of people. The large social unit, having a life and purpose of its own, can exist and fulfill its purpose only as the smaller systems and groups which are its components can maintain their own existence, and coordinate themselves to further the general welfare.

In this sense a giant social institution such as General Foods, Du Pont, or the United States Air Force (and small institutions as well) is not at all unlike a single human being. As a physical being, a human possesses purposes toward which every system, every organ, and every cell must work, each subordinate unit coordinating with all the others to integrate the whole. And just as a human is a multiplex arrangement of interdependent systems or organs, so is a business enterprise. A corporation must recruit and retire its members, trying to keep them in good physical and mental health while they are a part of its body. It must procure and schedule materials, sell products, develop new ones, keep books, plan advertising, foresee the future, schedule production, arrange shipping, and make certain that its key employees have transportation from place to place. The integrated whole is a coordinated arrangement of many interdependent parts.

The responsibility of mutual interdependence, however, works in both directions. While the whole is dependent upon each of the parts, so is each part dependent upon the whole and upon every other part. Even as the health and vitality of the whole man depends upon the functioning of heart, lungs, circulation, and other organs and systems, so the heart cannot successfully maintain itself if the circulation is blocked or the man as a whole is diseased. Similarly, advertising cannot be vital if sales does not produce income to finance it, nor can accounting be a healthy department if the entire organization is sick. The well-being of each employee and of each department or division depends upon every other and upon the success of the institution as a whole.

Thus, while competition may be the stimulus to progress and success in the economic world, cooperation is the final key to survival.

37

Each of the components of an organization has its own identity

Although every sub-group or system of an organization exists to contribute to the purpose of that of which it is a part, each in fact has a purpose and an identity of its own. This fact was interpreted in an address to the Catholic Hospital Association by William Baumer, special assistant to the president of the Johnson and Johnson Company. Calling each sub-group an "island of activity," he pointed out, "There are in the hospital doctors, nurses, trustees, an administrator, engineers, technicians, the auxiliaries, the patients. Each has its own world, its own ideas, and these islands do not easily connect." And a hospital is not unique, for the same sort of islands can be found in almost any institution of any size or complexity, each forming a small, unified social group having its own life, purpose, customs, and loyalties. Each member may feel a primary allegiance to his group, sometimes even at the expense of loyalty to the institution as a whole, and often in rivalry, competition, or conflict with other groups. Carl who works in inventory auditing may identify with his corporation as strongly as Jack, who works in production control, yet each cannot escape seeing their common interests from a different point of view. Each takes on some of the characteristics of the group of which he is a member, of its culture and its frame of reference.

Just as each group of people has its own identity, so does every individual within a group. Each has an identification with the parent organization and an identification with his group, yet each also has a personal set of goals and a unique viewpoint which sets him apart. The uniqueness of each individual depends in part upon his personality and temperament and in part upon the kind of work he does. As Charles Redfield of the University of Chicago has observed, many working in industrial and professional assignments do not strongly assume the role of organization man, and therefore display a greater independence of thought and action than their colleagues in other posts. Typical of this class would be industrial research scientists, master craftsmen, non-resident physicians attached to a hospital, and "customers' men" attached to a brokerage firm.

The degree to which members of a group or island identify themselves with one another and with the parent organization, will have an effect on communication within the group and with the rest of the organization. Dr. Jackson has noted that, "When any particular communication is sent to a number of sub-groups in an organization, each group may extract a different meaning from the message, depending on its significance for the things the group values and is striving to accomplish."[9] Similarly, each individual will send or receive messages in terms of his own interests, his identification with the group, and his identification with the organization. A true "organization man" identifies closely with his employer or corporation, and this may make communication with him easier than with a more individualistic employee.

The structure of an organization is a pattern of relationships held together by communication

If you will visualize the structural chart of an organization, usually a pyramid with the chief officer at the top and subordinates of various grades arranged in successive layers beneath, you will mentally note that each office or person is related to others by chart lines. These lines denote responsibility and accountability, both of which are implemented by communication. The lines of communication make the organization what it is, for if they did not exist, only an unorganized, unrelated collection of individuals would remain. In truth, an organization IS communication.

Actually, we must recognize that two sets of communication lines exist in any organization. The first is the formal or official communicative structure shown on the organization chart. Here the lines of communication are neatly and clearly marked, indicating who reports to whom, and suggesting how messages flow up, down, and across the organization.

The second is the informal network, sometimes called the "grapevine," but actually consisting of something more than a web of message-bearing lines of communication. It is the way in which the interaction of people tends to transcend, ignore, or even destroy the formally established or official communicative relationships. It has been described in these words:[10]

---

[9] Jackson, p. 17.

[10] Burleigh B. Gardner and David G. Moore, *Human Relations in Industry, 4th Ed.* (Homewood, Ill.: Richard D. Irwin, Inc., 1964), pp. 19–20.

39

Behind the formal, paper facade is another organization consisting of a group of people from various walks of life —people having varying interests, needs, and ambitions, and all of whom are making adjustments to the formal tasks which they are called upon to perform, adapting their own interests to the demands of the people with whom they are thrown into daily contact, making friends, and acquiring enemies. This is the realm of feelings and emotions, scuttlebutt and rumors, cliques and washroom repartee. This is the human side of doing business. Observing it, we get the "low-down," so to speak, on how organizations with all their "paper" dignity actually work.

Within both the formal and the informal networks are definite communicative patterns of varying shapes, sizes, and arrangements. Members become structured into various patterns of relationships, based on work performed, on non-business interests, on authority or status, on prestige, on friendships, or even on membership in car pools. These patterns penetrate the entire organization, resulting in a vast, interlocking series of networks along which communication flows.

Each person in a business or industrial organization can be thought of as a "station" on at least one major and probably several minor networks, with lines of communication running between him and a number of other persons or "stations," which form some kind of communication web.

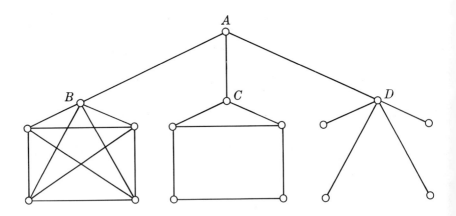

You may derive a better understanding of the communication networks from the accompanying diagram, which illustrates some of the basic differences to be found among groups of similar size. In the diagram, station A represents the chief of a work unit who has three subordinates reporting to him, indicated in stations B, C, and D. Each subordinate has charge of four workers, but the lines of communication within each group are arranged differently. Assuming that each line represents two-way communication, you can see that the relationships of subordinates to workers and of workers to workers will be different within each group.

The differences which exist among various types of networks will in turn have an effect on both the persons involved and the amount and nature of the work performed by the group. Writes psychologist Harold J. Leavitt on this point:[11]

> Some communication networks allow for *faster* operation than others, but the advantage of speed may be gained at the cost of accuracy and/or morale. People are *happier* in some networks than they are in others, and some networks therefore are more likely to keep going longer without blowing up, but these networks may be slower or less accurate than some others. This conflict between "morale" and "efficiency" may indeed turn out to be a generalized conflict in industrial organizations. Some networks have fewer errors than others. Some are more flexible than others. All these words may have something to do with what we mean by "efficiency."

It is not our purpose here to go into detail on the characteristics and relative advantages or disadvantages of the various forms of communication networks. But you should be aware of the fact that such networks exist, for it is as a part of similar networks that you will do much of your talking and listening.

Organization is a function of communication

Usually we think that an organization requires communication only as a tool. As we look at an organizational chart, we are apt to see a

[11] Harold J. Leavitt, *Managerial Psychology, 2nd. Ed.* (Chicago: University of Chicago Press, 1964), pp. 233–34. The chart on page 41 suggesting various types of communication networks is adapted from Leavitt with permission.

static and logical arrangement of parts served by lines of communication. The organization-communication relationship is reciprocal, however, and when people begin to communicate, some kind of organization surely emerges, placing individuals in relationships and assigning functions to them. Thus, we must also see the organization as a live, dynamic thing, feeding on emotions as well as logic, and created, at least in part, by the very communication which presumes to be its servant. And the people who as individuals created their organization through communication, assume roles as operating elements of the thing they created.

Thus, three interrelated factors appear which shape the dynamic thing we call organization. One is the network structure which formalizes communication, establishes working relationships, and influences the communicative behavior of individuals; another is the character and personality of the individuals who make up the structure; the third is the potent energy of the communication itself, as information and understanding course throughout the whole, serving the purposes of the organization as well as of its members. Each factor affects the others, finally determining the morale, the accuracy, and the efficiency of the organization.

Consider a group which becomes authoritarian in structure because communication flows only between the boss and each individual worker. The efficiency of such a group could be high, its morale low. If the boss is secretive or close-mouthed, linking the workers below him with the manager above but restricting the messages delivered, he could damage the effectiveness of the entire group. Again, rivalry between two office workers for an advancement could send conflicting messages through the network as each tries to impress the manager responsible for promotion. In situations like these, even an efficient network is hampered by communicative blundering on the part of some who occupy stations within it. On the other hand, people who as individuals are effective speakers and listeners can be severely handicapped by having to work within poorly structured communication networks. An imaginative and articulate technician may make no impression on an organization which provides him no opportunity to talk to key people. Two competent production workers who, by talking things over, might solve a production problem, never have an opportunity because they work on different shifts. An institution such as a hospital, which operates three shifts around the clock, may have especially troublesome problems. Each shift may have satisfactory communication networks, but too little communication may take place between shifts.

In short, organizational communication *cannot* be thought of as a telephone system which is unaffected by the messages which flow throughout it or by those who use it. Organizational communication affects and is affected by both organizational structure and the persons who do the communicating, just as the latter two also affect each other. Each organization is not only a living, functioning whole, but is also unique. And as David Berlo of Michigan State University observes, "People who do understand how a system works can use their knowledge to improve the efficiency and effectiveness of their communication."[12]

The individual is the key to the communicative effectiveness of the whole

We are told that a chain is no stronger than its weakest link. We may conclude that similarly the communicative health and productivity of an organization depend on the people, separately and individually, who *are* the organization. Communication, oral or written, is the joint product of two persons at a time, for even a speech is heard by *individuals* who have gathered together to listen, and a company publication is read by individuals, even if it reaches thousands.

In an organization, each employee relates himself to others through communication, while the manager or administrator performs his functions solely through communication. He consults with others, receives information, makes decisions, issues directives, delegates responsibilities, coordinates activities, and tries to effect or control behavior. Through communication he attempts to guide and regulate the organization or some part of it. In the words of Lawrence A. Appley, former president of the American Management Association, "Communication is the means whereby management gets its job done."

It would be a mistake, however, to assume that even the top officer can direct an organization of any size with precision, for the organization takes on a character of its own, independent of any one

[12] David K. Berlo, *The Process of Communication* (New York: Holt, Rinehart, and Winston, Inc., 1960), p. 152.

43

person. Murray Lincoln, president of the Nationwide Insurance Company, has observed, "I used to think that once I had charge of an institution I could make it do anything I wanted it to. But after an organization grows to a certain size it has a life of its own and you can't *make* it do much of anything, however much power you have to hire and fire. You must work constantly through education, persuasion, and demonstration to get your own people to do what you think ought to be done."[13]

From this examination, three principles emerge. First, improvement in organizational communication begins with upgrading the communicative skills and abilities of individuals, since it is *individuals* who communicate. Second, managers communicate to get their work done, and that their communication is an effort, through others, to influence or control the organization. Third, such control can rarely be perfect, for the organization is more than the sum of its parts, and therefore resists being controlled as a puppet, even as do the individuals who make it up.

Organizational communication is subject to breakdown

We have noted already the obstacles which may impede communication between two persons, and we must now appreciate that organizational communication can be similarly distorted in additional ways.

Since the individual is the key to organizational communication, it follows that one or more individuals can create communication problems for any institution. Bad relations between two or more people can affect an entire group and impair its relations with other groups. Lack of communicative skill not only can create misunderstanding and confusion, but, as indicated in Chapter 1, can waste many collective man-hours of work. An individual who does not understand the importance of good communication may delay or withhold information or send useless messages.

Individual "bottlenecks" often screen, delay, or stop information from passing their stations in the formal structure of the organization. Studies made in 17 companies by the Opinion Research Corporation led to the recognition of several types of organi-

---

[13] Murray D. Lincoln, *Vice President in Charge of Revolution* (New York: McGraw-Hill Book Company, Inc., 1960), p. 297.

44

zational bottlenecks, each personally motivated to distort communication. Among these bottlenecks are the "gatekeeper," usually a second in command, who filters through only what he wants others to hear; the information "status seeker," who hoards information, fearing that to divulge it would make others his equal; the "job rival," who secretes information from anyone he feels may threaten his job security; the "temperamental boss," who behaves in ways which discourage subordinates from approaching him, or insists on talking when he should be listening; and the "buck passer," who wants to make his group look good, and therefore carefully withholds anything which might work to the contrary.

Conditions in the organization itself may work against productive communication. Among such conditions, inadequate channels or media should first be noted. As already pointed out, when more than one shift is at work, inadequate communication between those on different shifts can be disruptive. When few departmental or group meetings are held, information may be shared only on a hit-or-miss basis, dissatisfaction may become grievance, and group morale may sag. In contrast, if any one member of an organization has too many meetings to attend, his time and effort may become so splintered that he cannot give serious attention to anything. And when key people cannot be talked with, understanding suffers. In many other ways, the lack of proper media, channels, or opportunity for communication creates a primary breakdown.

Distance, or size of an organization, may establish another barrier. The West Coast representative of a company with headquarters in Michigan may be able to telephone his home office, yet if he personally knows no one to whom he talks, fullness of understanding is seldom achieved. The very size of an organization such as the Shell Oil Company or the University of California, makes productive communication extremely difficult. Yet communicative distance may be psychological as well as physical, for the same conditions which permit two people to be neighbors in a huge apartment without knowing one another, can also operate in a large organization. Any experienced teacher knows that he can establish greater real understanding in a small class than a large one, for he can come to know the students he is teaching.

To organizational distance we must add complexity as a barrier to communication, especially since distance, size, and complexity often go hand in hand. Communication between or among line, staff, and systems personnel is inadequate or overlapping in some companies. Those who should receive certain information are sometimes overlooked because distribution lists are incomplete or subject to change. In contrast, some officers get so many messages that they are not able adequately to digest, coordinate, and act upon them. Timing becomes a problem in complex organizations, it being necessary to insure that key people have needed information at a precise time in relation to others and in relation to a given operation.

The climate of an organization has a strong effect on its communication, and often may cause blockage. An authoritarian climate may facilitate a downward flow of communication but discourage an easy upward flow. It may encourage a thriving grapevine in which rumors circulate freely. On the other hand, a democratic climate may facilitate an upward flow of messages, sometimes to the point that significant ones become lost in the flood. A climate of extreme permissiveness can dampen work-centered communication by encouraging too much chit-chat among personnel. Organizations may be static or dynamic in climate, optimistic or pessimistic, selfish or humanitarian, friendly or cold, rigid or flexible, and so on, with the climate in each instance exerting an influence on the kind and amount of communication.

Finally, change in an organization may in itself be communicatively disruptive. Change not only gives rise to rumor, keeping the grapevine busy, but it creates other difficulties. Relationships among persons in an enterprise are constantly in a state of flux. Personnel change means that new and sometimes unknown people occupy communicative stations, and their behavior can be unpredictable at best. Information wanted by the former manager goes unnoticed by the new man. One supervisor makes it a habit to keep his workers fully informed; his successor seems to withhold information. One man seeks advice, another shuns it. Change creates a parade of innovation—change of people, change of purpose, change of product, change of organizational structure, change of office layout, change of market. All this means that new channels must constantly be opening as old ones close, that new routines must be adopted, and that different methods of supplying and obtaining information or of issuing instructions must be established.

From this brief survey of some of an organization's communication problems, you can easily identify a few of the more common kinds of breakdown. *Chain loss* sets in when messages are passed from person to person, each in turn making some alteration of the message as received, so that the last one to get it may have an understanding significantly different from the intent of the original sender. *Bad timing* results in people's getting information too late for it to be useful, or otherwise out of synchronization with the rest of the organization. *Overload* is a consequence of too many messages given to an individual within a short time, making him unable to respond effectively to any one. And *omission* results from the failure of one person to see that all who should receive a given message do get it.

The reason for all this examination of the social matrix in which business, industrial, and professional communication takes place should be plain. The matrix is the social structure in which you will work. You will become a station—a "relay" perhaps—in the overall organization, receiving messages, sending messages, forwarding messages. You will be a part of a network of communication, subject to the climate, the complexity, and the change which fix its character. You will be exposed to the pressures it generates, and in your own way motivated to add to or subtract from the productiveness of the whole. The things you say will not be isolated occurrences, but parts of larger units of activity within a social structure. If you do not appreciate something of this structure, you may harm both yourself and the organization which employs you. If you do understand something of the social system of which you are a part, you are in a better position to improve the quality and productiveness of your talking.

You may object that as a small businessman or a professional person, you will be unaffected by these considerations. True, you may not be an integral part of a great corporation, but you cannot escape involvement with corporate structure. Some corporations may be your clients, some will be your suppliers, some will have officers or managers who belong to professional organizations with which you are affiliated. In many ways your business or professional life will be affected by the social structure of organizations, big and little. A corporation man talking *outside* of his corporate structure still carries the influence of the society of which he is a part. A lone attorney is a member of an organized bar association, practices within the structure of the court system, and does business with men who are representatives of various organizations.

You are, of course, a citizen of the United States and of several of its political subdivisions, a member of the society which makes it up, and a part of the culture of the West. The entire range of your communicative and personal life is a small part of the national

47

fabric, affecting and being affected by it. You cannot escape the climate and the purpose of the larger society of which you are a part.

SEVEN PRINCIPLES OFFER GUIDES
TO BETTER SPEAKING

The complexity of the communicative process, the obstacles which can arise to prevent understanding as one person talks to another, and the degree to which communication can break down in an organization may sometimes seem appalling. In the face of the hazard and uncertainty of success, some may reasonably contend that it is not possible to reduce an activity so infinitely varied and so complex as speech to a few essentials. Experience, however, shows that through the application of certain understandings and principles, people can learn to achieve an increasingly higher degree of success with their talking. For study and practice, therefore, we must begin with the following basic fundamentals, hoping they will lead to a progressively fuller understanding of the more complex and sophisticated aspects of speech communication.

Be aware of the communication process, its obstacles and break-downs, and of your function as a communicator in any group

Just as you can drive a car more skillfully through the maze of modern traffic when you understand both the flow of traffic as a whole and your own functions and responsibilities in that flow, so you can be a better speaker when you understand your part in the total process of communication in a modern business or professional setting. The purpose of this chapter has been to make you aware of the process and to introduce you to the setting in which it functions.

Choose well the time and place to speak

To the degree that it is possible for you to control both the moment and the surroundings for your speaking, do so. Success may sometimes hinge on these factors. Inappropriate times, places, and sur-

48

roundings can reduce your ability to reach an understanding with others, either because you or they are not ready, or because you or they are not prepared to give full attention to the task.

Have your purpose or objective clearly in mind

It has been estimated that half of the failures in communication result from the fact that one or both parties had not beforehand clearly defined the precise purpose of the exchange. Talk is not aimless self-expression nor the exposure of ideas; listening is something more than passively waiting for a chance to speak. Both are for the purpose of effecting *some kind of behavioral change in the other person or of altering one's own behavior,* and the exact response desired must be definitely established before productive communication can be expected. In order to hit the bull's-eye, you must first clearly see it.

Be sure of your message

Not only must you know the effect you want to produce by your talk, but you must also determine what message will secure that effect. Your talk will, in most instances, deal with ideas. These ideas must be clear and definite in your own mind before you can hope to make them equally clear to someone else. Dr. A. T. Weaver of the University of Wisconsin spent a lifetime driving home to students the lesson, "Speech is first of all a thinking process," and it follows that to speak clearly you must first *think clearly.* In succeeding chapters we will be vitally concerned with appropriate messages and effective thought-patterns.

Understand your respondent or respondents

Since your talk must be purposive in terms of others' behavior, and since your ideas must be clear to them as well as to yourself, you must understand those with whom you talk. You must be aware of their degree of readiness to respond and their ability to receive your ideas. You must know as much as possible about their needs, wants, and interests, about their way of life and the manner in which they

49

are accustomed to receiving messages. You must understand how they are different from you, and be ready to modify your own attitudes and thinking to reach common ground. Your talk will have to be adapted to the receiver, it will have to be sent on a wavelength which he is capable of receiving, and it will have to motivate him to listen and respond. At the same time you must be sensitive to your own background and motives as they relate to those of your respondent.

Package your message with skill

Having identified your purpose, clarified your message, and gained as much understanding as possible of the respondent, you must then carefully plan your talk to make it conform to the specifications. It must be framed in terms of reception and listener response. The ideas must be expressed acceptably, arranged in the best order, and put into words which are both clear and evocative. Your whole effort must be tailored to the time you have available, and delivered to fit the respondent's customary ways of receiving communication. And it must be appropriate to the *form* of speech involved, whether it be conference, interview, public address, and so on.

Verify the degree of your success

In both speaking and listening you must take every available measure to find the degree to which a common understanding has been accomplished. When you speak you must assess how well you are understand by asking questions, by observing listener response, or by formal testing. When you listen you must verify your own understanding by asking questions or by restating the ideas and feelings of the speaker accurately and to his satisfaction. In short, as a speaker you will use feedback by becoming a listener-observer, and as a listener you will provide feedback by talking—all, of course, within the limits of opportunity provided by the situation.

From the discussion in this chapter and from the seven basic principles, you have now discovered that, although you first set out to learn how to *speak* better, you will also have to improve in *listening* as well. You have learned that speaking and listening are reciprocal parts of the single process of *speech communication.* Seldom will you do nothing but talk. Even as a "public" speaker, you will have to listen before, during, and after a speech in order to plan for maximum success and to know the degree of your success. Always you will have to be an alert observer as you speak, and in most forms of speech communication you will constantly alternate your predominant role as speaker and listener.

From all this you may distill a unified point of view to speech communication. In your role of listener, your task is to *understand others as fully as possible without necessarily evaluating them.* And in your role as speaker, your ultimate task is to *persuade those who listen to you.* All speech is for the eventual purpose of predictably affecting behavior, and even when your purpose is only to get others to understand, you must persuade them to want to understand. Basically, speech is a method of mutual adjustment and accommodation, a way of relating to and living with others which makes possible the concert of human activity we call society.

Chapter 3

The People with Whom You Talk

The biggest trouble with industry is that it is full of human beings. The longer you are president, the more firmly that fact will be riveted in your mind. That is why you will lose sleep. That is why your hair will turn gray, then get thin, and then fall out altogether, unless you are lucky. You will learn to your sorrow that, while a drill press never sulks and a drop hammer never gets jealous of other drop hammers, the same cannot be said for people. You will learn that a turret lathe may run one part for ten years without affecting its ability or its willingness to be switched at any time to another part. But men are not that way. They develop habits and likes and dislikes.

You will learn that you have with people the same general problems of preventive maintenance, premature obsolescence, and complete operational failure that you have with machines. Only they are much harder to solve.[1]

JOHN L. McCAFFREY, *President*
International Harvester Company

OVER A PERIOD OF TIME YOU WILL TALK WITH A WIDE VARIETY OF people.

The bank executive from whom you want to secure a loan.

The professor whose class you cut yesterday.

[1] John L. McCaffrey, "What Corporation Presidents Think About at Night," *Fortune*, XLVIII, No. 3 (Sept., 1953), p. 128.

A native of India studying in this country on a scholarship.
A waitress who has brought food you didn't order.
A co-worker who has just discovered a mistake in your work.

With each person you will talk in a different manner. You will do so because in each case you are involved in a unique relationship not duplicated in any other. Sometimes, as when you talk with the waitress, the relationship is transitory and your status is one of relative authority. At other times, as when you talk with the man who has power to loan you money, the relationship is more prolonged and your status is subordinate. Each relationship into which you enter differs from all others in the nature of the complex forces at work to establish or modify it, but all relationships are created, maintained, strengthened, or weakened by your talk.

Speech communication, then, is not concerned alone with the sending and receiving of messages. It has to do with the way one person relates to another or to a group, and therefore with the way people behave toward one another in specific situations. It has to do with the way you relate to those in one of the communication networks described in the previous chapter. It has also to do with the forms and patterns of speaking to be discussed in later chapters, for these have evolved culturally from man's experience in relating himself to others under specific kinds of conditions.

People do not talk in the abstract, however, but always *in relation to* some event, condition, situation, or person, or to some combination of these, and while speech is a major element of their behavior, it cannot be isolated from the whole. Speech does not take place in addition to other manifestations of behavior, it is rather, an integral part of the whole process of a person's behavior. *With this understanding, we can view speech as any fraction of behavior which (1) conveys a message (whether intended or not), and/or (2) expresses an attitude toward the subject of the message, the self, or the listener. The effect of the behavior, (again whether intended or not), is (1) to modify or affect the behavior of others, (2) to establish the bases for modifying one's own behavior, or (3) to establish, modify, or terminate interpersonal relationships, their nature, or their intensity.*

To understand speech better, therefore, is to understand behavior better. Conversely, if we can improve our understanding of human behavior we can improve both our understanding of speech and our ability to speak (or behave) appropriately and with purposeful effect. In the preceding chapter some of the psychological factors involved in the communication process were identified, and their effect on speech can now be illustrated by referring to the hypothetical situations which opened this chapter.

In each of the five hypothetical relationships, motivation is at work. Each person talks and listens in the light of what he feels is at stake. He has, or thinks he has, something to gain or lose. You may be concerned with your grade as you talk with your professor, with your sense of self-importance or your desire to impress another as you talk to the waitress, or with your personal sense of security as you talk to your co-worker. And the professor, the waitress, and the others likewise converse in terms of the anticipation of benefit or harm which motivates them.

The motivation in these instances might be called extrinsic, since the expected benefit or harm will be a consequence of the talk. Sometimes, however, people talk to each other because of the intrinsic benefits of the conversational relationship. Thus, you might find talking with the student from India to be in itself an interesting and stimulating experience.

The most common extrinsic motivation is the desire of the speaker or listener to influence the behavior of the other person. As you are interviewed by the bank executive, you hope that your talk or your behavior in listening will influence him toward granting the loan you seek. Similarly, in a job interview, you would like to influence the interviewer to think favorably of your capacity to fill the available job.

In all such interpersonal situations, each individual is profoundly affected by the attitudes he brings to the occasion, including his attitude toward himself as well as toward the respondent and toward the subject and purposes of the talk. Attitudes in turn may be influenced by the role each sees himself playing, and the role he sees for the other. Beyond this, each possesses a set of expectations— the things he hopes or unconsciously predicts will happen during or as a result of the conversation.

Motives, purposes, attitudes, roles, expectations—these are but some of the many psychological factors influencing people who talk to one another. Yet they are perhaps enough to show that proficiency in speech communication demands some understanding of human behavior, to which this chapter is devoted.

At the outset we must recognize that there is a difference between studying the behavior of people in the aggregate and

54

understanding the behavior of a single person in particular circumstances. Scientists can predict with neat precision the gross behavior of a billion billion molecules, but they cannot foretell how any given molecule will act. They can foresee reaction only in the mass. Similarly, we can understand the probable behavior of people in statistical quantities, but rarely can we be certain of how any one person will act. Nevertheless, what we do know about human behavior in general will help us to understand and to work with individuals.

The general processes and patterns of behavior arise from the fact that all of the family of man are fundamentally alike. Each individual, whether the child of upper class American parents, of South American peons, or African tribesmen, is born with a physical inheritance similar to every other child. His brain grows and matures after birth in a way unlike the brain of any other living creature. For years he is helplessly unable to survive alone for any extended time, again much unlike other creatures, making his growth and survival dependent upon his parents or upon other adult members of his society. And the elements of his behavior are similar to those of any other human being—all have wants, needs, hopes, and fears. All learn their specific patterns of behavior from the society and culture in which they are reared.

We also know that no two people are identical. You, yourself, are unique, and from the beginning of time to the end there will never be another human exactly like you. While each person is formed according to the common pattern of the species, each possesses a singular combination of talents and capacities, and each lives in a world which no other can totally share.

These facts mean that we must learn to look for both the similarities and differences among people. The similarities will suggest ways in which people are likely to behave in a predictable manner, while the differences will warn us that we must not treat all alike. Most of this chapter deals necessarily with ways in which people behave similarly, considering the principles, the elements, and the patterns of behavior. Let us first, however, look at some facts about differences among people.

EFFECTIVE SPEECH MUST TAKE ACCOUNT OF INDIVIDUAL DIFFERENCES

To begin with, nature has given each human being a unique physical make-up. No one duplicates exactly the inherited physical structure of another. We know this is true of finger prints and in general of the external appearance of people, yet we some how seem to forget that humans are unlike on the inside, too, and that this can make a great difference in their behavior. Main arteries running from the heart, for instance, may vary in number from two to four, and each artery may vary in size, permitting one man three times the blood-carrying capacity of another. The blood itself varies in chemical composition from one person to another. If we consider the entire number of physical factors which can be significantly variable—muscular structure, skeletal form and structure, glandular size and capacity, and so on—we can understand why each human being is a unique historical event, never to be repeated.

Since physical make-up is the organic basis of behavior, we can appreciate that each individual also has his own singular combination of potentials and capacities. One man is created with the physical equipment to run faster than others, a second is made more sensitive to sound. Theodore Roosevelt was given the equipment which enabled him to read a page at a time and to remember what he read, and John F. Kennedy was reportedly able to read vertically. Mahalia Jackson's singing must be traceable to unusual vocal equipment, while Willie Mays' baseball skill depends upon neuromuscular coordination. Albert Schweitzer was gifted alike at the organ console and with the surgeon's scalpel.

Each unique combination of physical structure and inherited potential accounts in part for unique emotional and intellectual behavior. Dr. Henry A. Barton, Director of the American Institute of Physics, writes, "Every person who knows he is unique by nature will be equipped to understand the inability of the scientist—be he chemist, anthropologist, physicist, or whatever—to recognize any 'established' way of thinking."[2] Within normal forms of thought

[2] *Saturday Review*, XL, No. 14 (April 6, 1957), p. 45.

each of us has individuality. Some are quicker of imagination, others of logical inference, and a few have strong intuition. No one is a university of talents, but among the normal or gifted each has his own knacks and aptitudes.

Beyond individual inheritance and potential, each human being also develops and matures in a world of his own. Indeed, he lives all his life in a complete universe of which he is the center. No one sees the material world which he sees, for no two people looking at the same scene will see it alike. Each accumulates for himself a store of experiences, memories, impressions, and "lessons from life" which lead him to live in a world inhabited by no one else. And each individual, therefore, will react only to a world-as-he-sees-it.

The facts of individual differences are intensified by the additional fact that each person in his world-as-he-sees-it is ever changing. There are times when the change is sudden and revolutionary, perhaps following illness, an accident, or some unusual experience. Yet more often the change is a slow, almost imperceptible process. Nevertheless, it does occur and needs to be reckoned with. The student who was dismissed from school last year may not be the same one who now seeks readmission. The manager who was creative on one assignment may be conditioned slowly into routine conformity by the environment of another, or the client who was uncertain yesterday may have grown firm by this morning. The world is inhabited by beings of infinite variety who live in a process of change, each in his own universe.

Communication, if it is to bridge the gulf which separates one man's world-as-he-sees-it from another's and bring people into desirable relationships so they can live and work together, must take account of the problem of uniqueness. The task is neatly expressed by Dr. Samuel J. Bois, Canadian industrial psychologist:[3]

My self and my world are one. Your self and your world are one. When I penetrate into your world, as I am doing now, I become subject to the climate of your world, to its laws and traditions. In your world things do not necessarily happen as they do in mine. . . . You cannot assimilate my world in its entirety, and I cannot assimilate yours.

[3] J. Samuel Bois, *Explorations In Awareness*. (New York: Harper & Row, Publishers, 1957), p. 92.

Our speaking, then, must be based on the principle that each person to whom we relate and with whom we talk is a unique whole. He cannot check any part of himself at the door when he enters a classroom, an office, or a factory. You cannot see the whole of the instructor in charge of your class, but he is there in his entirety. He is the sum total, as the poet puts it, of "all that he has met," including every student he has ever taught. Likewise, he may see you only as a "student," but in the classroom as a part of you is the home from which you came, as well as all the experiences of the twenty-three hours a day when you are not in class. Into the classroom both of you bring the triumphs and failures of yesterday and the hopes and fears for tomorrow, and they are a part of your behavior.

Thus the talk that goes back and forth in the classroom does not involve just the messages of the hour, but it involves all that makes up every person present. Every memory, conscious or unconscious, and every expectation exerts its influence upon the human interactions revealed largely in talk. And what is true of the classroom is true on the job. The worker is more than a time-clock number. The salesman is more than the "keystone of the American industrial system." They have homes, families, sickness, indebtedness, children, weddings, friends, bowling leagues, and so on indefinitely. The "economic man" who is concerned solely with pay checks and time schedules simply does not exist. If you try to talk to such a man, you are wasting your breath, for he is man who never was. You may be talking to the man who won the sweepstakes in a giveaway contest last week, whose child was taken to the hospital last night, or who is wondering if his vacation schedule will fit the best fishing season. But you will not be talking to an economic automaton.

As a speaker, your responsibility is to make sure that your talk and action are guided by the "laws and traditions" of the other person's world. And as a listener you need make every effort to decode the speaker's symbols in terms of both his past experience and his present intentions rather than assuming that the meaning you yourself assign is the proper one. Only as you match the elements of your world with those of your respondent to find relatively common bases of understanding, can divisiveness be overcome and identification be increased. The communion of people who share common parts of separate worlds builds and maintains organizations and institutions.

With the principle of individual uniqueness and difference in mind, let us turn to the elements of communicative behavior, recalling that from here on we are talking about people in the mass.

THE STUDY OF BEHAVIOR IS BASED
ON CERTAIN ASSUMPTIONS
AND PRINCIPLES

Some of those interested in the application of the behavioral sciences to business management have lately been talking about "Theory X" and "Theory Y." While the nature of these two conflicting theories is not essential here, interest in them indicates that managers do seek some kind of theoretical framework which can be useful as a guide in the daily conduct of their work. The same can be said for professional people as they establish relationships with clients, colleagues, and associates. So I shall put together in the following pages an eclectic theory which can be used to explain human behavior as it relates to speech. The elements of this body are drawn from various schools of psychological thought, both new and old, with the single purpose of providing a satisfactory explanation of speech behavior and one which you can use to develop your own communicative skill.

Behavior is caused

Mary has been a highly satisfactory laboratory technician, both dependable and loyal. Without prior warning she announces that she intends to leave her job at the end of the month. And Tim has proved an effective student during two years of college, but in the present semester his instructors notice that he is growing indifferent and that his work is not up to his usual standards. If Mary's boss or Tim's advisor decide to talk to them about their behavior, it will be on the assumption that the behavior was not random or accidental. It will rather be on the assumption that the behavior was the result of causes which may somehow be discovered.

Fundamental to the study of human behavior is the idea that it is caused, that just as physical change in the world is the result of a combination of forces, so behavior is the result of forces acting on the individual. The forces may lie within the individual, as illness,

59

or without, as perhaps an intense experience or a set of constraining environmental factors. Although we commonly speak of heredity and environment as the two basic influences which shape what a person is and how he acts, we sometimes forget that speech is one of the most pervasive of environmental forces. We use it to influence the behavior of others, and are in turn molded by what others say to or about us.

The causes of behavior are complex

It would be simple if we could say that Mary has been offered another job at a higher salary, or that Tim has fallen in love. Each of these might be true, yet employees have often remained on the job despite offers of more money, and students have fallen in love without allowing their studies to suffer. Money and love could well be important causes, but by themselves they do not necessarily explain the behavior. How a person acts is determined by a combination of causes, just as the weather is formed by a number of variables.

We have difficulty in predicting behavior because we cannot always recognize the significant causative factors. Some lie in the circumstances of the immediate environment while others may stem from occurrences long in the past and buried in memory. Behavior results from the interaction of the individual with the world-as-he-sees-it, and even normal human beings do not always recognize the well-springs of their own behavior.

Behavior occurs in situations

Even though some of the influences which determine behavior lie within the individual, including the memories, expectations, wants, and energies which motivate him, the individual nevertheless is always responding to specific situations in the world-as-he-sees-it. We may say that Nick "has a temper," but we must not forget that his temper is the visible response of his inner workings to what is going on about him. While Nick may have an explosive temperament, he does not explode unless there is something to touch him off. The stimuli which trigger behavior lie in specific situations.

At times our difficulty in understanding Nick arises from the fact that we do not see things as he does, hence we may feel that he shouldn't lose his temper. The situation does not affect us as it does Nick, and we are quick to judge him rather than understand. We shall do better if we try to see the situation as he sees it before we evaluate.

A corollary of the principle that behavior occurs in situations is that frequently *we are a part of the situation* in which another is behaving. Would Nick "blow his stack" if we were not present? Even though he may not vent himself *at us,* it is possible that a burst of temper may be *in response to our presence.* One person may act as a catalyst, precipitating behavior which would not normally take place in another under given conditions. Thus a supervising teacher may induce behavior in a cadet teacher which would not occur if the latter were alone with the class. You will find this corollary noted in Chapter 6 as it applies to your talking in face-to-face situations.

In Chapter 11, too, you will find outlined a method of motivating others by revealing or describing situations in which they are involved, thereby arousing wants or desires which impel them to action.

Behavior is directed toward goals which satisfy wants, needs, or desires

A man suffering from thirst will direct all his available energies toward the finding of water. Similarly another man possessed by an unsatisfied desire for recognition may work night and day to build a business which will carry his name in flashing neon. The water and the neon constitute the goals which each man perceives as satisfying *his* need or desire. He is therefore motivated to attain them.

When a desire or need within the individual becomes linked to specific goals which promise satisfaction, a tension is created which impels the individual to move toward those goals. Some goals may be easily and quickly achieved, the tension is relieved, and the individual, having found satisfaction, is no longer motivated to behave as he did. In contrast, the desire for other goals may persist throughout a lifetime. On occasion the achievement of one goal only sharpens the desire to move on to succeeding goals. Lord Acton's famous statement, "Power tends to corrupt; absolute power corrupts absolutely," stands as a commentary on the lifetime pursuit of

61

goals. Fortunately, many men seek goals which are more constructive than the pursuit of power. Nevertheless, human behavior can be seen as a continuing movement toward goals.

The forces which energize people are called motives

The exact nature of motivation is still unsettled by psychologists, but for our purposes we may identify motivational forces as the springs of behavior. They are the physical and psychic energies which drive people in the pursuit of goals. Some say that behavior is caused by the effort to get rid of tension, to reach a state of equilibrium or balance. Basic to this notion is the concept that unattained goals or unsatisfied desires create a tension or imbalance which the individual seeks to overcome. In more formal terms, motivation has been defined as "a mobilization of energy within the individual for the attainment or restoration of a pattern of desired social or biological states."[4]

We need not fully understand the inner nature of motivation, however, to observe its results or to apply it in our speaking. We need only to appreciate that people are impelled by wants, needs, and desires, and that these wants, needs, and desires are aroused by dissatisfaction within the individual with the state of his existence. Behavior to relieve this dissatisfaction is seen as the result of motivation.

Persuasion is effected when wants or desires are aroused, when needs are revealed, or when tensions are created, and when the goals of the speaker thereby become the goals of the listener. Specific kinds of wants or needs which arouse goal-seeking behavior will be detailed later in this chapter.

People tend to behave by habit and to seek a state of equilibrium

We have already noted that people seem motivated to overcome tension, to behave in ways which will enable them to find satisfaction by reaching goals. The converse of this is the principle that people seem by nature to seek a satisfying and balanced state of

---

[4] Wayne C. Minnick, *The Art of Persuasion.* (Boston: Houghton Mifflin Company, 1957), p. 205.

being. Having come to terms with the world-as-they-see-it, they find any upset of this world to be emotionally disturbing, involving as it does an interference with achieved goals or satisfactions. Thus a young man is angered when his plans for the evening do not meet the approval of his date, the manager loses his calm when a mechanical break-down upsets the production schedule, and an old man is irritated when his pipe and slippers are not in the accustomed place. In each instance the disorganization has upset a state of equilibrium, resulting in emotional disturbance.

The principle of equilibrium applies to both the intellectual and emotional components of behavior. Reflective thinking, we are told, begins whenever an individual becomes aware of a difficulty. When he recognizes that something is amiss he must try to analyze the situation, discover the nature of the problem, and seek a workable solution. Thus, a shopkeeper will run his store by habit until he discovers his volume and profit are falling. Then he must set about to correct the situation. The disturbance of routine is unwelcome, not only because it is emotionally annoying, but also because the mental operations involve extra effort. Nevertheless, having sensed a difficulty, the individual is moved to reduce or to eliminate it that he may return to a normal state of intellectual and emotional equilibrium.

An application of this principle can be found in Chapter 6 where it is suggested that in working with people the technique of "presenting problems and asking for solutions" can be advantageous. The principle also appears in conferences, for conferees must be involved in difficulties if they are to be motivated to take part in the search for a solution, which is the business of the conference.

The principle of equilibrium also explains the resistance to change which characterizes so many people, and which is a continuing problem in wide areas of business and industry. Change threatens each man's individual world, it disturbs his comfortable habit patterns, and it upsets his emotional equilibrium. One of the great problems of talking with people occurs when things must be changed.

Normal people are neither wholly rational nor wholly irrational

Most of us like to think that our behavior is directed by facts and logic, that we are highly rational beings governed by intelligence and good judgment. And while some may be unwilling to grant it, we often tend to think that others allow their behavior to be directed by their feelings and emotions, that others are irrational beings governed by impulse. Neither extreme accurately reflects the make-up of the average man. Even the most hard-headed purchasing agent or the most precise scientist, each taking delight in his logical behavior, is moved in part by the very feelings he associates with his logic. Most of us are a blend of the rational and irrational, and your speaking must take this into account.

A successful man is one whose behavior is appropriate

"Success" is a word which has as many meanings as there are people who use it, but we shall here make it apply to the individual who lives a well-integrated and sanely adjusted life. He is successful as a human being. His ambition may be to achieve a continuing series of constructive goals, and his drive to achieve those goals stems from a mature balance in his emotional life. He does not exhibit behavior patterns characteristic of childhood or adolescence, but meets the problems of daily life with self-command and perspective. His speech behavior is appropriate to his outlook on life and to the circumstances in which he speaks, as well as to those who hear him. In sum, he represents the best combination of the characteristics to be viewed in Chapter 4.

These eight assumptions and principles provide the foundation for our study of speech behavior. In their light we can now take up a more detailed examination of the essential elements or components of behavior.

THE ELEMENTS OF BEHAVIOR PROVIDE A BASIS FOR UNDERSTANDING PEOPLE

The accompanying diagram, which I have called "The Behavioral Pyramid," represents the elements of behavior which furnish the basis of our study. The elements are arranged in an ascending order, which is roughly the order in which behavior seems to happen, with sensation as the foundation for all response. Of course, there is a great deal of interaction among the elements, for a person behaves as an integrated whole rather than in a series of episodes as the pyramid might suggest, and at any given moment each of the elements may be affecting others. Yet the pyramid should nevertheless give us a useful notion of behavior. If we accept it as a conceptual model and not insist on making it an accurate representation, it will serve very well.

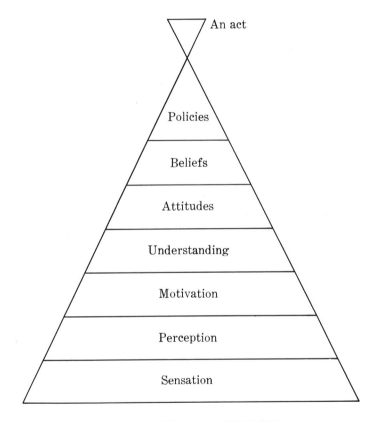

THE BEHAVIORAL PYRAMID

Within this concept a specific sequence of behavior may be understood to originate when a stimulus of some kind touches off a response by exciting the sensations. The responding behavior may continue upward through the layers of the pyramid, ceasing at any level which provides adequate satisfaction to the respondent. This

65

level of adequate and satisfying response we may call, for our purposes, terminal behavior, for it may identify the nature of the response our communication is designed to evoke. If the behavior continues all the way to the top, it issues in an overt or observable act of some sort, indicated by the small inverted pyramid. This is located outside of the basic pyramid to indicate that the elements which make up the latter are largely implicit or covert and cannot necessarily be seen by an observer. (Of course we realize that many covert forms of behavior can be detected by outward signs although the behavior itself is essentially internal.)

Recognizing, then, that the elements of behavior cannot in reality be separated in a living person as we have separated them here for analysis, let us nonetheless now consider them individually. They do make a useful way of talking about behavior, allowing us to appreciate that speech is directed toward their modification and control.

Sensation

News of the outside world reaches us only in the form of physical stimuli which impinge upon our sense receptors. Light waves and sound waves, our two major links with the world, beat upon us without ceasing. We are also assailed by odors which come to our nostrils, sunshine which warms our skins, and food and drink which stimulate our taste buds. The five external senses together with two internal ones have been popularly referred to as the "seven doors to the mind."

News also reaches us from within, for we are made aware of our own bodily condition and our internal reactions by stimuli which originate in various parts of the body. The feeling we get from riding an express elevator, for instance, is a result of internal stimuli. We also stimulate ourselves externally, for we are guided in the production of sound for speech by hearing our own voice as well as by subtle muscle tensions in the speaking mechanism. Such feedback is vital to the control of our own physical behavior, and constitutes the parallel which cyberneticists see between humans and automated mechanisms.

We noted in the preceding chapter that light waves and sound waves are the only true media of communication in speech. Of what practical use is this information?

Recall that the sensory stimuli to which we are subjected are infinite and endless, and that therefore we are never aware of most of them. We become aware of a given stimulus only when it crosses the "threshold of intensity," usually by change of intensity or by otherwise becoming differentiated from other stimuli. If a noise is loud enough or persistent enough we become conscious of it. We say that it catches our attention, by which we mean that we have "tuned in" on it.

As a speaker you are essentially a source of stimuli—of light waves and sound waves. To succeed in communicating you must first of all compete with various other stimuli at work, both in the environment and within those you are talking to. You must attract and keep the attention of your listeners. Unless you can succeed in getting them to "tune in" and stay tuned in, you are not being received. Attention can be defined as *the process of focusing on any source of stimulation and the shutting out of all competing stimuli.* As a speaker, you must be seen and heard in such a way that your listener will focus upon you, disregarding all else.

As a listener you are, conversely, a receiver of stimuli. You must, therefore, tune in by focusing your eyes and ears upon the speaker for the best reception. Good listening may be said to begin when you *act like* a listener.

Behavior, then, and specifically speech behavior, begins with sensation. Both the speaker and the listener must be aware of the stimuli they exchange, in the sense that they give one another undivided attention. Although it is usual to consider it the speaker's obligation to catch and hold the attention of the listener, good communication requires that the latter assume an equal share of the common responsibility. Much of your skill in speech communication will depend on your ability to hold the favorable attention of others, and upon your skill in attending to subtle stimuli—those which reveal how a person feels and thinks as well as what he is saying. We shall refer to this principle in later chapters.

Perception

Sensation may be thought of as essentially a physiological process, for it is merely the reception of stimuli and their transmission to the brain. The incoming nervous impulses are without significance until they become associated somehow with past experience which

67

assigns meaning to them. The operation of attaching meaning to stimuli we call perception. By it we select, define, organize, and interpret the multitude of varied sensations which come from within and without.

A person cannot stay focused on a specific and constant stimulus for more than a short time. His span of attention to one stimulus is normally limited to a few seconds, which means that you must, as you speak, constantly renew your listener's attention. You can achieve this in part by appropriate variety in the substance of your message as well as in your manner of speaking. But attention cannot be renewed by devices alone; the listener must perceive meaning and significance in your message. He must become so interested that he is impelled involuntarily to attend to what you have to say. Favorable perception by the listener, then, is an immediate prerequisite to continuing attention. Indeed, sensation-attention-perception are virtually simultaneous elements of a single process.

But perception is more important than simply a prerequisite to meaningful attention, for the way in which a person perceives stimuli governs his entire reaction to those stimuli. For this reason we need to examine the nature of this element of behavior and some of its implications for speech communication.

Were an Icelander to speak to you in his native tongue, all you would get would be an unintelligible confusion of sound—unless you understand Icelandic. Otherwise you are not equipped by prior experience to assign meaning to the sound patterns of that language. On the other hand, you are so accustomed to hearing the pattern of American speech that you are seldom aware of your active involvement in perceiving the sounds as meaningful talk. The same principle is true of what you receive through other senses; you assign meaning to everything you see and smell, feel and taste, in terms of your past. The world-as-you-see-it is a product of your unique perception of things.

Perception is in part a physiological phenomenon by which you relate and orient yourself to the physical world. By it you determine to your own satisfaction the relative sizes and shapes of things, their apparent distance from you, and so on. The color of a passing auto or the loudness of a person's voice are determined for you by your perceptions. Another person seeing the same car you do, or hearing the same voice, might dispute with you about either the color or the volume. Because of differences in perception, both could be "right." Different people perceive nearly identical stimuli differently.

Perception is also a psychological process; by it you attribute significance, value, or meaning to objects, persons, and relationships. It is said that Ebenezer Bryce's first remark on seeing the canyon which now bears his name was, "What a terrible place to lose a cow!" Today thousands of people visit Bryce Canyon to admire the mystifying beauty of its natural formations. Their perception is different from that of Mr. Bryce. Similarly, what to one person is a friendly smile is perceived by another as a leering grin. Clothing which may seem the height of fashion to those of America's jet-set might well be seen as ostentatious and artificial by a midwestern farmer. It has truly been observed that, "Beauty is in the eye of the beholder."

What leads people to perceive as they do? What leads two or more to perceive a given event differently? For one thing, the surrounding world is bombarding each with stimuli, too many to be noticed. The individual, therefore, is selective in his perception. He ignores some stimuli, but attends to others, selecting only those to which he can attribute meaning. This screening process, called abstraction, is a universal human characteristic, necessary if one is to "make sense" of the world, yet treacherous because it can lead to confusion and misunderstanding among people.

One critical factor in selective perception is memory. Since perception is based on prior experience, the influences of the past are vital to our perception of the present. We tend to be influenced more by those events of the past which were pleasant than those which were not, regardless of whether we are conscious of their influence or not. We also remember better those experiences which were originally vividly intense and those which have frequently been recalled or repeated. Consequently some events of the past sensitize us to particular stimuli, while other events cause us to ignore other stimuli.

We also tend to perceive what we are looking for, and thus we accept those stimuli which make up a pattern consistent with our expectations as well as with our memory. If you expect that a merchant may try to cheat you, you will perceive signs of dishonesty in his every action. The very language you use not only describes the world as you see it, but by naming your expectations it in part determines what you see. Your observations at a given institution might be quite different, depending on whether you were visiting a "lunatic asylum" or a "state hospital for the mentally ill." The label applied to something effectively shapes and colors our perception of it, and consequently our attitude and behavior toward it.

People not only perceive what they expect to, they also tend strongly to perceive what they want to. Because of this they project meaning onto people and events about them. A fearful salesman will perceive signs of rejection in every word of a prospective customer, while a baseball fan is apt to find in every poor pitch signs that the offending pitcher is headed for the showers. Doctors must be careful in diagnosis lest they judge an ailment quickly and then perceive symptoms which support their early opinion.

People also refuse to perceive what they do not want to. Recently a local office-holder became the center of a bitter political controversy: his opponents declared that he was "bullheaded, uneducated, rigid, and uncooperative," while his adherents affirmed that he was "kind, considerate, generous, and firm." Members of each side saw only what they wanted to, and refused to see anything more. Harold J. Leavitt states that as a rule, *"People perceive what they think will help satisfy needs; ignore what is disturbing; and again perceive disturbances that persist and increase."*[5]

The forces governing perception are not necessarily rigid, however, and the interplay of expectancies, attitudes, and communicative interchange can sometimes change perception during the course of an event. S. Howard Bartley, psychologist, provides an example of perceptual change during the course of an interview:[6]

> Soon she was in Mr. H.'s office talking to him, and listening to what he had to say. In the midst of this she realized how changed several things had become. She had changed while waiting to see Mr. H., and a part of the change was the way that things about her were perceived. Now she saw that Mr. H. looked very different in his present role than he had seemed on other occasions. She had heard that he was a little hard to please, but what she was hearing him say, and the way he was saying it, convinced her that her fears in this respect were ungrounded. His whole face looked different to her than it ever did. His voice was not what she expected, either.

[5] Harold J. Leavitt, *Managerial Psychology, 2nd Ed.,* (Chicago: University of Chicago Press, 1964), p. 33.
[6] S. Howard Bartley, *Principles of Perception* (New York: Harper & Brothers, 1958), p. 442.

The experience of this woman emphasizes what was said in Chapter 2, that in communication the factor of perception cannot be ignored. It is a major determinant in the behavior of people, strongly affecting what they talk about, how they talk about it, and the way they relate themselves to others through speech. We can listen carefully to others to help understand how they "see" things, and when we speak we can try to present our ideas in terms of the other's perceptions. In this way, to use Dr. Bois' expression, we can adapt ourselves to the climate of the other person's world.

Nor must we forget that character or reputation may also hinder or facilitate communication, since people will tend to perceive what they have been led to expect. If you should become known as the wise-cracking "joker" of a group, others would find it nearly impossible to "see" you in a serious role. The boy in Aesop's fable who cried "Wolf!" when there was no wolf was not believed when the wolf did come. The manager who, over the years, creates an image of an unsympathetic individual, will be unable to get others to talk to him frankly when the need arises.

Differences in perception, then, can create disagreement among people, even over the "facts" of a situation to which all are a party, to say nothing of the meaning or significance of those "facts." In a very real sense the function of communication is to enable people to "see" things in a similar way, to get them to arrive at common meanings. If a lawyer can get the jury to see things as he does, he will win his case. If a salesman can get the customer to see the benefit of purchasing his goods, he can make a sale. If a parent can understand how his child sees the world, he may be able to advise him wisely. Communication is the effort of people to see "eye to eye."

Motivation

We have already seen that each act of speaking or listening must be motivated, and we have established the principle that motives are the forces which energize the behavior of people toward goals. In later chapters we shall consider some of the methods of effecting motivation in specific speaking situations. Here we shall take up the more specific nature of the motives which actuate people.

Let us start by recognizing the two major bases of relationship between and among people by which one person can influence the

71

behavior of others or by which concerted action can be directed. The first relationship is based on power or authority, and the second on persuasion, the exact dividing line at times being obscure. A third relationship in which individuals unite or coordinate behavior voluntarily by agreement based on common understanding and shared goals, we shall exclude at this point.

Power establishes relationships on a coercive basis ranging from physical force to organizational authority or social status. The military hierarchy exemplifies one form of authoritative relationship, a counterpart of which exists in many if not most industrial and business organizations. In such organizations the power may not be naked, but it nevertheless exists, and is a potent factor in directing the behavior of people. Wherever there are rules of conduct, whether written or unwritten, and some means of enforcement, there are coercive relationships.

Persuasion arises from the ability of one person to evoke desired behavior voluntarily in another. "Leadership," it has been remarked, "is the ability to get someone to do what you want done because he *wants* to do it." The third form of relationship, participative association, mentioned above, may begin in persuasion but ultimately transcends it.

This book is based on the premise that persuasion is to be preferred to power, and that even when an authoritarian structure exists, the former should be sought before orders are given or authority invoked. You should read parts of Chapter 6 with this premise in mind, while remembering that in many situations authority remains, should persuasion fail.

But to be persuasive, we should understand the wants and needs of men, thereby increasing our ability to enlist these forces in directing the behavior of others. An understanding of motivation can also better enable us to know ourselves.

The basic wants and needs of men are those requirements which seem necessary if the individual is to develop and sustain himself as a human being in the fullest sense of the term. The needs are to his ego what vitamins and food are to his body, and each individual seeks to satisfy his self-nourishing needs as he does his physical needs.

Behavior, then, is seen as motivated by a feeling of want or need *within* the individual. In order to satisfy needs, men endeavor to reach goals which they see as promising satisfaction. As a hungry man will seek food to satisfy his need, so will a lonely one endeavor to find suitable companionship. And although the number of basic wants may be few, the number of goals which appear to satisfy them can be countless, such goals being largely culturally or socially determined. To satisfy a need for recognition, an Indian warrior might display the scalps he has taken in battle, a foreman might adopt a loud and bossy attitude, a businessman drive an expensive car, a laborer continually find fault with working conditions, or a surveyor become a collector of antique glassware. In each case, behavior can be understood as the effort of the individual to satisfy an inner want by attaining a perceived goal.

The following classification of needs draws significantly from psychologist Abraham H. Maslow, whose work in the field has strongly influenced current thinking. It is, however, modified by the work of others in the field of industrial psychology, and is based upon a classification of needs as essentially physical, personal, and social, depending upon the kind of goals which satisfy them.

These motivational needs seem to function in a hierarchial manner, those named first taking precedence over those later in the list. On this basis, the physical needs come first. Until they are satisfied, a man generally does not seek to fulfill his personal needs, nor does he seek goals to satisfy his socially-gratified needs until his personal ones are met. For instance, hunger is not a pressing problem for most of us, and so our eating behavior is motivated by personal or social needs rather than by primary physical ones. Eating provides satisfaction for our tastes or for our desire for companionship rather than meeting only our physical requirements. Again, demands by workers for higher wages seem to represent goals which satisfy status or ego-enhancing needs, not merely physical subsistence. In our civilization, most behavior apparently derives from needs which are satisfied by socially or culturally determined goals, whereas in some lands poverty and hunger prevail, making the satisfaction of physical needs paramount.

Here is the classification of needs we shall use, for it provides a useful explanation of behavior as related to speech communication.

Physical needs

Man's physical needs arise from the physiological functioning of the body, beginning with the need for food, optimum environmental conditions (temperature, humidity, air, etc.), sexual gratification, and the avoidance of physical discomfort. These are the needs whose gratification is derived from the physical world, and in the main, those which sustain a desirable level of physical existence. Included, of course, is the need to be free from pain and sickness, which motivates our visits to doctors and dentists, our annual consumption of aspirin, and some, but not all, of our dieting. Worthy of special note among the physical needs are three which seem to have special relevance to our interests.

1. SAFETY FROM ETERNAL DANGER. In a world of high speed transportation, complex and dangerous machines, and increasingly polluted air and water, sensitive men are more and more aware of threats to their well being. Automobile seat belts, research in safer air transportation, smog control, a nuclear navy, industrial safety campaigns, and drives to reduce indiscriminate use of pesticides are all motivated by this need.

2. ACTIVITY. Confinement to desk or office, the routine of the production line, the tedium of many jobs tend to create a need in many people for some form of physical activity, either as recreation or as a way of compensating for unbalanced living patterns. To satisfy this need, many take up golf or bowling, go hiking or camping, or find satisfaction in do-it-yourself jobs around the house.

3. SENSORY PLEASURES. The taste of broiled steak, the sigh of wind through pine trees, the salt odor of breaking surf, or the strains of a well-loved melody suggest that some behavior can be understood as a search for satisfaction of the senses. A person's desire to escape the anxieties and frustrations of living heightens the pleasure he finds in delighting his senses, giving rise to an increase in pleasure boating, affording patrons for good restaurants, and stimulating the growth of parks and vacation sites in locations of natural beauty.

Personal needs

After a man's indispensable physical needs have been met, he seems to turn next to the satisfaction of those needs arising from the fact that he is a human being and must, even unconsciously, strive to

74

fulfill his humanness. In order for life to be meaningful, he must assure himself of personal uniqueness and importance; but he must satisfy, not only the requirements of being himself, but also the requirements of having escaped, in the evolutionary journey, the limitations of being an animal. As an "emergent creature" endowed with mind, symbolic language, and a sense of abstract values, man senses that there is more to life than mere existence, and despite the brutishness of much about him, he responds to the vague impulse toward truth, beauty, and justice.

Each individual strives to fulfill himself, both as an individual and as a member of the family of man. To do so, he is impelled to satisfy in some degree these four specific needs.

1. SELF-RESPECT AND HUMAN DIGNITY. Man's first craving is to be able to look at himself with respect and dignity. He even prefers to "die with his boots on," if die he must, but before that he lives to maintain the integrity of both mind and body. He wants to be able to recognize himself as a human being, worthy in his own eyes to take his place in company with all other human beings. This is one reason he cherishes his own name and revolts against the trend toward becoming merely a number—whether a time card number, a social security number, a military serial number, a bank account number, or a number in line at the meat counter. It is one reason he battles against the anonymity of development housing or fears the growing facelessness of modern life. A man is eager to follow any path which promises him self-realization and a feeling of personal pride. He reacts against that which reduces his ego.

2. INDEPENDENCE. Allied with self-respect, humans want a relative degree of freedom and independence in carrying on their own affairs. They want to be able to make their own decisions, to escape the confining pressures of others, to stand upon their own feet. They seek self-confidence as the prerequisite to independence, and they are dissatisfied with decisions and policies in which they have had no voice.

American freedom and democracy, nurtured on the frontier and bequeathed in tradition from generation to generation, makes the desire for independence perhaps stronger in our nation than in many others. Yet the age-long history of man's struggles against tyranny suggests that indeed it may be an inborn need. At least the need for independence is basic, not only to our political system, but to the entire concept of private enterprise; and it explains the behavior which strikes out against whatever constrains the individual contrary to his consent.

3. OPPORTUNITY AND EXPRESSION. "What a man *can* be, he *must* be," writes Maslow, affirming that a significant human want is to find one's potential or capacity and to develop it. For ages men have found satisfaction for this want in their daily work, and many still do, despite the fact that modern conditions of work often tend to frustrate rather than to fulfill the need. Under these conditions some seek satisfaction in hobbies or avocational pursuits, while others suffer dull frustration. Many women find opportunity and self-expression as homemakers, and many others in civic or service activity.

Recent expansion of adult education can be accounted for, not only as a way of keeping up with rapid technological change, but also as a door to personal opportunity, for learning is a path to expression. The lives of creative workers in all fields—painting, literature, music, scientific research—are often dominated by the need to satisfy the desire for self-realization.

4. SECURITY. A man wants security, not only in his work and in his relations with others, but also in a deeper and even more fundamental way. He needs to live in an orderly and predictable world where he can have assurance of events and relationships, and where he is not physically threatened. We have seen how his perceptions are shaped by this desire for orderliness and consistency, and how resistance to change arises from the need for security. Man spends his lifetime putting the world-as-he-sees-it into a meaningful pattern, and anything which threatens this pattern is a threat to him.

"Self-preservation is the first law of nature," is a market-place maxim which is too often interpreted to apply to physical survival only. Equally strong, if not stronger, is man's desire to survive in essence, and his essence is something more than the physical body. Anything which threatens the meaning he has created for himself— his very ego—is a threat to his security. Man's behavior seeks to maintain both physical and spiritual security.

Social needs

The third cluster of men's needs are those whose satisfaction derives largely from association with others. Just as man must have strength and assurance in his own eyes, he must have approval from others. Man's gregariousness is more than a desire for company of his own kind, it is a consequence of the fact that he is a social being, that he finds something of his own meaning in his relationship with others. He cannot, as a human, survive alone. As a result he needs positive and constructive relationships.

Society itself is a pattern of relationships among people. Made up of individuals, it is more than their sum total, for it is the matrix in which life is conducted and from which each draws part of his own significance. Hence men are motivated to belong. They want to know that they are accepted, that their effort has contributed to the group's success, that they are "a part of the team."

Specific needs are manifold, but we shall notice four major ones.

1. LOVE. Every evidence indicates that love is essential to the full development and maturing of the normal human being, that man is not complete unless he loves and is loved by others. After forty years in the field of psychiatry, Dr. Smiley Blanton testifies:[7]

> To say that one will perish without love does not mean that everyone without adequate love dies. Many do, for without love the will to live is often impaired to such an extent that a person's resistance is critically lowered and death follows. But most of the time, lack of love makes people depressed, anxious, and without zest for life. They remain lonely and unhappy, without friends or work they care for, their life a barren treadmill, stripped of all creative action and joy.

We are not talking about the love of one sex for another, although this is a part of the whole. The larger love is that described by Saint Paul, which may be defined as an affirmative identification with other people, a "conscious acceptance and a thorough under-

[7] Smiley Blanton, *Love or Perish*. (New York: Simon and Schuster, Inc., 1956), p. 2.

standing of our relatedness to all other human beings." Men's need is reciprocal in that one must both accept and bestow regard and affection to be fully nourished as a healthy personality.

Deprived of love, or unable to give it, men grow resentful, narrow, suspicious, or bitter. Having been cut off from sustaining relationships, they grow negative or antagonistic, creating problems in the home, on the job, or wherever they may be. Motivated by love, men have done heroic deeds, provided for the unfortunate, founded hospitals and clinics, created homes, taxed themselves for the general welfare, or suffered silently for others.

2. APPRECIATION, RECOGNITION, ESTEEM. "Man's deepest craving," wrote William James, "is to be appreciated." All of us have felt the desire to be recognized for our achievements, to know that others have found us worthy, to be accepted as peers in our own company. A word of appreciation or recognition can be a strong force to motivate behavior or to strengthen personal relationships.

If an individual cannot win recognition in a constructive way, he easily turns to other methods of gaining attention. The misbehaving boy in the fifth grade may be only seeking attention. As a teenager he may turn to drag racing on main thoroughfares, and when he reaches adult years (if not behavior) he may be known for his loud talk and exaggerated statements.

Desire for approval can motivate long hours of study to make the Dean's list, great feats on the athletic field to win the crowd's applause, or many extra calls a day to become a Blue Ribbon Salesman. Across our nation are many college halls named for the one who gave funds for their construction, testimony to man's worthy hope that his accomplishment may be deserving of permanent recognition.

3. STATUS. Allied with the need to be recognized for accomplishment, is the one to be known for position, rank, or standing in a group or community. Men seek to occupy a place of acknowledged importance, and they find satisfaction in the signs or symbols of that place. Vance Packard's best-seller, *The Status Seekers,* is compelling testimony to the motivating force of the desire to display the trappings of position.

Moved by this desire, men buy houses in socially-approved sections of town, join country clubs, lodges, and professional organizations, drive the right kind of car, and vacation in selected locations. Some have even been known to choose a vocation on the basis of its prestige value. Of particular importance to us is the fact that the very person one talks to may provide status value. This is one of the reasons behind the fact that some people tend to talk more often to their superiors than to their peers or subordinates.

Studies also show that a speaker with an ascribed status is apt to be more successful in persuasion than one without status. Men not only seek status and its symbols, but they also tend to accept more readily one who possesses those things.

4. DEPENDENCE. Although man wants independence, at the same time he finds life the meaner if he cannot be dependent on others. In many circumstances he prefers not to "go it alone," but feels the need for the confidence derived from the support of others. This may be particularly true as an individual faces problems and decisions which seem to thwart his power to best them; the testimony of many executives, including Presidents of the United States, agrees on the feeling of loneliness which is a part of the cost of high office. But the need for the faith and support, and sometimes the advice, of others is not limited to those in high posts, for every worker recognizes his desire for good leadership, and depends upon it.

The need for dependence can become a power to motivate behavior particularly when the person offering leadership or support is perceived as being helpful to others *in attaining their own personal goals*. A follower does not find full satisfaction in depending on leaders whose personal goals are incongruous with those of the followers. Motivation can be effected when each member of a team or group identifies himself with the group goals, and consequently feels dependent upon others of the group to help achieve the common goals.

This three-fold classification of the wants and needs which motivate behavior is not intended to be exhaustive, but to be one useful to the needs of business and professional speaking. You should appreciate that similar classifications exist in great variation, and while there is general agreement, each writer brings his own experience and purpose to the task. Many a list of wants is so comprehensive that its very length is self-defeating.

You should appreciate, too, that while the needs we have named appear common to all mankind, they exist in different combinations and different intensities in each individual, making his behavior understandable only in terms of a particular convergence of forces. In the words of Aldous Huxley:[8]

> Human beings are immensely complicated creatures. . . . Each individual is unique and, in a number of respects, unlike all the other members of the species. None of our motives is unmixed, none of our actions can be traced back to a single source and, in any group we care to study, behavior patterns that are observably similar may be the results of many constellations of dissimilar causes.

An individual's behavior depends not only on the number and intensity of the desires which may motivate him, but also upon the direction in which they impel him. Like a sailboat, the direction of his behavior depends upon the way the winds blow, the intention of the helmsman, the size of the waves, the depth of the water, the cut of the boat, and the skill of the crew. It is possible for two opposing drives to cancel each other, leaving the person undecided or immobile. A few years ago a study was made of the purchasers of life insurance. These men were discovered to hold a deep-seated hostility to the whole idea of insurance even though they were consciously aware of the love and security needs which could be satisfied by its purchase. Subsonsciously, however, they displayed anxiety concerning the purposes of insurance agents, the desire of the beneficiaries (usually their wives) for an estate, and the thought of death. Insurance was unknowingly perceived by them as a threat to their own independence and security. Conflicting motives of this sort must be handled by a salesman if he is to be successful.

When we talk with others we will find our success increasing as we (1) increase our ability to understand the motives of those with whom we deal, and (2) are able to present our ideas and purposes as goals which will satisfy the perceived needs of those to whom we talk. The first of these depends in part upon our ability to be good listeners, and the second upon the skill with which we plan what we have to say.

[8] Aldous Huxley, "Drugs That Shape Men's Minds," from *Collected Essays* (Harper & Row, 1959), p. 336.

Understanding

Referring again to the behavioral pyramid, we should note that so far as communication is concerned, we have not yet been considering what we have called terminal behavior. That is, sensation, perception, and motivation do not normally in themselves constitute the goal of communication. An exception is when one speaks only to entertain, or simply to establish a pleasant social atmosphere or to enjoy the relationship made possible by the talk, the latter function being called phatic communication. In these exceptions, attending to and participating in the talk is in itself satisfying. But when we turn to understanding as a form of behavior, we are dealing with understanding as the desired response to speaking.

When we communicate to affect the behavioral elements above the level of understanding in the pyramid, understanding ceases to be terminal and becomes a means to a further end. A speaker may find it necessary to get response through each level to reach those above it, as, for instance, when he finds it necessary to gain understanding before belief or action can be secured.

When understanding is the ultimate purpose of speaking, we say the talk is to inform or instruct. We give directions, issue orders, present lectures, or deliver reports or briefings. Or we may be on the receiving end and find it necessary to listen that another can get us to understand.

In either event, understanding must be motivated. When you speak to get others to understand, you must be certain either that your listeners *already want to know* what you plan to tell them, or that you *create a need* for the material before you present it. The basic content of your talk must be seen to fill needs of which the listeners are aware.

You may have attended more than one lecture which you privately thought was dull and dry. If so, the lecturer was perhaps at fault for not creating in you a desire to know what he had to say. He may have shown no connection between the subject of the lecture and your personal needs or wants. Still, although it may not have been the most brilliant lecture ever delivered, the fault may in part have been yours if you didn't *want* to understand. You may have had a negative attitude toward the speaker which effectively walled you off from what he had to say. Although a speaker has the primary responsibility for arousing in his listeners a desire to hear his message, the latter also must recognize their obligation to take an active part in the communication process.

What do we mean by understanding? What happens when a person understands? Essentially it is the process by which new perceptions, new experiences, new information, and new ideas are received by an individual and are integrated meaningfully into his old and established patterns. It is a cognitive goal-related process by which the new assumes relevance and meaning in terms of the old. At times a fusion takes place which reveals old ideas and old perceptions in a new light, or which rearranges old patterns into new structures. If this recognition or rearrangement occurs swiftly it can be called *insight*. But always the new learning must be based on past experience.

For instance, if a stranger in town asks you for directions to reach a given address, you cannot get him to understand by reference to familiar landmarks. You cannot say, "It is four blocks from the art museum," for his experience does not include either the location or the appearance of the art museum. You must therefore get him to understand in terms of things he does know. You have to say something like, "Follow this street to the third traffic light. Turn right and go two more blocks, then turn left and follow that avenue as it curves to your right again. You will cross a small bridge, and your destination is just beyond that bridge." Traffic lights, city blocks, and small bridges are presumably within the experience of a stranger, and you can thereby get him to understand.

Communication to develop understanding may take one of two forms. The first is through direct first-hand experience, based on the principle that people learn by doing or seeing. One *knows* the shattering impact of an automobile accident by having lived through it. The principle of learning from experience may sometimes be planned by a communicator as a way of gaining understanding. This is the laboratory method in teaching, yet it may be applied outside the classroom. Clerks learn how to fill out sales slips by practicing on fictitious sales, or parachutists learn how to hit the ground by dropping from towers.

The second way of developing understanding is by the use of words or symbols only. We *tell* people what we want them to understand (assuming that we have created a desire to know) ; the understanding is vicarious, depending entirely upon the listener's prior experience and our skill in telling. The listener may then be said to *know about* the subject as one may know about the same shattering impact of an accident by being told.

Since direct experience is normally a more effective way of learning than verbal instruction, speakers often try to come close to the reality of first-hand experience by using illustrative anecdotes, word pictures, descriptive physical action, films, displays, sound effects, and models. Skillful use of words which recall sensory experience in the listener (the principle of imagery) can be effective in gaining either understanding or belief. According to Wayne C. Minnick of Florida State University :[9]

> Although one cannot expect the audience to perceive his verbally reconstituted experience with the same sense of reality as they perceive an actual event, he can expect, if he is skillful in the use of words, to elicit a response that is very nearly the equivalent, or in some instances is the exact equivalent, of that produced by direct contact with environment. This happens because people tend to respond to words with the same response they accord to the real things the words stand for.

It should be clear that when you speak to get understanding, you must begin at the listener's level of readiness, for understanding begins when you effectively manipulate the prior experiences of the hearer. Be certain that any unfamiliar words or terms are made clear. Go carefully from point to point, frequently using a system of enumeration to make the order of your material clear. You will often find it useful to give your listener a skeletonic *preview* of the points or sections which make up the structure of your message. Then as you supply the details, he has a prior mental impression of the whole to which he can connect the details. A final summary will also help fix in the listener's mind the things you want him to remember.

We cannot leave this section without noting that there are times we wish to affect behavior at the level of learning without being involved in the cognitive aspects we have so far been talking about. These are the times when we would like to have another simply strengthen or retain a response he has made, or would like to eliminate one. Perhaps we want a subordinate to learn that trucks should always be as clean as the one he has just washed, or that

---

[9] Minnick, *The Art of Persuasion*, p. 178.

fifteen minutes is too long for a coffee break. In such situations the principle of *reinforcement* can be used.

Fundamentally reinforcement is a way of conditioning behavior. When a given response is followed by a reward (anything which satisfies or reduces an existing need), the likelihood of that response being repeated increases. Conversely, punishment or negative reinforcement tends to inhibit a response. It should be noted, however, that punishment does not appear to have more than a temporary effect in stamping out undesirable behavior, whereas unreinforced behavior tends toward extinction. Thus the principle would be to *reward behavior which you want another to learn or repeat, but make sure that undesirable behavior is unrewarded.*

This principle can be applied to person-to-person speaking and in group situations. An approving word, a nod or smile, or other encouragement is often enough to reinforce desirable behavior, while the absence of approval tends to discourage it. Expressions of disapproval, especially by several in a group, tend to suppress undesirable behavior.

Attitudes

Beginning with understanding and continuing upward in our behavioral pyramid, each of the levels may by definition constitute a form of terminal response. Following our model, you should remember that, in general, to evoke any desired form of terminal behavior a speaker must deal in sequence with the elements below it, beginning at the base.

Although we have placed attitudes on the level above understanding because the latter seems to have an effect in determining attitudes, to some degree the relationship is reciprocal, in that attitudes also tend to condition understanding. An individual with a negative attitude toward evolution, for instance, might have difficulty understanding the subject because his attitude unconsciously closes his mind to it.

We may define an attitude as an habitual tendency to respond in a general way toward a given object. The object toward which the attitude is directed may be a person, a group or class of persons, an institution, a physical object or class of objects, an idea, or a situation. The attitude itself may be positive or negative or indifferent, and it may exist in varying degrees of potency although the indi-

84

vidual rarely is conscious of possessing it. You yourself have an accumulation of attitudes, for example, towards objects such as a co-worker, retail sales people as a class, "The Company," cats, tea parties, and poetry. Toward such objects you are preconditioned to respond favorably, unfavorably, or with unconcerned disregard, and your responses may be in varying degrees of intensity.

We must not overlook the fact that you also have an attitude, or perhaps a set of attitudes, toward yourself, which tend to determine your relations with others, and hence your effectiveness in speech. There may be times when a person is indifferent to himself, but as a rule, self-attitudes are either positive or negative. An individual with strongly positive attitudes toward himself may speak with exaggerated humility, pompously, flippantly, cynically, or with indifference to others. One with strongly negative self-attitudes is apt to communicate indifference, uncertainty, withdrawal, affectation, or overly compensatory aggressiveness. Neither extreme creates satisfactory relations with others. The effective speaker possesses a positive self-attitude only intense enough to give him appropriate confidence and an objective outlook.

Attitudes are created and modified by the experiences of life or are adopted from the revealed attitudes of other people. Since attitudes contribute to how we "see" things, they may be thought of as related to perception, and like perception, they can be changed or modified. Such altering of attitudes can be important in communication, either as a condition prerequisite to affecting other elements of behavior or as an end in itself.

An attitude can rarely be changed by a direct approach. "You ought to change your attitude," is a common but futile piece of advice. Seldom was anyone argued out of a negative attitude toward salmon loaf or women bus drivers. A person whose attitude is challenged tends to cling to it stubbornly, for by defending his attitude he defends his own integrity. If attitudes are to be modified, it must be by indirection rather than command or injunction.

First-hand experience can be as important in changing attitudes as it is in forming them. A negative attitude toward dentists, for instance, can be significantly lessened by an agreeable experience in a dental chair. An industry holds "open house" so the citizens of the community, as well as the families of the workers, will have first-hand knowledge of the plant and as a result desirable attitudes toward the industry will be nourished. Words must take the place of experience when one hopes to change another's attitude, but the words should be used to describe or explain instead of to command or admonish. Speech to modify attitudes should as a rule conceal its purpose, and should abound in illustration and word pictures.

Group speaking situations, as noted in the chapter on conferences, can also be effective in altering attitudes. When the situations provide for free interaction and are geared to creative learning, participants are influenced by the expressed or implied attitudes of each other. Conferences cannot effectually be employed to implant predetermined attitudes (unless they are "rigged" and not truly conferences), but they do allow an opportunity for the participants to change their own. As Cortright and Hinds of Wayne State University put it, "We do not pour ideas and attitudes into learners. We awaken their desires, confront them with problems, make available facts and knowledge for their use, and hope they will change as a result."[10]

In speech-making, the good-will or public relations talk discussed in Chapter 9 is increasingly used to establish or change attitudes. This kind of speech seeks to create favorable attitudes toward a company, an industry, or an individual by presenting information consistent with desirable attitude patterns. Speeches to stimulate may also aim to develop desirable attitudes; for instance, a speaker at the ceremony opening a new factory might hope to develop favorable attitudes toward company policies.

As you speak, you should be alert to the attitudes of your listeners toward you, toward your subject, and toward your perceived purpose. Appreciating these attitudes, you should adapt your speaking to them, so that both you and your message appear consistent with them. You should also be aware of your own attitudes, building positive ones toward your listeners, your message, your purpose, and yourself.

As a listener you should similarly be aware of your attitudes toward the speaker and his message, so that you are neither unduly influenced by your own positive attitudes nor prevented by negative ones.

You should be aware, too, of the fact that words can be used to trigger attitudes, favorable or unfavorable, which can either facilitate or hinder communication. Such words are known as "loaded," "slippery," or sometimes "incendiary." It makes a difference

[10] Rupert L. Cortright and George L. Hinds, *Creative Discussion*. (New York: The Macmillan Company, 1959), p. 267.

whether one says *surgeon* or *butcher, statesman* or *politician, new-fangled* or *modern,* for each word puts the object in a different context and invokes a different pattern of attitudes.

Beliefs

Whereas attitudes can be described as generalized, diffuse, and unthinking, belief is a more specifically focused and conscious form of behavior. People are often more aware of their operational beliefs than of their attitudes, and are able to offer reasons for possessing the former. Belief can be called behavior which gives assent to a proposition. It is conscious recognition of an idea or claim, accompanied by agreement that the idea or claim is valid. To believe is to accept a proposition as true. If your neighbor says that he has seen a flying saucer and you are sure that he did, you believe. If your mayor announces that the city's financial condition requires a cut in the number of municipal employees, those who agree are believers, while those who do not are dissenters.

Since beliefs are, or can be, verbalized, and since the propositions with which people agree or disagree are expressed in words, belief can be described as a form of symbolic behavior. The significance of this fact is that belief does not necessarily, therefore, result in overt physical behavior. A man can believe sincerely that he should visit a dentist twice a year, but this does not mean that he actually does. Similarly, an individual may have beliefs which are entirely false to fact, and may even act upon them to his own harm. Mature behavior occurs when one's world of symbols is an accurate representation of the world of reality.

Each of us possesses a countless number of beliefs, not all of which are mutually consistent. A person might believe, for instance, that the government should not interfere with business, and also believe that Congress should increase the tariffs protecting his own product. Since beliefs operate on different levels of abstraction, and since an individual at any given time is aware of only a small fraction of his beliefs, he is usually not aware of his inconsistences. So long as inconsistent beliefs are held in "watertight compartments," the individual suffers no inconvenience or stress. But when an individual does become aware of two mutually inconsistent beliefs, he must, to avoid frustration or embarassment, either dismiss one or rearrange his thinking to achieve a satisfactory congruity.

The many beliefs of an individual likewise exist in varying degrees of intensity. Those of low intensity exert little or no effect upon his overt behavior, while those of high intensity determine to a large degree how he acts. The degree of intensity is the "energy power" associated with a belief. If you believe that smoking endangers health yet continue to consume two packs of cigarettes a day, your belief has a low *vitality*. If you switch to a pipe because you feel it would be less dangerous to your health, your original belief has a higher degree of intensity. But if you stop smoking altogether, your belief possesses a maximum intensity, all other things being equal.

As infants and children, people acquire beliefs uncritically from their parents and family, from playmates, and from teachers and others with whom they associate. Many of these beliefs persist throughout life. As they grow older, they continue to derive many of their beliefs from others whom they consider authorities. In primitive tribes, the witch doctor may be the source of beliefs. In contemporary America it is the scientist, the specialist, the expert, or the newspaper headline.

Experience, both direct and vicarious, also determines belief. We tend to believe what we see, forgetting that our experience is apt to be only fragmentary and colored by our perceptions. Alex, for instance, believes that a certain foreign car is uncomfortable, since he rode three blocks in one on a cold, wintry night. Experience, either direct or verbal, helps us arrive at beliefs by reasoning or inference. One might be led to believe that education is a productive investment for any nation as a result of examining statistics showing that the economic health of a country varies directly with the amount spent on schooling.

Two factors condition an individual's acceptance of beliefs from these sources, however. The first is that *a person tends to accept any idea which is presented to him unless that idea is inconsistent with a belief or attitude he already holds and is aware of.* Since children have not accumulated a great store of beliefs, it is easy for them to accept fairy tales, Santa Claus, and all the folklore of childhood. As they grow older and their stock of beliefs accumulates, it becomes increasingly difficult for them to accept new ideas. Ideas which are incongruous with beliefs already held tend to be rejected, while congruity facilitates acceptance. If Walter has believed for years that the health of an institution depends upon its taking in more money then it spends, he cannot accept the idea of an increase in the national debt, despite the explanations of the economists he calls "egghead radicals." Similarly Julia, who has a negative attitude toward what she terms "longhaired music," will refuse to believe that a symphony concert would be enjoyable, although she takes pleasure in many popular selections adapted from serious compositions. She accepts only what is compatible with her existing attitudes and beliefs.

The second factor conditioning the acceptance of ideas is that *a person tends to believe any idea which promises to satisfy one of his felt needs.* Experimental evidence strongly supports Brigance when he says, "We tend to see what we want to see and believe what we want to believe."[11] This accounts for the thousands of people who each year spend millions of dollars for fraudulent cures for cancer and arthritis, sink hard earned money in investment schemes which promise high returns, or buy dream homes at prices beyond their means.

When you speak to persuade, or to induce belief, you should understand as fully as possible the nature of your listeners' existing beliefs, and the relation of those beliefs to the proposition you intend to offer. That relation will, as a rule, be one of three kinds.

First, your central idea may be one which the listeners already believe. Your task then is not to induce new ideas or to change opinions, but to increase the intensity or power of beliefs currently held, to renew or revitalize old faiths, or old beliefs. Some of Winston Churchill's war speeches are magnificent examples of the power of speech to renew faith and keep alive hope. You yourself may want to increase enthusiasm, to generate determination, to arouse people to action, and this you may do by kindling the motives which energize people.

When we talk to arouse this kind of behavior, we say that we are speaking *to stimulate.* A manager talking to his salesmen, a minister addressing his congregation, a political candidate speaking to members of his party, an editor addressing a meeting of journalists may all face a similar task, that of speaking to listeners who already believe, but whose belief is feeble and must be restored and reinforced.

Second, your central idea may be one toward which your listeners are not committed. Either your proposition is new to them,

[11] William Norwood Brigance, *Speech: Its Techniques and Disciplines in a Free Society,* 2nd Ed. (New York: Appleton-Century-Crofts, Inc., 1961), p. 112.

or if known, one upon which they have made no decision. We say then that your purpose is *to convince* them. Under usual circumstances, a lawyer addressing a jury, an engineer presenting recommendations for a change in production methods, a witness testifying before a legislative committee, or an advertising executive trying to get approval of a new campaign from a client exemplify talking to convince. The procedure is sometimes deliberative, and the persuasive method consists essentially in showing that the proposition will satisfy the wants of the listeners and is congruent with their existing attitudes and beliefs.

Finally, your central idea may be inconsistent with the existing beliefs of your listeners. Again, your purpose is *to convince*, except that instead of simply making a decision, you must get the listeners to change their minds. This is a delicate undertaking, not only because people will not accept an idea which is incongruent with those they already hold, but also because the change may be perceived as a threat to their security or identity.

You must, first of all, avoid saying anything which will tend to make your listeners opponents. Once they take conscious opposition to your point of view, you will have virtually no chance of winning them. Persuasion can be effected, however, by removing or modifying the beliefs of the listeners which conflict with your proposition, and by so arousing their wants that the new idea will be more appealing than the conflicting old one. An appliance salesman, for instance, trying to sell a food freezer to a couple who believe they cannot afford it, might remove the objection by showing that they cannot afford to be without it, since they will save money by purchasing food in quantity and storing it. He could then appeal to the desire for freedom and independence by vividly depicting how the number of shopping trips to the supermarket would be reduced, repeating his theme that the freezer would help them save money.

Since authority, experience, and reasoning are important determinants of belief, your persuasion is enhanced to the degree that you are able to establish your own authority to speak on a subject, that you can make your proposition consistent with the prior experiences of the listeners, and that you can support your proposition with facts and evidence. But above all, persuasion is accomplished by showing that your proposition will satisfy the eager desires of those who listen.

Policies

"Policy" is not a term commonly used by psychologists to describe an element of behavior, yet it is one I think appropriate to indicate a particular sort of belief. The word itself is familiar to you, for it indicates a settled course of action, a generalization for governing behavior in future situations. Individuals, groups, and institutions establish policies as a matter of course, whether those policies are formally stated or not. A housewife may make it a policy not to buy from door-to-door salesmen, a group of men in a car pool may follow a policy of having the next-in-turn drive when the regular driver is ill, or a company may have a policy of promotion within the ranks rather than bringing in a new man when a vacancy occurs.

A policy is symbolic behavior which sets the conditions of future action, and because it is verbal may be classed as a belief. To set policy is, however, a matter of more serious concern than simply to believe, since setting policy implies accepting the consequences of that policy, together with a commitment to act in an established way. It is a more public matter than a private belief.

For these reasons the process of establishing a policy generally involves a greater amount of deliberation than that of accepting a proposition which will constitute belief. Deliberation means that the decision is made critically and as a consequence of balancing advantages against disadvantages. Frequently the deliberation of policy will incorporate a comparison of several lines of action before fixing upon the final one. Although this demands reflective thinking and rational speaking, motivation is still important to deliberation, for policy makers hope to display wisdom, and the desire to display wisdom is itself motivating. Yet logical argument is likely to have a more prominent place in deliberative speaking than in other forms of persuasion.

The purpose of distinguishing policy from any other form of belief lies in the desirability of knowing clearly the behavioral aim of any talk. If you know precisely what is to be accomplished, you begin with greater chances of success than if you do not. Whether you talk, whether you listen, or whether you exchange ideas, you should know that a policy is a conscious prelude to action, that it

91

calls for commitment, and that its consequences may be more significant than the policy itself.

An act

As we think of it here, an act is a single overt form of behavior, such as voting, donating to the One Fund Drive, attending a professional meeting on the ninth of May, or buying Brand X on the next shopping trip. An act takes place at a given time and in given circumstances, and is the result of both motivation and opportunity.

Many writers do not distinguish the several sub-divisions of speech purpose, preferring to group the influencing of attitudes, beliefs, policies, and actions within the general category of persuasion. The view of this book, as expressed in the previous section, is that your chances of success in communication are better when you know the precise goal you seek as a speaker and the exact kind of behavior expected of you as a listener. I have therefore differentiated the persuasive purposes of speaking into influencing attitudes, revitalizing old beliefs, establishing new beliefs, creating policy, and securing definite action. The first two may be called stimulation, the second two, conviction, and the last actuation.

What, then, sets actuation apart from the others? The difference lies in the fact that when you want action you must clearly and definitely specify the act you are urging upon your listeners. Often you must stimulate and perhaps convince in order to get action, but unless you name the desired act, you may fall short of your goal. If I ask that you keep your car in good mechanical condition, I am trying to get you to adopt a policy, not perform an act. If I want you to *do* something about it, I will have to specify some particular action, such as having your car inspected tomorrow. I will have to be precise in naming the action wanted, and I will be more successful if I tell you *when* and *where* to do it.

People who must secure action by speaking will be more effective, too, if they make every effort to see that the requested action can be done easily. They will see that the order form is at hand, the petition is waiting to be signed, the merchandise is on the counter, or a car available to take voters to the polls.

The foregoing eight elements of human behavior provide us with a basis for increasing our understanding of the people we talk with and the role of communication in affecting behavior. Speech is directed toward the modification and control of these elements, which comprise the ends of speaking or the means of securing the ends. Because of the unpredictable forces which influence human behavior, you may not always secure the results you are after, but you will almost certainly not induce given behavior unless you know exactly what results you are after. In later chapters you will find an application and elaboration of some of the principles set forth here.

But before we end our consideration of the people you talk with, we should turn our attention to some kinds of general behavior patterns.

SPEECH BEHAVIOR IS OFTEN AN EXPRESSION OF MORE GENERAL BEHAVIORAL TENDENCIES

As I have already pointed out, the whole man responds to every situation as he sees it. Included in the situation are the people present, the group, organization, or affiliations which exert an influence, the events which are happening, and the physical setting. All these, together with memories and expectations, form a universe at the center of which is the whole man. He organizes the kaleidoscopic elements into a pattern, and then responds to that pattern. His response may be based on the memory of an event in days long since gone, on what he expects to happen in the next moment, or on some unknowable combination of the elements of the situation as he sees them. *Talk is a portion of this fluid behavioral situation.*

Psychologists recognize typical ways of responding to a situation or to a continuing condition. Each individual in the course of his lifetime tends to develop habitual patterns of response which are variations of the recognized ways of behaving. Such patterns are the ways in which the elements of behavior are integrated into a manner of meeting life, part of which may be expressed by the content, form, and manner of speaking.

Our analysis is based upon the classification of situations and responses outlined by Eisenson, Auer, and Irwin, in their book, *The Psychology of Communication.*[12] They see behavior in three basic patterns. The first is a fear response aroused by situations which

[12] New York: Appleton-Century-Crofts, Inc., 1963.

threaten an individual's security, and which often arise unexpectedly, and are new or strange. The second is an anger response aroused by situations which prevent the attainment of a goal or which prevent an individual from behaving in a way he finds satisfactory. The last is a pleasure response aroused by situations which permit the satisfaction of needs and desires or which remove threats to an individual's well-being.

In these pages we shall recognize some typical forms of behavior which can be associated with each of the three basic responses. We must keep constantly in mind, however, that we greatly oversimplify the delicate and complex problem of analyzing human behavior, even though it may be helpful in understanding why some people talk as they do.

Fear responding behavior

One form of response to a fear-provoking situation is either avoidance or escape. The first of these is intended to prevent a fear-provoking situation from arising, the second seeks to evade the consequences when it does arise. Thus a man will follow orders to avoid reprimand or punishment, or may attempt to shift the blame for an error from himself to another in order to escape penalty.

A second form of response to a threatening situation is anxiety, a state in which the individual becomes physically or emotionally disturbed when he cannot avoid or escape the conditions which arouse his fears. A salesman may become anxious when he finds himself unable to meet his quota, a teacher may become anxious when she cannot control an unruly class, a child may become anxious when separated from its parents, or a manager may become anxious when he perceives signs that someone else may get the promotion he has been looking forward to. Under conditions of anxiety people often have difficulty eating and sleeping, their normal behavior may tend to disintegrate, and, if conditions are prolonged, they may develop ulcers or other physical ills.

A sense of inferiority may be classed as a form of anxiety, since it arises from a feeling of inadequacy in specific situations, or in life itself. Commonly over-emphasized by the popular term "inferiority complex," attitudes of inferiority are said by some psychologists to constitute a normal rather than an abnormal trait.

Individuals suffering from negative self-evaluation can be touchy, tense, or edgy, quick to feel slighted, their feelings easily hurt, and resentful of criticism. Or they may be nerveless and colorless, asking in their behavior for reassurance.

Over-compensation for a sense of inferiority can make a person outwardly strong, even rigid and tyrannical. Such an individual needs to prove to himself that he is able, and to do so he must show others that he never makes a mistake. He cannot admit his own weaknesses, even to himself. In extreme cases he may become a miniature Hitler.

A third way of meeting fear-producing situations is to attack and overcome them, or to attack the fear itself. This may be viewed as a variation of avoidance behavior, but it is aggressive, not defensive. A student fearing failure in a course may so vigorously set himself to study that he achieves a worthy grade, or an individual fearful of the necessity of making speeches may take himself in hand and conquer his stage fright by actually doing the thing he fears.

Anger responding behavior

One form of behavior in response to an anger-producing situation, and perhaps the major one, is frustration. Frustration occurs when an individual's normal goal-seeking behavior is delayed or thwarted in some manner. Prevented from reaching goals or from behaving in a comfortable and satisfactory manner, the individual becomes disturbed and is likely to behave in unproductive ways. A child, prevented from possessing some object his heart is set upon, may cry or sulk. A young man whose girl friend is late for an appointment may begin to cast his eyes at other girls. Behavior may regress to patterns of childhood, as when a man kicks the automobile which refuses to run. Some people find more satisfactory ways of reacting to frustration, such as the woman whose hopes of marriage have not succeeded, and who sublimates her response by working for charities.

We all suffer minor frustrations from day to day. As a result we develop a certain amount of tolerance for frustration, some of us more than others. It is the more prolonged frustration which characterizes important behavior patterns. A scientist whose search for financial support for his research is fruitless may become a dejected routine laboratory technician. A young actress whose hope for fame seems gone may try an overdose of sleeping pills. Many who cannot find a satisfactory meaning or purpose in life become alcoholics. Some find alternate goals or forms of behavior which adequately replace those denied, while others silently and perhaps resentfully endure, and still others give up the struggle. A few suffer complete demoralization.

A second form of behavior in the face of anger-provoking situations is aggression. Some psychologists hold that aggression is invariably a consequence of frustration, that the two behaviors are virtually inseparable. For us it will do to recognize that situations which arouse anger and produce frustration do also give rise to aggressive behavior. Few of us have not felt like breaking the television set when it failed to work, or like kicking ourselves when we blew a two-foot putt. Frustration does often create an impulse to strike out in same manner.

Aggression may grow into an almost permanent behavioral tendency. Ray, for instance, small in stature and with a limited education, has spent his life driving for recognition and power. He has bullied and blustered his way into a branch managership, from which there is no promotion without the educational experience he does not possess. His drive for advancement and power is now blocked, yet he cannot give up. Consequently his voice becomes louder and his actions more violent. His aggression takes the form of browbeating both his subordinates and his family.

Aggression may take several forms and issue in different directions. It may be directed at the object or situation which created it, and may become constructive rather than destructive in nature. An individual may work endlessly to overcome the competition which has prevented him from getting what he considers his share of the market. Another may labor on an invention to overcome the obstacles he faces. In many ways, aggression underlies constructive motivation.

In other ways, aggression may be directed destructively at objects or at people who are innocent of any connection with the anger-causing situation. One man throws things when he cannot achieve an immediate goal. Another, frustrated by company policy, takes his aggressive feelings out on his office associates and becomes hard to work with. When destructive aggression promises to bring further undesirable consequences, it may issue in some more subtle form of behavior. It can be seen in spiteful conduct, in name-calling and rumor-bearing, in the faint praise which damns, in a tendency to be argumentative, or in cunning opposition to the suggestions of colleagues.

This form of behavior shades into the third manner of responding to anger-provoking situations, revenge, which is a measure of retaliation or repayment, usually directed at persons perceived to be the cause of the difficulty. A grade-school boy, unable to succeed in his school work and therefore failing to get the attention of others, set fire to the school during vacation. His action was found out because he could not resist bragging of his way of "getting even" with school authorities. Workers in years past have been known to destroy the machinery which replaced them on the job. Verbal abuse, snide remarks, or an uncooperative attitude are more common forms of aggressive revenge.

Pleasure responding behavior

Psychologists have been unable to find a generally more satisfactory explanation of behavior than the pleasure-pain principle, which postulates that humans seek behavior which provides them satisfaction and pleasure, and avoid that which results in irritation, discomfort, and pain. The two types of behavior we have just considered are negative patterns of response to situations which humans would like to avoid. In contrast, pleasure responding behavior is the pattern of reaction which results in a feeling of gratification and which is therefore attractive.

Whatever offers satisfaction of men's wants and desires bestows pleasure. Consequently people tend to acquire and to repeat behavior which they find pleasant, or which aids in desirable adjustment to the situations causing it. This rewarding effect we have identified as positive reinforcement, and have suggested that it offers a useful approach to understanding behavior and to constructively guiding it, either through speech or otherwise.

Reduced to its simplest, this means that you can encourage desirable behavior in others by rewarding it when it occurs or by withholding reward when it does not occur. Similarly you can offer the promise of pleasure or reward for future desirable behavior, or the promise that no reward will be gained in the absence of desirable behavior. The effectiveness of this motivation is based on two assumptions, first that your own behavior is sincere and your promises within your power to keep, and second, that the reward will satisfy a need actually felt by the other person and not one which you only presume exists.

Teachers use positive reinforcement, both for academic achievement and for desirable conduct. They offer words of praise or criticism, display work of high quality, organize honor societies, bestow prizes, and ensure a feeling of gratification for quality performance. Managers, too, praise initiative, post competitive records, and offer encouragement to their workers. Sales managers run contests and offer bonuses, while delivery people reward efficient handling. Wherever responsible leaders must control behavior, the pleasure principle is put to work.

Let us re-emphasize that negative reinforcement, the use of punishment, fear, or anxiety, produces questionable results, although it, too, is frequently invoked. Reprimands, fines, the loss of privileges, suspension, threats, physical punishment, or the loss of personal liberty produce a dampening effect on undesirable behavior, but seldom achieve a substitution of improved patterns of response. The satisfaction produced by the original but objectionable behavior is rarely offset by what is called aversive control, which, indeed, may bring about hostility, a revenge response, or a deliberate repetition of the punished behavior. Positive reinforcement is to be preferred, for, as psychologist Robert Lundin remarks, "The proper use of positive reinforcement cannot only act for the better interests of the individual but for the whole of society as well."[13]

We should finally note that attractive and repulsive forces may operate simultaneously on an individual, producing tension, inner conflict, or ambivalent behavior. The latter, a product of opposing feelings in the same person at the same time, may make an individual uncertain of what behavior is appropriate, or may make him inconsistent in his behavior over a period of time. Nathaniel Cantor lays stress on the human need for both dependence and independence, indicating that these opposing motivations may result in ambivalent behavior. On the job a man may feel dependent upon positive, constructive leadership, yet have a deep desire to assert independence. His ambivalence may take the form of criticizing his

[13] *Personality, An Experimental Approach* (New York: The Macmillan Company, 1961), p. 418.

superiors at intervals, or of occasional erratic insistence on doing things his own way.

Good speaking is not born of destructive aggression, of withdrawal, of anxiety, or of inferiority. The most effective speaking and listening must be predicated on a mature and capable personality which responds to life situations in positive and productive behavior patterns, some of which we will take up in the next chapter. Yet many people behave in negative and non-productive ways, and these are some of the people with whom we must establish relationships and do business. Our responsibility is not to judge them, but to understand them. And, as psychologists Menninger and Levinson have put it, "Recognizing that people are different—that everyone has his own strengths and abilities, his own weaknesses and limitations—is the first step in understanding people."[14] If we can add a positive desire to create respect and good will, our talk will succeed more often than not.

[14] William C. Menninger and Harry Levinson, *Human Understanding in Industry* (Chicago: Science Research Associates, Inc., 1956), p. 20.

Part Two

THE PERSON

Chapter 4

The Responsible
Communicator

The first necessity is to be a good man—to know your product, to believe in it, to understand and believe in people, to have sound ethical standards, to be reliable, to deserve a reputation for standing on your word. This is what "stands over you and shouts so loud I can't hear what you say to the contrary." Unless you are worthy of trust and respect, no amount of skill in speaking will ever fool many people for very long.[1]

DR. ROBERT T. OLIVER, *Chairman*
Department of Speech
The Pennsylvania State University

WHAT KIND OF PERSON DOES IT TAKE TO BE A GOOD SPEAKER? WILL you, as an effective communicator, be expected to possess special personal qualities which distinguish you from other people?

A few years ago a research team at the Ohio State University set out to find answers to questions such as these. Specifically, they wanted to know if *professional* communicators possessed characteristics which distinguished them from other professional people. So they interviewed 248 professional people at length. Part of them were teachers, clergymen, journalists, broadcasters, and lawyers, all of whom made their living by communicating. The others were professional engineers, who made up a control group against which the professional communicators were compared. All were asked the same set of questions.

[1] Robert T. Oliver, "Who Says You Should Be a Better Speaker?" *Today's Speech*, XI, No. 2 (April, 1963), p. 17.

103

What was the conclusion of the study? The researchers found that no significant difference could be determined between the people who made their living by communicating and those who did not. They also discovered that many of the engineers were required to do a great deal of communicating! And so they reported that "the professional communicator, as a person, may not be greatly different from the nonprofessional communicator."[2]

This survey, in short, seems to affirm the ancient maxim, "the measure of the speech is the measure of the man." We can similarly affirm the obverse, "the measure of the man will be the measure of the speech." The ultimate effectiveness of communication does not rest upon any set of attributes which is unique to speakers or listeners, but stems squarely from the kind of person doing the speaking or listening. In the words of Sarett, Foster, and Sarett, three of the most respected writers in the field of speech, "This principle states the belief that true excellence in speech can be achieved only by a person who is exercising and developing his power to become an excellent person."[3]

The principle can be extended to apply to almost any area of human endeavor. If you will consider carefully the greatest teacher under whom you have studied, you will, I am sure, come to the conclusion that his or her greatness was derived from unique and strong personal characteristics. That teacher was first a great human being, and as a result of human excellence, a great teacher.

The same is true of physicians, lawyers, engineers, managers, public servants, and businessmen. Those who stand out do so because of strength of human character. They put their individual excellence to work in a specific field of endeavor. Abraham Lincoln was a great man who put his abilities into service as President of the United States. Henry Ford built an empire on insight, mechanical skill, and determination. And men noted for power of speech have been first of all, and in some significant way, men of greatness whose speaking was an instrument of their virtues and attainments —Winston Churchill, Franklin D. Roosevelt, Clarence Darrow, Peter Marshall, John L. Lewis, Eric Johnson, Bishop Sheen, Clarence Randall.

[2] Dayton Heckman, Franklin Knower, and Paul Wagner, *The Man Behind the Message* (Columbus: The Ohio State University, 1955), p. 113.
[3] Lew Sarett, William Trufant Foster, and Alma Johnson Sarett, *Basic Principles of Speech*, Third Ed. (Boston: Houghton-Mifflin Company, 1958), p. 41.

From this principle it follows that if you are to seek excellence as a communicator you will find it by seeking excellence as a person. To this you must add skill in the arts of speaking and listening, but skill alone can at best produce only temporary victory or transitory fame. Your speech cannot escape being an expression of what you are, and therefore it cannot rise to greater heights than the sum of your character and personality permits. Your speech behavior may at times fail to represent you adequately, but it can never be more than the measure of your life. The development of your power of communication, consequently, requires nothing less than the full development of your potentials and capacities as a human being.

To accept this challenge may add much to the enduring satisfactions you can find in life, but to avoid making the discussion seem like a sermon, let us attend to only one practical and relevant question. Will your employer (and most of you will start your careers as employees) be concerned with your excellence as a person? Indeed, yes. In a world of hard-fisted practicality and swift-paced competition he will be looking for a *whole man,* and will therefore be imminently concerned with your qualities as a person. Whether he is a single proprietor, a corporation, an agency, or whatever else, he will be able to get an increasing share of the work done by automated processing. His employment needs will best be filled by co-workers or employees whose performance will be of high calibre. He will be looking for people able to share in the direction of an enterprise with vision, integrity, and intelligence. Those who most nearly meet the highest standards, those who stand above the mediocre, those of demonstrated excellence, will be chosen. A worthy person skilled in communicating has the best chance for selection and advancement.

What do you have to offer? How can you best develop yourself? A final answer to either question will never be found, but some firm directions can be charted.

BEGIN WITH HONEST SELF-APPRAISAL

As a responsible individual, you should be concerned not only with improving your skills in speech communication, but in seeking growth and maturity as a whole person. The starting point for the second of these goals lies in taking a direct and candid look at yourself. What do you have to offer, not only to an organization which may employ you, but to society at large? What are your liabilities and assets as a human being? What traits and qualities need to be cultivated, and what ones discouraged? How can you most constructively relate yourself to your several environments—the worlds of people, ideas, and things—within which you must work and live?

Let us adopt the concept that the responsible and able person is one who has come to satisfactory terms with his total environment in such a way as to become a contributing member of society. To make an effective self-evaluation based on such a concept, we should have some kind of a check-list of factors to be considered. One furnished by the American Council on Education provides a list of specific personal characteristics and capabilities, each of which is balanced by an equivalent but contrasting item.[4] Taken as a whole the scheme inventories the elements of a satisfactory dynamic relation of the individual to his environments. You may find it useful for your initial self-appraisal.

On the one hand there are:	These must be balanced against:
1. One's assets.	1. One's liabilities.
2. One's own assets.	2. Assets of others.
3. The giving of affection, sympathy, and understanding.	3. The receiving of affection, sympathy, and understanding.
4. Enjoyment of work.	4. Enjoyment of play.
5. Enjoyment of activity.	5. Enjoyment of rest and quiet.
6. Enjoyment of working cooperatively.	6. Enjoyment of working alone.
7. Enjoyment of success.	7. Ability to accept failure.
8. Seeing failure as due sometimes to one's own limitations.	8. Seeing failure as due sometimes to environmental difficulties.
9. The ability to think.	9. The ability to feel.
10. The ability to be a leader.	10. The ability to be a follower.
11. The ability to use one's own powers to the utmost.	11. The ability to recognize that there are powers beyond our control.

[4] *Counseling for Mental Health*, Series VI, No. 8, (Washington: American Council on Education, 1947), pp. 25–6.

12. The recognition of conscious factors as important in our motivation.	12. The recognition of unconscious factors in our motivation.
13. A respect for the mind.	13. A respect for the body.
14. The import of one's own sex.	14. The import of the opposite sex.
15. One's worth as an individual.	15. The vastness of the universe.
16. The realization of the present.	16. The realization of the past and future.

You may recognize that this framework, since it directs attention to the relation of the individual to his environment, is particularly appropriate to our interest in communication. This is true because, as indicated in Chapters 2 and 3, a group, or even society at large, is simply a system of interpersonal relationships made possible by communication, and because the development of the individual himself is largely a matter of creating satisfactory relationships through communication with his various environments.

As you weigh the several factors of the list, you will notice that the first pair of items calls for personal self-examination. How well equipped are you to undertake specific and increasing responsibilities? The range of human potential is great, and you will have to determine for yourself whether your endowment is rich or scant. It is yours to discover and cultivate whatever unique combination of talents and powers you have been furnished. Yet one thing should be kept in mind, and that is the principle of compensation. You are a combination of strengths and weaknesses, and in many cases the former can be employed to compensate for the latter, particularly when the weaknesses cannot be directly overcome. Wilma Rudolph, for instance, American Olympic star, spent a third of her life a cripple, unable to walk. Courage and determination were the assets which enabled her to overcome her liability. Arturo Toscanini's eyesight was so poor that he had to memorize the score of every work he played or directed. Was he thereby freed to use his other gifts more completely? Four young blind people are now studying at my university; perhaps one will emulate the blind attorney who pocketed his courtroom notes in Braille, and with hand in pocket was able to direct his full speaking power to a jury.

Using these or similar beginning points, you may then begin to look forward to the process of self-development. It is impossible to plot the path toward a distant goal until you know the spot on which you stand.

But before you move ahead, you must recognize certain of the difficulties with which you must contend.

YOU MUST SATISFACTORILY RESOLVE FIVE PROBLEMS

A phrase much used by thoughtful people in recent years is "the predicament of modern man." Those who use the phrase refer in the main to crucial issues upon which man's survival seems to hinge, and regarding which he must make decisions. In a parallel way you will become aware as you read further that you will face a series of decisions. They concern matters which may not be as imminently critical as the major issues of our day, yet they have serious implications for your own future. Some you may be able to make now and firmly, and some may trouble you for life, but none can really be escaped.

What you will read later in this chapter and throughout the book will, implicitly or explicitly, take a position on these issues. Please do not think, however, that the objections you or others may raise have not been recognized. What you read has been set down after preliminary critical examination by philosophers, speech experts, and students. The opinions given are my considered answers, and the fact that you may, and probably will, raise some questions, simply confirms the fundamental premise, that you are a free man engaged in making decisions.

Let us, then, briefly examine the alternatives.

Ideal or practical?

"After all," it is said, "why should I be concerned with my stature as an individual? Will it not be enough that I gain skill in the methods and techniques of speech? Aren't we after hard, practical results? If I can sell my product, isn't that enough?"

Here we are confronted with the measurement of man as a speaker. Is a successful man the one who wins the most converts to

108

his position? Or is a successful man one who may lose in a cause he considers right? We must grant that many an individual seems to make a good living on little more than a "gift of gab." Why, then, should we strive for more?

Your answer must be predicated upon the kind of life you intend to lead, and upon the degree of your concurrence with Lincoln's statement that "you can't fool all of the people all of the time." The belief advanced in these pages is that the ideal is ultimately practical, and that the final triumph of a great man's speaking is not always immediately visible, especially by that speaker.

This dilemma, of course, is not limited to the matter of speech communication, but threads throughout both your academic work and the world at large. The world as it "is" or the world as it should be? You must make your own answer.

Specialist or generalist?

Business and professional leaders in increasing numbers utter warnings against the dangers of specialization and point to the need for men of broad vision in top positions, men with generalized education which enables them to cope with the vast range of social, economic, political, and cultural involvements in their responsibilities. In contrast to this cry is the reply, "How can I get a job if I do not specialize? Employment officers everywhere are looking for people with specific training. They are little interested in breadth of culture, but highly concerned with particular skills."

The choice between specializing or generalizing has a paler ethical coloration than the one mentioned before, yet it is also a difficult decision. As a rule college students seem to see higher education as the entry way to a rewarding job, which it may and should be. Consequently their selection of studies, and indeed, the way they tackle learning, is determined by their immediate vocational goal. They have small interest in poetry, history, and philosophy, and great interest in accounting, quantitative analysis, or production control. They are less concerned with *being* than with *doing*.

This issue is not easily resolved, but ultimately you will make a choice, consciously or unconsciously.

Rule or exception?

For every principle laid down in these pages you can find an exception. Seldom has any speaker followed all the principles advanced in any good book on speech. Nearly every man held up as great in accomplishment also had a weakness of some kind. Statesmen have cheated, great literary figures have been morally weak, outstanding industrialists have ignored their families or circumvented the law, and outstanding musicians or noted artists have been drug addicts or alcoholics.

"What then of all the good advice," someone says. "Look at these exceptions to the rules. Joe Jones didn't follow the rules, and look what he did! Every genius was crazy in some way, wasn't he?"

What rules to follow and how far to follow them—this is the decision you must make. Simply remember that the exception *tests* the rule; if it weren't for exceptions, we wouldn't understand the principle. If it were not for evil, we would have difficulty understanding the nature of good.

Leader or follower?

Many of your books discuss with you the qualifications for leadership. Conferences are held on developing leaders for this or that enterprise, and speakers exhort each generation of students to rise to the demands of the new leadership. Yet somewhere in your mind may be the idea that you are not going into a society of all chiefs and no Indians, which poses the question of whether you should expect to be a leader or a follower.

Fortunately this alternative may be more easily resolved than some of the others, for every organization is made up of individuals of various ranks and grades, each of whom may be a leader when he faces one direction, but a follower when he faces another. Your own answer may lie in deciding the degree of leadership you hope to attain, and in determining how much effort you will make toward developing the qualities of a good follower.

This book takes the position that if you strive for excellence as a person you will move toward the level for which you are best suited. Beyond that, the decision is yours.

Individualism or conformity?

William H. Whyte, Jr.'s best-selling book, *The Organization Man,* brought into public consciousness the degree to which group pressures influence the behavior of those who belong or who wish to belong to given organizations or who live in certain circles. Its publication dramatized a growing reaction against conformity in this country, and the dilemma of individualism or conformity continues to face our people.

To what degree should you resist the pressures of your associates in order to assert the uniqueness of your own being and the individual creativity of your own thinking? To what degree should you comply with the habits and the opinions of others, gaining a comfortable security in the anonymity of the group?

In an evolutionary sense, the deviant is socially necessary to challenge conventional thinking and to create unusual approaches to persistent problems. Yet such a person is often lonely and frequently misjudged. Before you resolve this dilemma, assess both your conscious and your unconscious motivation if you hope for a satisfying outcome.

As I have already indicated, these choices are based on the premise that you are a free man, living in a free society. The rationale of the premise makes up the succeeding section of this chapter.

FREEDOM AFFORDS OPPORTUNITY FOR EXCELLENCE; EXCELLENCE MAKES FREEDOM SIGNIFICANT

Free men collectively, in affirming that for their own good each should have what Seymour St. John termed "the freedom to be one's best," thereby declare their belief that only in a free society can man attain his greatest excellence. We have liked to call our nation a "land of opportunity," and despite the ugly fact that some of our

111

people have not found the opportunity we proclaim, we cannot overlook the equal fact that as a nation we have constantly sought to convert our ideal into practice. We do so because we believe in individual worth—that the individual should be paramount, and that the state, and indeed all social groups, exist to further the humanism and dignity of man. This faith, fundamental to our heritage, affords to each an opportunity for excellence which we feel cannot be matched in any other kind of society. We believe that a free society is one dedicated to the principle that every individual deserves and should have a chance to discover and develop his unique talents in the search for a good life. This is the best, and probably the only climate in which excellence can truly be nurtured, and therefore is the necessary foundation to your own personal development.

Free men collectively, however, equally believe that the growth and progress of their society—even its very survival—depend upon individuals' creative impulses and drive for excellence. They see this principle as an explanation of the extraordinary civilization developed in the Greek city-states of the Eastern Mediterranean more than two centuries ago, and they see it as a leavening factor running throughout the history of Western life. This belief asserts that the individual is important to society because the great achievements of mankind have come from individual human minds, that the great advancements of mankind have come from free human beings working in voluntary association, that the recognition of individual worth offers the only power which can unite all men in constructive enterprises, and that the hope of the future lies in individual hearts. In short, we believe that the challenges which confront a society are met by the creative responses of individuals, that human evolution must be consciously achieved, and that the accomplishment comes from individuals, not from any overriding group-mind. Thus the individual, granted an opportunity for excellence, has an obligation to make the most of his talents, not for himself alone, but for the sake of those who have made possible his fulfillment.

These beliefs lead to the paradox which chronically bedevils freedom, that the individual given the opportunity to make the best of himself may elect to make the worst. A man who is free may choose to be base and mean, may mistake freedom for license, may fail to respect the rights of others, may make himself a brute instead of a being capable of knowing what to do with the secrets of the universe which he commands. This paradox is the hazard of

112

freedom, the calculated risk which a free society must run in order to affirm its belief in itself.

Indispensable to this philosophy of freedom is the principle that free men, governing themselves in a free society, must be effective communicators, since the judgments and decisions of men living in voluntary association depend upon the free exchange of ideas and opinions and the free deliberation of choices. For this reason freedom and the art or science of discourse were born together and the cultivation of skill in communication has been important wherever democracy has flourished. Aristotle, who trusted that "men might discover the good life and lead it," was one of the first to systematize the art of persuasion. Today his *Rhetoric* still furnishes a substantial basis for current theories of public address, although modern communication theory has advanced beyond the limitations of his learning and culture. But from his time to ours, free men have necessarily concerned themselves with discovering and teaching the principles and practices of effective communication because it is essential to their way of life. The only alternative to deliberation and persuasion is authority and force.

In sum, freedom provides the opportunity for each to develop himself to the limits of his capacity. A free society can flourish only when its members assume the responsibility of being their best, a free society has an optimum chance for survival and advancement, and no society can remain free if its members lack either the will or the ability to consult and to deliberate on all matters of common concern.

Since man, then, must have freedom if he is to pursue the development of whatever potential he possesses, since the individual who achieves excellence does so because he has been free to seek it, we come face to face with the question *What is freedom?* The answer provides a foundation to examine the pursuit of excellence, and is offered in terms of the basic nature of a free man.

The free man is one who makes his own decisions and judgments. As Herbert J. Muller wrote after long study of the problems of freedom:[5]

> A man is free in so far as he can do something or choose not to do it, can make up his own mind, can say yes or no to any given question or command, can decide for

---

[5] Herbert J. Muller, *Issues of Freedom* (New York: Harper & Brothers, 1960), pp. 5–6.

himself the matter of duty of *for* what. He is not free in so far as he is prohibited from following his inclinations, or is obliged to do something against his own volition, whether by direct coercion or by fear of consequences, even though it might be better than his heart's desire.

Thus the free man's choices are not imposed upon him by pressure, ignorance, prejudice, or servitude of any kind. His uses of freedom lie within himself, and in this sense freedom is more than a simple absence of restraint. The free man cannot be like a toy balloon released from the hand of a child and at the mercy of every wind that blows. He must be able to choose his direction regardless of the gales.

Choice, then, implies the determination of goals, the knowledge of a destination, the possession of a set of values. The free man directs himself toward one or more destinations selected in the light of his scale of values. Furthermore he must have the power to move himself toward his destination, else his freedom is a worthless abstraction. These three elements describe the essence of freedom— the making of choices, the selection of goals, and self-propulsion toward the chosen goals.

Granting that we have vastly simplified a complex and involved concept, and granting that, as we earlier noted, a free man may make evil, ignoble, or disastrous choices (Hitler himself was a free man although every other German became subject ot his tyranny), the free man who strives for excellence will not knowingly do so. He is responsible to himself as well as to his fellow men. With these things in mind, let us examine the characteristics of man in pursuit of excellence, noting some of the implications for superior communication.

THE RESPONSIBLE COMMUNICATOR SEEKS EXCELLENCE AS A PERSON

Excellence means quality. From this definition we might agree easily that excellence is desirable and still not have a common understanding of what characteristics or abilities we should try to improve. Let it be understood, then, that in these pages we are discussing excellence in those capabilities which mark free men, and that excellence itself means the highest quality of performance possible as a human being, performance which marks a good individual life and which makes the significant contribution both to one's employer and to society as a whole. We are therefore concerned with performance as an individual, as a member of one or more organizations, and as a citizen at large, and with performance which can be viewed in the following principles of behavior.

The responsible communicator strives for sound decisions and judgments

A man at his best must make decisions which are as valid as can be made within any given set of circumstances, and which are calculated to accomplish ultimate good, both for himself and for others. Such an ability to make sound decisions and judgments is not inherited; it is acquired by careful nurture of whatever capacities of mind and temperament he may have been born with.

A decision or judgment is a choice. It is, or should be, the rational act of selecting among alternatives, many of which are simply a matter of polarity—yes or no? Should I study biology or math? Should I enter the bowling tournament or not? More choices, however, are complex, involving many fine distinctions of gradation and difference, and forcing consideration of intangible values and of consequences which may not become apparent until long in the future. Should I buy, rent, or build a home? In what direction should we aim our research? Where should new distribution centers be opened? How can the design be improved? Some of our decisions are trivial, but others are of critical consequence and the individual must employ all his resources if they are to be sound and valid.

The first thing an individual must have in order to make sound decisions is the ability and the willingness to think. It is incorrect to assume that the product of a man's mind is directly proportional to the "intelligence" with which he was born. Leaving aside the question of the nature of intelligence and the degree to which it may vary during a lifetime, the fact remains that there is evidence to show that most people do not use more than a fraction of their available power. The opportunity for improvement is vast and largely uncultivated.

The power to think involves the process of reasoning. It includes the ability to possess, relate, and evaluate both facts and ideas. It includes the ability to draw valid inferences from established facts and credible opinions, and to test those inferences before accepting or acting on them. And it involves the ability to state and arrange materials clearly both for oneself and for others. Much of the material in this book is related to your ability to infer, state, and arrange ideas, and is therefore concerned with the improvement of your power in thinking.

Thinking involves not only reasoning, but other powers as well. The productive thinker is apt to have a lively curiosity; he has a desire to learn and grow. He may also have a lively imagination, the power to visualize what *is not* or what *might be*. His mind is not constrained by what the great Francis Bacon termed idols, or false ways of looking at things. He knows that his imaginings are not real, that he possesses a built-in bias toward his private point of view, that he may be too easily swayed by popular or group opinion, and that custom, tradition, and culture can produce a rigid and dogmatic mind.

But the *power* to think is not enough. An individual must also have substance to think with. He must have knowledge and understanding. He cannot choose among alternatives unless he is fully cognizant of the range of the alternatives and of the distinctions which separate them. He must be able to estimate the consequences of each, and the relative weight of the various factors to be considered. The superior man relizes all this and constantly strives to enlarge his area of relevant knowledge and understanding. He realizes that in no way can he afford ignorance which restricts his thinking or prejudice which paralyzes it. The complexity of our civilization means that a man whose knowledge and understanding is narrow will necessarily be able to make sound decisions only in a limited area of action. It is for this reason that specialists often cannot be entrusted with broad judgments and that men of wide responsibility find it increasingly necessary to grow as generalists.

And the man who would be truly excellent must spend a lifetime growing! The rapid proliferation of knowledge and the increasing rate of change pointed out in Chapter 1 mean that a man cannot cease to learn. Simply to do a job satisfactorily he must keep up in at least one dimension, and to forge ahead he must grow in several dimensions. The necessity of continuing growth has been pointed out by Crawford H. Greenwalt, President of Du Pont:[6]

[6] Crawford H. Greenwalt, "The Culture of the Businessman," *Saturday Review*, XL, No. 3 (Jan. 19, 1957), p. 13.

How many of us can look back upon the day we became college graduates and say that, on that day, we were
educated people? I am sure I cannot, and I know few who
can. An education is not a simple entity, developed in a
few semesters of study and delivered with our diploma—
it is a never-ending process built up over years of exposure
and experience. How well we are educated, it seems to me,
is simply a matter of . . . whether we have enlarged our
horizons or have been content to vegetate within a narrow
valley.

The man who cannot continue to grow is quickly obsolete. He is
unaffected by new ideas, inflexible, and unable to meet change.
"Unfortunately, most businessmen just aren't interested in ideas,"
Peter Barth has written in the *Saturday Review* (Sept. 14, 1963, pg.
78), and we must hope that he exaggerates, for history is a record
of men's ideas. Ford had an idea which reshaped our society. Keynes
had an idea which altered the economic thought of the world.
Einstein had an idea which split history as it split the atom. Automation is forcing us to rethink, not only our production processes,
but our entire social structure. Businessmen, industrialists, professional folk, all must keep alert to new ideas or they will be swept
under by the tide of change.

Considerations of this nature lead the business and industrial
world to stress the continued education of its members. The American Savings and Loan Institute and the American Bankers Association both operate flourishing education programs for their people.
General Motors, General Electric, and Bayuk Cigars are notable
examples of firms which provide training or encourage employees to
develop themselves technically or liberally. The American Management Association offers more than 1200 courses, conferences, and
seminars a year. In our nation we no longer talk about *adult*
education, but term it *continuing* education.

Beyond the ability to think and substance to think with, the
man of excellence must also have a set of serviceable and creative
values. Such a set was referred to by Grayson Kirk, President of
Columbia University, during the centennial convocation of the University of Denver. According to Dr. Kirk, a worthy sense of values:[7]

derives from an ability to discriminate not only between
right and wrong, but also between the significant and the

[7] *Vital Speeches*, XXX (May 15, 1964), p. 472.

trivial, between that which is cheap and shoddy and that which has integrity and beauty. To put the matter in another way, an educated man should have a well-developed and refined "good taste" which he uses as a yard-stick in making his moral, social, and aesthetic judgments.

Values become operative as an individual formulates any judgment or makes any decision, for every choice is affected by standards of good and evil, by things considered more or less important. If a person's choice is to be productive, his value system must be consistent with the highest standards of our civilization, and he needs to be aware of it.

Enduring, creative, and productive values are found not only in the great religions of mankind, but in the accumulated experience of civilization as well. Fortunate is the man who can and will read, for he can become what Count Korzybski has called a "time-binder." That is, he shares the experience and wisdom which is available to him from those who have lived before, learning what life has taught them. "Learn from the mistakes of others," we are told, "for you won't live long enough to make them all yourself." By living vicariously but richly through the lives of others in all sorts of books, the man of excellence can help himself to learn the price involved in every significant decision. His value system tells him what he *should* do, balancing the alternatives in the scale of human experience.

Such a choice demands still another quality. The exceptional man must have courage, or as President Harold W. Dodds of Princeton University put it, "a moral boldness which readily assumes the burden and risks of decision, together with a courage to stand on what may be an unpopular and lonely spot, once the decision has been made."[8] If he is to decide wisely, the individual must weigh the advice of others, attending to words which may be distasteful to him as well as to those which echo his own opinions. Such listening does take courage, for in doing it the individual exposes himself to change—he may find that he was wrong, the admission of which is a courageous act. And having decided, he may have to announce and defend his judgment, for few decisions do not affect others. "I have directed the armed forces to prepare for any eventualities," President John F. Kennedy told the American people in October, 1962. His statement revealed a decision made in full view

8 *Vital Speeches*, XXII (Aug. 15, 1956), p. 653.

of the potential consequences, but with the resolution that that decision must be made and must be announced and supported. "Without courage, whether it is an individual's or a nation's, there can be no success, whatever other virtues one possesses," said Richard H. Amberg, publisher of the St. Louis *Globe-Democrat*.[9]

There are requirements other than these four which might be added to the prerequisites for making sound judgments and decisions; among them are a sane and objective evaluation of the environment and the ability to distinguish between statements of fact and statements of inference. You yourself may wish to add to the prescription. Yet we have considered what may be deemed the minimum qualifications, and these are sufficient to suggest a connection to the characteristics of effective communication.

Because he thinks clearly, the exceptional person speaks clearly, the first being necessary to the second. His command of language, an indispensable tool of thought, his ability to organize and arrange ideas, and his skill in assessing relative values lend order and unity to his messages. Others have little difficulty in following his train of thought.

Because he recognizes the incompleteness of his own knowledge, the man of excellence is an eager listener, seeking thereby to enlarge his own understanding. And equally recognizing the bias and incompleteness of another's information and perception, he is a critical listener, intent to hear yet not hasty to believe. He possesses an inquiring mind, but not a credulous one.

Because he has thought well and deeply, because he has formulated his conclusions only after thoroughly examining them, the man of excellence is a convincing speaker. He presents his ideas with the force of one who knows and believes in what he is saying. Further, he can support his conclusions with facts as well as with the fervor of commitment. When they are aware that he has sought the truth and that his sense of values will lead him to speak the truth as he sees it, his listeners tend to accept what he has to say. They believe him because they believe in him. His persuasive power goes deeper than an outward show of salesmanship. It is based on the confidence his listeners have in him as a man of clear thought, sound knowledge, and high ethical values.

Because he is committed to sound judgment, the excellent individual does not assess the quality of his speaking solely on the

---

[9] *Vital Speeches*, XXXI (Dec. 1, 1964), p. 123.

standard of measurable results. Important as this may be, he is also highly concerned with the inherent value of what he is communicating, not dealing in surface appearance to obtain an effect. He knows that excellent communication is more than a collection of techniques, that it manifests what he is as a person, and he insists on being a person of integrity and substance.

He aims for worthy goals

Implicit in our concept of the man seeking excellence was the notion that his freedom was more than an absence of restraint. He must be more than *free from,* he must be *free for.* The judgments and decisions of the man seeking excellence must be made in relation to a constructive purpose, a goal, a destination toward which he is self-directed.

The nature and vitality of a person's goals give meaning and purpose to his life. Recall again the outstanding men or women of your acquaintance, and inquire if they have not visibly been possessed by a sense of direction and purpose which marked their lives. Then ask yourself if the sense of personal assignment may not have been significant in contributing to their quality as a person. *Life* magazine, in a special issue on Japan, described the achievements of Konosuke Matsushita, that nation's leading industrialist and one of her wealthiest men. Clearly emphasized was the fact that he has dedicated his enterprises to a purpose, that of furnishing prosperity and abundance to people.

It is probably no coincidence that Matsushita is known also as a philosopher and as a writer whose books have been among Japan's best sellers. Goals and purposes imply a philosophy, and no man lives who does not have a philosophy of some kind. The only question is the nature of that philosophy, the degree to which it is productive of worthy consequences, and the clearness with which it is understood. Matsushita's philosophy is both creative and explicit.

In a society which is admittedly materialistic and highly competitive, the pursuit of creative goals may to some seem discouraging. Yet a man who seeks excellence will need a sense of purpose based on a constructive and to some extent a spiritual interpretation of life. Such an interpretation rejects mechanistic explanations of the meaning of man as incomplete if not erroneous, rejecting with them the concept that man is nothing more than an automated, computer-like communicating machine. Regardless of any specific creed, the man of excellence cannot escape the Greco-Judeo-Christian tradition of the West and its emphases on personal responsibility, individual worth, and a conscience animated by something higher than group norms.

Within some such philosophy the man of excellence seeks goals which satisfactorily fulfill his personal motivation and provide him opportunity to attain his finest potential in the art of living. He seeks to become a whole man and not just a splinter, a rounded man and not just a narrow functionary. His job may be the center of his existence, but it is not its circumference. Vocationally he may be a professional auditor, truckdriver, clerk, designer, or member of the board of directors, but he is equally a "professional" human.

Practically, man in pursuit of excellence sets attainable short-term or intermediate goals as well as long-term ultimate ones. The short-term goals are worthy, each in its own right, but contributory to the larger end. Knowing himself as best he can, this man realizes that his level of aspiration may be higher than his level of achievement, and finds satisfaction in reaching attainable short-term goals, avoiding the frustration which may come when ultimate goals are set too high, or are otherwise out of reach. He prefers to light a candle than to curse the darkness. Nor does he always estimate his success in terms of distance covered, but often in terms of effort made toward worthy ends. Equally, he knows that desirable ends are not served by undesirable means, and that he cannot increase his own stature by diminishing that of others.

The man of excellence, in seeking worthy goals, reveals a sense of purpose, perhaps even of dedication, in his speaking. In turn, this tends to command understanding and faith and to stimulate the best in others. Compelling the respect of others, the man of excellence removes many barriers to effective communication.

He maintains a reservoir of energy

The making of sound judgments in the pursuit of constructive goals, however, is not sufficient for the man of excellence. He must have energy or power to move himself toward his goals. The skipper of the finest ship, knowing his destination, having the most exact charts, and possessed of the greatest skill in seamanship, is not free to follow his course unless, when he signals command, the engines respond. To pursue his destination he must have power.

There are many varieties of power, one of which is the authority vested in the rank or station to which a man is appointed. Power may also be said to derive from wealth, family, status, or some similar source. These are not the varieties of power with which we are now concerned; we are concerned rather with the sources from which an individual energizes his own behavior, and from which he may derive a persuasive effect with others. Such energy is essentially of two kinds, physical and emotional, each of which is mutually dependent upon the other. Physical vitality is greatest when an individual's emotional tone is aroused and positive, and emotional health and buoyancy are sustained in part by strong physical resources.

Because of the need and because of the interdependence of sources, the man of excellence maintains both his physical and emotional energy at ample levels. (And in using the term *emotional* here, we must let it stand for *mental-emotional* energy.)

The first of these is beyond the scope of our treatment. Let us only note that contemporary emphasis on the need for improved physical fitness goes back, not unlike other principles we have noted, to the early Greeks who stressed the importance of physical excellence to a well-rounded life. Superior business and professional people today respect their bodies and try to meet the requirements of sound living. The experience of every veteran speaker testifies as well that good health is necessary for the most productive speaking.

The man seeking excellence also respects the well-springs of his own mental and emotional health, beginning with the fact which we noted in Chapter 3, that all men live as a whole. He cannot successfully live a fragmented life. He does not leave part of himself at home when he goes to work, nor can he shut the door this morning on what happened last night. Each role that a man plays is a part of the indivisible person, and each has its effect on him in every other role. Therefore the superior man strives for integrity in his life, for consistency in his behavior, and for unity in his approach to the problems he faces.

The person who cannot live life whole exposes himself increasingly to the dangers of internal conflict, and while the splintering of life certainly does not cause all intrapersonal conflict, it is a contributing factor. The man who becomes a "walking civil war" dissipates his powers in useless internal discord which he otherwise could use to purposeful and productive ends. And mental and emotional conflict arising from any cause, leading toward the disintegration of the individual, deprives uncounted thousands of people of the resources they need for a healthy and productive life. Employers are concerned with the mental-emotional condition of their employees, for according to the editors of *Life* magazine :[10]

> Psychologists have known for a long time that one of the greatest problems in business and industry is the disturbed worker—the man or woman who is in such bad shape emotionally that happiness and efficiency on the job are almost impossible. A pioneer study at a Connecticut silk mill showed that mental and emotional disturbances caused more loss of time and money than all contagious diseases and accidents put together.

The superior man, realizing with D. Maurice Allan that "an integrated personality is the essence of mental health and the mark of maturity,"[11] therefore strives in various ways for harmony within himself and for ethical consistency in his relations with others. For one thing, he may inventory his conscious desires and try to determine ways in which he can achieve their constructive satisfaction. Although dollar income is important, he selects a job which he also feels will offer him the fullest personal reward in terms of self-respect, the esteem of others, and creative opportunity. And he interprets his work in terms which provide real and durable satisfactions rather than viewing it as so many hours of labor. Like Matsushita he prefers to sell happiness or security instead of only gadgets, or to build homes, not simply houses.

Furthermore, the man of excellence endeavors to sustain an affirmative attitude toward himself and toward the world at large. Despite the scoffers, he is assured that there is more power in positive thinking than in negative, and more strength in positive emotions. Without surrendering his privilege of righteous indignation, he cultivates to the fullest extent feelings of faith, hope, gratitude, and compassion as contributory to his well-being, and restrains his impulses toward despair, jealousy, bitterness, and envy.

[10] Ernest Haverman, "The Psychologist's Service in Solving Daily Problems," *Life*, XLII, No. 3 (Jan. 21, 1957), p. 90.
[11] Denison Maurice Allan, *The Realm of Personality* (New York: Abingdon Press, 1947), p. 80.

An affirmative attitude can be manifest in an honest sense of humor. The superior man is able spontaneously to laugh at himself, consistent with the ancient code of the British naval officer, "Don't take yourself too damned seriously." A sense of humor may be taken as a sign of healthy balance, free alike from either egotism or servile humility.

An affirmative attitude is likewise manifest in an abounding enthusiasm, a buoyancy of spirit which releases and sustains man's physical vitality. The superior man's being rises to the challenges of living. He is absorbed by his interests and gives himself to his undertakings with zest. "Nothing great was ever achieved without enthusiasm," wrote Emerson, and his words have become a credo to encourage the energies of superior men. An unknown writer has affirmed, "Enthusiasm is faith in action; and faith and initiative rightly combined remove mountainous barriers and achieve the unheard of and miraculous." And John M. Fox, President of the Minute Maid Corporation told the Sales Executives Club of New York, "Enthusiasm and a positive attitude are an important part of the balance required of a leader whose judgment and decision-making activities will be tested from the day he assumes important managerial responsibility."[12]

The man of excellence, however, does not act with completely unrestrained enthusiasm. In contrast, he integrates his intelligence, his sentiments, and his character, knowing that intelligence alone may make him calculating, sentiment alone, susceptive or foolish and character alone, dogmatic. These three aspects of behavior complement one another, resulting in controlled and purposive energy.

Finally, the man of excellence guards against mental-emotional exhaustion by retreating periodically from the day-to-day tensions. In doing so he is able to reassess the facts and values of life, to gain fresh perspectives, perhaps to allow his subconscious mind to assert its powers. He employs the principle Toynbee advanced to explain the survival of great civilizations, the principle of withdrawal and return.

In practice withdrawal may take varied forms. For some it may be retreat to a wilderness sanctuary, an isolated cabin, or a seaside haunt. For others it may be a regular hour when the office door is closed to all comers, or only forty minutes in the commuter

---

12 *Vital Speeches*, XXII (April 1, 1952), p. 377.

train to lean back and think. Some find it in a churchman's retreat, and some in a sabbatical leave, for as one experienced observer of the business world has declared:[13]

> Each executive who shows promise of heroic leadership should be allowed ample time to think. Perhaps once every five or seven years he should be given a year off with pay so that he can read and study and perhaps even write. When it is possible to organize his time and responsibilities, he should be given time off to think, to get away from his office and become aware of the broader possibilities found in studying literature, art, and the social sciences.

Maintaining in these or other ways a reservoir of energy, the man of excellence enhances his abilities as a communicator. His vitality energizes others when he speaks, his enthusiasm becomes outwardly manifest as physical animation, and his drive toward vital goals becomes infectious. Being a whole person, he does not suffer the eroding effects of conflicting purposes or the enervation of unnecessary emotional stress, but is able to devote himself single-mindedly to his interaction with others. What he is adds impact to what he says.

He is also a better listener, not being too tired to attend to others, nor too irritable to make the effort to discern their intended meanings. His is the calm self-possession which is denied to those who must use up the last ounce of energy to meet their daily responsibilities. He applies the ancient aphorism, "The archer hitteth the target partly by pulling and partly by letting go," and meets the duties of his job with power in reserve.

He respects people

Aware of the forces which tend to depersonalize contemporary life, the man of excellence is equally mindful that he cannot establish sound and productive relationships on such a basis. He realizes that his decisions and judgments involve people, that his goals must be pursued within a social milieu, and that if he expects to earn their cooperation and loyalty he cannot manipulate humans as he might

---

[13] Eugene Emerson Jennings, "The Anatomy of Leadership," *Management of Personnel Quarterly*, I, No. 1 (Autumn, 1961), p. 9.

cattle or machinery. Consequently he holds human life in the highest esteem, revealing in his behavior interest in and respect for all men. He does not feel obligated to like every person he meets, but he cultivates an attitude of respect, not as an instrument for attaining his personal ends, but because he himself is involved in humanity.

The superior man sees something of himself in every other human being. He unreservedly accepts membership in the human race, perceiving clearly the things he has in common with all mankind. Among these things is the common wish for the dignity with which he is certain human existence has been endowed, a wish which seemingly cannot be extinguished despite the anonymity, the degradation, the meanness which has been imposed upon countless people. He feels that the uniqueness of the human status is more spiritual than animal, and that this uniqueness is recorded in those works of literature, art, music, and science which mark man as something more than an accidental combination of chemicals.

Our man is concerned with individuals as individuals. He is aware that no human life can duplicate another, and that differences arise not only from the varieties of human experience but also from the effect of diverse cultures. He therefore respects diverse backgrounds and cultures, being more concerned with understanding them than with judging them. He therefore considers himself inherently neither superior nor inferior to others, adopting the state of mind described by Alfred Adler, "The ideal, or rather normal, attitude toward society is an unstrained and unconsidered assumption of human equality unchanged by any inequalities of position."[14]

Because he is concerned with individuals, the excellent man is eager that others enjoy the essential opportunities and privileges that are his. He cherishes his right to think for himself, to discover and develop his own endowments, to grow into independent and well rounded maturity, to search for his place in the world, and to exercise the maximum control of his own destiny. Therefore he affords to others the same rights, recognizing that as he guards the liberties of others he is guarding his own.

Involved in mankind and respecting others as individuals, the man of excellence equally respects himself and presumes to receive from others the respect he freely gives. He does not feel defensive in the presence of others, but meets them on a basis of equality. And

[14] Alfred Adler, *The Science of Living* (New York: Greenberg, 1929), p. 16.

when he does not receive the respect he should, his attitude is of forebearance, rather than reproach or anger.

Meeting others with respect and as individuals rather than as stereotypes or ciphers, the superior man establishes sound lines of communication. He earns an open mind from the person to whom he speaks. In the sense that communication is a process of establishing common meanings among people, he is a capable communicator because he actively seeks the common denominator which joins him with others. And because of his attitudes, he is a good listener. He concentrates on understanding, not only what another says, but what he is, trying to see things from the other's point of view. He builds his communicative venture on the solid foundation of making it a joint enterprise.

He willingly accepts responsibility

The man of excellence willingly accepts full accountability for his role as a free man, declining to shift his burdens to others. He assumes initiative for making the decisions which fall within his area of responsibility, whether on the job or in his capacity as a human being, and he holds himself accountable for the consequences of his decisions. He willingly assumes liability for his total behavior.

He is first of all, responsible to himself. He performs his duties without constant supervision, yet always as if he were in full view of his fellows. He is aware that his decisions will have personal consequences for which he alone will be answerable. He does not excuse himself when things go wrong, alibiing to himself, rationalizing, or engaging in sentimental overdramatization. He doesn't tell himself, "That was a bit of bad luck," or "I wouldn't have done it if Sam had kept his big mouth shut," or "Can I help it that I was born clumsy?" On the contrary, his personal response to bad judgment is more akin to the famous paraphrase, "We have met the enemy and he is us."

Nor does he shrink from his responsibility to others for his behavior. His decisions and judgments rarely have personal consequences only; most, in fact, have social consequences. Even though he has every right to make and express his own judgments, he does not have a *right* to be wrong. This does not mean that he will always be correct, but that he does not formulate a judgment or decision until he has made every effort to collect available evidence and to evaluate it before arriving at a conclusion. He bases his judgments on established fact and clear thinking because he accepts a public accountability for them, and he therefore holds himself morally culpable if he has not subjected them to critical examination. His decisions have consequences for others whom he does not want to offend or injure.

Accepting this responsibility, the man of excellence may make mistakes, but he does not make excuses. He accounts for his judgments, and is willing to acknowledge his errors, not trying to shift the burden to a scapegoat. He does not say, "You were in such a hurry that I couldn't understand what you said," or "The shipping department got things fouled up again," or "Everybody else was driving that fast." His motto is the one reportedly displayed in Harry S. Truman's executive office, "The buck stops here."

Nor does he fear to be mistaken and therefore try to avoid responsibility. He does not put a committee in charge of things he should take care of. Nor is he so other-directed that he takes his cues only from the thinking of those about him. To the contrary, he willingly stands for what he feels to be right, and voluntarily shoulders a share of responsibility for the common welfare.

The excellent man is therefore a responsible speaker. He fulfills his obligations to say only that which can reasonably be verified, and to differentiate clearly fact from inference. He disdains to deal in rumors, gossip, or half-truths, or to reap advantage of the credibility of a listener. Availing himself fully of his right to freedom of speech, he does not go beyond the point where freedom becomes license.

Because he accepts the burden of proof for every claim, the man of excellence is known for the soundness of his arguments. The respect in which his words are held gives him persuasive power. And because he is responsible, this man in listening assumes a full share of the communicative task. In all speaking situations he intends that communication shall be meaningful and productive, and therefore he meets his obligation to help make it so.

He works for the common good

The man of excellence understands John Donne's statement "no man is an island," for he recognizes that his fate is indissolubly involved with that of others. As a rule, he gets what he wants only through others; rarely can he reach his goals without their aid and approval. Few of his problems are purely personal matters, and most of them he faces in company with others. From birth to death he is a social being, his triumphs and failures being largely the triumphs and failures of the human groupings of which he is a part.

In fact he, like all people, is to a large extent made by those about him, for from them he derives his own meaning and the justification of his existence. A leader cannot be a leader without followers, a teacher cannot be a teacher without students, nor can a foreman have a job without both management and labor. In the give and take of interdependent men personality and character are formed. The man of excellence may well consider that he alone may be able to develop his capacities, but that he rarely can do it alone.

Against dependence upon those about him, the superior man balances his desire to escape and to assert his independence. The individualistic, assertive drive, strengthened by the American frontier tradition of independence and the Puritan ethic described in Whyte's *The Organization Man*, directly contrasts with the notion of comfortable conformity to the pressures of the group, giving rise to the dilemma described earlier in this chapter. If the superior man cannot develop his singular capacities, if he cannot exert himself as an individual, both he and society are the losers. Yet if his capacities are allowed to develop along non-social lines, both he and his fellows are likewise ultimately harmed.

The man of excellence often establishes a productive balance by choosing to work in community with his fellows, promoting voluntary cooperation toward mutually beneficial ends. Recognizing that his own best interests are often most effectively advanced when the interests of others are advanced, and that at times the welfare of the group must supercede his own, he devotes himself to the common good, integrating himself constructively into organizational or community purposes. He identifies his own personal goals with the goals of others, he is sensitive to joint problems, he seeks and promotes mutual concerns, and he helps others interpret their personal aims in terms of the common welfare. In sum, he does not passively accept group membership, but assumes an active role of collaboration with his fellows in guiding the destiny of all.

A man seeking excellence knows that effective speech is indispensable to productive collaboration. Although its members may desire common goals and mutual understandings, the free society is not made up of people with unanimous opinion. It is pluralistic, composed of groups and individuals of many diverse beliefs, opinions, and attitudes. Disagreement among free men is a natural and normal condition, and talk is the instrument by which differences may best be reconciled or compromises effected, enabling the society to find strength in diversity.

Seeing communication not as an end in itself, but as the means by which free men relate to one another and by which they acquire common understandings, solve mutual problems, and arrive at workable decisions on group or public policy, the excellent man appreciates the importance of skill in speech and that he use it for the common good.

He knows that freedom of speech is not a comfortable tradition, but an indispensable right which he must use vigorously if he is to protect the other freedoms he cherishes. He values his own right to express opinions, to criticize and to dissent, but his understanding of free speech does not end there. He values, perhaps even more highly, the right of others to express themselves and to dispute what he firmly believes, for if he listens only to those who agree with him he learns nothing, whereas if he listens to his opponents he may discover his errors and improve his opinions.

In fact, the superior man sees continuing dialogue, public or organizational, as one of the critical ways by which he may find truth, and truth is necessary if judgments and decisions are to be sound. He holds with John Stuart Mill that if all other people are wrong and he is right, it is his function to speak out against errors and try to make clear the truth; that if all other people are right and he is wrong, he may learn the truth from them; and that if he and others are each partly right and partly wrong, the truth will ultimately emerge from the clash of dissenting opinions.

In sum, the man seeking excellence will not only direct himself toward the development of the foregoing six elements of performance, but he also cultivates skill in the arts of speaking and listening, and uses his skill productively. He speaks that he may help command his own destiny and the destiny of the group or society of which he is a member, and he listens that he may be able to understand others, to learn, and to improve his opinions.

Personal implications

You, either as a leader or follower, look to find your place somewhere in business, industry, or a profession. In any function, the effectiveness of your speech commnuication will begin with your qualities as a person. In turn, the speaking-listening habits you develop, good or bad, will influence your development as an individual. Since speech is a part of your total behavior, the effect is reciprocal. Your determination should be to make education in speech an important part of your development as a person.

With this in view, recall that Harry A. Overstreet, in his book *The Mature Mind*,[15] tells us that humans are born helpless, ignorant, irresponsible, inarticulate, self-centered, of diffuse sexuality, and into a world of isolated particulars. We have our choice of growing up or simply growing old. By inaction and indecision many choose simply to grow old. Those who would grow up must make themselves capable, understanding, responsible, articulate, socially sensitive, wholesomely heterosexual, and must find the wholeness in a world of splintered complexity. That's quite a job. But you have the opportunity as well as the responsibility to work at it every day of your life.

[15] Harry A. Overstreet, *The Mature Mind* (New York: W. W. Norton, 1959).

Chapter 5

Listening for Communication

Volkswagen's success did not come because of any ballyhoo about our product or any saturation techniques over television or radio. Our success came because this product answered the needs of many people. These people told others, and we, the manufacturers, listened carefully to what they said. We responded by making improvements. Changes were made, not to be different, not to make people talk about our product, but to correct the weaknesses—weaknesses we learned by listening to our customers, and to those who did not like our product.[1]

DR. HEINZ NORDHOFF, *President*
Volkswagenwerke, Wolfsburg, Germany

GOOD LISTENING CAN BE VITAL TO YOUR SUCCESS AS A STUDENT AND to your career in business or a profession. Consider the hours you spend in class, and estimate the amount of information and understanding you are expected to derive as a listener. Consider the information, directions, orders, suggestions, and advice you receive, or will receive, on the job. Your grades and your job performance will be determined to a significant extent by your skill in listening. Listening *is* communication.

These facts clearly indicate that you are concerned with the things to be taken up in this chapter.

[1] *Vital Speeches*, XXIX (Dec. 1, 1962), p. 115.

THE LISTENER SHARES RESPONSI- BILITY FOR PRODUCTIVE COMMUNICATION

In Chapter 2 we described the communication process as a joint interplay of four elements, two of which were the sender and the receiver. Elsewhere listening has been termed the counterpart of speaking. No matter how we put it, the fact insistently emerges that it takes two to communicate, that the speaker by himself may talk but he alone cannot establish communication. His message—the code—must be acted upon and interpreted by the receiver if meaning is to be created.

With communication depending upon the establishment of a common meaning between sender and receiver, the listener should be an active collaborator in the mutual concern. When listening improves, communication improves, and a good listener can often made an inept speaker into an effective one.

The effect of purposive listening on communication is exemplified in the following report of a student who was assigned to listen carefully to a speaker whose reputation for being worth listening to was dismal.

> I respected the man, but couldn't help thinking of him as being meek and too lifeless himself, a type of person who doesn't say much, do much, or think much.
> Today, due to this assignment, I made myself listen. . . . Surprisingly enough, the words, thought, and ideas on the subject of the day were excellent. . . . This speaker certainly wasn't the man I thought. No, he was a man with real interests and convictions, and obviously a hard worker, as the subject matter showed.

A real difference between earlier occasions when this listener had received no message and this occasion when the message came through was the intention of the listener to assume a share of the responsibility in the communication process. While the incident may show that listless public speaking repels listeners, it also shows that active listening is important to effective speech communication.

We must not assume that the principle is true only for public speaking situations, for it is perhaps even more importantly true in conversations, interviews, and conferences. Irving Lee, late professor of speech at Northwestern University, observed and analyzed more than 200 meetings of various boards and committees. He came to a number of conclusions to explain the failures he discovered in communication, and as a result he suggested:[2]

> Committee members need exercises in listening. They must learn not how to define terms but how to ask others what they are intending to say. Our advice: Don't blame the speaker alone for misunderstanding. The listener is involved, too. It takes two to make communication.

Thus you need to make yourself an active collaborator in every speaking situation, for you are a part of the communication process as a speaker or listener, and have a full share of responsibility for its success.

LISTENING IS A SELECTIVE MENTAL-EMOTIONAL ACTIVITY

What happens when we listen? The answer is not nearly so simple as one might think at first, for even the experts do not agree when they try to define what the term "listening" means to them. One investigator has analyzed more than a dozen definitions found in the literature of listening, coming to the conclusion that, ". . . the definitions have remained vague and speculative. No definition or description can be termed right or wrong. . . . It therefore becomes necessary for each writer and investigator to attempt to make as clear as possible the meaning which he assigns to the term."[3]

Of one thing we can be comfortably certain; *listening* is more than *hearing*. It is perfectly possible to hear another so well that one can repeat back all or most of what was said, and yet fail to understand the meaning of the words. The hearer may perceive sounds, and may even recognize the words, but fail to assimilate or interpret meanings. Instead of actively wrestling with the incoming signals,

---

[2] Irving J. Lee, *How To Talk With People* (New York: Harper & Brothers, 1952), p. 3.
[3] Charles R. Petrie, Jr. Unpublished manuscript. Used by permission.

he passively absorbs them with the deadening effect of an acoustic ceiling. Hearing is the first step in listening, but only the first step.

Nor can we assume that a listener receives only the audible code. Quite to the contrary, he gains much of his impression of an incoming message from visible signals—from what he sees in addition to what he hears. To test this, try turning off the picture on your television set and attending only to the sound. What a difference it makes to your comprehension or appreciation of the program! Sound alone does not provide the full spectrum of communication necessary if we are to gain the maximum meaning possible. This is one reason for psychotherapist Carl Rogers' insistence that the best speaker must give an impression of congruence. That is, the meaning derived from his actions should be perceived to match the meaning derived from his words, enabling words and actions to reinforce one another and enrich meaning. This, indeed, partly explains the premise in Chapter 4 that the responsible communicator be a well-integrated individual.

Good listening also derives meaning from silence, for often the moment before a person utters a word, the pauses between statements, or the moment following a statement may be fraught with significance. From such silences a listener may form a part of his total impression. Other impressions may come from sources aside from the speaker but making up a part of the entire situation. One writer suggests that all sensory perception is part of the act of listening, including smell, taste, and touch.

Listening begins, then, when the receiver "tunes in" and begins to pay serious attention. At this moment he must become selective by concentrating on the stimuli which seem important or relevant and by excluding from his attention all others. He may concentrate so completely, for instance, on the words being uttered by a speaker that he may not even hear his own name being called by someone else. Simultaneously with tuning in, the listener becomes selective mentally. That is, he puts aside thoughts which might interfere with full reception, that he may attend exclusively to the immediate task of interpreting what he sees and hears. To listen well he cannot let his mind drift off to other things.

As he selects the signals to which he will pay attention, the listener at the same time begins to interpret those signals, supplying the meaning as he perceives it. This meaning is derived from both his memory of past experiences, and the expectancies he has for the future, for no one has more to hear with than these. Even the recognition of words as words depends upon the memory of experience with those words, and the richer the memory, the more meaning can be attributed to the language symbols. As pointed out earlier, however, this does not mean that the listener's interpretation will be that intended by the speaker, for each brings to the word which passes between them a different set of experiences. Only as both can use the word to recall similarities of their experiental background can real communication be approached.

The process of associating expectancies and experience with words possesses both intellectual and emotional elements. We might say that it operates on two levels, although we cannot determine which level may predominate. One level is intellectual, comprising the recall of first-hand experience, the association of definitions and concepts, and the remembrance of contexts in which the word being interpreted has been previously used. The other level is emotional, involving the feelings, attitudes and even prejudices which the listener consciously or unconsciously associates with the word. Each level may interact with the other, augmenting or diminishing the fullness of interpretation, facilitating or hampering communication.

For instance, the defending lawyer in a murder case may petition to have the trial moved to a court some distance from the location of the crime, contending that the rights of his client are in jeopardy in the local court. If the case has aroused the public and if it has been sensationally publicized, he may be right to feel it difficult to secure a local jury able to hear the evidence and argument objectively. Its members, regardless of their intention to remain unprejudiced, would be unable to separate themselves from the emotional conditioning produced by inflammatory publicity, and would hear the trial against a background of intensified feeling.

As the listener bestows meaning to the words he hears, to the tones in which they are expressed, and to the behavior of the speaker, one great hazard is that of assigning meanings which were not intended by the speaker. Sometimes communication miscarries because the listener has decided beforehand what the speaker will say, and fails to concentrate on what is actually said. Sometimes it miscarries because the listener perceives only those things in the message which he subconsciously *wants* to, thereby distorting the message as a whole. And sometimes it miscarries because the listener draws erroneous conclusions, attributing to the speaker ideas which were not at all a part of the message. Much unnecessary interpersonal conflict arises out of such miscarriages of communication.

From the foregoing we can conclude that listening is essentially a perceptual skill. It begins with focusing attention on the speaker, and continues by recognizing and interpreting the stimuli, both visual and audible. The listener assigns meaning in terms of his total experience as well as in terms of what he expects to result from the communication. The assigned meanings will always be congruous with the listener's world-as-he-sees-it, and only to a certain extent similar to those intended by the speaker. The listener must always be aware that the meaning he takes will not be identical to that intended.

The more we become conscious of listening as a perceptual mental-emotional skill, and the more we are able to use that skill in a purposive way, the more productive will be our speech communication. The following will help you listen to greater purpose.

BY OBSERVING GUIDE-LINES YOU CAN IMPROVE LISTENING

Although a considerable amount of research has been done in recent years on various aspects of listening, we are still not at all certain of the basic principles which can be applied to improve the skill. Yet in general the eight recommendations made here reflect a consensus of current understanding.

Control your attention

The first step in improving your listening skill should be to bring yourself under conscious control so that you *act like a listener*. Alert yourself. Look at and see the person speaking. Be sure you can hear him comfortably, and pay conscious attention to what he is saying. Sit upright but not stiffly, avoiding a posture of indifference. If you are conversing, watch your respondent without staring enough to make him ill at ease. Physical self-control will not automatically make you a good listener, but you cannot become one without it.

As you bring yourself under control to listen, you should also, so far as you are able, bring your environment under control to establish the best possible listening conditions. In an audience, when you are with others who may tend to be noisy, tactfully suggest that there are those who would like to hear the speaker. If extraneous and distracting sounds drift in from outside, see if doors or windows can be adjusted to cut off the sounds. If lighting is bad or air stuffy, take it upon yourself to try for improved conditions. If a meeting drags on and people become uncomfortable and restless, suggest a recess.

You cannot always control environmental conditions, of course, but when you are sensitive to their effect on your listening, you will find more opportunity for control than you had imagined. Dr. Wesley Wiksell illustrates this by referring to the Director of Research at Stephens College, who was known as an excellent listener. In Wiksell's words:[4]

> Dr. Charters was asked how he ever happened to be such a fine listener. "You noticed that, did you?" said he with a twinkle in his eye. "Well, it was like this: Early in my career, I asked people what they didn't like in their bosses. In nearly every instance the answer was, 'He never listens to me.' Since this was so prevalent I decided that I would be a good listener. I examined my own listening habits. I soon found that it was absolutely impossible for me to listen while sitting behind my desk. The papers, telegrams, articles, and other materials pulled my attention to them like magnets. I could not get away from them. So, I did what you no doubt noticed. I left my desk when you came in. I pulled out my pipe or cigar. I drank water. I walked back and forth until I had cleared my mind. Then I came over and sat down by you in what I called my *listening chair*. There I had my back turned to my desk. I gave you one-hundred percent of my attention. I worked with you all the time I sat there with you.

As Dr. Charters suggests, there are also distractions which arise *within* the listener—competing thoughts, ideas which rap for attention, anticipation of things which must be attended to within the next hour or next day. These must be dismissed from attention so that you may concentrate fully on receiving and understanding what is being said. Literally or figuratively, you should "clear your desk" of whatever might tend to draw your attention from the

[4] Wesley Wiksell, *Do They Understand You?* (New York: The Macmillan Company, 1960), p. 106.

immediate business at hand, leaving your mind free to work with the speaker and his message.

To control and concentrate your attention will not always be easy, for you may be beset by sounds which cannot be shut out, or irritated by an uncomfortable chair which you cannot leave. You may be fatigued, you may even have a headache. It is often possible, however, to compensate for handicaps and still listen effectively. You may decide to heed the advice of a wise old teacher to a student who complained that he couldn't get his work done because he didn't feel well. "Young man," said the teacher, "never forget that half of the work of the world is done by people who do not feel well." Good listening is not a passive activity. It takes hard work and concentrated energy, and begins with very real, and not pretended, control of your attention.

Cultivate an affirmative attitude toward listening

Experts agree that negative attitudes toward listening create major barriers to productive communication. They lead the listener to tell himself, in effect, "I don't care what this person has to say. I know before he opens his mouth that he isn't worth listening to." Having such an attitude, the listener has figuratively taken his phone off the hook but refused to place it to his ear.

Negative attitudes of many sorts can be identified, but we will content ourselves with noticing five representative types and the people who hold them. Let us call the first kind of individual the *know-it-all*. Before listening he knows what the speaker is going to say and decides that because he already knows all about it, there is no point in paying attention. His is the attitude of superiority which leads him to remark, "That's old stuff. I've heard it before." He never finds out whether he was right or not.

The second type we may call the *rationalizer*. He doesn't try listening because it's hard work, yet he must have some reason to justify not making the effort. In school he's the one who says, "I don't like that subject." (It may be math, biology, art appreciation, or English—the subject itself seems not to make much difference.) In committee meetings or elsewhere he says, "This is tough—I don't get it." In either case, having provided himself with an excuse, he is content to sit back and tune out.

The *dogmatist* is the third type of individual with negative attitudes. He goes one step beyond the know-it-all by deciding in advance that the speaker is wrong. Consequently he listens for one purpose only, and that is to expose the errors of the speaker. Attending a speech, his mind is so busy with answers that he cannot fully comprehend what was actually said. In conversation, he is so busy thinking of what he wants to say in reply that he seldom really understands what he is replying to. He can be identified as the one who says in effect, "You're wrong, and I'm the one who can put you right."

The fourth person we may call the *playboy*. His prime object is to be entertained, and he is usually fearful that the speaker or program won't be up to entertaining him. "This is going to be dull," he remarks on the way to a meeting. And as he sits, his expression and posture telegraphs to the speaker, "I dare you to interest me!" At a luncheon meeting he entertains himself by drawing pictures on the tablecloth.

Finally we have the *snob*. A half-brother to the rationalizer, he finds his excuses for not listening in the speaker's dress, manner, or delivery, or in some part of the situation itself. "This man's a crank," he says, "Look at that hair cut." Or perhaps, "He can't talk. All he does is read from notes." Or again, "Why do they have to meet here? I know a better place to have a meeting." His attitude, like that of the other four, effectively prevents him from allowing his mind to contemplate a message.

To become a better listener, you must not only avoid attitudes like these, but you must also cultivate affirmative ones. You must enter a communicative situation in a positive frame of mind. As Oliver, Dickey, and Zelko put it, "Good listening commences with an objective interest in other people and in the ideas, emotions, and attitudes that they may express."[5] It is not enough to discard negative attitudes. You must replace them with affirmative ones.

One way to cultivate such desirable attitudes is to remind yourself always of the positive benefits of good listening. Recall that no one, yourself included, can ever know enough about anything. Recall that somewhere in another man's experience is an important fact, idea, insight, or feeling which can be significant to you if you will only listen to understand it. As Arthur K. Watson, President of

[5] Robert T. Oliver, Dallas C. Dickey, and Harold P. Zelko, *Essentials of Communicative Speech* (New York: The Dryden Press, 1949), p. 147.

International Business Machines, remarked, "We must remind ourselves that the talker educates but the listener learns—and there is much to learn."[6]

Better listening can improve your grades. It can help you become a better employee or a better manager. It can help you make better decisions based on the information, opinions, and experiences of others. It can improve your relations with others as you get to know and understand them and as they grow to have greater confidence in you. Consideration of these and other benefits should improve your attitude toward listening and help you involve yourself actively in that part of the communication process.

In short, you should cultivate the attitude of wringing the last ounce of information and understanding out of every opportunity you have to listen. Listen as if every time someone spoke, you were about to hear good news!

Consider why you are listening

Elsewhere in this book we consider the purposes of speech communication from the standpoint of the speaker or by looking at the process as a whole. Here we need to consider that you as a listener will do better in each communicative situation if you are aware of the purpose of your listening. You should ask yourself the question, "Why am I listening?" and with your answer enhance the purposiveness of your effort.

It is unlikely that we can, in these pages, indicate the *specific* purpose of your every act of listening, for specific purposes will depend upon the circumstances of each particular situation. It will be better, then, to examine five *general* purposes of listening, allowing you in any instance to know the *kind* of listening which may be appropriate.

In the first place, you may decide to listen for simple *enjoyment*. In this category you may put those occasions when all you expect from the experience is recreation. Many an after-dinner speaker, for instance, can top off an evening with some high good humor and nothing more. You watch a comedian or a famous mountain climber on television with only one motive, that of pleasure. Or

[6] Arthur K. Watson, Letter to the Editor, *Saturday Review*, XLVI, No. 34 (Aug. 24, 1963), p. 31.

you converse with friends during the course of a social evening simply to enjoy the fellowship of good talk. Listening of this kind does not demand that you be able to recall what was said, nor apply a message to your life and work. All it requires is attention, which you are likely to give without effort.

At other times you may listen to an orchestra playing a Beethoven symphony, you may attend a Shakespearean play, you may listen to a commencement speaker, or you may be one in an audience listening to a panel discussion of recent advances in space exploration. Occasions similar to these call upon you for something more than sheer enjoyment if you are to gain a maximum benefit. We may call this listening for *appreciation*. Beyond giving your full attention, you should expect an emotional understanding to emerge, or an evaluation of either the content or performance, based on an understanding of what you heard, and including perhaps an appraisal of the competence of those to whom you listened. If you attend a play, for example, your listening might be geared to seek answers to questions such as *What was the author's purpose? To what degree was he successful? Did the director and cast catch and enhance the drama?* Or as you listen to a speaker on some ceremonial occasion, you might ask yourself *Is he interpreting the mood and spirit of the event? Are his ideas appropriate to the occasion and audience? What is he trying to do for us who listen?* You may not find it necessary to do a great amount of appreciative listening in connection with your business or professional career, but it may make up a considerable part of the full life context in which your career is set.

Much more common, and of extreme utilitarian value, is listening to *understand*. In college you attend lectures and take part in discussions. On the job you may attend briefings, participate in conferences, receive instructions, get directions, and in a host of ways be expected to receive, comprehend, and use information which is given to you orally. You must be able not only to grasp the full import of the material, but to retain, recall, and apply it.

Listening to understand undoubtedly may take a variety of forms, and any comprehensive treatment would be impractical at this point. We can safely generalize by saying that you will need to determine *what* you are expected to understand, and *why* you are expected to understand it. The way you receive and treat what is said will depend greatly on your answers to these points. In some instances, for example, you will want to take notes, whereas in others you will do better to make an outline of what you hear. (By notes I mean random jottings of the significant things you hear; by an outline I refer to a systematic record in skeleton form of what was heard.) Often, however, you will depend solely on your memory. At times you must listen to grasp and relate specific details, but there are occasions when the details are significant only as they illustrate vital ideas, and it is the ideas themselves which you must comprehend. When you must be absolutely certain of your understanding you will want to repeat back all or part of the message as a way of verifying your comprehension. This will be especially true of many instructions and directions. In short, only when you know the *what* and the *why* of the message will you be in a position to determine the most productive way of receiving and fixing it in your mind.

The fourth general purpose of listening we may call that of *critical appraisal*. When you attend meetings and conferences, when you listen to salesmen and advocates, and when you participate in some interviews, you will listen to men who are advancing a point of view they hope you will accept. They would like you to agree with them, to believe them, or to make a decision in favor of their cause or case. You must, often in downright self-protection, listen to determine the truth of their arguments, the validity of their claims.

Listening to evaluate the statements of others, like listening to understand, can be so varied that it defies adequate treatment here. Much of what is said in other chapters of this book can be applied to this kind of listening. Here let us note only some fundamentals. Your first task should be to identify clearly the main proposition and the supporting claims of the speaker. With these in mind, you should next determine the evidence you deem acceptable in support of the claims. Then you need to assess the relationship between the evidence and the claims, establishing in your own mind the degree to which the evidence warrants your accepting the claims. You will be helped here by your knowledge of logic and reasoning. These three elements—claims, evidence, and reasoning—form the logical structure upon which your decision should rest.

At the same time you should be aware of the degree to which your personal wants and your attitude toward the speaker may be influencing your listening. Are you inclined to accept what he says at face value because of his ostensible authority or status? Does your desire to believe make you more impressed by data favoring his point of view than you might be by equally good data opposing it?

To the contrary, does a negative attitude make it difficult for you to give fair consideration to what is being said? The emotional side of your listening is difficult to weigh, but plays an important part in your reception of a message.

Finally, you must evaluate to some degree the language being used by the speaker. Does it represent a reasonable reality in terms which are objective? If necessary, can the speaker's statements be validated by the observation or testimony of others? Or is his language abstract and general? Does it include many words which inflame attitudes and arouse emotions? Does it over-simplify an involved and complex reality? Does it represent a fair and considered treatment of the topic? If you are to give your assent to the speaker's proposition, you must make sure that it is given only after a critical appraisal of the language of his presentation as well as of his reasoning and his appeals to your wants and attitudes.

The final purpose you may have in listening is in nature quite different from the others, for it calls upon you to understand the speaker much more than to understand what he is trying to say. We call it listening for *empathic understanding*. This kind of listening requires you to be sensitive to the feelings, the unspoken thoughts, the perceptions, and the attitudes of the talker. It requires you, in effect, to identify yourself so closely with him that you can appreciate, not only what he is saying, but why, and how he feels about it. You are not required to agree with the speaker, but to see things as he does, and to understand why he sees them that way.

Listening for empathic understanding is more common in face-to-face conversation than in group or audience situations. It is especially appropriate in counseling interviews, in handling grievances, in talking with employees or colleagues who are troubled, or in any delicate situation when matters must be handled with tact or caution. These are the situations in which, at least at the outset, you must do much more listening than talking, and in which you should avoid making responses which indicate your own approval, disapproval, or evaluation of either the speaker or what he says. Rather, you should assist him with helpful questions, with statements which repeat or reflect what he has said, or even with "eloquent and encouraging grunts."

Empathic listening has a cathartic value to the person being listened to. It permits him to purge himself of pent-up or hidden feelings by expressing them to someone who indicates understanding and who does not censure their expression. Beyond this, it helps

144

the talker to verbalize and to recognize his own ideas and feelings, enabling him thereby to evaluate them more objectively than he might were they unspoken. Frequently just being listened to is all an individual with a grievance really wants, and finding an empathic listener removes pressure which otherwise could mount to explosive proportions. Empathic listening often helps the speaker to communicate with and understand himself. Being listened to is a road toward sane and mature adjustment for distressed or discontented persons.

Listening with empathy also has positive values for the listener. Since it may be a form of release for the talker, and since it may enable him to understand himself better, the listener finds himself ultimately conversing with a person more able to talk rationally and in a better mood to solve problems or make decisions. Empathic listening also helps the listener to understand the motives of the talker, thereby understanding possible causes of the latter's behavior. Frequently it is more vital *why* an individual is saying things than to know *what* he is saying. Empathy is a way of putting yourself in the other's shoes and understanding the motives which produce his speech behavior.

You will be unable to derive the most value from empathic listening, however, unless you do it with sincerity. The speaker as a rule is able to sense the difference between true empathic listening and the cool and detached listening of one who views the process as a manipulative tool. Unless the speaker feels that his auditor is genuinely trying to see things from his point of view he will not open himself to vital communication.

As you determine which of the foregoing purposes describes your immediate listening aim, you should also reflect that very often you must listen for a combination of purposes rather than for one of the five alone. You may need to be alert to some speaker who seems to be only an entertainer but who is subtly attempting to propagandize, in which case you will need to appraise critically what he is saying as well as to enjoy it. Or you may find that information is being used to persuade, and again you will have to discriminate between your functions of understanding and appraising. And in the give and take of conversation you may find it needful to listen for different purposes at different times. In short, do not assume that only one kind of listening is appropriate in a specific communicative situation.

Be aware of your biases

In the preceding section we noted that when you listen critically you need to be aware of the effect of your wants and attitudes on your reception of the speaker and his message. This was saying that each of us possesses biases which make us eager to hear what is congruent with our predispositions, but which close our minds against that which seems incongruent. These biases are formed not only by wants and attitudes but by all our perceptions, our feelings, our prejudices, and our experiences, and create a filter through which we tend to allow only personally desirable ideas to pass.

Unfortunately we are in no position to know how important or desirable an idea may be until we have listened carefully and understood it. Yet we filter out those things which do not immediately seem congruent with our feelings and beliefs, thereby depriving ourselves of the opportunity of adding to our understanding, or of improving or correcting our thinking. This is the reason Walter Lippmann once observed that every statesman should pray to be delivered from his friends, but not from his enemies. The former say only what the statesman would like to hear, whereas the latter, by pointing out the dangers and weaknesses of political policy, can warn of disaster—if only they are listened to. The same is true in business, for every manager or administrator should listen more carefully to his opponents than to the yes-men who tell him only what they think he would like to hear.

Emotional filters can make us stop concentrating on what is being said, and can put our whole attention on what *we would like to say in return*. As a result we may miss something which could put the whole matter in a different light. As Nichols and Lewis have observed:[7]

> The over-stimulated auditor usually becomes preoccupied by trying to do three things simultaneously: calculate what hurt is being done to his own pet ideas; plot an embarrassing question or refutation to hurl at the speaker at the earliest opportunity; enjoy mentally, prior to its realization, all the discomfiture visualized for the speaker

[7] Ralph G. Nichols and Thomas R. Lewis, *Listening and Speaking* (Dubuque: Wm. C. Brown Company, 1954), p. 20.

once the devastating reply to him is launched. With all these things going on it is little wonder that subsequent passages of the discourse are tuned out, with comprehension of them sinking to near zero level.

Another effect of our filtering is that we tend to translate what we *do* hear into terms of what we *would like* to hear or what we *expect* to hear, thereby altering the speaker's meaning. The speaker may say, "Perhaps we should take the matter up with the president," but we hear, "Take the matter up with the president," because these words are what we would *like to hear*, and we assume that the speaker has committed himself, when in fact he has not.

Because of these and other effects of biases on your listening, you should take steps toward building sound habits which will overcome or compensate for them. First you need to be sharply sensitive to the fact that bias does make you an inferior listener, and alert yourself to become increasingly aware of the way your biases may be operating. Second, you should cultivate the habit of dampening your emotional reaction to what you hear so that you can more objectively attend to what a speaker is saying, hearing him out for the duration of his remarks. Third, suspend evaluation or judgment of what you hear until you are certain that you fully and accurately understand the point or message.

In addition, analyze the extent to which you seem to find that other people are "wrong." If it seems that another or others are "wrong" most of the time, you should thoroughly reappraise your own thinking by deliberately seeking facts and evidence contrary to your own opinions. One of the best ways toward an open mind is to conduct a personal and private campaign against your own beliefs. When you can honestly entertain all contrary argument and still hold to your opinion, you are a strong and open-minded individual.

Be aware of inferences

The poet Heine once remarked that, "The arrow belongs not to the archer once it has left his bow; the word no longer belongs to the speaker when it has once passed his lips." Applied to the process of listening, Heine's declaration can be taken as a reminder that the listener too often *thinks* he hears statements which were never actually made. He draws inferences from what was actually spoken, jumping to conclusions which are erroneous. The common practice of transcribing the verbatim text of important conferences, the records of legal proceedings, the statements made in critical press conferences, and even at times, vital telephone conversations, is evidence of the need for guarding against listeners who claim to hear words which were never uttered.

A woman walked into the emergency room of a large urban hospital not long ago and complained of stomach pains. Apparently a routine case, she was instructed to wait for attention. An hour and a half later she told an attendant that she had accidentally taken rat poison, and shortly thereafter she died. The attendant who originally interviewed her had inferred that her case was not serious. Granting that the woman was partly at fault, the fact remains that the attendant had acted on his inference rather than immediately seeking more complete information. He had listened carelessly.

All instances of listener inference are not as tragic as this one. Neighbors dropped in at the home of Lillian, age 6, who was eager to tell them of an impending visit by her Grandmother. "And where does your Grandmother live?" inquired one of the visitors. "In the hen house," replied Lillian. "Not really," commented the adult, "you must be mistaken!" "No," said the child. "My Daddy tells the truth, and he says she goes to bed with the chickens."

In both of these cases, the listener reacted, not to the actual words uttered by the speaker, but to the ideas in his—or her own head. Similarly, listeners can jump to conclusions from what they see of a speaker, or from his tone of voice, as easily as they can from what he says. A sudden twinge of neuralgia caused a member of a conference to grit his teeth as he was making a point about the proposal under consideration. Other conferees immediately inferred that the speaker was bitter in his remark, and accused him of taking a more extreme stand than his words by themselves could be construed to mean. The disagreement which followed was unnecessary because the inference was unjustifiable.

Trouble also arises when a speaker offers an inference as if it were a statement of fact, and fails to recognize the difference between the two. The trouble can be compounded if the listener likewise fails to discriminate. We shall take the matter up again in Chapter 7, for it is a frequent cause of unnecessary confusion and conflict. A statement of fact is one made about events, relationships, or phenomena in the physical world, and usually is verifiable. A statement of inference, on the other hand, is a conclusion or an opinion, and as such it is entirely a subjective evaluation. "Student

A is lazy," "Subordinate B is a deadbeat," and "Manager C is egotistical" are all statements of inference. They are statements which evaluate and which, if assumed to be statements of fact, can lead to communication failure.

Of these statements Dr. William M. Sattler has written:[8]

> Student A is not *lazy* simply because he asks to be excused from taking Course 300—two of his "required courses" may be scheduled at the same hour; Subordinate B is not necessarily a *deadbeat* merely because he failed to keep an appointment—he may have a legitimate reason; and Manager C is not *egotistical* if he fails on occasion to greet his employees—he could at these times be pondering helpful plans for employees. While it is probably true that we shall at times entertain such value judgments, depending upon our moods and inclinations, we will be better thinkers if we remind ourselves to *keep factually oriented.*

We cannot leave the matter of inferences without noting that they are a common and necessary part of many conversations. Frequently a speaker wishes to communicate something when tact suggests that the matter should not be bluntly stated. Consequently the idea is *implied* in carefully chosen words, so that the listener can *infer* the message. Marshal Foch, French leader of World War I, was once told by a companion that, "Etiquette is nothing more than a lot of air." "Mais oui," replied the Marshal, "nor is there anything but air in a pneumatic tire, yet how wonderfully it eases the jolts along life's highway!" How much more tactful a reply than simply, "Sir, you are wrong."

Inferences, then, have a legitimate place in talk, more so than this brief discussion can indicate. As listeners we must, however, beware of making inferences not intended by the speaker, and must learn to discriminate between statements of inference and statements of fact. Otherwise we create communication failure.

Use your spare time productively

It is estimated that Americans on the average talk at the rate of about 125 words a minute. Public speakers are apt to slow down at times to 100 words per minute, or speed up to 200. In contrast, a

---

[8] William M. Sattler, "Talking Ourselves Into Communication Crises," *Michigan Business Review,* IX, No. 4 (July, 1957), p. 28.

person can easily listen at double those speeds. Investigation indicates that thought speed, or listening speed, will mount to 750 words a minute or more. Thus an important differential exists between the rate at which you can listen and the rate at which a speaker talks to you.

This differential is deemed by Dr. Ralph G. Nichols, pioneer scholar in the problems of listening, to be a major barrier to good listening. Typically the listener fails to utilize productively the "spare time" offered by the differential. In effect, the old story of the hare and the tortoise is repeated time after time. The listening hare races mentally far ahead of the speaking tortoise, and then sits down and goes to sleep. Meanwhile, the tortoise speaks on, saying things which the sleeping hare never hears. Of course, the listener's "sleep" is usually a mental sidetrip into his own thought-ways, but his mind is as much detached from what the speaker is saying as if he had truly nodded off.

How, then, can you use your listening "spare time" productively? The answer can be put succinctly in four words: *anticipate, analyze, relate,* and *review.*

First, anticipate what you think the speaker will say next. If you are listening to an address, what point will he take up after this one? If your guess turns out to be right, you have reinforced the impression made by the speaker when he arrives at that point. If you are wrong, you have the opportunity to compare your own thinking with his, and in the comparison to enrich your impression of what he has to say, and perhaps to modify your own ideas. Meanwhile, you have been actively grappling with the talker's thought patterns instead of merely absorbing his words. You have been involved in the communication process.

Next, use your time to analyze the message and your reaction to it. Apply some of the suggestions and cautions of this chapter. Remind yourself of the purpose of your listening, discovering if at any point you should revise that purpose. Sense the biases that could be at work to distort the message as you receive it. Consciously be aware of inferences, and if possible translate them into statements of fact. Give mental emphasis to the points being made by the speaker, and swiftly analyze his proof and supporting material. Bring the emotional elements into objective focus, and note whether you seem to be much too irrationally affected. Appraise the structure of the message, and if it seems to lack reasonable order, create your own order from the speaker's chaos. And establish in your own mind the theme and purpose of the speaker as the central point to which all else should connect.

Third, relate what you are hearing to the general body of your own experience. Does it agree or disagree with the events through which you have lived? Is it consistent with what life has taught you? How does it compare or contrast with the speech you heard last week on a similar subject, or the book you read two months ago? If the talk is not consistent with your own experience, can the difference be reasonably explained? Has the speaker a background culturally or environmentally different from yours, causing him to see things in a different light? Has your own experience been narrow or limited in any way? If the message and your experience do agree, what is the speaker saying that can broaden and enrich your own thinking? What is he adding? Since you will be able to understand and retain what you hear only in terms of your own background, this way of using your spare time can be highly productive.

Finally, from time to time use the differential to go back and review what you have heard. Quickly summarize each point as it is made by the speaker, and if listening to an address, cumulate your summarization as each major part of the talk is ended. Continual recapitulation will not only help to fix the parts of the message in mind as they are presented, but will enable you to see more clearly the pattern of the talk as a whole. You will have used your spare listening time for productive purposes.

Delay judgment

A few pages back, in discussing the effect of your biases on listening, the point was made that you should suspend evaluation or judgment of the speaker and his message. The reason is that when you make evaluations of what the speaker is saying, or when you formulate a judgment of the speaker himself, you tend to commit yourself to that judgment. Hence you cannot thereafter listen with an open mind to the whole of the message. You cannot both evaluate and receive fully at the same time. Immediate evaluation puts your mental filters into action, so that what you then hear is colored if not distorted as it filters into your mind.

Walter attended a meeting devoted to the problems of unemployed youth. When the speaker took up the causes of the high rate of unemployment, Walter heard him say something about

151

"putting the responsibility on the youngster himself." "Nonsense," he thought to himself, "I know several unemployed young fellows, and it's not their fault they can't get a job. This man just isn't well informed. He's another theorist." And having judged that the speaker didn't know what he was talking about, Walter failed to hear him say that "placing the blame for unemployment" was a waste of time, and that society should energetically bend itself to solving the problem—ideas which significantly altered the tenor of the speech from what Walter had thought he heard. Immediate evaluation had made him deaf to statements which followed.

This is not to say that you shouldn't evaluate what you hear, for you must do that, of course. The question is *when* to evaluate, and the effective listener delays his judgments until he has carefully considered all that the speaker has to say. And if he is impelled to evaluate as the speaker talks, he does it only in the form of a mental note to which he will return. He does not allow it to distort or interfere with full comprehension.

Strive for understanding

"I just can't stand the professor," complained the freshman to his counselor. "He's a nut of some kind. All he does is walk up and down and talk about things nobody can understand. I can't get a thing out of his lectures. No wonder I got an F in the last exam!"

"We've tried about everything else," said the counselor after a brief moment of thought. "Now let's try this. When he says 'Yes', *you* say 'Yes.' When he says 'No,' *you* say 'No.' Try to get inside his mind and see what's going on there."

Three years later the student was graduated with a major in the subject he hated as a freshman, and was enthusiastic over his choice.

Admitting that the account has been simplified, the content remains just as it was told me by the counselor, and emphasizes the most fundamental principle of good listening. *Understand the full message on the speaker's terms.* In order successfully to accomplish this purpose you will have to put to work the seven guide-lines we have established up to this point. And unless you do achieve full understanding, it will be entirely beside the point to attempt applying those seven, for their purpose is to assist in getting the message.

152

Carl Rogers calls this the principle of listening *with* understanding. "It means," he says, "to see the expressed idea and attitude from the other person's point of view, to sense how it feels to him, to achieve his frame of reference in regard to the thing he is talking about."[9] Only as we do this can we fully comprehend what it is we are giving our attention to.

We can assist a complete understanding in a number of ways. The first is, of course, to refrain from interrupting the speaker if the situation is conversational. Let him have his say in all respects. You can even go further by encouraging the talker to expand on his theme—a nod, an understanding glance, or a simple, "And what else?" will do. Also, we can ask questions, especially covering details, technical points, or items we would like to have clarified in the speaker's own words. Asking for things to be repeated may be indispensable if we will be expected to remember them, or to carry out instructions or orders. Again, we can repeat back to the speaker what we have understood him to say, sometimes paraphrasing his remarks, sometimes using his own words, but always seeking verification of the degree to which we have comprehended his intentions. These three, elaboration, playback, and feedback, are helpful techniques as one strives for understanding.

Listening to understand may also include an appreciation of the person being heard and of his motives for talking. In an article in *Nation's Business*, Nathaniel Stewart points out some of the types of people who may try to reach a manager's ear—the chartists who insist on visual display, the manualists who are quick to cite organizational policies, the idea-stiflers, the logicians, the visionaries, the philosophers, and others. Each of these may deserve a hearing, and each may have something to contribute, and the manager will have to determine how to allocate his available listening time. Yet in listening, he is called upon to understand the men without necessarily approving or disapproving of their ideas.

Understanding, then, is the first imperative in good listening. Evaluation can come later, criticism can come later, response can come later. These depend upon the completeness and accuracy of your listening to understand. It is not a simple task, and you will have to give it your undivided attention, and do so with an open mind. As John W. Gardner has observed, "One needs to cultivate

---

[9] Carl Rogers, *On Becoming a Person* (Boston: Houghton-Mifflin Company, 1961), p. 331 f.

patience, discipline, and a deeply rooted interest in others to listen alertly and intelligently."[10]

In this chapter I have put you almost exclusively on the receiving end of the communication process, yet that position can be vital to you. Not only will you be likely to be spending more time listening than talking, but also the success of the speaker himself may well depend on how effectively you attend. Furthermore, as a speaker, you need be aware of the part your listener plays in the success of your efforts, and be sensitive to his attitudes and hidden responses. As we begin to take up the specific forms of speech communication in the next chapter we shall continue to stress the dynamic interplay between the sender and the receiver, with specific emphasis on the way they relate as individuals.

[10] John W. Gardner, "The Art of Listening," *Saturday Review*, XXXIX, No. 27 (June 2, 1956), p. 45.

Part Three

INTERACTING WITH
PEOPLE

Chapter 6

Person-to-Person Speaking: Human Relations

This multidimensional tool that the administrator needs, I call "human relations." It is designed to help persons to deal with concrete situations in which they are involved. It provides them with a useful way of thinking about such situations. It provides them with a skill of diagnosing such situations. It helps them to understand, to become more sensitive about, and then to respond more skillfully to what is taking place as they interact with people in face-to-face relations and as members or leaders of a group. In particular it helps them to see the effect of their behavior on others and vice versa. Thus it helps them to learn to accept their own feelings as well as the feelings of others.[1]

F. J. ROETHLISBERGER
Harvard Graduate School of Business
Administration

WHAT FORM OF COMMUNICATION WILL YOU USE MOST OFTEN? You will probably not have to reflect long to come up with an answer—person-to-person speaking! You may make speeches, read and write letters, attend conferences, send memos, plan interviews, and post notices, but most of your communicating will be made up of plain talk—person-to-person talk. Part of it will be semi-social "small talk," perhaps at the water cooler or in the cafeteria, and the

[1] "The Territory and Skill of the Administrator," *Michigan Business Review*, VI, No. 6 (Nov., 1954), p. 9.

rest will be more strictly related to the demands and functions of your job. Yet all of it may have a very positive bearing on your effectiveness as a member of a going enterprise. Because of its importance, person-to-person speaking is the first of the four basic forms of speech communication treated in this book.

Person-to-person speaking makes up the great bulk of the contacts in the life of a person or an organization. Think of your own situation and the multitude of personal contacts it undoubtedly involves. Upon such contacts the success or failure of a person or an organization may rest. There are instructions, directions, and orders to be given, complaints to be heard, requests to be made, coordination to be accomplished, information to be discovered, successful relationships to be established, and valid decisions to be made. Some of these contacts may be formal enough to classify as interviews, which we will take up in a succeeding chapter, but most of them are informal and unexpected, the kind of speech situations which fill the lives of all of us.

For instance, John is a teller in a bank. Early in the morning he comes in and exchanges greetings with his co-workers. During the morning most of his time is spent in talking with customers on routine matters. He has to handle a complaint made by a customer whose monthly statement contains an error. Later he takes time to explain to a new client how the schedule of charges on a checking account works. At lunch John talks with some fellow members of the Junior Chamber of Commerce about the details of a pancake dinner the group is sponsoring. In the afternoon, amid more routine, he finds it necessary to ask the vice president of the bank for a decision, to request some assistance from an associate, and to make a suggestion to the janitor before it is time to close his books for the day and make a report. As one banker observed, "Much of a teller's job involves a great deal of face to face interaction which should be conducted in an atmosphere of friendliness and helpfulness."

John's experience is repeated by hundreds of other people in the same small city and by thousands in a larger one. The building inspector ranging the city, the doctor making his rounds in the hospital, the high school principal managing his school, the receptionist greeting clients, the foreman working with crew, supervision, and materials handlers, or the heating contractor estimating new installations, engage in personal talk with a host of people.

All this talk is inescapable and indispensable, both for the individual and for the organization of which he is a part. The human interaction it provides is as much a part of an enterprise as machinery, laboratories, tools, or furniture; physical equipment is designed only for the use of human beings who are directed and related through communication. Person-to-person talk, allowing for back-and-forth interaction as noted in Chapter 1, establishes conditions necessary for the fullest understanding and for the maximum personal satisfaction from the communication.

As our first form of speech communication, person-to-person talk is characterized as a kind of good conversation wherein we respond to one another. You talk while another listens, and then he talks while you listen, until each of you knows, or thinks he knows, what is on the other's mind. The situation is spontaneous, often unexpected, and may be as brief as the conventional morning's greetings or the exchange of impressions with a roommate. In this kind of talk the sort of interpersonal relationship being established, modified, or terminated may be of greater moment than the actual messages being exchanged. Indeed, the messages themselves may at times be significant only as they bear on the relationship of those doing the talking. And since some inter-personal relationships endure for the greater part of a life-time (although others may be as fleeting as your conversation with the girl at the check-out counter), person-to-person talk sometimes takes on the character of a long and continued but interrupted dialogue.

Because person-to-person talk is spontaneous, interruptive, and often unexpected, it can rarely be planned and it defies the logical structuring of content, the basic principles of which can be applied to other forms of speech. You have almost no opportunity to organize your message; in fact, you may be hard put to know what to say first or last. You may have to listen more than you speak. You may be, in short, "flying blind."

Since this is the case, it would be fruitless to look for guidance to the doctrines taken up in later chapters. Rather we shall attempt to arrive at a set of precepts to guide our relationships with others, and to develop a functional understanding of language as it affects those relationships. To the first of these matters this chapter is devoted; we shall consider language in the next chapter.

HUMAN RELATIONS IS PSYCHOLOGY IN ACTION

People in business, industry, and the professions know that they are deeply concerned with the development of good human relations. Yet despite wide-spread acknowledgment of the importance of building good human relations, evidence indicates that too many business and professional people are inadequate in their relationships with others. Said Dr. William C. Menninger, Secretary of the Menninger Foundation, "Many individuals . . . don't get along well with the people about them. They account for a major part of the employee turnover in every business. Repeated surveys have indicated that 70 per cent of all dismissals are the result of social incompetence and not more than 30 per cent from technical incompetence."[2] A study of executive failure made at Stevens Institute of Technology concluded that "personality lacks" accounted for failure over "knowledge lacks" by a ratio of ten to one. Among the personality lacks was "inability to cooperate with others." Dismissed employees and failing executives, unable to relate well with others, simply fail in the basic person-to-person communicative relationships which are created and maintained by talk.

In chapters 2 and 3 of this book we looked at the principles of communication and of human behavior. It should be sufficient at this point to indicate the way in which those principles apply in building relationships with others.

Human relations are based on psychological principles

Among other things, good human relations seek to break down the barriers which impede the fullest possible communication and to promote the maximum understanding by establishing conditions favorable to that understanding.

Both of these goals may be approached only through speech which conforms to the way people behave. Each party to conversation should have an accurate perception of his respondent, an understanding of the attitudes which at that moment may be influ-

[2] *Vital Speeches*, XX (Dec. 1, 1953), p. 124.

encing his respondent's behavior, and a strong sense of the wants and motives which energize that behavior. Each should be aware that his respondent's speech behavior may be understood in terms of goal seeking, and that the other brings to the encounter a unique world-as-he-sees-it which is different, possibly to a significant degree, from his own.

Each party should similarly be aware of his own perceptions and of the fact that they may be faulty. He should know that his own attitudes and expectancies predispose the way he will talk, and make allowances for possible error. He should recognize his own conscious motives and appreciate that motives of which he is unaware may be influencing his behavior. He should further appreciate that understanding can be obtained only as his world and his respondent's are brought into congruence.

Each must be alert to the fact that something in the situation may be seen by the other as a threat, or, indeed, that he himself may be seen as a threat. Each should work to reduce negative motivation of this kind and to promote positive motivation toward mutually acceptable goals. And, of course, each should affirm the individuality and integrity of the other even as he maintains his own.

In short, every principle of communication and behavior we have so far considered may be an element in the human relationship involved when one person talks to another. Successful person-to-person speaking demands that these principles be productively employed.

Human relations are a complicated interaction

Although human relations are founded on psychological principles, we must not gain the impression that when I talk with you my only task—or yours, either—is to be sensitive to the basic psychology of stimulus and response. Human interaction is not that simple. In the last century Oliver Wendell Holmes with rare insight laid down, in *The Autocrat of the Breakfast Table,* the dictum that any person-to-person talk involves at least six people, though only two may be visible. If we express the Autocrat's notions in more modern language, those six people are:

1. The real me, whom no one really knows.
2. The me I think I am; the role I assume at the moment.

3. The me you think I am; the role you see me playing.
4. The real you.
5. The you you think you are.
6. The you I think you are.

Human relations may be said to be the delicate balance of relationships established and maintained among these six people. The significant fact to emerge is the concept of *role*. I talk and behave in *the role I see myself playing* (which may be one I think you want me to assume) in relation to *the role I see you playing*. You do the same with regard to me. If there is reasonable and mutually satisfying correspondence between these roles, our relationship may be productive; if not, we may fail to maintain a good relationship.

Any individual may play a series of roles, depending upon the circumstances and the people with whom he is relating at the moment. At home he may be "husband," "father," "breadwinner," or "patriarch." At work he may be "boss," "colleague," "elder statesman," or "yes-man." (Recall some of the communication "roles" noted in Chapter 2.) At the lodge he may be "brother," on the bowling team "partner," and at church "deacon." Each role creates a set of expectancies among those to whom he relates; that is, others expect him to talk and behave consistently with the role he has assumed or developed. *The effectiveness of some relationships may depend on the degree to which each person understands his role as others see it, and fulfills their expectancies.*

When an individual plays a role others do not expect, or when he puts others in roles they are unwilling or unready to assume, good human relations may suffer. For instance, the "boss" at work may have interpersonal difficulty when he comes home and maintains his "boss" role with his teenage children. Or one who is the "chief" at work may suffer if he tries to be "playboy" after working hours. Promotion to a new and more important job frequently demands that an individual assume a fresh role, and it is undoubtedly true that some people do not meet the demands of new assignments because they cannot fulfill the role expectancies of those with whom they must work.

Beyond the importance of roles in human relationship, we must look to the basic character of the relationships themselves. Fundamental is the fact that to exist, *a relationship must provide mutual satisfaction of certain needs or wants for those involved.* In some cases the relationship is *in itself* satisfying, in others it satisfies wants or needs to which *it is only an instrument*. A recent and notable volume on human interaction,[3] for instance, recognizes four basic types of relationships according to their function. The first is a relationship formed for the purpose of fulfilling itself, such as friendship or marriage. The second is one created so that one or both of the partners may facilitate the finding or development of his "self," either personally or socially; an instance might be that of a young boy who finds that associating with an older one gives him a sense of being "grown up." The third kind of relationship is effected for the purpose of creating change, as exemplified by the interaction of teacher and student or father and child. The final relationship exists to further a goal or task, as viewed in the reciprocal behavior of doctor and nurse or pilot and co-pilot. The first two of these may be seen to provide inherent satisfaction of personal needs, the second pair to be instrumental is satisfying such needs.

In another way, relationships may be termed symmetrical or complementary, according to their nature.[4] The first of these is a relationship between equals who recognize their equality, exchanging an equivalent sort of behavior. The second is one between unequals, effective when those who are different complement one another to form a united whole, and when the differences are accepted, the superior member of the relationship defining its nature and the inferior member accepting the definition.

From these brief explanations we may be able to generalize that good human relations can be developed according to the following principles:

1. Each person should assume a role which is appropriate, and should strive to understand the role of the other.
2. Each should understand and accept the nature of the relationship and his position in it.
3. Each should understand and accept the function of the relationship.
4. Each should see his partner as an individual in his own right, not merely as an instrument of personal satisfaction.

---

[3] Warren G. Bennis, Edgar H. Schein, David E. Berlew, and Fred I. Steele, *Interpersonal Dynamics* (Homewood, Ill.: The Dorsey Press, 1964).
[4] See Paul Watzlawick, *An Anthology of Human Communication*, (Palo Alto: Science and Behavior Books, Inc., 1964). Tape and text.

5. Each should recognize the right of the partner to personal satisfaction from the relationship.

6. Neither should sacrifice his personal integrity for the sake of the relationship.

These generalizations must be taken as tentative, and not understood as validated by experimental evidence.

Human relations are instrumented by speech

The instrument by which the principles of psychology are brought alive and by which human beings are brought into various relationships is, of course, speech. Saying the right thing, in the right tone of voice, at the right time, and for the right motives creates sound and productive relations, while saying the wrong thing, in the wrong tone of voice, at the wrong time, and for the wrong motives creates bad human relations.

By carefully examining a man speaking, we can know him for what he is. Our voice, the words we use, the ideas we have to offer, and the physical elements of our utterance open doors into our background, our inner being, and the culture from which we came. Our speech discloses our attitudes toward others, our aggressive drives, our motives, our resentments, our hidden insecurities. Ben Jonson knew and affirmed this truth years ago when he wrote, "Speak that I may know you, for speech most shows the man." And as we reveal ourselves to others by our speech, so they reveal themselves to us.

By analysis, however, we may discover that "speech" in the sense of total communication between human beings takes place on three distinct levels. The first of these is the level of basic relationship in which whatever is communicated tends to establish the nature of the association, whether it be symmetrical or complementary, whether the partners will tend toward cooperation or conflict, and so on. The second is a contextual level which tends to provide meaning for the communicative signals which are exchanged, the meaning being taken in part from the total field of the exchange as well as from the identities or roles of the individuals themselves. Thus the words, "How are you?" will take on a different meaning when spoken by a doctor in his office than when uttered by the same doctor at a dinner party. The third level is the message level, in which information is presumably exchanged and the meaning has to do largely with evaluations of the physical, intellectual, or emotional world. These levels strongly reinforce the point made earlier, that human relations are a complicated interaction, for they add another dimension to the concept of speech communication. The person to first utter words in a conversation may not be initiating a stimulus-response pattern, for his words may come in response to what he perceives, and on the predictions he makes concerning possible response to his words. Whatever the partner says in reply may then tend to reinforce the original speaker's verbal behavior, or to significantly modify it. Thus human relations are not simply a matter of effecting a desirable response, but an intricate process of stimulus, response, reinforcement, and modification of behavior, the beginning and ending points of which cannot be precisely determined. The instrument for all this is speech.

Good human relations serve five functions

Sound and productive relationships between and among people are plainly desirable in themselves, yet perhaps their importance can be more fully appreciated by identifying several specific outcomes which may be expected from their cultivation.

THE PRACTICE OF GOOD HUMAN RELATIONS CAN CREATE VIABLE AND PRODUCTIVE INTERPERSONAL RELATIONSHIPS WHICH MAKE FOR A MORE SATISFYING JOB CLIMATE. As John, the bank teller, exchanged morning greetings, he may well have been nourishing relationships which make his work more pleasant as well as more productive. Like John, each of us spends more than a third of a lifetime on the job. The nature of the work environment is largely determined by the relationships among the people brought together in the organization. An environment filled with tension, friction, suspicion, or hostility can force a person to live a major part of his life under the most unpleasant circumstances. Conversely, an environment of relaxation, permissiveness, confidence, and relative friendliness can make work-life much more worth living. In the words of Elizabeth and Francis Jennings:[5]

[5] "Making Human Relations Work," *Harvard Business Review*, XXIX, No. 1 (Jan.-Feb., 1951), p. 30.

Environment is not just the physical plant and surroundings; it is also the mental and emotional atmosphere
inside the plant. It is the sum total of the contributions of
experience made by every individual in the plant from the
doorman to the president. It is the total of all the invisible
contributions of voice, clothing, gesture, word, report, and
report of report which every morning are behind every
bench and desk, every ledger and typewriter, every wheel
and tool of the organization. And every individual reacts
according to the way his experience in his environment
makes him feel. If he feels comfortable, mentally and
physically, he will react favorably; if he is uncomfortable,
his reaction will be unfavorable.

By developing constructive human relations, then, you can help
make your job climate warmer and more comfortable, you can help
make your work more pleasant, and you can add to the total
satisfaction you and others take from your careers. The same can be
said for your relationships at home, or in any group or organization
of which you are a member.

THE PRACTICE OF GOOD HUMAN RELATIONS HAS AN IMPOR-
TANT EFFECT ON THE RECEPTIVITY OF PEOPLE TO THE MESSAGES
YOU WANT TO COMMUNICATE. The second function of good human
relations is, as already indicated, to create a satisfying rapport
between and among people in which the fullest communication can
take place. Abraham Lincoln once said, "If you would win a man to
your cause, you must first convince him of your sincere friendship.
. . . Attempt to dictate to his judgment, or to command his action,
and he will retreat within himself, close all avenues to his head and
his heart . . . and you will be no more able to pierce him than to
penetrate the hard shell of a tortoise with a rye straw." A listener's
mind is not open to the instructions, the suggestions, or the persuasion of another when a reasonable degree of mutual respect and
personal understanding does not exist between the two. When friction, tension, or mistrust exist, communication which results in full
understanding is difficult if not impossible. Research done by Dr.
Eugene Jennings at the University of Wisconsin revealed that a
direct correlation exists between the respect a worker has for his
foreman and the clarity with which the worker understands the
foreman's instructions. Summing up this research, industrial con-

sultants Laird and Laird assert that, "A large share of 'denseness' in catching on to directions is just a hostile interaction. . . . Communicating is a human relations problem as well as a problem in the clear expression of ideas."[6]

In your own experience you have undoubtedly discovered that you can communicate more easily and clearly with people when mutual respect or strong friendship exist between you, thus proving to your own satisfaction that successful person-to-person talk depends upon good human relations.

THE PRACTICE OF GOOD HUMAN RELATIONS TENDS TO HEAD OFF MANY PROBLEMS WHICH MIGHT OTHERWISE DEVELOP IN THE WORKING OF AN ENTERPRISE. Among people who work in an atmosphere of respect and confidence, problems and conflicts are apt to be few and far between. According to an old adage, an ounce of prevention is worth a pound of cure, and people who enjoy satisfying relationships are little inclined to let friction or conflict develop. They are more prone to listen carefully to one another, to suspend judgment, to understand one another's motives, and to search for mutual adjustment to a problem or an issue. The enterprise, which is a social system, is possessed of a greater "team spirit," and functions better because of it. When John the bank teller found it necessary to seek a decision from his vice president, it was easier for him to accomplish his task because his relationship with the man was one of mutual and friendly respect. They worked *together*. This is the key to the cooperation and teamwork which prevents problems. It is also the key to good customer relations.

THE PRACTICE OF GOOD HUMAN RELATIONS CAN HELP SOLVE PROBLEMS WHEN THEY DO ARISE. The fourth function of good human relations is to relieve or solve problems, diminish crises, and resolve conflicts. Tactful person-to-person talking, based on sound human relations behavior, is imperative to reduce or settle complaints and grievances, mediate disputes, and adjust differences. When difficulties arise, the "mending of fences" may become the necessary object of talk. If John is dealing for the first time with a complaining customer, he must use all his skill in person-to-person talking to find the road to agreement or resolution. He must listen

---

[6] Donald A. and Eleanor C. Laird, *The New Psychology for Leadership* (New York: McGraw-Hill Book Company, Inc., 1956), p. 12.

carefully, somehow overcome hostility, get the customer's mind open to his own message, and establish an effective communicative relationship which will lead toward satisfaction while preserving the rights and interests of both bank and customer. All of these are part of the mending function of the cultivation of good human relations when things go wrong.

THE PRACTICE OF GOOD HUMAN RELATIONS IMPROVES ALL FORMS OF SPEECH COMMUNICATION. Although we are looking in this chapter at the practice of good human relations as a part of person-to-person speaking, we must not overlook that the same principle undergirds productive speech regardless of the social form in which the talking takes place. Thus good human relations are necessary in participating in an interview, in taking part in a conference or meeting, or in making a speech to a group of listeners. In spite of custom, social arrangements, degree of formality, or any other determinants of the kind and structure of talk which is appropriate, in every form people enter into interpersonal relations in which the three levels of communication occur. You will need to apply the basic precepts of good human relations any time you speak.

This brings us to the critical question: How can you improve yourself in the practice of good human relations?

First, let us remind ourselves that we are thinking of good human relations as the art of relating one's self to others in such a way as to make the relationships mutually satisfying, and contributory to a more perfect interpretation of messages. We are thinking of good human relations as the art of living in a healthy interpersonal or social environment which one has himself helped to create. We are NOT thinking of them as a "be nice to the other guy" approach to people, nor as a glib or sophistic set of techniques. Certainly we are not thinking of them as a method of manipulating others solely to our own ends, for as Reuel L. Howe remarks in *The Miracle of Dialogue*, "The purpose of communication is not to seduce or exploit persons, but to bring them into responsible relation to the world of persons and things."[7]

Second, let us realize that the behavioral sciences have not yet taken their study of speech communication and interpersonal dynamics to the point that specific prescription can be made on the

[7] New York: The Seabury Press, 1963, p. 56.

basis of experimental findings. The suggestions which follow have been derived from pragmatic evidence, from the accumulated experience of people who have found that *as a rule* they tend to bring about productive results. These suggestions are consistent with the basic principles of psychology and human interaction, and by putting them to work you may expect similar results.

Finally, you may find your own improvement in the practice of good human relations a stiff challenge. This may be so in the first place because for you, as for the rest of us, the universe is ego-centered. It revolves around each of us individually, and we are so used to looking at things from our own center that we assume it to be part of the nature of things. Yet good human relations call for us to *see* another and to treat him within the framework of the way he sees things. As Will Rogers is reputed to have remarked, "You can never tell what a man is thinking when you are looking at him. You have to get behind him to see what he is looking at in order to understand him." If we wish to encourage the voluntary rather than the antagonistic cooperation of others we must discipline ourselves in the art of understanding them.

Beyond the challenge to our ego-centered natures is still another challenge, this one to our innate self-acceptance. Once we do get behind the other man to see what he is looking at, we may find to our dismay that he is looking at us, and that the cause of his offending behavior may be our own. William Thackeray wrote, "The world is a looking glass, and gives back to every man the reflection of his own face." Yet when our interpersonal relationships are unsatisfactory, our own self-esteem leads us to place the blame anywhere except on our own behavior. Many corporations in recent years have put employees into courses for "sensitivity" training, the purpose of which is to develop the individual's sensitivity to the way in which he is perceived by others, thus helping him improve his relationships with them. If those with whom we deal are to become the kind of people we would like to work with, we must help them become such people.

It should be axiomatic that to be understood we must understand, that to be listened to we must listen to others, that to control others we must control ourselves, and to create healthy relationships we must be healthy persons. Toward these fundamentals and toward the practice of good human relations the following sections are aimed.

GOOD HUMAN RELATIONS CAN BE CULTIVATED BY PRACTICE

Satisfying and productive human relationships cannot be gained by reading about them, talking about them, or thinking about them only. These things build a useful foundation, but good human relations come about solely as your daily behavior helps create them. To consciously control your behavior, and to help make it productively a matter of habit, you will need a systematic approach more usefully simple than the whole complex body of theory. The approach here offered is founded on four basic precepts, each of which can be put into practice in various ways. Four specific methods of implementing each precept are suggested; you will find it possible to discover other ways of implementing the precept as you put it into practice. The list of precepts and of methods of implementation is a purely arbitrary arrangement which reflects the accumulated experience earlier referred to. It provides a manageable approach to the human relations part of person-to-person speaking, and one which you can immediately put to work.

Respect the dignity of others; never diminish a person's human dignity

We have already established that every individual has within himself a deep desire for self-respect. He wants to see himself as a worthy member of the human race, endowed with attributes in which he can take pride. Whether this desire is innate or learned is irrelevant; the fact remains that it is a motivation with which we must take account, for, as Dr. Menninger remarks, "Perhaps most important for all of us is the desire for a sense of personal worth and dignity."[8]

In dealing with others it is basic, therefore, to do or to say that which will honestly nourish the other person's sense of human dignity. If we can do this, we will improve relations and begin opening the mind to our messages. On the other hand, if we injure

[8] Menninger, p. 124.

the other's personal dignity, if we humiliate him in his own eyes, if we debase him in any way, we create resentment or animosity and close the door to what we would like to communicate. Dr. Rensis Likert, in an interview in *Nation's Business,* stated that, "Every person in the organization should have experiences which increase the sense of his personal worth and importance. The desire to make a mark in the world, to have a feeling that what I am and what I do makes a difference is a powerful force working in every person. The managers who are getting the best results in American business are making use of this motivational force."[9]

To illustrate, Evans Jackson walked through the door of a unit of one of the nation's largest clothing chains. Two clerks saw him across the expanse of the store, and one shouted loudly to the other, "I've got him!" Jackson turned around and walked right out again. Later he said, "I want to buy in a place where the customer is something more than a salesman's target. I didn't like their attitude." Both the salesman's tone and words were damaging to Jackson's sense of personal worth and dignity, and resulted in the loss of a possible sale.

As we turn to ways of implementing this first precept, know that the illustrations are all taken from actual occurrences. You can add further amplification from your own observation of human relations.

MAKE THE OTHER PERSON RIGHT IN SOMETHING. This is a rule of conduct practiced by many salesmen whose livelihood depends on effective communication. Even though you may disagree with another's opinion, the beginning step in the search for agreement is to pinpoint something in which he is right, to emphasize that something, and to carry on the conversation from there. All too often our first impulse is to make the other person *wrong.* "You're mistaken," we say, enhancing our own egos, but at the expense of the other person's ego and at the expense of sound relationships. We must resist the first impulse, and search for that in which the other is right. As the French philosopher, Pascal, wrote in *Pensees,*

When we wish to correct to advantage, and to show another that he errs, we must notice from what side he views the matter, for on that side it is usually true, and

---

[9] "How to Raise Productivity 20%," an interview with Rensis Likert, *Nation's Business,* XLVII, No. 8 (August, 1959), pp. 31–2.

admit that truth to him, for he sees that he was not mistaken, and that he only failed to see all sides. Now, no one is offended at not seeing everything; but one does not like to be mistaken.

To adopt Pascal's advice is to recognize the limitations of any individual's perceptions, including your own, and to find what there may be in another's experience which leads him to make statements you consider erroneous.

Simon, the manager of an auto dealer's repair shop, found it necessary to tell a customer that the best cure for a damaged motor would be the installation of a used but rebuilt one. His customer exploded at the idea of putting an unknown and used motor into his car.

"Of course you don't want an unknown used motor in your car," said Simon, thereby making his customer right at the very beginning. "And neither do we. But the motor won't be unknown to us." He went on to explain where the motor would come from, and how it had been selected and rebuilt. By making his customer right at the outset, Simon was able to maintain good communicative relationships and have a customer willing to listen to the rest of his message.

AVOID COMPLAINING OR FINDING FAULT. This may be one of the most important implements for nourishing sound and enduring relationships, for the chronic complainer and the habitual faultfinder destroy all reasonable relations. The nagging wife and the complaining mother-in-law may be acceptable as the focus of crude humor, but their counterparts are completely unacceptable in business or the professions. Such verbal behavior may indeed be symptomatic of an unhealthy personality—at best it is a gross lack of tact.

Fault-finding often grows out of dealing with the mistakes of others, and is best avoided by following the maxim, "Fix the error, but not the blame." Clarence Darrow expressed the basic idea when he said, "I hate the sin but not the sinner." When Ralph's secretary typed an error into a letter, he avoided fault-finding by simply stating, "Christine, the figures in this letter are inaccurate. Will you please do it over so we can send a correct estimate?" Although the man she works for sets high standards, Christine is a loyal secretary, for he treats her with respect and dignity, as the example shows.

The person who habitually complains or finds fault betrays a negative and defensive outlook on life, the opposite of the positive outlook suggested in Chapter 4 as characterizing the excellent communicator.

AVOID ARGUMENTS. A certain way to diminish the dignity of another is to correct or argue with that person, clearly implying that he is ignorant or mistaken. Engaging in argument establishes a clear-cut conflict, developing antagonism and causing others to close their minds to later constructive communication. As Dr. Samuel Johnson observed nearly 200 years ago, "Every man will dispute with great good humor only upon a subject in which he is not interested." If you want to make a man into an opponent, thereby damaging productive relations, tell him he is wrong.

The wise Benjamin Franklin made avoiding arguments one of his rules of behavior, writing in his autobiography that he developed the habit by

> never using, when I advanced anything that may possibly be disputed, the words *certainly, undoubtedly,* or any others that gave an air of positiveness to an opinion; but rather say, I conceive or apprehend a thing to be so and so; it appears to me, or *I should think it so and so....* I wish well-meaning, sensible men would not lessen their power of doing good by a positive assuming manner, that seldom fails to disgust, tends to create opposition, and to defeat every one of those purposes for which speech was given us.

By being modest in advancing our own claims and by avoiding telling others they are wrong, we can reduce the unnecessary arguments which are so damaging to good interpersonal relations. Jerry had just completed checking a consignment of goods from Buffalo into the receiving room when he heard an office supervisor comment, "I'm glad that shipment from Chicago is in." Jerry's impulse was to hurry to tell the supervisor he was mistaken, that the Chicago shipment had not arrived. Then he checked himself. There was little to be gained by immediately contradicting the man, and good relations could be harmed. He avoided argument, knowing that it made small difference whether the supervisor was right or wrong. Later he made sure that the supervisor saw the invoice of the shipment, discovering for himself that he had been mistaken. The point was made, but Jerry had avoided challenging the supervisor's

173

opinion. He is perfectly able to defend his own convictions, but he does not cultivate a controversial attitude.

ADMIT YOUR OWN MISTAKES. A final way to implement your respect for the dignity of others is by frank admission whenever you are mistaken or wrong. If you are willing to admit that you are human enough to make an error, the person with whom you are talking finds his own image taking increased stature. The tactful individual may not go about advertising his own mistakes, but he is not reluctant to be honest and admit them when he can thereby promote improved relations with another. The admission of an error can reduce the sense of insecurity for both parties, thereby promoting improved communication. According to the English satirist, Jonathan Swift, "A man never should be ashamed to own up that he has been in the wrong, which is but saying, in other words, that he is wiser today than yesterday."

When Ellen, a first-year teacher, used the wrong formula in tabulating the final averages for her students, the principal called her to his office. "Ellen," he said, "you made the same mistake on those averages that I did years ago. The formula you used didn't give me the right result then, and it doesn't give the answer we need now. In order to come out right, you'll have to . . ." and he explained the proper formula for deriving the needed averages. The sting was taken off the error for Ellen because her principal thoughtfully opened the conversation by admitting his own mistake. He helped motivate her to do the job over the right way.

When you have committed an error, quickly and freely admitting your mistake is often the best way—or the only way—to meet the situation. You thereby deprive a challenger of both the opportunity for an argument and the opportunity to nourish his own self-esteem, leaving him only the opportunity to adopt an attitude of magnanimity.

Develop an honest interest in other people

The second basic precept for developing viable relations with others calls for us to face firmly the previously-mentioned fact that our human nature makes us see everything from a personal, and frequently from a selfish, point of view. It is said that a person may enter a room with one of two attitudes. One is expressed as "Here I am," and the other as "There you are." The second of these attitudes characterizes the person who has an honest interest in others, who thereby cultivates effective human relationships, and who is able to communicate clearly with others because he sees them as individuals and understands the people with whom he talks.

Gordon Smith, Vice President of Remington Rand, reveals the "There you are" attitude of one of the major figures in American industry:[10]

> I was working for I. B. M., and one day the Board Chairman, Mr. Watson, came for a field visit. I studied hard to have all the right statistics and answers, but to my surprise after a few questions about sales, he started asking about me, and then about my men—what was their background, were they married, how many children did they have, what were their health problems, how was the man's wife who had been ill, and so on. During that three-day visit, I saw first hand the genuine interest, fairness, and consideration which had built the business. Why was the Board Chairman taking all this time with me? It was because he was sincerely interested in me and my men, and in our success and well-being.

Such an attitude not only gains the respect of others which is needed for the most productive communication, but it also enables one to know those with whom he deals, to understand them, to treat them as individuals. Here are some ways of cultivating that attitude.

BE AN INTERESTED LISTENER. We have already considered listening as participation in the process of communication, and have stressed the importance of empathic listening. Now we must note that careful listening in face-to-face situations not only nurtures the dignity and self-respect of another, but evidences as well an interest in them on the part of the listener. And to assume this virtue with honest intent will help one become genuinely interested in others, thus leading to effective working relationships.

The Scoutmaster had been listening intently to one of his youngest scouts, who was describing with enthusiasm but at great length his collection of butterflies. The young scout's mother, who had overheard the monologue, later thanked the Scoutmaster for his kindness to her son, and added, "But wasn't it boring?" "Yes, you might say so," replied the man, "but if we're going to work with

<hr/>

[10] *Vital Speeches*, XVIII (May 1, 1962), p. 442.

your son and help him grow, we have to be interested in the things which interest him." This Scoutmaster's rapport with his boys is built on unfeigned interest in them, which leads him to be a good listener. If you are interested in others you will encourage them to talk about themselves.

Become sincerely concerned with the needs, desires, and interests of others

The Scoutmaster in the preceding section was concerned not only with the young scout as an individual, but with the things which seemed vital to the youngster. This did not mean that he himself must become wrapped up in butterflies, but that he must appreciate the other's interest. We must understand that it is not always necessary to *approve* or *like* another's needs and interests, but that we must be concerned enough to *understand* them and be able to work with and through them. The springs which drive behavior lie within the individual, and his behavior cannot be modified except from within.

Jack Worth was foreman in a steel mill. One of his workers, a man named Leshinsky, was so irregular in reporting for work that he became a real problem. "Fire him," said the supervisor. But Jack decided that first he would try to find out why Leshinsky was so frequently absent. During an interview he discovered that the man was within two years of retirement, that his wife had died, and that in his loneliness he too often had found a bottle to be his only companion. On the "morning after" he would be unable to make it to work. On the basis of these discovered facts, Jack was able to modify the man's attitudes and get him to report with regularity. "He wanted to get his full retirement benefits," said Jack, "so I was able to keep a skilled worker, and I felt a whole lot better about the matter. I hated to see him lose his job without trying to find out why he was absent so often. And if I hadn't found out what made him tick, we'd both have lost."

Please note that the incident also reveals good human relations precepts at work in an interview situation, because the talk was deliberately planned by the foreman with a specific goal in mind.

SMILE HONESTLY AND OFTEN. How do others perceive you? Frequently a genuine smile may be the surest way of indicating

176

good will on your part, and a method of helping others perceive that in a given communicative situation you do not constitute some kind of a threat. (It is interesting to note as an exception that a study made of waitresses in night spots on the West Coast turned up the fact that some did interpret a customer's smile as a threat. It was concluded that to get good service in such places, a customer should not smile at a waitress when ordering!)

Still a smile is, as a rule, more than a warm gesture of friendliness; it is a signal of recognition and appreciation. Some individuals become so wrapped up in their own thoughts that they actually may not see others. Recognition and a friendly gesture are habitual accompaniments of interest in others, and to cultivate the habit of smiling is to engender the more fundamental habit of being interested in individuals. Ed Hegarty, formerly Manager of Sales Training for Westinghouse, declared that he made it a practice to smile at his audiences before beginning a speech. The manner in which he evidenced an interest in a group of people can equally demonstrate your own interest in any one person.

ASK QUESTIONS FREQUENTLY FOR THE PURPOSE OF UNDER-STANDING OTHERS. As a means of developing an interest in others, a question can be valuable, for the asking of it requires you to take specific action in their direction. Furthermore, it offers the person questioned the opportunity of revealing himself, thus providing you with an invaluable means of knowing and understanding him. Since one of the major benefits of person-to-person talk is the feedback it provides, allowing the speaker to evaluate the responses of the one he is talking with, it is only good judgment to ask questions frequently in order to encourage that feedback. In this sense, questions should be put for the purpose of getting better acquainted with others and of understanding them; there are times when questions may become a form of verbal attack, which is quite the opposite of trying honestly to develop an interest in other people.

Lee noticed that one of the men who worked with him in a large law office had a new and unusual decal emblem affixed to the windshield of his car. One morning in the parking lot Lee observed to his colleague, "That's an interesting emblem. What does it stand for?" He did not miss in this casual conversational encounter the opportunity of asking a question to help him better know his co-worker. At the same time he was evidencing his interest in others and aiding himself make that interest habitual.

Recognize individual uniqueness and worth

The third precept of good human relations, which has been stressed throughout this book as the principle of dealing with individuals as individuals, is that of specifically recognizing the uniqueness of each, and of searching for the good qualities which each possesses as a person. Business and professional relationships are liable to suffer when all engineers are dealt with alike, or all farmers, all secretaries, all customers, all supervisors, all patients, all artists, or all salesmen. Although we commonly give lip service to the fact that no two people are alike, many neglect that fact in dealing with others, particularly those with whom they are not intimately acquainted. As a consequence, their human relations tend to deteriorate.

We fail to take into account the uniqueness or individuality of a person when we *label* that person and then talk to him or behave in his presence as if the label were an accurate description. Just as there is no living "average man," so there is no man who fits the characteristics suggested by such a label as "waiter," "clerk," "painter," or "truck driver." When people are important to our personal needs we tend to treat them with respect as individuals, but when we do not see them as significant to us we are often careless. The man who has run out of gasoline on a snowy night will see a filling station attendant as a highly important individual; on a routine stop he would likely never look at the man's face. Unfortunately, such behavior becomes habitual, undermining good human relations. Regardless of status or position, each person wants to be known as an individual in his own right, and sound relationships are built on that fact.

Sometimes we brand others with evaluative labels, a practice which is even more dangerous than using descriptive ones. We say this man is "good" or "bad," that man is "right" or "wrong," and the other is "disgusting" or "likeable." This distorts the truth. No one human being is wholly and unalterably at one end of the spectrum in any quality or characteristic, and all are a blend of many characteristics. It is important for us to realize that our dearest friends or our closest companions are imperfect, and that we tend to respond to their excellent qualities and to overlook their imperfections. We suffer from the so-called "halo" effect ("The King can do no wrong"), and allow ourselves to perceive only the good qualities. In truth, our friends are a mixture of strengths and weaknesses, but we see only the strengths. More unfortunately, we do the same for those we do not like or do not get along with, and because of the halo we can see nothing attractive or desirable about them. Consequently our attitude toward them is completely negative, as it is completely positive toward our friends. We need to realize that those whom we dislike are not totally evil or repulsive, and that it is possible to discover in them some quality or characteristic which may be respected or admired. Productive human relations are built on facing these facts, and are improved when emphasis is placed on the strength and excellence of others.

In short, we need to see people as individuals, and to respond positively to their better aspects, although not failing to understand their less desirable qualities. We can implement this kind of behavior in the following ways.

GET NAMES RIGHT AND USE THEM OFTEN. Every person has a name which designates his uniqueness. Addressing another as "Hey, you!" or "boy" may be expedient in an emergency, but when it becomes a habit it leads to unsound relationships. The elevator boy in the office and the broompusher in the shop have names, and would prefer to be called by them, as would your best customer or most cherished friend.

James A. Farley of the Coca Cola Company, one of the master political leaders of the century, is celebrated for his ability to remember names and to use that ability to create a great political organization. "Value each person you talk to," he has said, "and that value helps identify him to you." Thus using names correctly and frequently not only satisfies the natural desire of another for recognition, but also aids you to identify him as an individual. And having the name in mind is the beginning point in understanding him; you have a mental "peg" upon which to hang your knowledge of him as a person.

If we are willing to work at it as Jim Farley did, we can apply his methods to our own cultivation of good human relations. Politics is but one of hundreds of fields in which sound human relations are important.

BE APPRECIATIVE AND QUICK TO GIVE APPROVAL. Being ready and lavish with appreciation builds good human relations in two directions. In the first, it opens the mind of the receiver by nourishing his feeling of esteem and worth; in the second, it trains the giver to be observant of the strong or desirable traits or actions of others, in addition to helping make him sensitive to individuality.

In a shift of assignments, Tad found himself working under a new advertising manager for whom he developed a dislike. The man was arbitrary, cold, and unattractive, and Tad grew to find the job climate distasteful. No longer did he enjoy his hours at work. And then Tad decided to find something about his new boss to approve. In a few weeks he discovered that the man was meticulous in detail, that he kept the departmental records in much better order than his predecessor whom Tad had liked, and that he was skilled in delegating authority. At an appropriate moment Tad mentioned to the new manager that he appreciated the latter's precision in detail, and from that moment an improved relationship began to develop. The manager became warmer and more relaxed, and Tad's antipathy began to wane. He still has a negative feeling toward his superior, but no longer is the office as uncomfortable as it had been. Life on the job became endurable, and improved communication was established between the two.

TAKE DESIRED BEHAVIOR FOR GRANTED. This is another way to give tacit recognition to another's worth. An ancient maxim asserts, "Give a dog a bad name and he'll live up to it." Conversely, if we give another a good name, he will be inclined to live up to it. If we act as if we expected certain results, the chances of securing those results is greatly enhanced. Tony, a foreman in a rubber company, discovered this by accident. A worker who had been a discipline problem in another part of the factory was transferred to Tony's crew, but Tony was not told of his bad record. Consequently Tony accepted the new worker with full confidence in the man's cooperation and loyalty, and he was not disappointed. The man was a good worker and there was no difficulty. Later, when he found out the reputation of his new man, Tony exclaimed, "It's a good thing I wasn't told. If I'd known he was a trouble-maker, I'd have been lookin' for trouble, and we'd have had a fight!"

Giving a person a reputation to live up to is simply a way of getting him to follow Hamlet's injunction to "assume a virtue if you have it not," for it then tends to develop. People can be given reputations explicitly or implicitly, the latter by acting as if the reputation existed. "You must have had the flu," remarked the chief to a field man reporting back to work after an absence of several days. He was taking for granted that the man would not absent himself for other than a good reason. The chief assumes the best of each of his men, and it is rare for one of them to let him down.

RESPECT THE RIGHTS AND OPINIONS OF OTHERS. Recognizing individual uniqueness in this way does not imply that we must always agree with the opinions of others—far from it, for we must maintain the integrity of our own convictions if we are to sustain our self-respect. But it does imply that we recognize the rights of others to hold opinions different from ours, and that therefore we refrain from belittling or contradicting them. It further implies that behind the expressed opinion of any man lies some amount of thought or experience which produces it, thought or experience which make that opinion a part of the individual. An opinion may be as much a part of the psychological or intellectual make-up of a person as blood is a part of the physical make-up. To refuse respect for an opinion is to deny respect to the individual. Productive interpersonal relations cannot be built by destroying some part of another.

"I don't think we should hire this candidate," said Martha Todd, a member of the Board of Education. The Superintendent of Schools favored the candidate, but he recognized the right of his Board member to have a different opinion, and realized that starting an argument might be disastrous. So he approached the problem by respecting Mrs. Todd's ideas. "Whatever your reason, Mrs. Todd," he said, "we would appreciate having you tell us about it in detail." Regardless of the outcome of the deliberations, the Superintendent's opening was an attempt to build good relationships and to secure an open mind. With the latter, he would be in a stronger position to present his own thinking.

Cooperate with the wants of other people

As I have continually stressed, in most situations it is virtually useless to try directing the thought and behavior of others by external pressures. Even the power of rank and authority has limitations, and a direct order may be so grudgingly obeyed that its performance in effect becomes sabotage. Behavior is energized and directed from within as a person attempts to satisfy his own wants or to solve his own problems.

181

If we would build constructive relationships with others, and if we would communicate with them on a basis of mutual understanding, we must therefore cooperate with the wants which motivate their behavior. We must align their wants with our purposes, and avoid even the appearance of denying or frustrating those wants.

There is a difference between *giving in* to the wants of another, and *cooperating* with those wants, as every parent sooner or later finds out. Insofar as we are able to grant others whatever they may want, we have little difficulty in building easy relationships, except that we run the risk of becoming merely the instrument to satisfy the desires of others or of seeming to curry favor by satisfying every wish. Such a position destroys respect, which is the vital foundation of sound relationships. The real problem comes when we must at one time deny to others what they see as satisfying a want and still hope to maintain a viable relationship. In such circumstances, cooperating with the wants of another would mean finding a substitute satisfaction for the one we must deny, or arousing a dormant want which will re-direct the motivation of the individual toward another form of satisfaction.

At a military post the conventional sign "Keep Off the Grass" was having little effect. To secure greater effect, the commanding officer had a new sign erected which touched off the springs of response among the men. It produced results because it aligned wanted behavior with the soldiers' basic wants. The new sign read, "Short Cut to K.P." Similarly, in face-to-face talk, human relations can be improved by aligning the wants of others with you, not against you. Aligning wants can sometimes be accomplished by a short but meaningful statement, such as, "This could be a feather in your cap, because . . . ," or "We have confidence in your ability to do the job," or "This will give you a chance to get home more often," or "Your name will appear on the list of contributors."

Good human relations, then, can be aided by understanding the desires or wants of others and by demonstrating a desire to help others satisfy those wants. Here are ways to implement the precept.

ENCOURAGE INITIATIVE. Initiative is the self-directed use of energy to move toward a desired goal. A person may often satisfy his wants for independence, self-respect, and recognition by displaying initiative, especially when successful initiative is reinforced by explicit appreciation. So long as the personal goals of an individual are compatible with the goals of your organization or office, to encourage initiative is to develop good relations and enthusiastic

182

cooperation. Great energy can be released by encouraging and tactfully guiding the initiative of others, particularly in the delegation of responsibilities.

Often an apparently insignificant statement or question can be used to encourage some one to independent and creative effort. "This is what we need to accomplish—can you see a way to do it?" "I'd like your advice on a question that came up this morning." "It sounds good. Why don't you try it." "We tried that last year and were disappointed. Can you think of another way?" These and expressions like them may contribute to the development of good working relationships when they offer honest cooperation with the wants of others.

HELP THE OTHER PERSON GET WHAT HE WANTS. Insofar as you can reasonably help another get what he wants, effective human relations can be furthered. When another sees you as *willing* to help him satisfy his wants, you have established an atmosphere of cordiality which is conducive to cooperation. Thus it is not necessary that you always fulfill another's wants, provided you are sincerely interested in helping. At times, however, you may find it necessary to discern carefully between what a man may *say* he wants and what he is *really* seeking.

The capacity to make this distinction may be especially useful in the frequent occasions when you must say "No" to someone's request; the ability to deny someone and yet maintain a productive relationship can be a real test of one's human relations skill. That ability is illustrated by the executive who said, "I am called on for more speeches than I can possibly make, but I always try to help the caller when I have to say 'No.' I suggest the names of two or three other people who might make the speech for him. I try to show him that I would like to help if I could, and so I give him some leads. After all, what he generally needs is a speaker to fill a program, and he happened to think of me." One of America's major hotel chains uses a similar policy when one of its managers must decline a request for credit. The manager carefully outlines the steps necessary to secure credit, and assures the applicant that if these steps are taken the credit will be granted. Theirs is a policy of helping the applicant get what he wants.

PRESENT PROBLEMS AND ASK FOR SOLUTIONS. When you must ask another for help, when you must give an order, or when you want to enlist someone's cooperation, you will often find it more productive to present a problem and ask for help in the solution than to make a request or issue an order. This procedure avoids the bluntness of "I need your help," or "George, I'd like you to do something." Neither of these approaches arouses a want in the other person, whereas presenting to that person a problem in which he may be involved acts as a stimulant and tends to enlist interest. Even if the problem does not directly involve the other, at least it may arouse his interest enough to create a desire to help find a solution. It may arouse some dormant want which will motivate him to cooperate as you hope.

Mark, in the traffic department, wanted a few days off to take a trip for the purpose of selling a house which he had owned for some time in another state. Rather than meeting his superior head-on with a request for some time off, he decided on the problem approach. "Mr. Souers," he said, "I have a problem I hope you can help me with. The home I owned before I came with this company has been for sale for a long time, and now I can close a deal on it if I can get back for a few days. I know you're reluctant to give time off at this season, and that's the problem. Do you think we can find some solution that will help me get back long enough to finish the sale of my house without disrupting the work in our department?" Mark's beginning displayed an eagerness to cooperate with his superior's wants, and at the same time invited the superior to cooperate with him.

PRESENT DOUBTS, OPINIONS, OR OBJECTIONS IN QUESTION FORM. Earlier we noted the undesirability of avoiding arguments. Yet there are times when of necessity we must disagree with another, if for no other reason than to maintain our own integrity. When such disagreement seems necessary, we can make it more objective and more palatable to others if we avoid a dogmatic or challenging attitude. By asking questions we may escape arousing resentment or starting an argument, and at the same time make our ideas influential. In addition, we may make our own position more secure or more comfortable. We should, in the words of former Senator Neuberger of Oregon, "Remember, the other fellow may be right."

Two partners in an architectural firm were going over the plans for a new home they had been commissioned to design. Roy's own opinion was that his partner's plan had a weakness, but he offered that opinion carefully: "Wouldn't the room divider, where it is in these drawings, be apt to interfere with traffic flow between the kitchen and the family room?" Roy's objections, put in this form, did not challenge the partner, nor put him on the defensive. If we can adopt the method of offering our opinions, doubts, or objections in the form of questions, we can encourage a cooperative attitude in others instead of a hostile one.

The foregoing four precepts together with their methods of implementation have served well the many business and professional people who have honestly applied them. Nevertheless, we must bear well in mind that the development of skill in effective human relations demands consistent and continual attention. Every one of us has good times and bad times in dealing with other people. Experience shows that for some, bad days appear in a pattern. Monday may be a bad day for one, Saturday for another. One man may be at his best in the morning, while his colleague finds the afternoon better. Still another finds that he damages himself by such patterns as turning to a customer in an aggressive mood because he has just finished an unpleasant telephone conversation with a supplier.

In any situation, productive speech is an attempt to cause others to behave in a predictable way as they respond to us by interpreting our behavior. If our speech is to create viable relationships and mutual understanding, it must reflect a reasonably accurate prediction of its effect. Most of us would have little trouble predicting that if we drove through heavy traffic at night with glaring headlights, we would cultivate few friends among other drivers. Yet many people "drive with glaring headlights" as they go through life complaining, contradicting, arguing, or otherwise revealing extreme insensitivity to the interests, attitudes, and wants of others. They fail to see themselves as others see them. Therefore, good human relations may be defined as the high art of being sensitive to other people.

Chapter 7

Person-to-Person Speaking: Language

As people become more mature they use language more and more responsibly to report accurately what they learn when they listen well and in all other ways observe carefully the facts that are of interest and concern to them. They demonstrate the language of responsibility in describing clearly and in detail what they themselves do and what others do that needs to be understood. They speak the language of who, when, where, what and then what, and of the various possible whys, the language of honest and full report and of disciplined explanation—of thoughtful understanding.[1]

WENDELL JOHNSON
Professor of Speech Pathology and Psychology State University of Iowa

YOU LIVE IN TWO WORLDS. THE FIRST IS THE TANGIBLE WORLD OF reality, the world of events, things, and people which the word "environment" probably brings to your mind. The second is the world of language, although naming it "the world of symbols" would likely be more accurate. This second world in truth makes up the greater and the more important part of your environment, for you are affected by it more significantly than by the world of reality. At the same time, you are probably less aware of the world of language as

[1] Wendell Johnson, "The Language of Responsibility." Reprinted by permission from *ETC: A Review of General Semantics*, Vol. XIX, No. 1; copyright, 1962, by the International Society for General Semantics. Pp. 83–4.

186

an environmental influence than you are of the tangible world. It surrounds and pervades you as does the air you breathe; it is so common yet so inconspicuous that you are apt to be unconscious of the way it directs and molds the way you behave.

Not only does the world of symbols constitute a major share of your daily environment, but it also mediates between you and the remainder of that environment, the world of reality. The events, things, and people of the physical world are explained (made meaningful) to you, or you explain them to yourself, in symbols, and you in turn respond to the symbols rather than to the physical reality which is before you. This kind of behavior is the outstanding characteristic which distinguishes human beings from other animals. It constitutes man's greatest achievement, yet at the same time one in which he ensnares himself, since he permits it to color and distort experience, conceal reality, magnify and transmit error, and delude his own thinking.

It is this world of symbols, or more to our immediate interest, the world of language, to which we turn in this chapter. Language is an essential in speech communication: It is one of the three codes of transmission discussed in Chapter 2, it is central to the notion of symbolic behavior recognized in Chapter 3, and it constitutes the normal core of messages exchanged between people in face-to-face talk as well as in other forms of speech communication. Through the centuries it has been used by man to influence man. Because of its importance we shall consider it the second area in which it is possible to improve person-to-person speaking, remembering that what is said in this chapter can equally be applied in subsequent chapters.

As you read further you should discover that language as a subject for study and understanding is much too vast to be covered in a single chapter. We must be content here to gain a greater appreciation of what language is, of how it operates, and of some ways by which we may exercise a more intelligent control over its use as a tool of speech communication, for it is indeed a tool in the service of human beings as well as a part of their self-created environment.

LANGUAGE IS A COMPLEX SYSTEM OF SYMBOLS THROUGH WHICH WE RELATE TO THINGS, PEOPLE, AND IDEAS

Let us begin by asking *What is a word?* In reality, a word is nothing more than marks on a page, like the ones you are now looking at, or a series of sounds uttered by someone in the presence of one or more others. The marks or the sounds are the physical substance.

It is what the word *stands for* which is important. The marks or the sounds are used by people to represent or symbolize something else. When I use the word "rat" I may intend it to represent a member of the rodent family or I may intend it to characterize a certain person whom I dislike. In the first instance the word acts as a pointer simply to designate the referent, but in the second it symbolizes my own attitude toward the individual fully as much as it may suggest some personal qualities of the one referred to. In either case if you and I could agree on marks or sounds other than "rat," we could communicate, provided we were able to agree that the new marks or sounds were to be assigned the same meanings as "rat."

Since we are, therefore, more concerned with meanings than with words, it will be useful to examine some *kinds* of meanings most commonly symbolized by words.

Some words are used to symbolize reality

We use many words simply to represent the things and events of our physical environment, such words as *tiger, pen, table, fire escape,* or *turnpike.* When we do this we are employing language in the pointing function, and using it to symbolize the world outside our skins, the world which is tangible and can be seen or felt, measured or weighed, manipulated or perceived by ourselves and others.

Such use appears at first glance to be a relatively simple and foolproof process, but the appearance is deceptive. We can become victims even in what seems to be an elementary language operation because we take for granted that we know what reality is and we assume that what our senses reveal to us is the same as that revealed by the senses of other people. That neither of these assumptions is necessarily valid can be tested by asking several witnesses of an event such as an automobile accident, a closely-contested play in football, or even a laboratory or industrial demonstration to detail what "really" happened. The discrepancies among various eye-witness accounts may at times be amusing, but they can be frustrating or hazardous to those who must make decisions based upon them.

Statements made by witnesses and using words in the pointing function may be called *statements of fact,* and when important consequences hinge on such statements, they must be validated. Validation may be attempted by comparing the observations of several witnesses to a given event, or by repeating the event when possible and under controlled conditions (the method of laboratory or experimental research) in order to learn if the original phenomena recur and were accurately perceived. The cashier at a check-out register regularly validates the statement on a roll of coins that it contains "$5 in dimes" by opening the roll and counting the money before dumping it into the register. In a corresponding fashion, we should recognize that all statements of fact are not necessarily valid, and that an alleged reality does not exist just because we have a word for it.

Some words are used to symbolize evaluations

As we use some words to symbolize things and events outside our skins, so we use other words to refer to what goes on inside us, in our nervous system, in our glands, or elsewhere. Thus when we say, "It's hot in here," we are not making a statement about measurable temperature but about the state of our comfort, and when we say, "The dinner was delicious," we are not pointing to any observable attribute of the meal, but are pronouncing our personal response to it. The words *ambition, wisdom, dignified, classical, canny, lucky,* and others like them are much more likely to symbolize a personal evaluation than to point to an objective and verifiable reality. When someone says, "The Browns are living in adject poverty," we are hearing an evaluation and not a statement descriptive of measurable fact.

Statements in which words are used to symbolize evaluations are known by some as *statements of inference,* to indicate that the message content is not a report of objective reality but at best is an inference derived from some kind of factual foundation. At worst it is, of course, meaningless and used to deceive. In Chapter 5 we noted the importance of a listener's being able to deal with inferences, and we shall return to the matter later in this chapter.

Some words are used to arouse feelings

Often words are used to stir up feelings or emotions in others instead of to point to a referent or to express the speaker's unbiased evaluation. Such usage is common by political campaigners, propagandists, promoters and salesmen, and persuaders of all sorts, and we have come to expect it in much of the language of international charge and counter-charge, where "capitalist warmonger," "people's republic," and "wars of liberation" have become common coin for the Communists. At home we have seen the words "liberal" and "conservative" fall into relative disuse as logical symbols referring to diverse political viewpoints, to assume a new symbolism employed to arouse emotions. Words used this way are sometimes known as "loaded words" because of the emotional bias they tend to evoke; the meaning they arouse is known as the *connotation,* in contrast to the *denotation* of a word which indicates its logical or substantive referent.

Loaded words are a common tool of persuasion, and you can find them everywhere. Indeed, you have probably used them yourself without thinking. When you are against a suggested change, you argue for the "tried and tested methods of the past," but when you are in favor of innovation you argue against the "ancient methods of the horse and buggy days." Your country has a "security force," but the enemy uses "secret police." When you were questioned, your reply was "diplomatic," whereas a similar answer by someone else was "evasive." Your department has "taken the matter under advisement," but the other departments are "stalling." Words used in this manner are evaluative in nature, but when used to evoke emotional associations they tend to short-circuit honest evaluation and logical appraisal.

Some words are used to symbolize abstract ideas

Chief among the abilities of the human being is his ability to build up abstract notions, concepts, or ideas which he holds to be true or false or to be useful in relating to or dealing with the world at large. He uses all kinds of mathematical, chemical, or other symbols to represent these ideas, among them being language symbols or words. You will have little trouble concluding that a great part of this book uses language of this kind, for a great part of it deals with generalizations about people, their behavior, and their involvement in speech communication. Similarly, much of what you study in other texts must employ words to symbolize abstract notions or concepts which you are expected to master in the process of growth and maturation.

Sometimes a single word can be used to symbolize a general notion, as *love, justice, circular,* or *progress.* The "One Hundred Two Great Ideas of the Western World," identified by Dr. Mortimer Adler and his colleagues at the University of Chicago, uses one word to symbolize each of the ideas. The degree of abstractness of each word may perhaps be appreciated by noting that Dr. Adler deals with the one word, *love,* in a book of several hundred pages. *Abstract* is in itself a word which symbolizes a general notion which you must understand if you are to become reasonably conversant with the uses and behavior of language.

Complete statements, however, are normally used to express abstractions and generalizations. This sentence itself is a good example of such a statement. Other examples can be found in the physical sciences, "A body immersed in a liquid is buoyed up by a force equal to the weight of the liquid displaced"; the behavioral sciences, "Anxiety has its origins in the relationships of people with one another"; or in popular history, "An aggressor cannot successfully be appeased." Statements of this nature have no commonly accepted name other than "generalizations," and so I have arbitrarily termed them "statements of truth" to indicate a similarity and yet a distinction between them and statements of fact. To me a statement of truth makes a claim relative to a generalized notion, while a statement of fact makes one relative to a specific and single event, relationship, or phenomenon.

Statements of truth cannot be validated like statements of fact, by measurement or reference to a specific event or to a single observable object or relationship. They cannot be compared with physical reality because whatever they symbolize is a notion abstracted from a wide range of physical realities, and as a rule such statements are probabilities only. (The physical sciences offer notable exceptions, yet even in the physical sciences abstract ideas are constantly subject to change and modification.) Statements of this kind can be validated only approximately by determining if they are consistent "with the shape of the whole," that is, if the claim is reasonably congruent with the accumulated experience of men in general.

While the foregoing description does not pretend to exhaust the ways in which words are used as symbols, it should be enough to suggest that language is employed to replace, explain, or interpret the raw materials of experience. With that we move to consider men's responses to symbols, and some of the ways by which the latter shape behavior.

LANGUAGE CRITICALLY INFLUENCES HUMAN BEHAVIOR

Language has been called a Frankenstein monster since it is a creation of man which can escape his control and turn to destroy him. Words, of course, are invented by men, but the inventors too often forget that the marks or sounds are only symbols. They unfortunately come to take for granted that *words* are *things,* or at least they do not distinguish between the two. Consequently they behave in the presence of words as if those words always were reality or always were true, a form of behavior which in extreme form can be symptomatic of mental or emotional maladjustment. To illustrate the way in which people respond to words instead of to reality, a colleague of mine filled a box which had contained "dog goodies" with small round balls of oat cereal which come in various colors. He then offered the box to his students, inviting them to munch a few. With rare exceptions, the students refused the invitation, responding to the *words* on the box instead of to the reality it contained.

To understand that people change the meanings of words as time passes, will help us to recognize that language is an unreliable servant. The word *square* is a current and common example. To apply this to an individual today is to say that he is thoroughly objectionable, whereas in your grandfather's day the intended meaning was quite the opposite. To say then that someone was a "square man" was a high form of praise. Similarly, "silly" once meant blessed, not foolish as we now use it to mean, "crummy" described someone of admirable qualities, not something cheap or worn-out, and "presently" meant right now, not "in a little while" as we use it today. All of this goes to show that words in themselves do not have meaning; they are used by people, and although the *words* themselves may not change, the *meaning* people assign to them often does.

Can we not, then, turn to the dictionary to find the "right" meaning of a word? The question itself would betray a faulty comprehension of the people who publish dictionaries. They do not create or legislate the meanings of words, and there is no totally "right" meaning for a word. The makers of dictionaries are competent surveyors of those who use language, of the writers and speakers whose usage indicates the meanings they intended when they wrote or spoke. Thus the dictionary is nothing more than an accurate reflection of what most people seem to mean when they use a word. The meanings of words reside in people, not in a dictionary.

All this means that men have created the world of words in which they live and that they are responsible for the consequences, both good and bad. Let us examine briefly some of those consequences.

Language shapes and colors the world in which we live

Let us begin by understanding that the world outside our own skins—the "world of reality"—is *not precisely what we think it is*. To us that world is *as we perceive it*, which is something different, sometimes slightly, sometimes importantly, from total reality. This is true because, as we have seen, we perceive not more than a fraction of what can be perceived. We normally view an event, a person, or a relationship from one perspective only, our perceptions are colored by what we want or expect to perceive, and our senses themselves can be faulty. Consequently our impressions do not accurately and completely represent whatever we may be attending to. Either we never see (or feel, smell, taste, and so on) countless details, or seeing them we ignore them. Examine the room in which you are now reading this paragraph. Scrutinize it carefully. Listen. Touch the walls, the desk top, the flooring. Study the contours, notice the effect of changes in lighting. Has anything been altered, added, taken away, or moved recently? Have you, at the end of twenty or thirty minutes, a more complete impression of the room? Can you say things about it which you couldn't have said before? How much more could you learn about the room if you were to continue your examination for several hours? What could a skilled detective, searching the room as if for evidences of a crime, tell you about it and the people who inhabit it?

We know by perception much less than can be known about the world, and yet we respond to and talk about our impressions as if they were a complete and total story. This process of ignoring many details, of responding to or talking about only selected details we call *abstracting*. Each word we use, then, is an abstraction from reality. Even the name which points to a specific individual, as "Frank Bowman," tells us very little about him, and when we use words which apply equally to any member of a class or group, such as *coat, policeman, bookcase,* or *rocket,* they tell us even less about either a specific member of the class or about the class as a whole.

The normal process of our behavior, then, is to perceive something, give it a name by abstraction, and respond to the name as if we were responding to the actuality. Our response may involve either talking with others or thinking. Thus the students in my colleague's classes, when offered the box containing breakfast cereal, named the contents according to the label on the box, "dog goodies," and in refusing to eat responded to the name rather than to the reality. This is a very simple illustration of the fact that so far as we are concerned, our world is what we call it.

Not infrequently we cause trouble for ourselves, sometimes seriously, by responding to words instead of things. In Hollywood, Florida, a ten-year-old boy died when the empty gasoline drum he was cutting with a chisel exploded. "This is an empty drum," he had told both himself and his companion who was burned in the explosion, "so we can cut it up and use it to build a boat." Unfortunately, the drum was not "empty" even though the gasoline had been drained. It was still filled with highly explosive fumes which were ignited by a spark from the chisel striking steel. Similar instances had earlier been noted by Benjamin Lee Whorf, a fire insurance official whose avocation became the analysis of language as it effects behavior, and who has pointed out that linguistic analysis of a situation strongly determines behavior. It seems to make little difference whether words are *uttered* or only *thought;* the meaning of reality is shaped and colored by the way that reality is described.

When we reflect that much of our world can never be known to us by direct experience, but only through symbols, we realize the extent of our dependence on language and the ways in which we may therefore be misguided. Consider what you may know of the Renaissance, or of life in Moscow or Guatemala—or Appalachia for that matter. Consider the predicament of an executive who must make a decision based only on reports coming from distant sources. How accurately have those on the spot perceived and verbalized the situation? How accurately have reports been transmitted through channels? Will the decision be based on a reasonably accurate description of the circumstances, or upon a verbalization which tends to distort and which in itself must be interpreted?

Clearly we must not omit the language element from any understanding of the environment to which we respond, either near or far. We must be aware, not only of what we do with language, but what it does with us.

Language enables us to share experience with others

In the preceding section our attention was focused on what language does so far as our own behavior is concerned. Now we focus more sharply on the communicative function, on language as it enables us to share experience with others, thereby communicating with them. The communicative function is plainly more obvious than that of molding behavior and therefore demands less elaboration.

What should be emphasized, however, is that communication depends upon a sharing of experience, that when those doing the communicating have experiences and outlooks which are strongly similar, a given series of words can evoke similar meanings, but that when the communicants have dissimilar experiences and outlooks a given series of words cannot evoke similar meanings. Thus the prime concern of communication is with meaning rather than with the symbols used to express or evoke that meaning. The use of language is an endeavor to create a common meaning in given circumstances. When you talk you are trying to get people to "see things the way you do."

There are those, therefore, who feel that in this sense the most effective function of language is metaphorical; that is, language which suggests with little effort that "my experience is similar to your experience" is apt to create the highest degree of shared meaning. If I were to say, for instance, "Beethoven's sonatas are beautiful" I would not be communicating much because I do not compare my experience with an experience of yours to produce a similarity of meaning. But if I say, "Beethoven's sonatas are ripples in the moonlight," I might evoke your experience at a quiet lake, relating it to my own with Beethoven's music, thereby creating some identity of meaning.

You will find the sections in Chapter 13 dealing with the use of supporting detail and of concrete words useful in helping you present your messages in terms of your listeners' experience. You have already discovered that as a listener, you must be conscious of the way your own experience relates to what you are hearing, and be aware of the possible differences in background between you and the speaker.

Language entraps us in misunderstanding and unnecessary conflict

We should not be surprised when two people who do not share identical experiences and who give different names to their perceptions of experience fail to understand one another, become frustrated, and perhaps disagree, even violently. We should be even less surprised at misunderstanding and disagreement when the people involved are unaware that the language they use may be at the root of the predicament. One of your purposes in reading this chapter should be to become more aware of language, and therefore to enable yourself to avoid unnecessary confusion or disagreement.

If we leave aside entirely the matter of individual perception and consider only the way in which language may represent physical reality, we immediately confront a problem of huge proportions. The world about which we talk—our environment of things, events, people, and relationships—is a boundless affair made up of phenomena impossible to count and each different from the others. In contrast, the number of words we possess to refer to those countless things is severely limited. We must make one word represent an unnamed number of individual things or instances; we have a limited number of words which must be used to represent a limitless number of things. Because of this, each word may be used in a variety of meanings. The vocabulary of basic English is made up of 500 words, yet those 500 words represent 16,000 meanings. Even the common word *run*, which should cause us little trouble, is assigned 53 meanings in Webster's Collegiate Dictionary. But the infinite number of things about which we may talk and the relatively limited number of words we use is just the beginning of the way langauge breeds confusion, misunderstanding, and conflict.

If we add to this the fact that the world of reality is also an endless dynamic *process*, whereas the terms we use to describe and discuss it are *static*, we find another source of trouble. Things change but we continue to refer to them with unchanging words. This bars the paths of communication by leading us into *classified* or *static* thinking. Heraclitus, the Greek philosopher, was expressing this problem when he made his famous statement that a man can never step into the same river twice. Neither the man nor the river is the same the second time. If you read these lines again tomorrow, you will not be the same reader you were today. The organization, the service, or the person we name with a word today is not the same as the one we named with the identical word yesterday, yet our language strongly tends to lead us inaccurately to believe it so.

This is certainly true of today's industrial and professional world, for change is one of the characteristics of that world. Art Cherry, a manager for one of the nation's giant rubber corporations, earned three promotions in the course of one year. Each change altered his outlook and thinking to conform to the requirements of the new job; with each promotion he took on a new and different role. Yet someone calling him by telephone and unaware of the changes would talk to the Art Cherry he had known before the promotions. Or if the caller were phoning to Art's first office instead of to him personally, the former would find himself talking to an entirely different individual. Yet change by promotion is common in most enterprises, as revealed by a recent survey based on Poor's Register of Directors and Executives. According to the survey, 62 per cent of the top executives and 74 per cent of the presidents of 38 major corporations had been put in office within the preceding six years. As a result of these changes and the resulting shift of personnel down the line in each company, none of the 38 corporations was the same corporation at the time of the survey as it had been a year or two before. As observed by K. L. Ede, Pittsburgh marketing executive, "We are talking and writing to a parade and not to a static audience."

People, products, services, organizations—none of them are the same two days in succession. Even the man who holds a job for twenty years is not the same man, for he changes from day to day. Yet our talk so often fails to take this fact into account and to represent clearly the world as it is at the moment of utterance. The directions which were given yesterday do not fit today's operations. The mailing list of yesterday does not match the people of today. Yesterday's problems have been altered by this morning. The facts have changed, and the language we use must be selected to take the change into consideration and to represent the facts as they are. Language which does not fit the world of reality breeds misunderstanding and confusion.

But if language dealing with objective things and events creates communication problems, language which expresses a subjective evaluation may create even greater ones. Two persons may face the same set of facts, yet find themselves in disagreement simply because of what they say about those facts—how they interpret them. Frequently the dispute arises only because neither recognizes that what the other says is a subjective evaluation instead of a statement of fact. "Don't drive so fast," says auditor Pete to auditor Lee, who is behind the wheel as they drive to the firm where they are to go over the books. "I'm not going fast," returns Lee, and the disagreement may be only a passing exchange or it may develop into a continuing source of friction all day. The speed of the car is identical for both, yet each fails to recognize that what has been said expresses a personal evaluation in response to that speed. Lee, behind the wheel, is comfortable; Pete, in the seat beside him, is uncomfortable. They talk as if they were referring to the actual speed itself instead of to their separate feelings about it.

Communication problems arising from statements which refer to evaluations made within the nervous system can be momentous. A lawsuit arising from an accident in which a man charges he received a "disabling injury" could involve huge sums of money. Yet a "disabling injury" is not an objective fact; it varies from individual to individual and from interpretation to interpretation. Batteries of physicians on either side of the courtroom can testify that a given injury is or is not disabling, and each physician could be stating the truth as he saw it. The critical factor to remember is that the statement, "This is a disabling injury," is not a statement of fact, but a statement of inference, an evaluation or opinion.

Similarly, generalizations, or as I called them earlier, "statements of truth" are a common cause of misunderstanding and conflict. Statements of this kind occur in many forms and varieties, but all have one characteristic in common: They are abstractions from reality which fail to take into account the exceptions, differences, and the complexities of human experience. Those who make such statements tend rarely to qualify their remarks, and having uttered them feel bound to defend them, a form of behavior which leads to conflict. "You NEVER wipe your feet!" accuses a mother, and her teen-age son, who distinctly recalls having wiped his feet not more than ten days ago, retorts, "I do SO!" Marriage counselors agree that *always* and *never* are two words which can be counted on to cause trouble in a family, and they can do the same in any work situation. "Burns, you're always late with your deliveries," can start interpersonal friction if it doesn't cause an outright argument.

Nor are generalizations concerning personal behavior the only source of misunderstanding and conflict, for any statement of truth can be a trouble-maker. "We're wasting money on that new program," "Raw material prices are too high," "Conservatives believe that any enterprise that doesn't show a profit is useless," and "Friends are thieves of time" are examples of statements which are loaded with potential misunderstanding. We must interpret them with care, for like all language, they may signal a misevaluation of the world and can easily result in distorted communication and unnecessary conflict.

From the discussion to this point, I hope you see that language may indeed be a Frankenstein monster, and that you can neither master it as a tool nor cope with it as environment in ten easy lessons. Yet you must make a start, and the remainder of this chapter will outline some guides to help in your person-to-person speaking. They also apply to other forms of speech communication.

FOLLOW THE PRINCIPLE THAT WORDS DON'T MEAN, BUT PEOPLE DO

When Mr. X talks with Mr. Y we can be sure of one thing, namely, that under normal conditions each intends his words to have a certain significance or meaning. We know that none of the words *in themselves* have meaning, and it therefore follows that if misunderstanding occurs we cannot look to the *words* to find out how communication has failed. We must look to the people who use the words. If Mr. Y cannot grasp what Mr. X is saying, he must carefully explore behind the words to discover what it was that Mr. X intended him to get. And if Mr. X feels highly insulted by what he thinks Mr. Y is saying, he will, if he responds in a mature fashion, take pains to learn what Mr. Y intended to mean before he replies. In short, each will be a better communicator if he applies the principle: words don't mean; people do.

If, for instance, Mr. X gives a set of directions to Mr. Y, who fails to understand, it will do no good for Mr. X to disclaim responsibility by saying, "But, I *told* you." It is virtually impossible to utter a statement which cannot be misunderstood; it is likewise impossible to utter one which will be equally understood by a large number of people. For this reason you should never assume that what you say is understood, nor that you fully understand what you hear another say. Clues taken from the communicative field, from the context, and from the physical and vocal behavior of a speaker are a necessary part of total communication and must be heeded in order to determine intended meaning. Even when these clues are considered it is often necessary to use questions or feedback to determine the degree of understanding or to improve that degree. Mr. X is not apt to improve his communication by giving the directions to Mr. Y a second time. As a matter of fact, to do so might make Y feel that he must defend himself against the implications of denseness, thereby creating a new communication barrier. A better procedure might be to invite Mr. Y to talk, or to ask him questions, thus involving him more deeply in the search for meaning.

In this process of searching for meaning in people, the following recommendations for dealing with language itself will direct attention both to the intentions of the individual and to the referents suggested by the words.

Look for the exact referent

According to Dr. Warren Guthrie of the Standard Oil Company of Ohio, "We are successful communicators if we can manage to put the 'word world' and the 'real world' together in such a way that we understand each other."[2] Dr. Guthrie is saying that communication is best effected when the specific referent of a given word can be objectively identified by all communicants. To use an analogy common among the students of general semantics, he is saying that language can be likened to the map of a territory. When the map accurately represents the territory, the various people using the map can orient themselves and relate to one another and to the territory in harmony and agreement. But when our language maps do not accurately describe a territory which we all can recognize, confusion and disagreement can ensue.

To use a simple illustration, the president of one of the Big Ten universities was scheduled to make an address at a college a hundred miles away. For an hour, with growing distress, the audience waited for the speaker to appear; just as people were beginning to leave the auditorium the speaker arrived, exactly one hour late. His school operated on standard time but the meeting was scheduled on daylight saving time! Neither party to the arrangements had thought to specify or to find out what the other meant when the hour of the convocation was fixed for 10:00 A.M. To each the meaning of the ten o'clock hour was perfectly clear, but between them communication failed completely. Their maps did not describe a common territory.

To emphasize that the language map must accurately represent the referent territory, general semanticists have suggested a number of techniques for refining word usage in our thinking and communicating. Two of the techniques apply here, the technique of indexing and that of dating.

Indexing is a way to insist on thinking and communicating about specific and meaningful referents instead of about general

2 "BUT—Is Anybody Listening?" (Holyoke, Mass.: Tecnifax Corporation, 1958), p. 2.

and perhaps senseless ones. By placing an index number after a word we remind ourselves that book₁ is not book₂, vacation₁ is not vacation₂, and Chevrolet₁ is not Chevrolet₂. Indexing means that instead of thinking and talking about books or vacations or Chevrolets, we should be as factual as possible, recognizing the differences between one book and another, one vacation and another, one Chevrolet and another. When we talk or listen, the habit of indexing mentally will help us visualize more concretely, think more exactly, and understand more fully.

For instance, I might easily start an argument by saying, "I stood on the American shore and watched the sun set over the Atlantic ocean." Some listener almost certainly would respond by saying, "You mean you watched the sun *rise*. It doesn't set over the *Atlantic*." But my statement can be made perfectly valid by indexing. Although the sun does rise over the Atlantic from American shore₁—the East coast of the United States—it sets over the Atlantic from American shore₂—the coast of Panama. Since the West coast of Panama in Central America is washed by the Atlantic, a glance at an atlas will show that the verbal map accurately represents the territory and that the statement is valid. American shore₁ in the mind of a challenger is not the American shore₂ in my statement. In this as in many other situations, unecessary disagreement can be avoided by asking yourself "What does the speaker mean?"

Like indexing, dating is a way of making words more meaningful, in this case by specifying the time element involved. Although we are quite aware of many changes going on about us, we too often think and talk as if change made no difference, and are influenced in this direction by the fact that as a rule names do not change. We need to take into account that Martha (1950) is not the same as Martha (1960), that Chicago (1923) is not Chicago (1945), and that labor unions (1930) are not labor unions (1965). Some people talk about "free enterprise" apparently without recognizing that free enterprise (1966) is not free enterprise (1890); they think and talk as if no change had taken place, expecting to make sense to all with whom they converse. Followers of Karl Marx, influenced by his opinions about the evils of capitalism, neglect the fact that Marx wrote of capitalism (1848), whereas they now live in the presence of capitalism today. The words have not changed, but the world has. To return to our earlier discussion of change in management personnel, an individual who does not distinguish between the "Great Eastern Corporation (six years ago)" and the "Great Eastern Corporation (this year)" or between "Rudy Fisher (divisional manager last week)" and "Rudy Fisher (executive vice president this week)" may easily find himself talking to or about the wrong corporation or the wrong man. The technique of mentally (or actually) adding dates to important names or other words can do much to help either speaker or listener understand the exact referent; it is another way of striving to find out what a speaker means. Misunderstanding and conflict often arise when people fail to take into account that things change when words do not.

Distinguish reports from evaluations

If communication breaks down when words are used to refer to something as factual as a stated hour of the day, how much greater the problem becomes when the speaker uses language to signify a subjective evaluation or an abstract concept! When an administrator says, "Morale is bad in our organization," exactly what does he mean by "morale"? And exactly what does he mean by "bad"? Is he referring to observable facts or to his personal impressions? When the doctor says, "This patient is cured," what does he mean by "cured"? Does he intend to say that the patient's illness has been completely ended? Or only suppressed? Is the patient in the same physical condition as before his illness, or is he simply at the point where he can function with reasonable normality? When the language of a speaker expresses an abstraction, an opinion, or an impression, our attempt to discover what the speaker means rather than what the words mean becomes even more important than before.

Possibly the greatest communication barrier growing out of the fact that words don't mean but people do occurs when words do refer to a subjective evaluation but are thoughtlessly interpreted to refer to something objective and factual. In instances of this kind the failure of either listener or speaker arises from the inability to distinguish statements of fact from statements of inference, a misevaluation which results in improper response. As we observed earlier, such statements as "the food is bad," "the service is poor," or "the nurses are careless" are subjective, and refer to feelings inside the speaker rather than to facts outside. The food is bad, the service is poor, or the nurses are careless *to the speaker*. The statements are sentiments, not observable facts. They are inferential in nature, meaning that they are conclusions which the speaker has reached from his personal experience with whatever facts are available to him, and in the light of his own unique background. All such statements are *relative to the speaker only,* and if unfortunate consequences are to be avoided, must be both offered and interpreted for what they are.

That statements of inference can lead to unhappy consequences is attested by Samuel Grafton, nationally-known commentator, who has written, "A young child who is called stupid by his teacher may take the word literally; he may not mention the incident to his parents, because he is afraid they, too, will discover his horrible secret—that he is stupid. He turns in on himself, in daydream and fantasy."[3] By failure to understand language, an individual may respond to statements of this nature in a total pattern of unhealthy behavior; response to language goes deeper than conversation only.

One way of guarding against the tendency either to offer or to interpret evaluations as statements of fact is to add to them, aloud or mentally, the phrase "to me." By this you can identify evaluations for what they are, expressions of subjective opinion. For instance, at great personal risk, and ignoring all the basic principles of water rescue, a young man pulled a drowning swimmer from the Ohio River. "That was a brave deed," asserted one of the spectators. "It was a foolhardy escapade," returned another, who was thoroughly trained in Red Cross rescue methods. If each added "to me" to his statement, the two might find it possible to understand one another and agree. But if each were doggedly to maintain his opinion, refusing to recognize that the other's statement was completely relative and not objectively factual, the failure to communicate could lead to verbal warfare.

Another way to avoid verbal conflict is to follow the caution, "Description should precede prescription." Another way of putting it might be, "Get the facts first. Talk about opinions, impressions, or conclusions afterward." Even though misunderstanding is possible when talk is concerned with factual content, there is always more possibility for understanding and agreement than when conversation is on a level of inference and evaluation. Wisdom, then, suggests that conversations should commence with facts, with a consideration of objective and verifiable referents. Experience testifies to this. After 36,000 grievances were appealed to arbitration under a two-year contract between the International Harvester Company and the United Automobile Workers, both management and labor

---

[3] "Teachers Who Make Children Hate School," *McCall's*, XCIII, No. 4 (Jan., 1966), p. 69.

came to the conclusion that 95 per cent of misunderstanding involved interpretations of facts, and that to avoid contention the first and basic thing to be done was to understand the facts.

In applying the principle of description before prescription, you may find it helpful to try assisting others to reach their own conclusions by arraying facts and asking for a decision. "The weather report predicts rain tomorrow. Should we still plan to play golf?" might be more effective than "Let's call off the game tomorrow." Or "There are four typographical errors in today's paper. What's wrong?" would be preferable to "You proofreaders must have been asleep again today!"

Even if misunderstanding occurs when conversation is on an objective level, neither participant will feel as personally involved as he might were his opinions or conclusions at stake. When the content can be objectively verified there is always a stronger tendency for the conversationalists to suspend judgment and to verify statements. Neither is likely to be placed in a defensive position wherein he must justify *himself* as he defends his statements.

Allow for what language leaves out

Earlier in this chapter we noted that no word tells all about a thing, and that language allows us to abstract from our experience and thus to generalize or conceptualize from it. By this we mean that we can separate certain elements or characteristics from an event, and by giving them names, we can think or talk about those characteristics entirely apart from any particular happening which exhibits them. For instance, there is in my neighborhood a huge and amiable dog named Dino. When I use his given name I point in effect to a particular dog, but I do not tell all about him. Even the name omits many things about him, and therefore is an abstraction at a low level. I could also say that he is a Great Dane, and in so doing I would point to certain characteristics he has in common with all of that breed, but I would at the same time leave out other qualities wherein he is unique. Again, if I said "He is a dog," I would refer to characteristics he shares with all canines, omitting those which are peculiar to Great Danes. Or I could call him an animal, thus classifying him with all other living beings, but also forgetting everything else about him. As I go from "Dino" to "Great Dane" to "dog" to "animal," with each step I leave behind a large number of significant details. Each level of abstraction therefore becomes less precise as a symbol and less meaningful in referring to concrete experience. As William James remarked about language, "Something always escapes," and the more we abstract, the more escapes us.

When we do not allow for what language leaves out, for the differences in our experiences which language does not account for, we endanger both accurate thinking and meaningful communication. We encourage misunderstanding and conflict. Because words or statements do not tell all, what is forgotten can be the cause of trouble. This is why the accusation, "You NEVER wipe your feet!" can start an argument. It omits the exception. The words *one, always, never, only, none,* or others which fail to allow for exceptions or differences are constant causes of disagreement. Nor must these words be expressed. "Joe's a troublemaker," implies ALWAYS and is therefore as misleading as if the word had been said. Moreover, it overlooks the fact that that's not ALL he is. There's more to be said of Joe than that he's a troublemaker, but the expression leaves out the other things. For exactness and understanding we must constantly remind ourselves of what language leaves out.

For one thing, we must remind ourselves that the abstract word itself is misleading. The act of abstracting causes us to place things in categories, to which we react as if every member of a category were like every other member. Furthermore, we tend to respond to the name of the category as if it were a discreet and tangible entity in itself, something which really existed rather than a name used to indicate some few common characteristics of members of a group. For instance, newspaper accounts of acts of vandalism are often followed by letters to the editor complaining of "irresponsible teenagers." These in turn are answered by indignant letters pointing out that all teen-agers are not alike, and that many have performed deeds of service and valor. The first letters indict the category "teenagers" as a whole, the second remind us to look for differences among members of a class.

Similar examples are common. Some people talk about "poets," forgetting that the category must include such diverse individuals as Dante Alighieri, Ogden Nash, John Keats, Robert Frost, John Ciardi, and Phyllis McGinley. Others talk about "capitalists," implying that John D. Rockefeller, Meyer Rothschild, Henry Kaiser, E. I. du Pont de Nemours, Cyrus Eaton, and several million American investors are all of a kind. We should constantly recall that words like these—words such as Democrat, socialist, Negro, Lutheran, professor, New Englander, hourly-rated worker, scientist, and American—denote kinds of people more notable for the differences than for the likenesses among them. When we hear or use such words we must exercise discrimination, remembering that not one of them accurately describes any one member of the group.

Another way in which language misleads us lies in the effect known as polarization. By this we mean that language tends to cause us to think in terms of opposites—polar opposites. We may be amused at the television Westerns in which every character is either one of the "good guys" or one of the "bad guys," but real life is not that simple. Nonetheless, language causes us to act as if it were, for we conveniently divide the world into good and evil and ignore all that may lie somewhere in between. Our language induces us to think and talk in terms of opposites: up-down, strong-weak, black-white, true-false, wise-foolish, success-failure, sharp-dull, honest-dishonest. Everything becomes either A or not-A, and consequently we find it easy to talk and think as if all people must be for us or against us, all speaking must be effective or ineffective, all steak must be tough or tender, and all judges harsh or lenient. Again we forget what language leaves out. After all, if a man is neither good nor bad, what is he? We seem to have no common word to help us remember that most people are probably neither good nor bad, but perhaps "just human," and so we neglect to make distinctions.

While it is true that we come to understand the meaning symbolized in a word by knowing that word in contrast with its opposite, it is equally true that unless we can distinguish degrees of difference between the opposites, we misevaluate and miscommunicate. Thus we know "insane" by contrast with "sane," but until we can think and talk about degrees of sanity and insanity, our verbal maps do not accurately represent the real world territory inhabited by people. Similarly, we may understand "loser" by contrast with "winner," but if we allow these words to polarize our thinking we have forgotten much of what life is made of. Verbal contrasts are useful, but we must learn to think and talk by using language which specifies where on a scale between the poles we wish to place our meaning. Thus we can avoid indiscriminate thinking, and perhaps arguments over whether "hard selling" is better than "soft selling," whether our organization is projecting a "favorable" or "unfavorable" image, or whether the action of the Rules Committee was "democratic" or "undemocratic."

There are still other ways in which language leaves out many of the facts of life, more in truth than we can justifiably take up in these pages. We can improve the productiveness of our talk, however, if we can make ourselves more sensitive to the principle that words do not tell everything and if we make greater effort to express our own meaning more precisely as well as to make allowance for inexactness in the words of another.

Make understanding your goal

A dog walks into a room and stares at his master until the master puts down his newspaper and looks at the dog. The dog then looks at the door, and the the master rises and lets the dog out. Without a word being spoken, full communication has been effected between them because both have contributed with cooperative understanding to the process.

The fullest communication among humans can be accomplished only when all parties share a mutual and earnest desire to reach understanding. Nevertheless, better communication than often now exists can be reached when even one of the parties takes pains to plan to observe the effect, and to improve the way he interacts with others. This is shown by an event in the national campaign against tuberculosis. When trucks were first used to bring portable X-ray equipment into towns which could not provide that type of examination, the operators found that a great many of their pictures were useless. Upon investigation they discovered that a large number of blurred negatives were caused by the way directions had been given to those being X-rayed. At the moment of taking the picture, the operator had said, "Don't move." He had intended the subject to be completely still, not even breathing. But the people being X-rayed didn't understand what the techician meant. They obeyed instructions as they interpreted them; they stood still but keep on breathing, thus blurring the negatives. When the operators changed the instructions, the results were greatly improved. The new directions were not only specific, they were positive. After explaining that breathing would distort the negative, the operator, when he was ready to expose the plate, said, "Take a deep breath. Hold it." Analysis of communication with the intent of being understood resulted in better pictures.

The same is true for all of us. One way to make certain that our face-to-face talk is both understandable and acceptable is to take greater care with the expression of what we have to say. Ed Maple amazed his friends and co-workers by the way he was able to arouse enthusiasm for his ideas and to elicit understanding and coopera- tion. They would not have been so amazed had they taken the time to observe the long moments he sat at his desk planning how to approach others with what he had to say. His conversations were fruitful because they were considered ahead of time instead of being clumsily improvised. He adjusted his talk to those with whom he spoke.

Since face-to-face talk is a give-and-take affair, it is also vital to know that you have clearly understood what the other meant. You have already learned that for this purpose a question is useful because it provides feedback. Use it to re-phrase an idea or state- ment in your own words and to offer your interpretation for veri- fication. "Do you mean that the transformer in the upper right-hand panel may be the trouble spot?" "You say this is a small operation. Would that mean that its annual gross would be about $200,000?" "If you were to offer this service to management personnel, would you include production foremen?" Questions like these indicate that a listener is concerned that he get the meaning with exactness.

Repetition of key words and ideas is another way to make understanding more certain, and may be used by both speaker and listener. Labeling of such key words may also help: "The essence of the job is speed. Speed is the first thing to keep in mind. We cannot afford to delay." Here a speaker not only repeats "speed," but uses "first thing" to give it emphasis. The listener might respond, "I get it. We must get this done quickly."

In this chapter we have examined some of the language princi- ples which can be used to make face-to-face communication more successful and more productive, together with suggestions for putting those principles into daily practice. If we look for meaning in people rather than acting as if words in themselves were mean- ingful, we shall improve not only our common conversations, but our interviews, conferences, and public utterances as well. And we can make our relationships with others firmer and more rewarding.

But the pay-off comes, not from what we know, but from what we do with what we know. The challenge lies in whether we learn enough to govern our behavior; we are concerned with more than merely knowing how we ought to speak. We are concerned with our daily speech behavior when we confront people in situations which may be significant to our jobs or to our lives. At that point you will know whether you have really learned or not.

Chapter 8

Interviewing

The executive engaged in the normal conduct of business devotes much of his time to interviewing. However, there is an appalling lack of effort given to systematic attempts at building improvements into this age-old process. Interviewing remains one of those activities which we think we know all about merely because we have been doing it so long we have been lulled by habit. It seems apparent that a modest effort aimed at an analysis of our interviewing techniques would yield generous returns.[1]

SAMUEL G. TRULL,
School of Business Administration
University of California

NO DOUBT YOU ARE ALREADY FAMILIAR WITH THE INTERVIEW AS ONE of the four forms of speech communication, for you have probably talked by appointment with school officials, admissions officers, counselors, advisors, employment managers, doctors and others. Your experience evidences that industrial managers are not the only people who must do a great deal of interviewing, and that the need for skill in this form of speech exists in a great variety of business and professional callings.

In many occupations, interviewing demands a major share of one's time and attention, and business or professional success hinges upon the ability to manage an interview successfully. Social case workers; criminal, insurance, and credit investigators; public

---

[1] Samuel G. Trull, "Strategies of Effective Interviewing," *Harvard Business Review*, XLII, No. 1 (Jan.-Feb., 1964), p. 89.

opinion and market pollsters; journalists; physicians; and lawyers spend much or all of their time interviewing others. Many for whom interviewing is not a major activity still find interviews taking a significant share of their attention. Among these, in addition to businessmen and industrial managers, are pastors, policemen, supervisors, school executives, teachers, government employees and public officials.

It follows that you can expect in the future to take part in many interviews. In some you will seek the interview, while in others one or more will want to interview you. In all these, the principles of good person-to-person speaking covered in the preceding chapters need be applied. Yet an interview is apt to be much less casual, more definitely structured, and more purposive than the form of speaking there considered. For these reasons, we shall take up here some basic facts and principles which will help to make your interviewing more productive. At the same time we must recognize that there is a wide variety of interview types, and that almost every business or profession has its own unique interviewing methods and techniques. Consequently you must understand that what can be said of one kind of interview, or of interviews generally, may not apply to another kind of interview or to a given situation. At this point we must be content with an overview and with the necessary fundamentals.

AN INTERVIEW IS A PLANNED AND PURPOSIVE CONVERSATION

In contrast to the chance nature of most of the person-to-person speaking we have been considering, an interview may be defined as an arranged event. It brings together two people, at least one of whom has sought or arranged the meeting, and more often than not the time, place, and topic have been set by mutual agreement. Consequently one person at least, and frequently both, will have had an opportunity to plan in advance. When he takes his place behind the counter, John, the bank teller of Chapter 6, expects to meet many people in the course of the day's business. Yet he rarely anticipates any one conversation, and so he cannot classify the talk as interviewing. To the customer, however, who enters the bank with the predetermined intention of talking with John about a certain matter, the event constitutes an interview.

The fact that an interview is premeditated suggests a second characteristic, namely that it is purposive. One or both of the parties looks forward to a specific outcome to be achieved as a result of the meeting. A student seeks advice, a salesman wants to sell his wares, a manager must see that some new policy is understood and followed, or two people must plan a program for which they are jointly responsible. In one way or another, one of the parties hopes to influence the behavior of the other. When the goals are mutual or congruent the interview may run easily, but when the purposes of those involved are incongruent or inconsistent the interview may follow a devious course.

Because of prearrangement and purpose, an interview is very likely to entail a higher degree of formality than a conversation which simply occurs, falling somewhere between the relaxed casualness of friendly chat and the decorum of a parliamentary meeting or an important public address. Social or professional convention may prescribe a standard of dress or a code of behavior which can be violated only at the risk of endangering success. For instance, you would not normally go to an employment interview in "come as you are" attire. And if you heed the advice of experts you will take extra care with posture, voice and diction, and appropriateness of thought and expression. Andersen, Lewis, and Murray observe, "all interviews are expected to follow certain ground rules, such as adhering to predetermined time limits, following some semblance of order, staying within agreed-upon content boundaries, and respecting the nature of possible confidential remarks."[2] Those who participate in interviews should be aware of the particular "ground rules" which may be expected in a specific meeting.

In an interview the person who has taken the initiative in arranging the meeting or who exercises responsibility for conducting the talk may be known as the interviewer. His opposite is the interviewee. It is frequently difficult to distinguish the roles, and indeed, they may seem to change during the course of an encounter. When two equals talk, as two vice-presidents of an organization, especially when the purpose is consultative, such distinctions are virtually meaningless. It is sometimes useful to refer to the one

[2] Martin Anderson, Wesley Lewis, and James Murray, *The Speaker and His Audience* (New York: Harper & Row, Publishers, 1964), p. 365.

exercising initiative at the moment as the interviewer, and to the other as the respondent. This last word suggests a more active role than "interviewee," and is therefore more appropriate in denoting the give-and-take which actually occurs. We shall use it frequently in this chapter.

It is the give-and-take which characterizes most interviews, and in this sense an interview is but a variety of person-to-person talk. It is adaptive and responsive, a fluid interchange and neither a question-and-answer session nor a speech to an audience of one person. (An exception may be the standardized data-collecting interview which seeks comparable responses to a uniform series of questions asked by a number of field workers.) Since it is this, with much of the talking-listening being relatively spontaneous and intimate, it is apt to require a higher degree of communicative skill than other forms of speech communication. Non-verbal communication may assume greater importance, with one or both persons having to interpret the significance of such signs as a puzzled expression, a deliberate delay in responding, uncertain tones or unusual vocal force, tensed muscles, unsteady gaze, or figiting. Each of the participants is likely to need a deeper understanding of his respondent's mind, purpose, motives, and attitudes than words alone will reveal; he must get the story behind the words.

Interviews are usually known as structured (directive) or unstructured (non-directive) in form. The latter are generally limited to counseling on personal matters or analysis and therapy in psychiatric cases, and require substantial professional training of the interviewer. Nevertheless, some non-directive methods can be useful in business and professional work. The structured interview is usual in most situations with which we shall be concerned, although within a permissive atmosphere, and merits our major attention. It is likely to be task-centered or subject-centered, whereas the unstructured exchange is likely to be person-centered.

Interviews as planned and purposive forms of speech communication can be classified according to kind or according to purpose. It will be convenient to examine briefly some of the kinds before looking at purposes.

THERE ARE MANY KINDS
OF INTERVIEWS

Contrary to rather wide-spread impression, the kinds of interviews are not limited to sales and employment, although these two are certainly among the most common. We shall recognize eleven kinds, classifying them roughly according to the use to which each is put. This classification should provide a means of appreciating the range of usefulness of interview techniques and the manner in which each kind serves one or more of the three recognized purposes. It will also be worth while to note certain unique characteristics of some of the kinds.

Consulting interviews

A consulting interview may function simply to exchange information and ideas, or it may be used for problem solving. The participants may be either of equal or unequal rank or status, but they meet to explore a topic of mutual concern or to consider a common problem. Thus two members of middle management in adjoining offices who converse regularly may at times find their talk assuming the status of an interview as they focus formally on a given subject. Many administrators maintain an "open door" policy for the purpose of encouraging organization personnel to consult them without the formality of an appointment. When two physicians get together on a challenging case, their purpose is consultation. Similarly, an advertising manager might consult an account executive from an advertising firm concerning plans for a promotional campaign. In most cases the consulting interview is likely to involve not only an exchange of information but also the appraisal of ideas and the evaluation of suggestions.

Counseling interviews

Whereas the consulting interview centers on a work or task problem and is usually for the purpose of aiding one or both of the partici-

214

pants do his job better, the counseling interview is normally directed as matters of a personal nature and the purpose is to help one of the participants ease or overcome some difficulty. This difficulty may be of interpersonal, psychiatric, social, economic, ethical, or similar nature, and consequently specialists of many sorts are involved in counseling. Among these are psychiatrists, marriage counselors, social workers, lawyers, physicians, school counselors, clergymen, industrial, prison and military chaplains, teachers, and even industrial managers. Some make a career of counseling those who are in trouble, while others find that counseling is a minor but necessary part of their responsibility.

Today there is less emphasis on industrial counseling than during World War II, yet the personnel departments of many organizations do try to assist employees. At least one firm, for instance, regularly schedules a series of interviews with employees before they retire to help them make a satisfying adjustment to the new status. Other firms have found drinking an increasing problem among employees and have begun counseling procedures at the level of supervision. All counseling requires deep empathy with others, skill and patience in listening, and the ability to refrain from offering advice in favor of helping a respondent arrive at his own evaluations and judgments. Work of this nature normally requires advanced training, especially in methods of non-directive interviewing.

Employment interviews

The employment interview is the first of a series dealing with securing, training, and developing employees, although it is undoubtedly the most common. Even though employment interviews are usually regarded as information-exchanging in purpose, many in fact become persuasive when either the applicant or the interviewer attempts to secure a favorable response from the other. Even so, the outcome must rest for either participant on a skillful presentation of relevant information or on skillful discovery and evaluation of needed data.

Because the employment interview is so common, and because the applicant is frequently inexperienced and the interviewer too often inadequately trained, many such interviews result in unsatisfactory associations. According to two experts on interviewing, "The growing body of research findings which indicate relationships between such communications skills (as interviewing) and the hard facts of turnover, absence, and industrial productivity provide important evidence of the contribution which good interviewing and communications practices can make."[3] Consequently larger corporations demand skilled personnel for interviews and make continuing efforts to improve selection methods. The ultimate purpose of an employment interview is to secure knowledge of the applicant or knowledge of the job and employer which will justify a prediction of how well the man will suit the job or the job suit the man.

Induction interviews

After an individual has been hired he is often interviewed by his immediate superior or supervisor for the purpose of providing orientation to the demands, the climate, and the routines of his work. This is a "breaking in" interview and is largely informational in nature.

Performance review interviews

An important function in many institutions is improving or upgrading the work of employees. This may be accomplished in part by interviews, ranging from the "three-week" interview shortly after a person is hired to regular semi-annual or annual performance reviews. Such events may also be known as training, progress, or development interviews.

Normally such interviews are conducted by the immediate superior of the individual whose work is under review, although in some cases it may be done by an officer of higher rank. The purpose is to make the employee cognizant of the quality of his performance, providing the spur of appreciation by recognizing elements of excellence, and seeking to encourage improvement in areas of weakness. For best results such interviews should be centered on specific

[3] Robert L. Kahn and Charles F. Cannell, *The Dynamics of Interviewing* (New York: John Wiley & Sons, Inc., 1957), p. 17.

activities or operations of the employee and not on his traits or personality characteristics.

Although performance reviews are often seen as persuasive in nature, the reviewer hoping to persuade his respondent to seek higher levels of achievement, the experience of many interviewers indicates that better results may be obtained when the interview is approached as problem solving. This method focuses on the problems of the job and on ways to overcome them, thus averting the tendency of the respondent to defend himself. As the employee involves himself in problem solving he may willingly modify his behavior in a desirable way, and is less apt to resent what he might otherwise take as unfounded criticism.

Correction interviews

Perhaps a more common term for this kind is "disciplinary interview" or "reprimand interview," but the use of "correction" suggests a more positive approach. It suggests that the purpose should not be merely to discourage undesirable behavior, but to encourage the substitution of desirable behavior.

When work is improperly or poorly done, when directions or instructions are not followed, when normal protocol is overlooked, when employees waste time or are chronically tardy or absent, or when they do not comply with necessary regulations, a correction interview is called for. It should be an occasion for an objective evaluation of the error or problem and a search for a remedy, in preference to an accusation or an indictment of the offending person.

The interviewer should avoid statements which tend to create embarrassment or resentment, which would reduce the respondent's sense of dignity or initiative, or would give cause for complaint over unfair treatment. To the contrary, in keeping with the injunction of the preceding chapter of "description before prescription," he should inquire into facts, seek mutual understanding, and make every effort to encourage the other person voluntarily to amend his behavior.

To accomplish these ends the careful interviewer chooses the time and place to provide privacy and an unhurried opportunity for a rational approach. Productively operated, the correction interview

217

can and should improve understanding, upgrade behavior, and avoid leaving the bitter after-taste of criticism and complaint.

Grievance interviews

This kind of interview may be thought of as a correction interview in reverse, with the subordinate seeking improved conditions or behavior rather than the superior. In corporations subject to union contracts, the regulations for submitting grievances or complaints are usually detailed and must be followed. Even so, a satisfactory outcome may be obtained more easily when good interview practices are observed in the early stages, preventing unnecessary escalation of an issue. Such practices should, of course, be followed in the many interviews not subject to regulations, in offices and organizations where complaints are easily and informally registered. If the principles of productive person-to-person speaking are observed, wants and needs considered, facts validated and understanding sought, a satisfying conclusion can be more easily reached. Although correction and grievance interviews are similar in nature, the status of the complainant in each case makes a difference, especially in the authoritarian structure of many organizations.

Exit interviews

This interview takes place between an employer or his representative, usually a member of the personnel department, and a departing employee. Its purpose is to enable the employer to find out exactly why the employee is leaving the job, and of course occurs only when the separation is the employee's decision.

Since hundreds or even thousands of dollars may be invested in hiring and training an employee, an organization normally hopes to retain those who are valuable members of its staff. Turnover of personnel can be costly, not only because of the loss of investment in the hiring and training process, but also because of the decreased efficiency of the organization during the time a new person is being fitted in. Therefore any firm is deeply concerned with the reasons for employees' leaving, and many make a practice of interviewing those who depart.

The most common problem lies in the fact that employees are

often reluctant to make known their real reasons for quitting the job, and the interviewer must therefore be aware of possible resistance and be prepared to meet it. In this fact, the exit interview poses a problem often met in information-seeking interviews, that of probing for knowledge which the respondent may wish to keep to himself. The successful interviewer must develop skill in establishing rapport, in asking questions tactfully, and in evaluating responses.

Sales interviews

For all practical purposes almost any persuasive interview can be considered a sales interview, for any individual who speaks with the aim of persuading another is a salesman. He is after a decision of some kind, whether he is selling an idea, a service, or a product. The nature of the decision may range from agreement with a proposed change in the color of a package to signing a contract for a million-dollar installation of automated equipment or consenting to give five dollars to the Animal Protective League. Sometimes the decision is indicated by a nod of the head and sometimes by signing an order, but regardless of the sign, the persuadee has made a decision. He may have decided between simple acceptance or rejection—yes or no—or he may have elected a preference—to buy Brand X instead of Brand Y—but he has made up his mind.

Although any persuasive interviewer is a salesman, when we speak of a sales interview we usually think in terms of professional selling. The profession in itself, however, exhibits a vast number of different and highly specialized types of selling, each calling for a distinct application of the general principles of interviewing. The retail salesman behind a counter faces a selling situation quite unlike that of an engineering salesman developing specifications for a five-mile system of conveyor belts, or of a door-to-door seller of brushes or cosmetics. Some must get an immediate decision, while others, such as a detail man for a pharmaceutical manufacturer, know they must be satisfied by answering questions which may be raised about their products and hoping thereby to influence the person to regard the products favorably and later to use them.

The principles of persuasion apply to all sales interviews, and despite the diversified types, no sales presentation should be a monologue but a true interchange of thought and feeling. The

219

salesman must not only know the points he wants his respondent to understand and accept, but he must also discover the effect of those ideas and understand the attitudes and wants of the prospect which may affect the outcome. And regardless of the fact that countless books have been written to help the salesman, that forgotten person, the prospect, is still a full partner to the interview, with rights of exploration and dissent to protect his own interests.

Data gathering interviews

Many people must secure information in the course of their daily work, and if you have found it necessary to talk with others to get information for a term paper or a report, you have had experience with this kind of interview. The nature of your future work will determine the extent to which you must depend on similar interviews. Managers must secure information from colleagues and subordinates to serve as the bases of decisions. Scholars must ferret out data in the course of research. Doctors and psychiatrists must obtain from patients information necessary for diagnosing and treating illness. Criminal and insurance investigators must glean information from many sources, while market analysts and opinion poll-takers conduct well-planned canvasses. For many people, the information-getting interview can be an effective method of acquiring needed data, sometimes from the only possible source.

The interviewer who seeks information is faced with several specific problems. He must first determine exactly what he wants to know, which may range anywhere from facts or observations to the feelings, opinions, and attitudes of those being interviewed. He is then confronted with the task of devising questions which will uncover the wanted data, not always an easy or obvious thing. Involved with this are both the element of motivation, for the respondent may not want to give information, and often the question of memory, for time tends to distort original impressions. Finally, he must deal somehow with the material he has obtained, often to classify it so it can be compared with other data, and always to verify its accuracy and relevance.

Order-giving interviews

For convenience I shall classify all interviews in which information and instructions are given as order-giving interviews; the similarities seem more significant than the differences. This kind of interview is common. Facts and estimates must be communicated to colleagues, instructions issued, explanations given, reports presented to superiors, and orders given. In all cases, the interview should provide opportunity for asking and answering questions to provide the interchange necessary for understanding and acceptance. In no case should such an interview become a monologue.

The person who gives information or issues orders must consider not only the factual material he wants to communicate, but equally the person to whom it goes. He must follow the aphorism, "Tell 'em *what* and *how* and *why*," for details are useless unless the respondent wants to understand, unless he sees how the information is relevant to his own needs and activities, and unless he is willing to act as directed. Thus the interviewer is involved with motivating the respondent. He may be concerned as well with the problem of getting the interviewee to remember at some later date what has been said.

Throughout the description of these eleven kinds of interviews you have undoubtedly noticed references to the three fundamental purposes of interviewing. It is appropriate now for us to examine these purposes.

AN INTERVIEW SEEKS A DEFINITE GOAL

At the beginning of this chapter we noted that an interview was purposive, and in this sense it is like a public speech or a conference. Speaking in all three of the following forms is used to affect the behavior of others, and sometimes the behavior of the speaker himself. The forms serve situations in which men try to get others to understand or in which they seek to understand others, in which one intends to persuade or dissuade another, in which two or more seek a solution to some problem or a decision concerning it, and so on. Each interview should be characterized and controlled in the light of one dominating and ultimate purpose, usually determined by the one who initiates the interview. At the same time, this person may have to reach intermediate goals in the pursuit of the ultimate one. Thus, he may have to persuade another to understand his message, he may use information for persuasive purposes, when understanding must be prelude to acceptance, or he may describe a problem, hoping the respondent will be motivated to want a solution. And there are times when an interview participant must abandon one ultimate goal in favor of another. In the light of these things, let us examine the three general purposes of interviewing—the three most common kinds of behavioral outcome desired.

To increase understanding

When the purpose of an interview is to increase understanding, the content, aside from necessary motivational elements, is likely to be information. The major direction of this information may be from interviewer to respondent (information-giving), or from respondent to interviewer (information-getting). Rarely is the direction of flow exclusively one way, however, for when either getting or giving information an interviewer must use feedback for various purposes, and in many interviews there must be a full exchange of information.

You must not think of information as limited to factual or objective data, such as the rate schedule for air freight or the current number of employees covered by hospitalization benefits. Indeed, useful information may range from objective data of this nature to extremely subjective information such as the attitude of the respondent to the interviewer, the interviewer's hopes for the growth of his department, or the worries or ambitions of either participant. Information includes facts, descriptions, impressions, relationships, sentiments, values, and much else.

In some cases, such as that of a scholar bent on learning the cultural significance of Hopi dances, information may be valuable in itself. In most cases, however, information is a means to some other end, having value as it makes possible better informed evaluations, judgments, decisions, or behavior of other sorts. A purchasing agent must know the comparative specifications and features of competing brands of dictating equipment before he can decide what to buy. A salesman must discover the wants and needs of his customer before he can make an intelligent presentation. The director of research and development needs to understand the physical qualities of a new material in order to evaluate its potential market value. One interviewer might want to get the respondent to understand the steps which should be taken in preparing a report, while another needs to learn the attitudes of members of his staff toward an impending change of organization before a final decision is made. As in these instances, the content of informational interviews generally serves a human functional or behavioral need, which is advanced by understanding that content.

To persuade

In a purely informational interview, the participants do not intend to exert control over the behavior of one another except as necessary to achieve understanding, viewing the impact of the information as a matter to be personally determined. In contrast, the persuasive interview is one in which one or both of the participants wants to influence the behavior of the other in some predetermined manner. Whatever information is exchanged is done so for that purpose.

Persuasion itself may vary from "high pressure" selling with the intent of securing an immediate and favorable response, to an unstructured presentation of ideas and information with no other end than helping another achieve an improved but not specified behavior pattern. A salesman with a prepared presentation and an unyielding determination to make a sale will conduct one kind of persuasive interview, while a guidance counselor, a teacher, or an industrial instructor, each attempting to get a respondent to see things in a new light, will conduct another.

Persuasion, then, may be aimed at modifying behavior in any one of the terminal elements of the Behavioral Pyramid of Chapter 2 except understanding. Therefore, sales interviews, induction, performance review, correction, grievance, and sometimes employment interviews may be considered persuasive. Teaching is often for the purpose of altering or modifying the behavior of the learner rather than for simply developing understanding, and discipline is better conceived as the improvement of behavior than as either reprimanding or the imposing of punishment.

To solve problems

In a problem solving interview, one or both of the participants seek a way to overcome a difficulty or resolve a problem, and the meeting is to provide help toward that end. Consulting and counseling interviews most naturally and normally fall into a problem solving form, but as we have noted, many other kinds can be organized on this basis, and often with more productive results. Among these are sales, correction, performance review, and order giving interviews.

Unlike either of the other two purposes, problem solving is *creative* in the sense that the outcome develops from the interaction of the two participants in a way which neither had specifically foreseen nor planned. When other purposes govern, one or both of those involved is hoping for a specific predicted outcome, whereas problem solving requires neither to be committed before the conversation begins. Obviously, the application of the problem solving form to such interviews as sales or correction, when one participant actually does seek an intended goal, establishes a deceptive atmosphere which can undermine good relations. When an interview is problem solving, each participant must be open enough to strive for a mutually satisfying conclusion.

The development of a problem solving interview will depend to a great extent on the degree of congruity with which the participants see the problem. If they come to it with strongly different viewpoints, values, and backgrounds they must take time to explore and understand these differences before going on to a solution. But if both feel equally involved in the problem, if they see it "eye-to-eye," they are ready and motivated to search together for an answer. A supervisor who must correct one of his men for failure to make a report in proper form is apt not to see the offense in the same light as the subordinate, and some initial and mutual understanding of values may be necessary. In contrast, two research chemists may consult on a problem in full harmony, both seeing the question alike.

Many problem solving interviews are organized on the basis of the reflective-thought sequence outlined and discussed in the next chapter. They are, in effect, conferences involving two people only, usually structured by the interviewer in the conventional pattern of creative thinking. This pattern becomes a tool to organize the interview. In contrast are unstructured or non-directive problem solving interviews, in which the exchange of ideas, attitudes, and feelings is allowed to develop without guidance or control, and with little or no effort being made to follow a plan. The use of the reflective-thought sequence can be learned without too much difficulty, but, as indicated earlier, non-directive interviewing demands special training.

Having examined the kinds and purposes of interviews, you will next want to take up the principles and methods basic to the practice of interviewing.

PLAN THE INTERVIEW CAREFULLY

Some people view the interview as an off-hand and impromptu speaking encounter. This impression may explain why many interviews fall short of success, for Samuel Trull notes in the *Harvard Business Review*, "The lack of adequate planning for an interview is the greatest single fault found in my studies of the interviewing process."[4] The interviewer who gets results bases his achievement on groundwork laid in advance, groundwork which includes an understanding of the purpose to be achieved, and a design for attaining that purpose based on as much knowledge as can be gained about the person to be interviewed.

Clearly not every person taking part in an interview will have had opportunity to prepare, yet usually one of the parties will have taken the initiative to arrange the event and therefore should have made full preparation. And many who cannot anticipate specific interviews, such as complaint adjusters or counselors, know they must be ready to talk, and can therefore be prepared with a general plan which can be modified to suit each situation. So far as possible, each participant should prepare by making written notes for himself to ensure thoroughness and accuracy. For your own interviews, those notes should include your answers to the considerations we now turn to.

Determine your objective

As in almost every other speaking situation, the first step in planning is to establish clearly in your own mind the precise object you

---

[4] Trull, p. 89.

hope to achieve. If the occasion will be primarily information-giving, what do you want the respondent to understand? If it will be largely persuasive, what is the nature of the response or decision you wish to gain? If it is a selling interview, must you obtain an order, and if so, for what? Will you, perhaps, be satisfied to establish a sound relationship which will enable you to call back later for the sale? If the interview will be information-getting, what facts, data, or other intelligence do you intend to secure? If it is to be problem solving, what is the nature and description of the problem and what sort of solution have you to suggest?

Consider, too, the possible necessity of selecting an alternate goal in the event that during the interview you find the original one unattainable. Will you be able to switch gracefully to the pursuit of another goal? Some salesmen, for instance, like to present a specific offering to clients, but are ready to adjust their requests to suit the customer. If you are seeking employees with the intent of selecting a number for further screening, what will you do if an almost perfect applicant presents himself? Or if you are interviewing for a job with the purpose of making a good impression and looking over prospective employers, will you be ready to sell yourself if an opportunity appears that you really want?

Although goal-setting is first of all the responsibility of the one who seeks an interview, the interviewee is not relieved of obligation. When a salesman calls upon you, for instance, what purpose will you set for yourself during the interview? If you have granted the meeting, you must have decided that you wish to examine his proposal. But will you be ready to go beyond investigation? Are you prepared to buy? If so, what specifications or conditions of purchase can you foresee? Whether you will be interviewer or respondent, you always protect your interests and lay the foundation for a productive interview by carefully forecasting your objective.

Analyze the situation

As you determine your purpose for the interview, you should at the same time analyze as fully as possible the situation which you will encounter. The elements of that situation include your route to your respondent, the respondent himself, and any portions of the general field which may influence the outcome. Goal-setting and analysis need go hand in hand, for the first is often determined in part by the second. For instance, it would be fruitless when applying for a job to hope for a decision from an interviewer who lacked authority to make commitments for his company.

The question of a route to the interview is sometimes irrelevant, sometimes crucial. Many interviews are quickly arranged perhaps by a telephone call or during a chat in the lobby of a building, especially among people who are acquainted. Others take nothing more than a formal request for an appointment. Some, however, require careful preparation to get the interviewer in touch with his respondent in a manner which will facilitate a productive meeting. For instance, writers and journalists not infrequently must "pave the way" to an important person to get the material they need. Salesmen, especially in highly competitive fields, often prepare an approach to a potential customer with great care. A person interviewing for an opinion survey of union members at a given plant would undoubtedly have to effect an "entry" to members of the group through one of their own men, a person known to professional interviewers as a "gatekeeper."

It is of prime importance, of course, to understand as fully as possible the person with whom you will be talking. Since the elements to be considered have been dealt with elsewhere in this book, we shall simply note here that you must consider attitudes, motives as they bear on your purpose, the way in which you may be perceived, and any special characteristics of your interpersonal relationship.

Similarly, you must anticipate and prepare to adapt to any factors in the field or setting which could influence the interview. Will your respondent be pressed for time so that you must pursue matters briskly? Are you likely to be interrupted? These questions represent the physical setting, but there is also the psychological setting. Is your respondent apt to feel himself speaking as a member of a group or "set," toward the members of which he may sense responsibility? Will recent or coming events have any impact on his sentiments during the interview? The interview itself will not be an isolated event, but must be seen in the setting of its larger context, physical, psychological, and even cultural.

Your analysis of the situation will lead you to decide whether your purpose will be furthered by submitting to your respondent in advance some kind of notice of the subject you want to discuss, whether it be an outline, a simple memorandum, or a set of questions. Some interviews could be facilitated by such an action, some hindered, depending in part upon the way your respondent likes to work. Even if you decide to send information in advance, however, you cannot ready it until you have completed the rest of your preparation.

Decide upon your strategy and tactics

Having established your purpose in the light of an analysis of the total situation, your next step should be to create a plan for the interview. Just as you would not think of making a speech without a carefully thought-out plan, so you should not contemplate an interview without a well designed scheme of procedure to attain that purpose. This scheme will incorporate the proposed content into the general interview form set forth later in this chapter, and you should read that part in connection with your planning. Within this broad structure, however, you will want to steer the conversation along lines which you have predetermined and which you estimate will secure your objective. This is the strategy of the interview, strategy being defined as the way you intend to make the best use of available resources.

During the conversation you will probably want your respondent to understand and accept certain ideas or items of information. These we may call the "points" you want to make. You may also want to obtain facts, ideas, or opinions, which are the items about which you will ask questions. Together these points and items cover the content to be discussed, and your interview plan will list them in the sequence in which you think they should be taken up. Experienced interviewers also suggest that a rough time allotment should be made for each item on the agenda, pointing out that if some attention is not given to blocking out the time, important matters may not be reached before the interview is ended.

Because the behavior of your respondent is not fully predictable, and because unforeseen circumstances can influence the course of the discussion, you cannot count on following your plan exactly. You may find improvisation and modification necessary, and should expect to adapt to whatever happens. Still, your chances of success will be better for having planned both what you want to communicate and what you want to find out.

The details of your plan and their sequence must depend, of course, on the situation analysis you have made, particularly on the readiness of the respondent to listen and to reply. His expectations, his attitudes, his motives, and his experience will all determine the items on your agenda, their order, and even the way you word them. In the light of these factors, jot down the points you want to make in the order you think they should be presented. These may be likened to the main points of a speech, each of which relates to the whole as governed by your purpose. You will not present them in a continuous discourse or monologue as you would a speech, but the intent may be similar. Each will be presented as a segment of the conversation, subject to interruption, modification, or elaboration.

Let us say that after a period of military service you are looking for a job. Investigation suggests that you emphasize the way your service has qualified you to meet a certain employer's needs. A simple outline of the points you decide to make during the interview might be:

1. Military service has given me the technical training needed for the work.
2. Having fulfilled military obligations, I make a dependable permanent employee.
3. Military service has given me the maturity necessary to meet the responsibility of the job.

Merely asserting these points, however, may not be enough. You must be prepared to elaborate or support each point in the course of the conversation. This means that you must accumulate and have in readiness a sufficient amount of *evidence* or *supporting detail* on each point to make that point clear and convincing to your respondent, the exact use of the detail being decided by the nature and direction of the interview. The matter of supporting detail, its kinds and uses, is taken up in Chapter 13, and you should study that material as it bears on interviewing.

Your plan must now be expanded to include what you hope to find out or obtain from the respondent. This means you should specify the items or areas of information you want to discuss. An employment interviewer, for instance, might want to inquire, among other things, into the reasons why an applicant had left previous jobs, what satisfactions he expected in a new job, and his health status and record. After placing areas or points of inquiry such as these into a satisfactory order, you should carefully devise the key questions which you feel will elicit the desired information.

The preplanning and even the pretesting of questions is sometimes of critical importance, particularly in such interviews as attitude and opinion surveys, employment, credit reference, exit, and some kinds of consulting interviews. A pointed matter-of-fact question often does not produce a valid or useful answer, which can only be secured by very skillful questioning. If a personnel manager were to ask a departing employee, "Why are you leaving?" the answer might be no more reliable than a teacher could expect from a high school sophomore asked, "Who threw the chalk in class today?"

The problems involved in securing information are concisely summed up by Walter Bingham and Bruce Moore in *How To Interview*. They tell us:[5]

> The usefulness of the personal interview for reliable fact finding with reference to data about external conditions and events is limited by the interviewee's knowledge, his memory, his ability to observe; by his understanding of what is wanted; and by his verbal capacity for clear and accurate expression of what he knows. Equally serious are limitations imposed by his feelings of self-concern and similar emotional complications which tend to determine his mental attitude toward the interviewer and his inquiry. He may be reticent or deceitful, fearing lest any information he discloses may be turned to his disadvantage; or he may be voluble and anxious to please, telling what he thinks the interviewer would like to have him say, as many a simple savage has done when an amateur anthropologist has asked him about his religious beliefs and tribal customs.

In the face of such problems, it should be clear that the art of asking questions to secure information is, as any lawyer can tell you, one which takes long and serious practice. This is true whether the desired information is objective and factual or subjective, involving attitudes, feelings, and opinions. We shall have to limit our consideration in a later section of this chapter to types of questions which are most commonly useful. That section, however, will aid you as you plan an interview.

Anticipate and prepare to cope with resistance

We have already noted that your respondent's purpose in an interview may not be congruent with yours, and may, in fact, be opposed.

---

[5] Walter Bingham and Bruce Moore, *How To Interview*, Third Edition (New York: Harper & Brothers, Publishers, 1941), p. 249.

The most productive interview is likely to occur when each of the parties has a common interest in the outcome, and the skilled interviewer will try to get his respondent to perceive their interests as identical. Still an undercurrent of resistance or objection can be expected in many interviews, arising from forces which may vary from vague insecurity or uncertainty regarding another's intentions to positive hostility toward another's purposes. The handling of such resistance cannot be left to chance or improvisation, but should become an item of planning. It is often as important to decrease resistance to your purposes as it is to promote them positively.

Resistance may arise from an individual's perception of the interview as a threat to his ego or status or to his position in a group or organization, such as when the accepted leader of a gang or work-group feels that his position may be undercut by the interviewer's purposes. It may develop as a personal reaction to the other's personality or official status such as when a misbehaving freshman is ushered into the presence of the Dean of Men. It may arise from a real or apparent conflict of purposes such as when a prospective customer feels that the salesman is more concerned with his own profit than the customer's interests, or when a patient feels that the doctor may prohibit his smoking. If resistance from these or other causes is not to defeat you, it should be anticipated and plans arranged to decrease or overcome it.

There is no formula for discovering what resistance you may expect. The best method seems to be that of putting yourself mentally in the other person's place, of assuming his role, and trying to assess his attitudes and feelings. You will not thereby unerringly recognize potential resistance, but with practice you may be able to improve your ability. Professional salesmen, of course, learn the general classes of resistance they are likely to encounter, and prepare themselves to deal with all expected objections.

Having satisfied yourself on what resistance you may expect, you must then plan tactics to deal with it as it arises. Potential resistance can perhaps be neutralized by a tactful opening of the conversation, for as Richard A. Fear of the Psychological Corporation remarks, "the first ten minutes of the interview are extremely critical since one normally succeeds or fails to establish rapport in this initial period." Other resistance or objection may have to be dealt with as it becomes manifest, but you should be ready. Will your respondent perhaps feel that you are after information which should not be divulged? Make clear the purposes for which you need

231

it, show that these purposes are not inimical to his own interests, and make sure that he is convinced that you are a person of integrity who will respect your sources of information. May he feel that you want to blame him for something? Prepare to emphasize facts and to assure him that you want to solve a problem and do not want to find a scapegoat. Regardless of the nature of the resistance, your methods of coping with it should be thought out beforehand.

If possible, arrange the timing

Since most interviews are probably held at a time and place mutually fixed, you should make every effort to know that the time of the meeting is one when you can be assured of the respondent's complete and favorable attention. For instance, if he will be in the midst of other affairs, if he has a succeeding appointment scheduled to which his mind may turn, or if recent events may have disturbed him, perhaps creating an unfavorable frame of reference in which to receive you, you should try to shift the meeting to a better moment. Similarly, you should try to avoid interviews at times when you yourself may be pressed or otherwise unready to give another your best attention.

If possible, arrange desirable physical conditions

When your meeting takes place in facilities provided by the respondent, you will have little or no control over the physical surroundings. But when you provide the place for the interview, you can arrange the setting with forethought, knowing that privacy, comfort, and an absence of distractions are desirable. The air should be clear and the temperature comfortable. Chairs should be arranged not only comfortably but so that each person can see the other conveniently. (Some people prefer chairs to face each other, others at an angle.) Clutter which may distract either person, such as papers on a desk or apparatus in a corner, should be placed out of visual range. The door may be closed, and the secretary instructed to hold incoming telephone calls. If note paper, refreshments, or reference materials seem indicated, they should be conveniently ready. Everything should be done to make the atmosphere conducive to permissive and unhurried talk.

Often the nature of an interview dictates where it will be held. Salesmen, for instance, normally call at the customer's place of business or residence, and a subordinate goes to his superior's office. Yet there are times when the selection of place has a bearing on the significance of the meeting or on its outcome. When a superior goes to his subordinate, a sense of urgency or importance may be communicated. At times a willingness to go to another person when normally you would expect him to come to you may communicate good will. (In some cases a "neutral" ground is advisable.) Since the choice of location may symbolize the significance of the topic, the relative status of those participating, or an attitude, this element should be considered during planning.

Prepare yourself personally

Few treatments of interviewing fail to give attention to matters of dress and grooming, and certainly these items can often be vital, especially when seeking employment, when selling, or when interviewing for information. *What your respondent sees* conditions to a large extent his reception of what he hears, and therefore it can be important that you make a good visual impression.

Cleanliness and neatness are paramount; the prescription for dress will vary from situation to situation. In general, your attire should fit the role your respondent may expect you to play, although as a rule it should be neutral enough that it does not demand his attention. Sport shirts, for instance, would be out of keeping in a business situation where convention calls for plain white. Although modest design should ordinarily be preferred, a salesman for men's clothing might be expected to wear the latest cut. For women, high heels could be appropriate in certain conditions, quite inappropriate in others. Jewelry should be in harmony with attire and situation. Your entire physical appearance should be appropriate and should honestly reflect you as a person.

If you have taken forethought and planned with care, you can look forward to an interview with much more confidence than otherwise. You are ready to talk with purpose, and fortified to meet contingencies.

THE INTERVIEW WILL BE STRUCTURED OR ORGANIZED

Even those who conduct unstructured interviews are likely to grant that such interviews do have some kind of organization. They are not absolutely formless. Most have an opening which may be given over to establishing rapport or to exploring the subject of the interview, a main part or body during which the purpose of the meeting is pursued, and a close or dismissal which rounds out or terminates the encounter. The same is true of structured interviews, the basic difference being that the latter are more highly organized within the main parts and are usually guided by the interviewer. An unstructured interview is generally allowed to develop a rough opening–body–closing pattern without great effort being made by either party to direct its course. Since the three-part structure is appropriate to either, we shall take up these parts in order, recognizing that our major concern is with the structured kind.

The opening should establish a workable relationship between interviewer and interviewee

Depending upon prior relationships between the parties, the opening phase of an interview may be brief or its development may require some time. Old friends can get down to business at once, whereas strangers or persons between whom relations are strained may find developing productive relationships to be time consuming. The over-all function of the opening is to establish the best possible rapport and to orient the conversation toward the content and purpose. There are three general methods of working toward these ends, and in your own interviews you may want to use one or a combination.

WORK FOR CONFIDENCE, EASE, AND A PERMISSIVE ATMOSPHERE. One of the interviewer's purposes at the outset should be to identify himself favorably, to put the respondent at ease, both physically and mentally, and to reduce any feeling of insecurity or threat which might exist. The aim should be to develop a sense of confidence and rapport between the two, in which both will feel increasingly free to speak without constraint. Specific methods will naturally vary according to the particular conditions. The interviewer may thank the respondent for consenting to the meeting. He may introduce himself and identify his role in the interview, as "I'm Vernon Widger, a staff writer for the *Daily Star*. Here are my credentials." He may indicate some identification with a friend of the interviewee: "Mr. Neff, I'm calling at the suggestion of Tom McCall. I believe you've known each other for several years." Or he may express a friendly interest in the other: "Mrs. Jones, you've been with us for three months now, and for your benefit as well as ours, it's time to see how things are going."

Ease, confidence, and a sense of security in surroundings which may be quite unfamiliar cannot, of course, normally be established by an opening sentence or two, and the interviewer may elect to pursue these goals for some little while. A few simple social amenities can reinforce his words and aid in adjustment. The interviewer may offer his respondent a cigaret or some refreshments, talk briefly about matters of mutual interest, or search for common ties. If he is genuinely at ease himself he can encourage a relaxed atmosphere.

When you are being interviewed the situation is naturally reversed, and your interviewer is likely to be concerned with putting you at ease. Normally the best course will be to follow his lead, but when it is appropriate, there is no reason for you not to suggest your interest in the topic of the meeting, thus taking the initiative in forwarding the interview.

In interviews, as in other human relationships, integrity is indispensable. Tactics suggesting hearty good will but actually used as devices to manipulate another are not only shoddy but often defeat their own purpose. Mary Whiting, a housewife, was called by a telephone canvasser who began by expressing what, for a stranger, was an excessive concern for Mrs. Whiting's health. Irritated, Mrs. Whiting ended the interview by hanging up even before she knew what her caller was selling. The canvasser's insincerity was only too evident.

ESTABLISH AREAS OF AGREEMENT. When the interview may have to deal with matters over which a conflict of opinion can or will emerge, the interviewer will often find it useful early in the meeting to build common ground. This may begin with a word of honest appreciation, a little bit of truthful praise. Making the other person right in something can improve rapport and help foster an attitude of reciprocity. With such an attitude both parties can explore matters of agreement. If both recognize that some difference of opinion will be involved, little can be lost by a survey of common outlook, after which it may be possible to go on to areas of potential disagreement with a view to searching for ways of resolving differences. To freely admit that one is searching for agreement may disarm suspicion and help head off resistance.

GET ATTENTION AND INTEREST; PRESENT A PROBLEM. Often the interviewer's first challenge is to secure the full and favorable attention of his respondent. This is likely to be true in most sales or persuasive interviews and in many consulting or information-seeking ones. In such situations you will find it helpful to talk with your respondent at the outset about something in which he is interested. Mention his goals, his wants or needs, the current challenge of his job, or similar topics, and encourage him to talk.

The subject of the interview may in itself be made of interest to the respondent if it can be skillfully identified with his own affairs. Many an interviewer has, in the planning stage, studied his respondent thoroughly to find out those things in which the latter may be interested, while others have obtained clues by alert observation or sensitive listening even while waiting in an outer office.

The methods of successfully beginning a speech outlined in Chapter 12 may be applied to getting attention and interest at the opening of many interviews. For instance, a thought-provoking question can get a speech off to a good start, and can be equally useful in an interview. A consulting interview might begin, "Jim, I wonder if you ever had an experience like the one I had yesterday?" and continue from that point.

Beginning a conversation with the respondent's interests, however, can create problems. Such an opening may serve very well to break the ice and to begin a pleasant relationship, but it can easily be overdone and consume more time than it is worth. Making a transition to the real subject of the interview can also be difficult, and if awkwardly handled may undo whatever good relationships have been established. When the opening is devoted to baseball, gardening, the new office decorations, the respondent's family, or similar irrelevant topics, there is apt to be the nagging under current, "Let's stop being pleasant and get down to business." Good

236

taste and a sense of the appropriate moment for shifting the focus of the interview are indispensable.

Often an interview can be opened effectively by a statement showing that the respondent is involved in a problem of concern to both persons and by inviting him to help solve it. Thus one of a group of merchants who had built a parking lot for their customers began consulting an associate by saying, "Tom, too many people are parking overtime in our lot and we're losing the good-will of customers who can't find a parking place." A salesman for heavy-duty light bulbs began an interview with a building manager by saying, "Mr. Manager, you are paying more in wages to a man to change bulbs when they burn out in your building than the bulbs themselves cost. If you are interested, I can help you cut this cost in half."

Regardless of which method or combination of methods you use to open an interview, remember that all this is preliminary to the major development for which you are preparing the way. Therefore, do not let the opening be obvious as a device, and do not let it consume an unnecessary amount of time. Under all circumstances both parties must realize that they are met for a purposive conversation, and the opening must be geared to this realization.

The body or development must accomplish the interview purpose

When the best obtainable rapport has been secured, the interview should be advanced into the development or main body. This is "where the work gets done." It is here that you make your points, ask your questions, exchange impressions and ideas, or achieve whatever interaction is necessary to attain your purpose. Let us consider the major elements of interaction.

MAKING POINTS. You have planned the points you want your respondent to understand or accept, and the order in which you think they should be presented. This plan must be subject to modification as the interview progresses, for you must adapt to your respondent. Do not destroy the interview by adhering rigidly to a fixed structure which may not prove appropriate.

Not only may you adapt to circumstances by altering the order of your points, but you may also adapt by care in choosing the method of developing each. You will find the inductive, deductive,

237

and combined methods explained in Chapter 13, and so we need not discuss them here. Each has its application, and you may select that which seems most appropriate.

Many times you may find that offering your point in the form of a question is better than making it as a statement or assertion. In this use, a question is a rhetorical device to imply your point, not a serious attempt to get an answer. A field foreman I once knew had little formal schooling, but he was marvelously able to work with people, and one of his habitual methods was to make a point by asking a question. "Why don't you take the time cards down to the main office?" he would say, avoiding the imperative form. In similar fashion, you can frequently communicate your point without making a flat statement, thereby minimizing the possibility of objection or resistance. Convert your points to questions, perhaps beginning with a phrase such as, "Wouldn't it help if . . ."

As you make each point, determine the degree of understanding or acceptance you have effected rather than contenting yourself with an uncertain impression. Use questions to elicit feedback, such as, "How would you say that in your own words?" or "Then you agree that . . . ?" Or summarize a segment of the conversation in your own words and ask your respondent to confirm that it accurately expresses the point as he understands it.

ASKING QUESTIONS. In many interviews your major task may be to ask questions, not of the rhetorical variety to secure agreement, but intended to yield answers you seek. As a rule, experience suggests that you should ask questions one at a time, and that often you will need to wait patiently for the answer. When your respondent does not reply immediately, do not obey the impulse to rephrase your question or to ask another, for to do so will be confusing and may inhibit a reluctant or slowly-developing answer. For this reason, too, do not interrupt an answer.

Experience also suggests that the most productive order of questions begins with the general and moves to the specific. Ordinarily the general questions are open-end, calling for narrative or undirected replies, whereas the more specific ones are direct and require less expansive answers. Preliminary or general questions may at times lead the interviewer to form an *hypothesis,* or tentative guess concerning a conclusion he suspects, and to devise specific questions to test that hypothesis. Thus in diagnosis, a physician may arrive at an hypothesis about the nature of his patient's illness, and then ask questions the answers to which will tend to confirm or deny that hypothesis. Similarly, a teacher might form an hypothesis concerning the reasons for a student's poor grades, a personnel manager might have an hypothesis about the causes of an employee's resigning, or a journalist might have an hypothesis to explain certain features of a subject he is investigating. In each instance, the hypothesis would suggest a line of specific questioning. The interviewer must exercise caution, however, against asking only questions which would confirm his hypothesis instead of those which would rigorously test it.

Let us now turn to some of the kinds of questions which can be useful in getting information.

1. THE OPEN-END QUESTION. This kind of question calls for a free and unqualified answer, and puts the respondent to the necessity of doing some thinking in order to reply. "Tell me something about your work." "Please describe the territory you traveled through." "You are interested in teaching high school English. How do you plan to do the job better than it was done for you in your own high school?" "What is your general impression of how effective the planning has been?" Questions of this nature are non-directive, and permit the questioner to note the respondent's behavior and the quality of his thinking as well as the substance of the replies.

The open-end question can be qualified to guide the answers into narrower channels and still allow room for freedom of answer. "What safety features of our product do you like?" focuses on a specific aspect of a subject, as does "Which of your studies in college do you think gave the best preparation for a job like this?"

2. THE DIRECT QUESTION. This calls for a specific reply on a definite topic, permitting the respondent little or no freedom of selection in his answer. "What is your favorite television program?" and "Why were you absent yesterday?" are examples.

The direct question can be narrowed to a yes-or-no dimension, "Did you see the memorandum when it was circulated?" or "Will you attend the convention in December?" This kind of question gives little opportunity to draw the respondent out, and is useful only for specific information.

3. THE YES-RESPONSE QUESTION. This type of question may be more useful in persuasive interviews than in informational, since its purpose is to encourage explicit agreement on a given point. It is

239

useful to the salesman, as can be seen in, "Wouldn't a gas-fired heater, giving unlimited amounts of hot water, be an improvement over your present installation?" A planned series of yes-response questions can be used to direct the respondent's thinking affirmatively toward a matter upon which agreement may be important.

4. THE LOADED QUESTION. This is a variety of leading questions, generally directed at a topic upon which the respondent may be "touchy," and designed more to elicit an emotional response than to secure information. To a football coach, "Don't you agree that sports are over-emphasized in our public schools?" could easily be loaded. This kind of question is used in "stress" interviews, which are employed to discover an individual's behavior under pressure.

5. THE MIRROR QUESTION. This type is used to return the respondent's thinking to a statement he has just made, and to encourage him to expand upon it. Since it avoids evaluating the statement, it enhances permissiveness. For instance, if a respondent has said, "I'm against parking on main streets," an interviewer might mirror the statement by asking, "You think we should prohibit parking on all main thoroughfares?" The mirror question is a neutral follow-up, and might be called a probe.

6. PROBES. The probe is an unplanned question used to explore an answer in depth and detail or to discover the attitudes and feelings of the respondent about what he has just said. Probes are used to get more complete answers, to discover implicit qualifications concealed in a reply, to achieve greater clarity of understanding, to discover the sources of a respondent's information, to verify specific details, or to discover the kind and depth of the respondent's sentiments related to an answer. They can be open, as "Tell me more about that." Or they may be specific, as "I don't quite see what you mean," "Will you give me an example of that?" "Where was the man when you first saw him?" or "Who told you these things?"

Skill in probing is a necessity for many interviews, and is acquired only through practice and by analysis of success or failure. The probe must normally avoid putting the respondent on the defensive, it must not limit freedom to reply, and it must avoid suggesting a wanted answer.

Since the question is used to invite or command another to talk, and therefore a device to direct the conversation, we might include

240

the "echo" as a form of question. An echo is an exact or a paraphrased repetition of a respondent's statement which in effect says, "I heard you. Go on from there." If the respondent says, "It was a lousy deal," the echo repeats, "It was a lousy deal."

ANSWERING QUESTIONS. In most interviews you will be answering as well as asking questions, and so some thought should be given to the principles of reply. The person who questions you may be as interested in the manner of your reply as in the content, for he may be examining you more than your words. Consequently you must often be as concerned with the purpose of his question as with the content of your answer.

To the great majority of questions you will want to give a reply which is substantial and to the point. Be certain at the outset that you clearly understand the question, and if you are uncertain, have the question repeated or explained. Once you understand, be definite in your answer, as a rule providing a short, specific reply before elaborating. A recent survey of 153 firms which do employment interviewing found that an indefinite response was deemed by them to reflect unfavorably upon the interviewee.

After you have given a succinct answer, you may elaborate as seems appropriate. Take your cue from your questioner, trying to add detail to the amount that he wants as well as that which will best advance your own purpose. Try to avoid extremes of brevity or elaboration, lest you give the impression either of having nothing to say or of having something to conceal.

If you are in doubt, either about the purpose of the question or about what you should say in reply, do not be hurried into a quick response. Take your time, observing the questioner to see if you can fathom the motive or the attitude behind the question, thereby gauging the nature of an appropriate response. Repeating the question will ensure that you have heard it correctly and will give you a bit of added time to consider your answer. Do not bluff, but if you feel that you must qualify your answer, do not withhold your qualification. If the question calls for a yes-or-no response and you would like to avoid a categorical commitment, qualify your answer before saying yes or no.

In most instances, you have the privilege of declining to answer a question, although tact and courtesy both suggest that you offer a reason for declining. The matter may be confidential or classified, you may be in no position to offer a valid answer, you may prefer not to involve someone else, the reply may take thought which you have not had time to give it, or you may wish not to commit yourself at the moment. Even if a question is surprising, rude, or sarcastic, do not bristle nor allow yourself to be pulled off balance. Remember that a calm posture gives strength to your position.

Remember, too, that human observation and memory are both fallible, and that you are human. Consequently, do not feel compelled to give positive answers when you are uncertain. It is better to admit that you do not know than try to explain later that you were wrong.

MEETING RESISTANCE. Resistance to some degree can be expected in a great many interviews. The prospect resists a salesman, perhaps because he objects to having anyone influence his decisions, perhaps because he is suspicious of this particular salesman, or perhaps because he doesn't want to spend his money on a given product. The client may resist his own lawyer because he feels insecure in the latter's presence. The subordinate may resist his superior because he fears to give away information which might discredit himself.

Often resistance is not expressed verbally, and can be detected only in the respondent's general behavior—in his manner, his voice, or his facial expression. When you sense restraint in another which might indicate resistance, it is generally useful to encourage him to do more talking; one of the ways of dealing with it is to try to get it out in the open.

Expressed resistance, or verbalized objection, falls roughly into two categories, one expressing honest doubt or indecision and another verbalizing an excuse. Salesmen very often handle an excuse by ignoring it or shifting the focus of the conversation, but they must meet doubt or indecision frankly. A sound way to do this without becoming argumentative is to go on the assumption that when the respondent *understands* more completely his objection will be ended. The assumption creates an explanatory attitude which helps build rapport.

Resistance, searching questions, and objections are a human and natural consequence of the fact that people do not think alike, and an evidence of the function of communication, which I defined in another context as the art of creating a common meaning. You must try to get people to see things the way you do. This means that an objection is not a frightening barrier, but an opportunity to know how the other person sees things. Having been furnished an important clue, you can then meet the situation constructively, perhaps by turning the objection into a reason for agreeing, perhaps by explaining things more fully, perhaps by denying the objection, or perhaps by getting the other to talk himself out of it.

LISTENING AND OBSERVING. Much of what was said about listening in Chapter 5 applies to interviews, and need not be repeated. You may be called upon during an interview to listen to understand, to listen critically, or to listen empathically. Your listening may be all for one purpose, or may vary from moment to moment as the interview develops.

The interview may, however, place special demands upon you to read the "silent language" of another's behavior, to interpret the meaning of his facial expression, eyes, basic posture, general bodily tonicity, animation or lack of it, particular habits or mannerisms, and so on. Such things as tightening or relaxing of muscles, blushing, blanching, change about the eyes, or even alteration of hand position may communicate unspoken feelings or attitudes which add meaning to what is said.

Only through learning from experience can you develop skill in observing and interpreting behavior, but it will pay you dividends. How does your respondent react to you? What does he "really" mean when he says something? Is he assuming virtues he does not possess, perhaps putting up a front? Is he thinking about something else? Is he answering frankly? Is he repressing ideas or feelings? Is he eager to keep your attention away from certain things? Does he adequately understand your point? Answers to questions like these can be obtained, in part at least, by observation when they cannot be gained from the conversation itself.

You must also remember that your respondent is observing you, perhaps so well that he can penetrate behind the image you may be trying to create. Your ultimate security then rests upon your character as a responsible communicator, discussed in Chapter 4.

The foregoing five elements of interaction are hardly restricted to the body of the interview, although we have been examining them as they apply to that part. Actually they continue from the first to the last word. At the moment, however, that you have accomplished your purpose, or at the moment you feel you have accomplished everything possible, it is time to effect a transition which moves the interview from the body into the close.

The close should round out or gracefully terminate the interview

When it becomes clear that the interview is no longer progressing, that further talk will not be productive, or when a specified time limit is at hand, one of the parties will take the initiative to bring the encounter to a close. This will normally be the interviewer, who presumably has been in control of the conversation, although there are times when the respondent (for example, in an unsuccessful sales interview) will end it. Prolonging the meeting past the period of its growth can even reduce or nullify whatever has been achieved. The close should clinch matters on which understanding or agreement has been reached, and should terminate the encounter with a feeling of mutual good will. As in the opening, one or a combination of three methods can be used.

REVIEW OR SUMMARIZE THE GIST OF THE MEETING. A lawyer of my acquaintance makes it a practice to end each interview with a client by summarizing succinctly the items which have been covered, and when necessary by indicating the action which either he or the client have agreed to take. Frequently he uses enumeration for emphasis. "First," he says, "it is clear that. . . . Second, you are to. . . . And third, I will . . . " In doing so he effectively reinforces the points to be remembered and signals dismissal to the client.

In a similar manner, you will find it useful to bring some of your interviews to a close by briefly reviewing the items which have been discussed, the conclusion reached on each, and necessary action to be taken by either party. For instance, at the end of an employment interview you are likely to want to know where you stand, what subsequent steps, if any, should be taken, and where the initiative may rest for resuming the conversations. When using this method, take particular care to note whether your respondent understands and is in agreement with you on the items, for this is the moment when you must be sure of complete understanding. Your summary has given the respondent a feedback, and you must watch the return from him to make certain of a meeting of the minds. "Do you have any questions?" can uncover a lingering uncertainty; if not, it may be an appropriate note of finality.

244

ESTABLISH THE BASES FOR FURTHER CONVERSATIONS. When the interview has involved negotiation or has covered material on which agreement has not been reached, it will be desirable or even necessary to go beyond a simple summation of accomplishment, and look toward the future. In order to do this constructively, it is often better first to clarify the issues which are still undecided, pinpointing unanswered questions, and to end by noting things which have been agreed upon and to arrange to meet again. Thus, a consultative interview might end something like this: "John, it looks as if we don't agree on what course of action should be taken, for we have different explanations of the trouble. But we do agree that something must be done to decrease the number of rejects that are coming off line three. Is it all right if we get together on this again Friday to see if we can reach a decision? In the meanwhile, we'll each look further into the causes as we see them."

It is easy under the stress generated by negotiation or disagreement for the exact issues standing between people to become hazy. For this reason a conclusion to such an interview should attempt to clarify the points of difference before they can seek final concurrence.

EXPRESS APPRECIATION OR INDICATE DISMISSAL. When the task of an interview has been concluded, there still remains the necessity of gracefully terminating the conversation. The individuals must play the role of gracious host or grateful guest. These roles involve the customary social amenities, and at times may require tact. The focus is on maintaining desirable interpersonal relationships more than on the substance of the interview. "Thank you for coming in," "Thank you for inviting me to talk this over," or "I've enjoyed talking with you," represent common but acceptable last words.

Dismissal can often be indicated by non-verbal means. Pushing back a chair or rising from it may signal the end of an interview. If the signal is interpreted correctly, either party can simply say, "Thank you," and the interview is ended. Or one of the parties, usually the one in whose home or office the meeting has occurred, may indicate that the time allocated to the conversation is up, and courteously accompany the other to the door.

When an interview involves a follow-up of some kind, referring to this becomes an apt way to bring it to a close. If an order has been secured or a decision gained, the interviewer can gracefully wind up his business by a reference to the delivery of goods, to a benefit the respondent can expect, or to some obligation he has assumed. An interviewer might say, for example, "Thank you, Mr. Goss, for agreeing to handle that part of the program. I will send you the memorandum tomorrow with a full outline of what is necessary, and I know you'll enjoy the experience." Reference to a subsequent meeting, offering of paper to be filled out, or a promise to check back when necessary can serve to round out an interview and bring it to a conclusion.

Regardless of the method or methods employed, the close of an interview, not unlike the close of a speech, must accomplish the two purposes indicated earlier. It must round out the structure of the meeting, concluding the business by reviewing or reaffirming the response secured, and it must bring the conversation as a social encounter to an end with good grace. Either party may initiate and guide the close, and in order to display good will either may stress the outcome as he thinks his respondent sees it.

INTERVIEWS MUST OFTEN BE FOLLOWED UP

While a follow-up is not part of the interview proper, one is commonly desirable if either or both of the parties is to secure the full benefit of the meeting. As noted earlier, during many interviews the necessity of a follow-up can be foreseen and arrangements for it made. For instance, a salesman who must leave without making a sale will want to arrange to call back on his prospect at a later date.

When an interview has involved information, particularly when notes have not been taken, one or both participants will want to review the information and get the results into written form as quickly as possible. Delay will result in memory loss and inaccuracy, especially when information must be interpreted or evaluated or when relevant items must be sorted out of a mass of detail. In instances of this nature, a follow-up consists of writing up the interview, perhaps filling out forms, and of studying and interpreting the data.

In many cases the memoranda of an interview must be transmitted to others or filed for permanent record, and again such material should be made out as soon as the interview is over. Marketing and public opinion surveys and similar information-seeking interviews often yield extensive data which require detailed evaluation of the written results.

Many an interview should be followed up by a letter, a note, or an unscheduled return visit. After some interviews a note of appreciation is a courtesy valued by the respondent. Many salesmen make it a point to call back on a recent customer to make sure he is satisfied with his purchase. United States Steel and the B. F. Goodrich Company are two which have taught many of their salesmen that "ensuring satisfaction" is the final step of the selling process, and that a callback is one way of making certain that the customer is satisfied.

When an interview has resulted in a delegation of duty, when an agreement concerning future action has been reached, or when instructions have been issued, a follow-up, if not always necessary, is commonly advisable. The person responsible will want to learn if the duty has been assumed, the agreement honored, or the orders accurately followed, and to do so requires some kind of continuing touch with events.

The person who, during an interview, issues instructions, furnishes data, or otherwise gives information will do well to remember that the most effective communication results when both oral and written media are used. Consequently he will follow his oral presentation with a written reminder. Similarly, a note or a telephone call can be used to generate feedback and find out if anything has become hazy with the passage of time.

An interview, then, is likely to be but an event in a continuing process of communication and interaction. As such, it does not end when the final word has been spoken, but may require effective and perhaps extensive follow-up to ensure maximum benefit. The method of the follow-up may be less important than the fact of well-timed action.

In this chapter we have made a survey of the kinds and purposes of interviews, have examined the general structure of an interview, and have noted the principles and techniques which apply to most. Your own skill in interviewing will develop with experience interpreted in the light of these things. You may find the following transcript of an interview helpful in understanding some of the things we have covered.

An Interview[6]

1. I : Well, good morning, Joel. How are you?

   R : Oh, pretty good, Mr. Blake.

   (I-1. This begins some informal introductory material, which extends through I-7. This introduction is considerably longer than that which has characterized some of the other interviews, and at first glance it might appear somewhat aimless and digressive. The supervisory role relationships which exist between the interviewer and respondent, however, make it necessary and desirable that the business of the interview not be entered into before some manifestation of personal interest occurs. Where a personal relationship exists prior to the interview, an indication of such interest is both natural and appropriate. Moreover, the interviewer uses this introductory material to give some structure to the interview. In I-2, for example, he indicates that the reason for this appointment is to discuss some job-related topics. It seems likely that the interviewer recognizes that the experience of a subordinate on being summoned to the supervisor's office includes some feelings of insecurity and concern, and the interviewer is attempting to offer some reassurance and establish an informal and comfortable atmosphere before beginning the interview proper.)

2. I : Fine. It's been some time since we sat down and had a talk about the job.

   R : Well, it has, but I guess you're a busy man these days.

3. I : Oh, yeah. Always things seem to pile up; more than they ought to, I guess. How's your family?

   R : Oh they're fine, they're fine.

[6] By permission from Kahn and Cannell, *The Dynamics of Interviewing.* Copyright © 1957 by John Wiley & Sons, Inc. Pp. 318–327.

4. I : Your boy home from college this year?

   R : Yeah, he's, he's out of school now.

5. I : Oh, swell.

   R : Trying to line up a summer job.

6. I : I was wondering. Got any plans, has he?

   R : Yeah, I think he's, ah, likely to be working down at the department store for the summer.

7. I : Oh, fine. Well I hope to get to see him sometime this summer. Haven't seen him in a long time now.

   R : Yeah, you wouldn't, you wouldn't recognize him. He's filled out a lot.

8. I : I bet—they do. Well, Joel, ah, as I was mentioning, it's been some time since we've talked about the job very much, and I thought it might be a good idea today to, ah, sit down and have a chat about, ah, about things, the way we do once in a while. Ah, how are things going?

   R : Well, I guess they're going all right. We're, we're all working hard. Doing our best.

   (I-8 begins the body of the interview. The interviewer repeats the statement made in I-2, that he wants to talk about the job, and poses his first direct question. This is put in broad, open form, permitting the respondent to answer in terms of any aspect of his job. In spite of the interviewer's efforts at informality and reassurance, the respondent's answer [R-8] appears to be defensive. He offers relatively little information, and instead makes a general assertion of virtue.)

9. I : Yeah, we've sure had a lot of work to do lately, haven't we? Things seem to be going pretty well?

   R : Yeah, I'd say they were going pretty well on the whole. We're getting a lot of work out.

   (I-9. The interviewer accepts the respondent's statement that he is working hard. Having done this in a reassuring fashion, he repeats the question. The question is not stated in as balanced a form as it was in I-8, but it reflects the respondent's previous statement that things are, on the whole, going satisfactorily.

(R-9 to R-11. In this series of interchanges the interviewer makes patient attempts to get the respondent to talk about the work situation. The respondent, however, continues defensive and appears unwilling to reveal any of his problems at this point. Implicitly, he continues to ask for reassurance and recognition of hard work. He is perhaps reacting to the interviewer as a supervisor rather than in the information-getting role. This supervisor-subordinate relationship poses a problem for the interviewer throughout the entire discussion.)

10. I : Yeah, Joel, I suppose your section does have a heck of a lot of work close to it, doesn't it?

    R : Well, it does. Course, course we're always busy but, ah, in the last few months it seems to have been especially heavy. I'll say this though, we've, we've got a good, good crew of girls this year.

11. I : Well, that's good.

    R : They, ah, they come in right on time. They, they tend to business while they're there. Some of 'em are, we've got some really fine typists.

12. I : Joel, I don't know about the typists, but I went by there the other day and you got some darn good looking girls, too.

    R : Ah-ha-ha. Well, we, we don't pick them on that basis. . . .
    (I-12 to I-14. The interviewer attempts again to lighten the atmosphere a bit. There is some suggestion here that the supervisor is attempting to persuade the subordinate that he is a "regular guy.")

13. I : Ah, Come on, Joel, you know that . . . (Laughter.)

    R : Well, it's no handicap.

14. I : Yah, that's right, if they can type, too, that's good. You're, ah, I gather then that you're able to keep up with the, ah, work pretty well with the crew you've got.

    R : Well, I'd say that on the whole we were. Course, ah, I don't like to ask to add to the crew. That raises costs and I know we gotta keep our costs down. I'd say that most of the time we keep up pretty well. Course there're some times of the day, late afternoon especially, where, where things really bulk up.

(I-14. Since the global questions [I-8 and I-9] did not produce much, the interviewer now tries a more specific question. It is possible that a better balanced wording would have improved it; however, the interviewer appears to be phrasing his question in a way that catches the content and implications of what the respondent has previously been saying. In any case, the question appears successful, and in R-14 it brings out some important material for the first time in the interview.)

15. I : Sometimes they kinda jam up on you at the end of the day, huh?

R : Yeah, they do and, ah, well, I suppose when, ah, when things jam up that way you can't make everybody happy.

(R-15. Here the respondent, encouraged by the interviewer's accurate reflection and acceptance of his previous expression, gives further indication of the nature of the problems which he has hinted at in R-14. It is in this response that we get the first indication of interpersonal difficulties.)

16. I : Sometimes they gripe to you, do they?

R : Well, I, ah, I don't like to, ah, say that, that anybody gripes really. I, I'm not complaining.

(I-16. The interviewer attempts to reflect the attitude which the respondent has previously conveyed, for purposes of encouraging further response. However, perhaps betrayed by his knowledge of what has actually gone on, the interviewer offers a stronger statement of the respondent's attitude than he is yet ready to accept. The interviewer's statement is factually correct, but it goes somewhat beyond the respondent's previous statement and leads to some temporary difficulties. In R-16 the respondent resists and becomes somewhat defensive about the implication that he is complaining about anyone.)

17. I : Yeah, I didn't mean that. I thought you, ah, indicated a few minutes ago that, ah, every once in a while they complain.

R : Well, as a matter of fact, you can't please everybody. I guess that's what it comes down to. I don't want to point the finger at anybody as, as complaining. Let's just say that when things bulk up the way they do sometimes in the afternoon, you can't make everybody happy.

(I-17. At this point the interviewer gets defensive, probably realizing that he has used an unfortunate probe. He emerges from his role and attempts to explain and justify his previous statement. The result is further defensiveness on the respondent's part.)

18. I : Yeah, I suppose, Joel, that on a job like yours, ah, you can't give everyone exactly what they want when they want it.

R : Well, we, we try. We try most of the time, and most of the time I'd, I'd say, ah, we're pretty successful. But what tends to happen is that sometimes we just get so loaded in the afternoon that something's had to go over to the next day.

(I-18. Here the interviewer has recovered. He no longer attempts to justify his own wording, but focuses on the respondent's previous less personal statement about the work situation. This more appropriate interviewing procedure is rewarded with the communication of additional material in R-18. For the first time, the respondent volunteers the basis of the current difficulty.)

19. I : Hm. Your work bulks up then the latter part of the afternoon, huh?

R : Yeah, I, that happens. Now I, I can understand how it is. Ah, people, ah, do a lot of writing and dictating in the morning, and then it starts, ah, pouring in to us after lunch. Sometimes the girls aren't very busy in the morning, and then, ah, the afternoon is awfully hectic.

20. I : Yeah, well, of course we've been pretty busy, ah, all over the place, and I guess, ah, a lot of the boys are feeling under, ah, some pressures. Ah, tell me more. What, ah, . . . Does this create special problems for you?

R : Well, frankly, it does. Of course there's always a problem when people feel pushed, I suppose, but the thing that makes it most difficult is that when people bring us work, nobody seems to know or care what other work is tossed at us. They're, they're just thinking about their own stuff, and, ah, sometimes it gets to the point where, well, where we just can't get it all out of the way in the afternoon. We have to tell somebody that they'll, they'll have to wait till the next morning.

(I-20. This again appears as a statement that incorporates unnecessarily in the interviewer role material which the interviewer has acquired in his role as supervisor. The interviewer has certain facts about the situation, and he is obviously laboring to get the respondent to bring forth material in the same area. Nevertheless, the question with which I-20 ends is well worded and effective. In R-20, the respondent begins to show the good effects of some of the reassurance which he has received, and he elaborates further the kinds of difficulties in which he has found himself.)

21. I : This must cause a real problem for you sometimes. How do the men, how do the men take this?

R : Well, some of 'em, some of 'em take it pretty well. Some of 'em understand that, ah, that we've got our problems, too. Most of 'em, I guess, ah, are thinking mainly about their, their own work and ah. . . .

(I-21. Proceeding with the funnel sequence of questions, the interviewer now asks a somewhat more restrictive question focused on the respondent's relations with other people in the work situation.)

22. I : Yeah, I suppose that's natural.

R : . . . wishing they could get it out. Once in a while we get a guy who gets pretty nasty about it.

23. I : Yeah, I guess that's right, Joel. As a matter of fact, one of the, ah, reasons why I thought we ought to have a talk this morning was, ah, one of the men was in yesterday, ah, saying that he was having some real problems, ah, getting some of the work out of your group. Ah, he thought maybe we ought to have a general talk to find out what kind of problems we're having, you're having with your operation. See if there is anything we could do.

R : Yeah. Well, I thought that might be it. Well, whatever you say.

(I-23. This is a rather defensively delivered bit of communication by the interviewer. From the beginning of the interview he has been in a situation in which he had a good deal of information regarding the respondent and regarding the specific difficulties in which the respondent found himself on the previous day. However, the interviewer has chosen, in his supervisory role, to keep this information to himself while attempting as an interviewer to get the respondent to discuss some of the same material. This has posed a problem which is more one of administration and interpersonal ethics than interviewing technique. At this point in the interview, the interviewer apparently has decided that he can no longer pretend to be uninformed on the topic. Apparently feeling some defensiveness at not having communicated the information earlier, he admits the episode which led to this interview.

In order to communicate this material, it is necessary for the interviewer to get out of his interviewing role and assume the supervisory role. The result of this communication is by no means good. The respondent answers in a way that emphasizes the supervisor-subordinate relationship. Moreover, the response [R-23] clearly suggests that the respondent had his own suspicions about the basis for the interview, and that these suspicions have now been confirmed.

It is certainly questionable whether the procedure that the interviewer is following here is desirable. On the other hand, it is difficult to predict whether the interview would have followed a more effective course had it begun with a statement from the interviewer as to the circumstances which had caused him to summon his subordinate. It is entirely possible that such an introduction would have created difficulties more serious than those which are here encountered.)

24. I : Well, as I say, I wasn't ah, I wasn't calling you in specifically for this, Joel. I don't want you to get the idea I brought you in here to give you hell or anything of this sort. But I know that when we, we have a lot of people working together like this, once in a while there's almost bound to be, ah, friction develop, unevenness of the work. It's particularly true when we've been working as hard as we have. We've all been putting in all kinds of hours, and I know as well as you do how hard you people have all been working. But I thought that, ah, it's been some time since we've had a general discussion and this, ah, just reminded me this might be a good time to talk things over generally. Ah, I just want to reassure you

that I'm not really trying to put the finger on you at all here. Why don't you tell me a little bit more about what went on yesterday, and we'll see if we can't work something out.

R : Well, I, I suppose if you come right down to it, it wasn't much. It was one of those things that happens. Ah, about four-thirty we were rushed as we could be. Johnson came plowing in with some work he said had to get out.

(I-24. The interviewer clearly feels uncomfortable about the material he has communicated and the respondent's somewhat resentful reaction to it. He appears not entirely certain what to say. He is still out of the interviewer role, but is anxious to leave his supervisory role for the more comfortable interviewer-respondent relationship. He does reassert the constructive purpose of the interview and his desire to bring about a remedy to any existing difficulties. In R-24 the respondent shows some acceptance of the situation. He appears to be somewhat reassured although still on the defensive.)

25. I : Well, just one of those things, huh.

R : Yeah, I, I guess that's, that's it. He, ah, he just kept yelling that work had to get out, and I began by not knowing how we could do it. I guess before he was done I sounded off a bit myself.

26. I : Well, Joel, I can see why this might have really got under your skin. Ah, I suspect it's not very pleasant, when you're doing a job, to have someone really land on you like this.

R : That's right, and I felt that he really wasn't justified. He stood there saying that he had to have the work out. Never thought to say "Joel can you get it out?" No. "I gotta have it!"

(R-26. The respondent appears to be considerably reassured by the encouragement and patience which the interviewer has shown. He is now communicating material, but it is material not wholly relevant to the objectives of the interview. Apparently the respondent wishes to talk about the personal aspects of the difficulty, whereas the interviewer's objectives require a discussion of the situation apart from the personalities involved.)

27. I : Well, Joel, as I said before, I'm not particularly interested in this, ah, problem between you and Johnson. Ah, I don't

want to get into that too much. What I am interested in is whether this represents a general kind of problem for you, and whether there's something we can do about it.

R : We're not servants just because we run a typing pool. We're a service section all right, but not a servant section, and it isn't up to him to treat us as if we were.

(I-27. The interviewer plays a purposefully directive role in getting the interview back on the objectives. It is especially important to the interviewer to redirect the content of the interview at this time, because in his supervisory role he wishes to avoid a situation in which one employee is reporting some series of hostilities with another. In R-27 the respondent does not pay much attention to the interviewer's attempt at reorientation. Apparently there is a good deal of emotion here, and he is intent on completing the ventilation process.)

28. I : Yeah. Well, ah, as I say, Joel, I can sure see why you would be upset by this but, ah, let's look at it more generally for a moment. Ah, is, is this problem of, ah, having to get out more work than you can at a particular time of day, ah, a general problem? I think that you've indicated before that the work tends to pile up, and I wonder whether there is something we may be able to do that would help out this situation.

R : Well, there're really a lot of things that could be done. If people would agree to do them.

(I-28. The interviewer makes a second attempt at reorientation here, and in the process reasserts the constructive purpose of the interview. Apparently the respondent [R-28] has gotten rid of enough emotion so that he can now listen and pay attention to the interviewer's attempts to move the conversation toward a more constructive outcome.)

29. I : Ah, will you tell me more? What kind of things do you have in mind here?

R : Well, for instance. Why, why can't we have a rule that anything that comes to our section after two in the afternoon doesn't get out till the next morning?

(I-29. With this question we move into a series of questions and answers in which both interviewer and respondent are clearly in the area of problem-solving. In this discussion the interviewer is restricting his conversation to general kinds of probe questions.)

30. I : Ah, well, that might be one possibility. Ah, let's explore this a little more. Do you have any other thoughts in mind that might help out things?

R : Well, I should think, ah, another possibility might be to have somebody make decisions about what's important and what can be delayed. If a couple guys come in toward the end of the day, each one waving a letter and saying that it has to be typed, and we only have time to do one of them, which one do we do?

31. I : What you're saying is that you'd like to have somebody who protects you from this, ah, problem of overload, so that you don't have to cope with that, is that it?

R : Well, I don't know whether I mean just protect, but there are decisions to be made and somebody has to make them so they'll be accepted.

(I-31. The interviewer asks a question that is essentially a reflection of the previous statements by the respondent, all of which imply that the solution to the problem lies in change on the part of others. Apparently the interviewer wants to see if the respondent is at all aware that the solution might involve action or change on his own part. It seems likely, however, that the interviewer has somewhat overstated the sense of the respondent's previous communications. The respondent [R-31] shows some tendency toward rejection of the interviewer's formulation, but on the whole he accepts the content.)

32. I : Yeah, I guess that's right. But let's, ah, let's look at it from another point of view for a minute. Ah, as I indicated to you earlier, I suspect, well, you know as well as I this kind of pressure is going to continue on us. Ah, is there anything that you think you could do in your section that might, ah, prevent some of the problems of this sort?

R : I suppose we could always have more girls working, but that gets kind of expensive.

(I-32. This question represents a further step-down in the funnel sequence, and requires the respondent to focus

257

specifically on the question of changes in his own operation. The respondent's answers in this area are meager
and grudging, but he does follow in the direction which
the interviewer's question suggests.)

33. I : Yeah, particularly since you indicated that, ah, sometimes
in the morning the girls weren't fully occupied as it is, huh?

R : Yes, I did say that. Of course, of course, it doesn't happen
very often, and I suppose that there is the possibility of, of
staggering the hours a little, of having some girls come in
later. We could even have a night shift. I don't know. The
girls don't like to work irregular hours. You know. Their
free time is pretty important to 'em.

(I-33, represents a statement on the part of the interviewer which is factually accurate but is undesirable
interviewing technique. Here he confronts the respondent
with an apparent inconsistency in his point of view. It is
difficult to specify what the intent of this question is, and
it may indeed have been quite benign. Nevertheless, there
seems to be some tendency to needle the respondent at this
point. The respondent [R 33], either because of or in spite
of the previous question, for the first time comes up with
a suggestion that involves meaningful change in his own
operation.)

34. I : Yeah, I can see why it might be. There is the one possibility
you've mentioned of the, of staggering the hours. Ah, are
there any other kinds of adjustments you think could be
made that will help out?

R : Well, I don't really know. I have thought sometimes about
having a night shift, or at least a skeleton crew on the second shift. It would raise some supervisory problems, but it
might be more efficient than overtime in the long run.

(I-34 and I-35. The interviewer attempts to make the most
of this line of response by stimulating the respondent to
think further about the problem and the kinds of solutions
which might be developed in answer to it.)

35. I : Uh-huh. This might be a possible solution. Is there anything
else that you think might help out?

R : Well, I'm just going to tell you straight out, Mr. Blake, but
I think the real solution doesn't lie in having the girls work

odd hours or getting more girls. It lies in, in having the people who hand work to us understand what we're up against and, ah, if that doesn't do it, in having some system of priorities that will even things out for us.

(R-35. Apparently the respondent has no further ideas to contribute and here returns to the assertion that the most appropriate solution to the problem lies with people other than himself. This is a further rejection of the notion that he perhaps needs to change.)

36. I : Well, I gather, at least the implication of what you're saying, Joel, is that, ah, the solution to this problem lies not with you at all but with somebody else entirely. Is that the way you feel about it?

R : Well, that, that, that's, I suppose it did kinda sound that way. I don't mean that there isn't something we could do too. I, I'm willing to meet the other men halfway on this thing.

(I-36. Here the interviewer attempts to summarize the respondent's attitude. The notion of a summary at this point, to which the respondent can either accede or take exception, is probably appropriate. It seems, however, that the interviewer has overstated the content of the respondent's previous statements. A more neutral summary would clearly have been preferable. The respondent [R-36] feels the needle and reacts by becoming defensive, in much the fashion that characterized some of the early exchanges in the interview.)

37. I : Yeah. Well, I didn't mean to say that there wasn't anything you felt you could do, but it seemed to me what you were saying is that the most of the adjustment was going to have to be made by other people, and I just want to be sure that's the way you really felt about it.

R : Well, let's put it this way. I won't say that most of the adjustment has to be made by other people, but the way it looks to me now, ah, it would be cheapest and most efficient if we could work it out on that basis.

(I-37. This represents a disavowal on the part of the interviewer of any aggressive attempt. If this were an earlier phase of the interview, the interviewer would have the problem of getting back into role and out of the supervisor-subordinate situation. As it is, he can move more definitely into the supervisory role and proceed to bring the interview to a close. This he does, beginning with I-38.)

38. I : Well, Joel, look. This, ah, this gives me an idea. I think you, you're perfectly right that, ah, when we get into things of this sort there's no simple solution in sense of one person changing. Ah, why don't we do this. Why don't we, ah, set up a meeting in the next two or three days and let me get together a couple of people who have the most call on the pool and somebody from Personnel and you and me, and let's sit down and see whether we can't work out some different procedures that will help us out in this. How's that sound to you?

R : Well, that sounds pretty good to me. I'm, I'm not anxious to continue the present hassle that started yesterday.

(I-38, with its clear communication of an administrative or action decision, conveys the words of the supervisor rather than those of an interviewer.)

39. I : Well, O.K. then. Suppose, ah, suppose I try to set this up in the next day or two and I'll, ah, I'll let you know as soon as we can get it set up. I think that's a good idea. Thanks a lot for coming in, Joel.

R : That's all right.

40. I : We'll be seeing you soon, then.

R : Yeah.

41. I : Swell. So long.

Chapter 9

Conferences and
Meetings

*It is no secret that a generous segment of Goodyearites are
something less than enthusiastic about meetings. In fact, some
quietly confess they think many of our meetings are a pain in the
neck. And that is too bad. It is too bad because in a big, modern
company like ours, the group meeting is essential for the following
very good reasons:*

> *Delivers information to a group—fast.*
>
> *Holds misunderstandings to a minimum.*
>
> *Saves time formerly spent writing and answering umpteen
> memos or letters.*
>
> *Produces immediate reactions and uncovers new ideas.*
>
> *Relaxes tensions.*
>
> *Gets conflicts, confusions, disagreements out into the healthy
> air of group discussion.*
>
> *Produces decisions that reduce chance of being wrong.*[1]

Goodyear Tire & Rubber Company

CONFERENCES AND MEETINGS HAVE BECOME AN INDISPENSABLE PART
of the ordinary conduct of any institution—so indispensable, in fact,
that a study made at the University of Michigan found some executives to be spending an average of ten hours a week in conferences,
or almost a quarter of their working time. Current trends toward in-

---

[1] "Let's Hold Better Meetings," by permission of the Goodyear Tire &
Rubber Company.

creasing specialization and decentralization, noted in Chapter 1, impose the necessity of conferring. Specialization requires that those of disparate training and responsibility get together to integrate their knowledge, skill, and authority in a common task, while decentralization imposes the necessity of coordinating the efforts of smaller units toward the purposes of the main organization.

Nevertheless, when you are called to a "conference," you cannot be sure of exactly what is going to happen when you arrive at the appointed place. The name does not tell you either the form or function of the gathering, for it is used loosely in a wide variety of meanings.

Consider the following statements, and the meaning implied by the word "conference" in each.

"Mr. Jones is in conference and can't see you for an hour." (Mr. Jones is in his office writing a report and doesn't want to be disturbed.)

"I had a conference with the boss." (I had an interview with him.)

"We went to a three-day conference at Atlantic City." (We attended a convention.)

"Joe is a conference leader at the Temperate Zone Corporation." (Joe is an instructor in the training department.)

"The manager has called a conference on the rock-cut separation of our earth-mover tires." (We've got a problem to solve on one of our products.)

From this array of meanings for the word "conference," two conclusions should be apparent. First, I must define the way in which the term will be used in this book, and second, you will have to understand that others will not always use the word in the meaning we assign to it.

In this book we shall use the word "conference" to designate a gathering of from 4 to 20 people who have convened to *think together as a team*. In theory at least, not one of them brings with him a predetermined opinion or stand which he is prepared to defend or which he hopes to persuade others to accept. On the contrary, each is prepared to help in the active search for, or creation of, the outcome which the session is organized to attain. Thus the conference is characterized by an attitude of inquiry, a spirit of cooperation, and a willingness to communicate fully and freely within a framework of reflective thinking.

In a conference, therefore, every person is an active participant throughout the entire session, interacting with every other in continuing dialogue. Although the conference is usually under the guidance of a competent leader, his function is not that of a master of ceremonies directing a program of arranged speeches. He can be thought of, rather, as a catalyst, in that he does not enter into the substance of the group reaction but is a prime means of effecting it.

When a conference is decision-making or problem-solving, its effectiveness is determined by the value of its product. When the conference is for learning, its effectiveness is determined by the quality of the process of thinking which takes place.

There are business and professional gatherings, however, which do not possess these characteristics, despite the fact that to an outsider they may *look* like a conference, even to the number of people gathered around a conference table. Such events are noncreative, and I shall call them "meetings."

Those who attend a meeting usually expect to be either active or passive participants. The responsibility of the passive ones is largely limited to listening, or perhaps to asking questions, whereas the active members arrive with a speech to make, an opinion to defend, or a predetermined objective to attain. They are not there to inquire, but to tell or persuade. The talk is apt to be a discourse or series of discourses, with possibly some argument back and forth, and although the leader is competent, he seeks a minimum of interaction. The ideas, the content, indeed, the entire session, may have been planned and packaged beforehand. It is not a decision-making group, although it may be a decision-confirming group, or in some cases a learning group.

From the foregoing description I think you can see that speech behavior which is appropriate in a conference is not appropriate at a meeting, and vice versa. When you are part of a conference, such as a committee of city council charged with the responsibility of determining how best to improve municipal port facilities, or a gathering of department heads to establish a budget for the coming year, you will discuss in a spirit of investigation. But when you are in a meeting, such as a gathering of sales employees to hear a manufacturer's representative describe a new product, or an assembly of office workers who will be told of plans for moving to a new building, you will listen and ask questions or you will make a speech.

On the basis of these distinctions, which are admittedly simplified, we now take up the problems and patterns of conferences and meetings.

A CONFERENCE IS AN OPPORTUNITY
FOR PEOPLE TO THINK CREATIVELY
TOGETHER

The conference can be a way of implementing the philosophy of participative management which has developed during recent years. According to Keith Davis,[2] despite problems of developing it, participation does have great potential for increasing productivity, improving morale, bettering human relations, and releasing creative thinking. To him the need of people to participate seems to be one of man's basic drives. Through conference processes men can release this drive, come to feel that they are shareholders in the real task of managing an institution, and know that they have some voice in determining their own destiny.

Participation through conferences can offer a number of benefits to an organization.

1. It can improve morale in the group by satisfying the basic want to belong.
2. It can result in better decisions by drawing on the knowledge and experience of many, thus helping to avoid unwise judgment.
3. It can provide a communication medium by bringing into face-to-face relationship a group of people who must share information and ideas.
4. It can help to improve or modify the attitudes of participants as they gain insight into the attitudes and viewpoints of others.
5. It can help develop a more willing acceptance of change, the members having a sense of participation in the process of change.

Conferences are not an unmixed blessing, however, as anyone knows after sitting through a number of them, for as one businessman remarked in disgust, "You sit, and talk, and adjourn." Indeed, waste of time and slowness of decision often constitute good reasons for avoiding conferences. There are, though, other disadvantages

[2] See Chapter 22, "Development of Participation," in Keith Davis, *Human Relations at Work* (New York: McGraw-Hill Book Company, Inc., 1962).

264

even more considerable. One of these is the fact that because a group's judgment must be bland enough to be acceptable to everyone, a group decision will sometimes not be as good as one man alone could make. When the decision must please everyone it is often one which displeases no one and therefore it may be timid and inconclusive.

There are times, too, when a committee is given the responsibility for a decision only because no individual is willing to accept that responsibility or because the person who should make a decision is afraid. When responsibility is divided, no person feels fully accountable.

The conference method may in itself limit its own usefulness, for it is essentially a democratic procedure and therefore incongruent with the authoritarian structure of many organizations. Furthermore, some subjects and some decisions do not lend themselves to judgment by discussion, being more suitable to objective inquiry, measurement, or executive determination.

After comparing the benefits and limitations of the conference, however, the editors of *Time* have concluded that, "Despite all the jeering and complaints, most businessmen agree that in a complex, highly diversified company, conferences are essential. . . . There is no doubt that conferences are likely to become even more solidly established as a handy management tool—if wisely used."[3] It is the purpose of this chapter to help you learn to use them more wisely. To do so, you should first become acquainted with the major applications of the conference method.

The conference method is applied in a variety of situations

We have defined a conference as a gathering of people whose function is to think creatively, and who must therefore talk together. The purpose of their talk is to solve a problem, to determine a policy, or to make a decision. At least seven major kinds of conferences can be identified, each having variations; some conferences combine characteristics of more than one of the major kinds.

STAFF CONFERENCES. By far the most common conference is the staff conference. In its typical form, it brings together a supe-

---

[3] "Company Conferences: The Perils of Table-Sitting," *Time*, LXVI, No. 26 (Dec. 26, 1955), p. 56.

rior and his subordinates at any level of organization, whether it be a president and his officers or a supervisor and his crew. The meetings are usually for the purpose of solving problems which face the staff as a unit, or for creating policy which the superior or executive will then administer. A variety of the staff conference exists when a group of equals meets under mutually selected leadership, sometimes with members of other involved groups participating.

COMMITTEES. For all practical purposes, committees are as common as staff conferences. A committee is a unit in an organization and is made up of individuals who do not normally work together, but who have been assigned to collaborate for a particular purpose. The work of a committee is usually a task which does not fall clearly within the responsibility of any given office or official and which can best be discharged by collective action. A committee may be a permanent part of the organizational structure or it may be a temporary force assigned to a one-time mission, to be dissolved when that function has been completed. As noted earlier, when a committee is set up to do something which should be done by an individual, committee action constitutes one of the weaknesses of the conference method.

PRODUCTION CONFERENCES. The production conference may be considered a special variant of the staff conference, except that its leadership is vested in a trained conference leader instead of residing in a superior line or staff officer. Originated in the stress of World War II, the production conference was a gathering of supervisors directed toward the practical solution of problems on the production line. It applied a simplified version of the problem-solving conference pattern which will be outlined later in this chapter, and the suggested solutions were forwarded to higher management for appraisal. In addition to the practical effect of improving production, the conference was found to be an effective method of communicating upward in the organization and a useful device for training foremen and supervisors.

TRAINING OR LEARNING CONFERENCES. The training conference is perhaps an updated version of the production conference, although it is now used at any level of management instead of only at the supervisory. It is usually a part of the operation of the

266

training, education, or personnel department, and is employed in developing desirable attitudes and understandings more than in presenting information. In this light the training conference based on a problem-solving pattern should be distinguished from one utilizing an informational design.

The problem-solving type of learning conference uses the same form and procedure as the normal conference, the reflective-thought structure providing the organization for each. The difference is that, whereas the value of the true problem-solving conference lies in the *product*, the value of the learning conference lies in the *process*. The participants learn through being involved in the process of solving a problem. The very act of exchanging information, of ventilating opinions, and of appraising and criticizing ideas constitutes a milieu in which learning and personal growth can take place.

There are several sorts of learning conferences, each a variation of the reflective-thought process, the difference largely being in the kind of problem used and the techniques of attacking it. In some an actual problem of the organization is considered and the conference carried through to agreement on possible solutions; in one of the major automobile manufacturing companies, for instance, one of the discussions centered on the abuse of shop privileges by workers. Other learning conferences use the case method or the incident method, the discussion stemming from a problem-situation chosen by the leader-instructor, the case or incident usually being real but selected from outside the organization for its potential learning value. Sometimes motion pictures, slides, or role playing situations serve to initiate the discussion, which is directed at principles involved in the situations portrayed. When cases, incidents, or situations provide the content, the conference generally does not attempt to arrive at agreement, but is content to explore principles, exchange ideas, and challenge opinions, allowing each conferee to reach his own conclusions. In all learning conferences the process is for the purpose of modifying attitudes, sharpening perceptions and broadening horizons, these being the learning outcomes desired.

The training or learning conference which does not use a problem-solving stucture can be organized in three basic steps: (1) The leader draws knowledge, facts, or experience from the conferees by means of questions, (2) the material thus elicited is appraised or organized by the leader, sometimes with the help of the conferees, and often principles or concepts are developed, (3) the possible use,

significance, or future application of the results of Step 2 is deline-
ated, either by the leader himself, or through the interaction of the
leader with the conferees. This is a method of reconstructing experience so that knowledge or experience takes on new significance. A
cashier for a savings and loan association, for instance, reports
participating in a learning conference in which the experience of a
number of cashiers was examined in such a way that the leader was
able to get the conferees to see their jobs in a new light, bringing
about an improvement in over-the-counter customer relations.

This kind of learning conference requires skilled leadership of
a different nature from the problem-solving sort. Here the leader
must know clearly what he intends to help the students learn, must
have an understanding of the students' background that he may
know the amount and kind of experience from which he may draw,
and must be skilled in leading the conferees to make the choices and
conclusions he would like them to possess.

The number of variations of these two types of learning conferences include the panel, the symposium, the forum, the collo-
quium, the Phillips 66 plan, and the buzz session, none of which we
have space to consider. We can only note the existence of these
variants, so you may be aware of them.

TASK CONFERENCES. The task conference is similar to a committee in that it brings together for a specific purpose a group of
people who do not normally function as a unit, but each of whom
has a responsibility toward the task to be accomplished by the
group. Frequently the members of the conference belong to different
organizations or institutions, each representing some facet of responsibility in the mission of the group and each charged with
contributing special knowledge or special competency to the collective outcome. An outbreak of rabies in the wildlife of an area of my
state created a need for a unified policy to meet the situation.
Consequently a meeting was called at which representatives of the
County Commissioners, the County Health Department, the State
Health Department, the County Prosecutor, the County Dog
Warden, and local veterinarians sought the best way to deal with
the situation. Similar conferences of specialists are becoming an
increasing necessity in our complex society as our problems outgrow
the ability of a single office or organization to meet them.

CONSULTATIVE CONFERENCES. When we face the realities of
business or industrial organization we must realize that there are

many situations in which a manager must be solely and personally responsible for a decision, and, as pointed out, there are situations in which one person can make a better decision than can a group. Under these conditions it would be an abdication of responsibility for one individual to turn his duty over to a conference or committee, or even to pretend to do so. Yet too often a conference is called under the pretext of making a decision when everyone knows that the real outcome will be determined by the leader.

Under circumstances like these, it is much wiser to admit the realities of the case, and to call the meeting a consultative conference. A consultative conference, then, is one in which the leader makes clear that he himself will make the final decision, but that he needs and wants the full advice of his staff or organization to help him assemble and appraise data, and evaluate all possible alternatives. Men will respond positively in an advisory capacity who would have a negative attitude toward the fiction of participating in the full decision-making process.

The consultative conference is, of course, a part of the normal procedure in many institutions, since it is well suited to their authoritarian nature. Some institutions, like the military, must, by their very character, have an absolute hierarchy of authority and responsibility, and no industrial or business organization can be a pure democracy. Within institutions of this sort the consultative conference can be a major instrument for helping responsible leaders make wise decisions.

CREATIVE VARIATIONS. With the purpose of increasing creative power through group inter-stimulation, two kinds of conferences have been developed which relate to the problem-solving process. The first, commonly called brainstorming, has been widely used in a wide range of settings. The second, termed "Synectics" by its inventor, William J. J. Gordon, is much less widely known and used.

Brainstorming is simply described as the solution-creating stage of the reflective thinking process. Under the stimulus of Alex Osborn and the Creative Education Foundation of Buffalo, New York, a set of rules has been developed and popularized, following which a dozen people or fewer can produce in a relatively short time from 50 to 150 ideas bearing on the solution to a problem. In action brainstorming is a free-wheeling "bull session." No idea is rejected, and even the wildest are welcomed, the purpose being to list many ideas as rapidly as they can be produced. No judgment nor criticism of any suggestion is allowed, but combination and improvement of ideas in a chain reaction is strongly encouraged, the process being termed "hitch-hiking." The basic rationale is that quantity and quality of thought go hand in hand, that if many ideas can be created a few will inevitably be good ones. Therefore the list of ideas produced in a brainstorming session is later evaluated, usually by one or more persons who were not a part of the session itself.

Although the popularity of brainstorming has apparently passed its peak, and although doubts have been voiced as to whether group creativity is actually superior to a single creative mind, the method has produced excellent results for many organizations.

Synectics, which grew form the efforts of Gordon and the Cambridge Synectics Group to discover the principles of creativity, is a group process dedicated to invention, creation, and discovery. It places greater stress on the emotional and irrational components of creativity than on the rational, attempting to invent by making the familiar strange and the strange familiar through methods of analogy. Recorded interaction among members of the group is important both to the Group's pure research into the process of creativity, and to the industrial applications of the methodology the Group has developed. Through interaction which helps reverse the strange and the familiar, new perceptions and new insights are created. The results of this process have been productive for a number of industries, among the products being a new closure for space suits. Unlike brainstorming, in which almost anyone can participate, the members of a Synectics group are carefully selected and trained.

THE CONFERENCE METHOD ORGANIZES THE INTERACTIONS OF PEOPLE THINKING TOGETHER

From our discussion thus far you can see that a conference is a particular kind of speaking situation in which you may be called upon to play a part. Your ability to behave appropriately in a conference will depend upon your understanding of the nature of the situation and the kind of speaking called for. Therefore, in this section we shall examine the rationale and functioning of the problem-solving conference, namely that those involved are expected (1) to think, and (2) to do so as a team. The kind of thinking needed is that commonly known as reflective or creative, a sort of thinking which you have unconsciously done whenever you faced a difficulty and deliberately plotted a way to overcome it. Such thinking begins with an awareness that something is wrong, it identifies the trouble, searches for solutions, and chooses the solution which appears to be most likely to resolve the difficulty. We can identify the stages of this process by asking four simple questions: What is the problem? What causes the problem? What are the possible solutions? Which solution is best? The production conference, already noted, employed a version of this pattern in three stages and a slightly different order. These were: What is the objective? What are the obstacles? What are the solutions?

You, yourself, probably have very little difficulty in using this thought-pattern, for with a little practice most people can learn to put it to work. For instance, suppose that you foresee an important engagement on the week-end and suddenly realize that you do not have a suitable pair of shoes. You have recognized the problem, and realizing that the cause is momentarily irrelevant, your mind turns to solutions. You can borrow your roommate's, have your own repaired, or buy a new pair. Since your roommate's shoes do not fit you and you can't afford a new pair right now, you elect the remaining alternative. You'll have your old ones repaired. Your mind moves from problem to solution smoothly and easily.

But suppose you held a conference on the problem? With several other people helping make the decision, the thought process becomes more complex. One thinks faster than you, another more slowly. One tends to get off the track by suggesting that maybe you ought to scrap your plans, while the joker of the lot insists that you go barefoot. The pattern of thinking which was simple for you alone has become complicated and devious only because others have participated in the thinking. Although our example is unsophisticated, it suggests that getting people to think *as a team* requires a concert of effort toward a common goal.

The thought process of a conference is conditioned by the interpersonal relations of those participating

From the foregoing you can see that you are involved with two elements in a conference. The first is the thought-pattern, which we shall take up in greater detail in the next section. The second is the intricate interplay of the people and personalities brought together into the conference. A successful conference must accomplish an integration of the two elements so that the desires and energies of the participants will be directed toward a rational solution of the problem rather than impeding it.

Harold P. Zelko of the Pennsylvania State University calls this interplay of people "discussion dynamics," and lists ten elements which contribute to the pattern of forces at work.[4] They are:

The individual backgrounds of each member of the group.

The status and position of each member.

The emotional involvement of each member toward the subject.

The relationship of the members toward each other.

The status and position of the leader in relation to the members.

The leader-group relationship in relation to the subject and outcome.

The relative amount of leader and of group participation.

The relative amount and type of participation of each member.

The effect of certain leadership methods, tools, and characteristics of the discussion.

The effect of physical surroundings on the discussion.

You can understand that almost everything which you have so far read in this book can be applied to your talking in a conference, particularly the chapters on understanding people and on person-to-person speaking. There are three additional observations, however, which have special significance to successful conferences.

The first of these is to recognize that in each conference there will be a personal "hidden agenda" for almost every participant. Despite the fact that there will be a conference agenda for the group's business, each individual will likely be guided or influenced by his personal goals—the things which he consciously or unconsciously hopes to obtain from the event. There will be unspoken thoughts, hidden attitudes, and concealed ideas. One person will be unwilling to give up a favorite solution. Another may be so beset by doubts and fears that in effect he is apt to sabotage the conference. A third hopes to obtain special advantages for his department by

---

[4] Harold P. Zelko, *Successful Conference and Discussion Techniques* (New York: McGraw-Hill Book Company, Inc., 1957), pp. 14–15.

influencing the decision, while a fourth nervously awaits the end so he can be about business he considers of greater importance. Sometimes participants bring items of hidden agenda to the meeting, and sometimes such items develop during the discussion.

There is no sure way of either detecting or dealing with the hidden agenda. Sometimes it can be handled effectively by bringing it into the open, while at other times to expose a hidden item could wreck the conference. Sincere and careful listening is always of supreme importance, as is avoiding emotional responses to the remarks of another. The best conference participation demands a high degree of discrimination and tact in dealing with what other people say.

The second observation is that a conference should be characterized by a permissive atmosphere. By this I mean that every person should feel free to speak his honest thoughts without fear of ridicule, condemnation, or reprisal of any kind. The conference will achieve its maximum productivity only when ideas are freely offered and fully and critically appraised, and such a vital examination of ideas cannot be obtained unless each participant feels free to offer his opinions and express his feelings. Securing a permissive atmosphere is the responsibility of every participant, including the leader, each of whom must respect the thoughts and feelings of others. Every idea should be given a full hearing and accepted or rejected on its own merits; the person offering it must not be given cause to regret his contribution.

The final observation is that a conference is more likely to be successful when the serious business is occasionally interrupted by moments of relaxation than when it operates under the continuous tension of grim efficiency. Humor has its place in the most earnest conference, and moments of good fellowship can frequently make possible another fifteen minutes of concentrated effort. After listening to two hundred conferences, Irving Lee wrote, "In some of the most satisfying discussions I have watched there was a continuous alternation of mood. The members swung between the serious and the playful, the relevant and the remote, kidding each other and laughing at the problem, with thrusts at the problem and inexplicable asides."[5]

The effect of interpersonal dynamics, then, can be critical in many conferences. As McCall and Cohen have observed, "Each

[5] Irving J. Lee, *How to Talk with People* (New York: Harper & Brothers, 1952), pp. 159–60.

person brings his total personality to the group, but some modification occurs due to the interaction with other members of the group. In short, the success or failure of group communication may often be attributed to the interpersonal relations between group members."[6]

When the interaction of participants is productively channeled into the reflective-thought sequence, the conference has its best chance of success. It is this sequence to which we now turn.

The conference structure follows the stages of reflective thinking

We have already noted that the process of creative thinking can be organized into a series of steps and it is the sequence of these steps which provide the structure of a conference. Ordinarily the conferees begin with the first step and arrive at an agreement on it, after which they go on to the next step, and so on. In practice, however, the steps are likely to overlap, and the conferees may find it necessary to retrace their path, returning to a step presumably settled earlier. There are digressions, too, as one or more men allow the talk to wander into by-paths. Yet the fundamental sequence remains, and provides the basic structure necessary to coordinate the thinking of all. We shall consider it as a series of six steps.

1. WHAT IS THE PROBLEM? A conference gets off to a strong start only when the problem itself is clearly defined and understood. Some people even prefer to call the conference a "problem-stating, problem-solving" meeting, to emphasize the importance of knowing unmistakeably the character and dimensions of the difficulty before seeking a solution or decision.

Under normal conditions it is undoubtedly preferable to name the problem at the very outset, using a declarative statement to express the difficulty. A common practice, and one which can lead to poor thinking, is to begin by expressing the subject of the conference in the form of a question. The question opening tends to direct the conferees immediately into a consideration of solutions, causing them to neglect a thorough analysis of the problem itself, whereas a declarative statement invites appraisal and analysis before solution.

---

[6] Roy C. McCall and Herman Cohen, *Fundamentals of Speech: The Theory and Practice of Oral Communication,* Second Edition (New York: The Macmillan Company, 1963), p. 202.

Thus it would be better to start a conference with the statement, "Too many employees are jumping the clock at quitting time," than with the question, "How can we reduce clock jumping among our employees?" The following list illustrates typical problem-statements:

The men in the shop are not utilizing waste materials.

Rest room privileges are being abused.

Trucks are forced to wait too long before unloading at our docks.

Our customers are complaining about the high cost of service calls.

Material on bulletin boards is not being read.

Down-time on machines in Plant X is increasing.

Noise in the building is distracting.

The simple declarative statement, however, is generally not more than a good beginning, for it is usually necessary to come to grips more fully with the problem. To do this the participants may find it helpful to size the difficulty up by objective measurement, to search for answers to such analytical questions as *Where? What? How? Who? When?,* or to inquire into the location, nature, extent, and significance of the problem. To return to the clock jumping problem, it would be useful to be more specific by at least determining that employees in the finishing department are losing an average of ten minutes a day by stopping work before the end of the shift, totalling a man-hour loss of sixty hours per month.

Good team-work in thinking, then, begins when all the members of a conference recognize that the problem to be solved affects each of them, when they can reach a common understanding of it, and when each sees that he will benefit in some way by helping find the best solution.

2. WHAT ARE THE CAUSES OF THE PROBLEM? The second step attempts to answer the question Why? There are times when the solution will be found by isolating and overcoming the significant causes of the difficulty, and even when the causes themselves cannot be overcome, knowing them will add insight to the deliberation. Ideally, all major causes should be listed, appraised, and agreed upon by the conferees.

Continuing with the clock jumping problem, we might find such items as these listed among the causes:

Time card racks contain so many cards that men quit early to avoid standing in line.

Time card racks are at a distance from work locations, so men get started toward them early to avoid waiting past the quitting time.

Cards are printed in small type, making men look carefully for the right card; this takes time.

Men avoid starting a new piece of work when they know the job will run past the quitting time.

3. WHAT ARE THE STANDARDS OF A DESIRABLE SOLUTION? This third step may not always be necessary, but it is more frequently useful than not, and is apt to be overlooked. If the group can agree at this point on the criteria or specifications of the solution for which they are looking, they may eliminate later conflict when appraising the solutions themselves. For instance, if they can agree whether the solution must cost not more than a given amount, they have a handy measure for judging the desirability of solutions. Or if they decide whether the solution should have an immediate or a long-range effect, they are similarly in a better position to judge.

Norman R. F. Maier makes a significant observation which is pertinent here. He writes, "Two different dimensions seem to be relevant in appraising a decision's potential effectiveness. One of these is the objective or impersonal *quality* of the decision; the other has to do with its *acceptance* or the way the persons who must execute the decision *feel* about it."[7] A quality decision which is not acceptable to a number of people may be ineffective, whereas a decision of lesser quality but of greater acceptability may be quite effective. These two dimensions may not be mutually inconsistent in every case, but they are worthy of consideration as important guides to a productive solution.

4. WHAT ARE THE POSSIBLE SOLUTIONS? In the fourth step, the conference becomes more creative, turning to the search for

[7] Norman R. F. Maier, *Problem-Solving Discussions and Conferences: Leadership Methods and Skills* (New York: McGraw-Hill Book Company, Inc., 1963), p. 3.

276

ways of solving the problem. This is the point at which a permissive climate is especially desirable. No potential solution should be overlooked because some member was unwilling to suggest it, being apprehensive about the consequences of his contribution.

There are two ways of proceeding at this juncture. One is to list in rapid succession as many potential solutions as can be thought of, with no attempt being made to evaluate or appraise each as it is suggested. This procedure divorces the creative from the judicial process, and is thought by some to be more productive. The other is to weigh and evaluate each solution as it comes up, in effect combining this step with what is next listed as the fifth. Either way can be effective.

We should note that while I have been using the term "solution" throughout this section, either "policy" or "decision" could be equally applicable, since we are examining the conference as a way of solving problems, creating policy, or making group decisions. The distinction lies only in the character of the outcome and not in the process by which it is produced.

Returning to the sample problem of clock jumping, we might list the following as potential solutions:

Eliminate the use of time cards altogether; make the foreman responsible for recording the presence of each worker, and assume that all work a full shift.

Have new time cards printed, using large, easily-read numbers.

Decentralize time-card racks and use smaller ones.

Pay workers by piece-rates instead of hourly rates.

Have foremen issue time-cards to workers just before the end of the shift, eliminating the need to search the rack.

Assuming that steps four and five have not been combined, the conference would then take up its judicial function.

5. WHICH IS THE PREFERABLE SOLUTION? If the standards of a desirable solution have been established, this step becomes a matter of measuring each suggested solution against those standards and choosing the one which best matches. If, however, no standards have been determined, the judicial process becomes a matter of assessing the several solutions in general, comparing them, and using whatever evidence can be secured to predict the productivity of each. During this process issues may emerge which

must be deliberated by the conferees in order to arrive at the final decision.

The decision itself may be by consensus or by majority vote. The former, involving a unanimous agreement among the conferees, is the more desirable method, especially if the degree of acceptability is a measure of the desired outcome. Consensus is frequently more possible than commonly supposed, especially if the group is not under pressure to reach a decision. Voting, the usual democratic procedure, is always an effective way of deciding, but it may leave an unsatisfied minority. Decision by negotiation or compromise is always possible in strongly divided groups.

6. WHAT SHALL BE DONE WITH THE SOLUTION? A group may not have finished its work by having arrived at a solution, for often there remains the task of putting that solution to work. Should the decision be reported? If so, to whom and under what conditions? Should the group take steps of its own to implement the solution? How far does the group responsibility go? If steps of implementation should be taken, what should be done, and who should make the effort? These questions suggest the final actions possible if the work of the conference is to bear fruit.

While the foregoing six steps can form the working structure of any conference, it would be a mistake to assume that a group will, in any one meeting, invariably follow this precise pattern. Many times the steps will form the pattern for a series of meetings, at each of which only parts of the structure will appear. At other times a group will take up a number of problems in order, repeating the pattern, or parts of it, for each item of business. There will be occasions, too, when for a variety of reasons, it is necessary to employ only certain of the steps. In short, the conference structure for creative thinking is a tool to be used appropriately in the service of the group. When it becomes a master, followed slavishly and mechanically, the vital spirit of inquiry and cooperation is notably missing.

Each participant must assume a full share of responsibility

The basic function of a conferee is to integrate his knowledge, ideas, and opinions with those of the others to create a stronger and more valid body of thought than would be possible by one person alone. In

278

so doing, the individual not only adds constructively to what others have to say, but appraises and evaluates as well. Moreover, every conferee may be able, because of his personal make-up, to add some unique quality to the work of the group as a whole. One man may be strong in coordination, able to clarify the relationships among ideas, arranging them in cohesive and meaningful form. Another may perform best by contributing from an especially rich background of information, supplying it as appears necessary, while still a third may be apt at harmonizing and reconciling divergent viewpoints, easing tensions which could otherwise trouble the conference.

There are, too, those with an equally unique knack for upsetting a conference. In addition to those who talk too much or too little, there may be the "yes-man" who is willing to agree with any superior, the manipulator whose desire is to pull strings to make the decision to his advantage, or the hard-shelled "standpatter" whose chief object is to resist the introduction of new ideas. These types do not exhaust the list of objectionable personalities, but simply suggest qualities you will want to avoid.

The following list of 12 suggestions for productive participation in a conference has been distilled from industrial, professional, and academic literature, as well as from experience. It should provide you with specific guide lines for your own efforts.

1. BE PROMPT AND REGULAR IN ATTENDANCE. Tardiness is rude, penalizing the entire group and often creating irritation which can grow into friction. Irregularity deprives the conferee of necessary continuity of understanding, and may cause the entire group to back-track so that one person can catch up. The constructive participant not only keeps appointments promptly and regularly, but also arrives quite ready to take part, having familiarized himself with the problem to be considered and having made a tentative survey of his own ideas, opinions, and solutions.

2. REALIZE THAT THE CONFERENCE BELONGS TO YOU, AND THAT ITS SUCCESS DEPENDS IN PART ON YOU. You are a part of the conference either because you possess some special understanding or capacity of value to the discussion or because you are involved in the problem and have some responsibility for its solution. In either case the conference is as much yours as anyone else's, and you are accountable for an equal share of its success or failure.

Realizing this responsibility is not enough, however; you must act on it. You should be mentally alert throughout the course of the conference, searching for significant ideas or relevant facts, integrating the fragments contributed by others, summarizing, suggesting transitions and relationships, and always trying to relate the business of the moment to the ultimate goal. In short, being an active participant means being active at all times, and not only when you are talking.

3. ENTER ENTHUSIASTICALLY INTO THE DISCUSSION, GIVING FREELY OF YOUR EXPERIENCE. Make yourself eager to take part without imposing what you have to say on others. Make your knowledge and experience fully available, but do not limit your participation to the offering of facts and ideas. Use your own background to appraise the contributions of others, taking care that you maintain an attitude of inquiry rather than of argument.

4. STICK TO THE POINT AND PROBLEM. You can promote a constructive conference by making certain that your remarks are always relevant, both to the point under discussion at the moment and to the problem and its ultimate solution. Many conferees tend to scatter the content or distort the structure by making unrelated contributions which disrupt both unity and coherence. Like most of the other conferees, you are likely to have certain ideas or opinions you are anxious to place before the group, but you should withhold these remarks until the moment they are pertinent. Keep in mind that a conference should be much like a good conversation in that it possesses a developing line of thought which may be lost if severed, and be alert to the need to "hitch-hike" on the contribution of the person speaking at the moment. Add on to what he says, expand or elaborate it, support it or point out the flaws or weaknesses, but help to keep the thought structure developing.

5. SAY WHAT YOU THINK, BUT DON'T MAKE SPEECHES. Admitting that you will participate in some conferences when it would be unwise to speak your mind freely, I must emphasize again that the best conferences take place in a permissive climate. You can help nurture such a climate by offering as fully as possible your honest views, and by behavior which encourages others to speak in similar vein.

This is not to suggest that you should talk at length at any time. Quite the contrary, your contributions should be short but clear, using the one-point method of contribution explained in Chapter 13. Remembering that you are in a conversational group, be sure that you but rarely direct what you have to say to a specific person. Instead you will find it good practice to address yourself to the group as a whole each time you speak, but in the manner of ordinary conversation. I hardly need add that it is exceedingly bad manners to carry on a private conversation with another conferee while the remainder of the group is trying to move along with the business of the day.

6. KEEP YOUR REMARKS IMPERSONAL AND FREE FROM PREJU-DICE. There will be times when you must disagree with others, but you should be tactful in doing it. An added reason for talking to the whole group instead of one individual is that the negative evaluation of an idea can be made more objective in that way. Speaking directly to an individual tends to make what you have to say take on increased personal significance, and too much sustained direct address can escalate a point at issue into a personal conflict. You can be objective and even negatively critical about an idea, promoting a productive conference, if you can remain on friendly terms with the person who offered that idea. If your attitude is objective and constructive, your manner is apt to be also; yet beware of a carping voice or a disparaging manner.

7. LISTEN ATTENTIVELY TO UNDERSTAND OTHERS. For detail on this suggestion refer to Chapter 5; the point is repeated here to emphasize that listening is a vital part of conference activity and that you should listen with the purpose first of all of discerning and appreciating the meaning intended by a speaker. Too many con-ferees seem to listen only so they may be able to comment on or criticize what they *thought* the other meant without first determin-ing if their understanding was correct or not. Test the accuracy of your listening before commenting or replying by paraphrasing the other's statement, "If I understand you correctly, you are saying that . . ." More conflict in conference develops from misunder-standing than from honest disagreement with another's views.

8. KEEP AN INQUIRING MIND; APPRECIATE THE VIEWS OF OTHERS. The constructive conferee seldom suffers from a harden-ing of opinions, but rather possesses what we might call a scientific viewpoint. That is, he values his opinions only to the degree that he

can support them factually, and is always willing to alter or amend them when new knowledge suggests a change in evaluation. His is not the vacant mind which is hospitable to everything, but the open mind which is willing to examine anything. As this kind of conferee you should seek, not only to understand clearly what your fellows say, but also to appreciate the viewpoint from which they say it. As you listen, try to visualize the angle from which the other man perceives the subject at hand, the experience which leads him to what he says. Even though you think another wrong, remember that no two people see the world alike, and that from where he sits his opinion may be reasonable.

9. Avoid Monopolizing the Discussion. While you should avoid being one of the silent members of the conference, you should equally avoid the opposite extreme as one of the loquacious. Take a full and active part in the deliberation without imposing on the time which belongs to another. There will be occasions when you will want to support your own ideas firmly and fully, as you should when there is inadequate evidence against them. But this does not mean that you must hold forth at length even in their defense. Quantity of utterance should not be confused with quality, and it is quality in both speaking and listening which marks the able conferee.

10. Assist in Reaching Conclusions. As a good conferee you should play an active role in the task of arriving at conclusions. Be alert for relationships among ideas presented, trying to discover how they may be substantively or structurally associated, reciprocal or inter-dependent. Watch, too, for ideas which are mutually inconsistent, helping to uncover what issues may lie beneath them, clarifying areas of conflict, and trying to obtain resolution of conflict through better understanding, adjustment, or compromise. All this is part of the creative function of the conference which demands your full concern.

11. Ask Questions Frequently. The well-put question can be one of your most effective conference tools. Even an individual with a minimum knowledge of a subject can be of real help in a conference if he is able to ask significant questions, for as every inquirer knows, the right question points the way to discovery. So use questions often, in many cases making your contribution in the form of a question rather than a statement.

There are many types and uses of questions. One of the uses, as suggested earlier, is to determine if you understand the meaning of another's statement. A feedback question of this nature might start with, "Do I understand you correctly to say that . . . ?" Questions can also be used to elicit information, determine opinions, or reveal reasoning, as "What is the capacity of that parking lot?" "How does anyone feel about gray as our foundation color?" or "Are you basing your conclusion on the similarities between the two cases?" A leading question can sometimes be useful to get something into the conference without making it as your own claim, as "Wasn't that proposal turned down last year because of the expense involved?"

A question can be employed as a tactful way of establishing your objection to a claim or to an opinion when outright rejection or contradiction would arouse hostility. Instead of saying, "That alloy won't work because it corrodes too rapidly," an individual could put his doubt as a question, "How long will that alloy withstand the corrosive effects of such an installation?" In an instance like this the question is an invitation to cooperate, whereas contradiction tends to create hostility; a conference should invoke as much cooperation as possible.

12. BE A GOOD SPORT WHEN THE DISCUSSION GOES AGAINST YOU. You cannot reasonably expect that in every conference your viewpoint will be accepted by the majority. Recognize that as a member of a minority, even when you are a minority of one, you will have fulfilled your responsibility if you have rigorously sustained a dissenting opinion, honestly held. You will then have the opportunity to earn the respect of others by accepting an adverse verdict with dignity and without rancor. Such earned respect will win colleagues willing to listen to what you have to say in other conferences. Remember that Babe Ruth was a strike-out champion as well as a home-run champion, and that his success came because he kept on trying, accepting his failures with good grace but always playing as hard as he could.

The leader coordinates the conference team

Most writers on the subject recognize three varieties of conference leader. The first is the dictatorial or authoritarian leader who dominates the conference, directing both the method and the con-

283

tent, and manipulating the conferees to the ends he desires. The second is the laissez-faire or non-directive leader, who sits by genially, allowing the group to determine its own direction and pace, and exerting little or no influence toward the outcome. The third is the democratic leader, who sees his function as that of providing every assistance to help the group arrive at its own conclusion. Each variety of leader may have a place in conference activity, yet in most situations the democratic leader is generally preferable. It is his kind of leadership which we will examine here.

The democratic leader is primarily concerned with the form and operation of the conference, and undertakes little or no responsibility for the content. He sees his job as that of a catalyst, making it possible for the conferees more effectively to think and decide as a cohesive team, and does not feel that he must exert influence over what they think or say. He does not attempt to guide the conference toward the decision he himself favors, but makes every effort to see that the decision is reached only after thorough consideration.

In accomplishing these purposes the democratic leader tries to facilitate group communication, to provide organization or structure to the deliberation, to pace the group, and to ensure critical evaluation of every idea. His desire is to stimulate thinking, to distribute the time fairly among the conferees, to clarify thought, and to help resolve issues. He facilitates decisions, but does not force them.

The democratic leader is concerned with the atmosphere and the interpersonal relations of the conference. He does everything possible to cultivate a permissive atmosphere, he sees that all the conferees are acquainted, and he takes what steps are possible to minimize any differences in status among them. He makes it his business to know the conferees as individuals so that he may anticipate and diminish friction which might develop among them. He familiarizes himself with the special knowledge or capacity of each individual, so that he may draw on it should the occasion arise.

Such a leader is pictured by Kenneth S. Davis in his book, *Experience of War*. Of General Dwight D. Eisenhower he wrote:[8]

> In the conference room, he could measure and respond to very slight changes in the emotional temperature

[8] From *Experience of War* by Kenneth S. Davis. Copyright © 1965 by Kenneth S. Davis. Reprinted by permission of Doubleday & Company, Inc., pp. 271–2.

and pressure. He could take his cue from a sign too slight for most men to notice. He could sum up a discussion, he could define a consensus, with clarity and force, bringing order out of chaos: conclusive action emerged out of what would otherwise have been separate, inconclusive expressions of opinion. He therefore often served the chairman's function, guiding and focusing discussion, even in meetings where the chairmanship was nominally assigned to another.

While it takes an exceptional person building on experience to provide leadership of this kind, the following suggestions paralleling those for participation offer guide lines for the occasions when you will assume conference leadership or for the moments you may be able to take on some function of group leadership.

1. PLAN THE CONFERENCE IN ADVANCE. Leadership begins well in advance of the actual conference, for arrangements must be firmly established before the conferees sit down. If the actual leader of the conference does not have responsibility for the advance work, he must at least be thoroughly informed. The purpose of the conference must be established, a roster of those who should attend drawn up, and each given adequate notice, including information necessary for individual planning. The leader must analyze the group and its members, prepare for himself a tentative agenda, perhaps circulating it with other information, and take whatever steps seem indicated to ensure needed materials and information. This may include seeing that one or more resource persons will be available to supply data as may be necessary. Arrangements for the physical facilities must be made, and this will include reserving the proper room and ensuring the comfort and convenience of the conferees. For some conferences coffee should be supplied, or arrangements made for meals. Only when the last detail of planning has been accomplished can the leader feel ready to meet with the group.

2. START THE CONFERENCE WITH A BRIEF CHALLENGING STATEMENT OF THE PROBLEM. The opening can be critical to the success of the conference, for this may be the moment when the conferees first become aware of personal involvement in problem and solution, and it is up to the leader to see that they recognize their involvement. The opening statement should do two things: It should

motivate the conferees to think by confronting them with a situation the solution to which will benefit each personally (see the discussion of the persuasive pattern, Chapter 11), and it should encourage group cohesiveness by presenting the problem as one which will not be overcome by the action of any one individual. The group should be problem-minded before it becomes solution-minded.

The opening statement should be short, and should carefully avoid any suggestion of a preferred solution or action. As a rule, the leader will follow his opening statement by establishing whether the conferees agree on the description of the problem, and by carrying the objective analysis as far as may be necessary to make certain that the problem is accurately understood. For instance:

> Leader: "Gentlemen, this bottle of dirty water represents the reason you have been invited to the meeting tonight. The water was taken today from the Blue River just below the Ann Street bridge, and it is not only muddy, but carries chemical and organic contamination. The condition of Blue River concerns all of us, for it is not the asset to our town it should be. On the contrary, it not only prohibits the use of the river as a recreation area, but it constitutes a health hazard and a deterrent to new industry. Is this a fair statement?"

3. ESTABLISH AN ORDER OF BUSINESS. After an opening which states and defines the problem and involves the conferees, the leader should next take measures to get a group agreement on the best way to set about arriving at a decision. He will, as suggested, have prepared his own tentative agenda, and this may be offered to the group as a potential basis of discussion, open to adoption, modification, or rejection. The agenda itself should preferably be in the form of a series of questions or issues which, when answered in turn, would lead to the ultimate decision. The question form encourages inquiry and provides for flexibility. It should be short but adequate to raise fundamental points; a proposed agenda for the conference on river pollution above might be:

> Is the Blue River truly a civic liability?
> From where does the pollution come?
> What can be done to make the river an asset?
> Through community action?
> By cooperating with other communities or agencies?

286

In attempting to establish procedure, the leader might say, "Here is a series of questions we could use to organize our discussion. Some of you may have other suggestions, but I think you'll agree that we can work more effectively if we have some kind of an order of business. Let's decide how we ought to proceed." In this way the leader raises questions, offers suggestions, but does not specify answers.

4. KEEP THE DISCUSSION MOVING TOWARD THE GOAL. Having obtained consensus on procedural matters, the leader should then help the conferees work according to plan toward a solution. He will need to discourage gently some who will tend to wander and others who will want to make speeches. After an irrelevant remark he will redirect the group's attention, perhaps seizing the opportunity to encourage a silent member to comment on the point under consideration. Always he will try to stimulate thinking, raising points, asking for new shades of opinion, or suggesting that facts or evidence would be useful.

The leader, however, should not concentrate so exclusively on the agenda and goal that he neglects his conferees as persons. He should be sensitive to fatigue, tension, or conflict, allowing moments of relaxation, humor, or even digression when the mood of the group indicates a need to unwind. Progress, he needs to remember, may come in spurts.

5. COORDINATE GROUP THINKING. A continuing responsibility of the conference leader is to unite the separate ideas and contributions of assorted conferees into a developing and coherent train of thought. To do this he must reduce statements which may contain two or three ideas to the one which is relevant at the moment, connect it to the point at hand, and place the irrelevant parts aside until they may be useful. He must clarify relationships, issues, and ambiguous statements, even while he sees that participation is well distributed among the members. Since thinking can often be better coordinated if members of the group can see their work as a common outline, the leader may use a blackboard or writing easel, placing the developing material where all can see it. Some leaders prefer to do this themselves, while others delegate the writing, including any note-taking, to a secretary or recorder, freeing themselves to give full attention to what is being said.

6. MAKE FREQUENT SUMMARIES.   To mark the progress of the conference, as well as to help coordinate the group, the leader should pause from time to time to summarize what has been said or accomplished. "So far we have suggested these causes of the problem. . . ." "The sense of the group, then, is that we should take steps within the department rather than involving others. Is that right?" "We have said that our object should be twofold, namely . . ." Statements like these not only succinctly emphasize the salient points of accomplishment and mark the stages of the conference, but serve as transitions as well, suggesting a point of departure from which to move to the succeeding stage. Summaries should be short, and frequent enough to stress coherence and unity, but not so often that they become monotonous.

In addition to occasional internal summaries and summaries as the group moves from one step of the reflective-thought pattern to another, the leader should, of course, provide a concise and balanced summary at the conclusion of the conference, indicating the solution or judgment agreed upon, and itemizing points of disagreement or minority opinion if such exist.

7. TRY TO SECURE HONEST AND VALID CONCLUSIONS.   Perhaps one of the most important functions of the leader is to make sure that the decisions and conclusions of the group are both honest and valid. In many conferences a continuing problem is the pressure toward conformity among its members, for a majority may insist on a decision of questionable value, an aggressive individual may overpower the resistance of his colleagues, or one with superior status may sway the group even without intending to. In such instances the conclusion may not represent the honest beliefs of those who are unwilling or unable to represent an opposing viewpoint. The pressure of time, too, can cause a group to find hurried agreement simply to get the conference ended. These pressures must be resisted by the leader, who should feel responsible that decisions represent both an honest expression of belief and the most defensible and valid conclusion possible. In order to effect such conclusions the leader should stimulate criticism, request facts and information in support of claims and assertions, mediate differences of opinion, and secure a test of conclusions. The task is difficult, but vital.

8. AVOID EXPRESSING YOUR PERSONAL OPINIONS.   By virtue of his relationship to the group as a whole, the leader can easily

influence the thinking of its members. In many business or industrial conferences particularly, the leader is the organizational superior of most or all of the conferees. Under such conditions his opinions have more weight with the group than those of any other individual, even if only because most people are unwilling openly to take issue with the boss. Therefore it is undesirable for the leader to express his opinions, lest he inhibit an honest examination of facts and ideas. When varying and critical views are not expressed, when ideas are not examined, the very purpose of a conference has been lost, for, as has often been said, "If both of us think alike, one of us is unnecessary."

This does not mean that the leader should see that his opinions are not considered, but only that they are not recognized as his. He must maintain an impartial posture. Even though his prime concern is the form of the conference and not its substance, he should see that every possible idea is explored, and if some member does not express the leader's views then the leader should see that they are considered. This he may accomplish by putting them in the form of a question—"Shouldn't we look at the manpower involved?"—or by attributing the thought to someone else—"I heard someone argue the other day that this office is not responsible for the situation." As a result of such methods the conference will recognize the view without being influenced by its source.

9. KEEP THE ATMOSPHERE FRIENDLY, INFORMAL, AND PERMISSIVE. Inter-personal rivalries, conflict, tension, and apprehensiveness about speaking out can disintegrate a conference, and it therefore becomes the leader's duty to minimize anything which could create these conditions. Aside from approving expressions of constructive attitudes and disapproving those of negative attitudes, the leader may facilitate a desirable group climate in part by controlling the flow and direction of talk. He should see that most contributions are directed to the group as a whole, since an exchange between two individuals can escalate into a conflict. At times he may choose to have remarks directed toward himself, drawing them away from another. He may insist that one member rephrase another's statement before answering it, thus promoting understanding before criticism. He may himself summarize or paraphrase a contribution, clarifying or softening it before permitting a response. He can attribute remarks to constructive motives, preventing a negative interpretation of intent. He can remind the group that the welfare of the whole or of the organization is the

paramount consideration. In these and in other ways, the leader can use his position to promote a constructive personal climate in which productive deliberation may take place.

10. ASK QUESTIONS OFTEN. Like any participant, the leader should use questions as a major tool. Some of these may be "overhead" or directed to the group as a whole, while others may be put to some particular individual. Questions of the latter kind should be used tactfully, however, for a participant can be embarrassed by an unexpected or an awkward question, perhaps becoming resentful or glum as a result.

The leader may use questions for the same purposes as the participant. In addition, however, he may employ them more often in procedural matters. "Which avenue should we explore first?" seeks to establish priority among alternatives. "Can anything else be said on this point?" may suggest that a decision or transition is appropriate. "Will you explain how that relates to Mike's idea?" may either gain clarification or focus the attention of the group on the main stream of thought.

A common mistake of some leaders is that of immediately answering questions asked by conferees, a habit which can limit or inhibit the participation of others. Group involvement can be encouraged when the leader mirrors or reflects back inquiries to the membership as a whole. "Can anyone answer Tom's question?" "Clara is saying that women employees have not been adequately represented. Would you agree with her?" In this way the leader can use questions asked by others to stimulate response by everyone.

Some leaders commonly fail to wait for answers to their questions. Uncertain, they either answer their own questions or follow one question with another. The first habit shuts off participation, the second only confuses the conferees. It is better for a leader to learn to wait, since a good question will finally be answered if the leader will only give his group time to think. So when you have put a question, avoid following it up yourself. Wait until someone volunteers a response.

11. BE ALERT FOR HIDDEN AGENDA. It is not enough for a leader to know that hidden agenda may exist; he must be sensitive to their actual presence. As part of his preparation he may have asked himself "What personal stakes may each conferee have in this problem? What private concerns may deflect each person's mind

from the business of the group?" If either question had an answer, he must be on the lookout for signs of a problem, either statements or behavior which may signal potential withdrawal or resistance. Dealing with these signs is a matter of tact for which no categorical rules can be made.

12. FOLLOW THROUGH PROPERLY ON THE RESULTS OF THE CONFERENCE. It will be the leader's final responsibility to see that the decisions of the group are appropriately communicated to the right persons or offices or are translated into action. Whether he does the necessary work himself, or whether he delegates it to another, the leader should assure himself that the job has been accomplished. Of course, as a prerequisite, he will have made certain that the conference produced the results worth following through. The bad name enjoyed so widely by committees is a result of the fact that "nothing happens." This can be avoided if leadership shapes the conference process toward reasonable and specific outcomes and then follows through on those outcomes.

Although in this discussion we have been thinking of leadership as residing in one person, we should broaden our understanding to realize that any member of a conference can and may from time to time assume some function of leadership. Each must be actively concerned for both good procedure and sound substance. You, yourself, either as an appointed leader or as a conferee, should be a constructive force in the deliberations of your group.

A MEETING IS AN OCCASION FOR PRESENTING PREPARED MESSAGES

We have seen that because of the confusing ways in which people use the word "conference" it has been necessary to set up an operating definition for use in this book. Similarly, I have indicated what I mean by "meeting" in order to distinguish between the two kinds of business gatherings.

You will recall, then, that for us a meeting is any gathering which is not devoted to inquiry or to creative thinking, or in which the pattern of reflective thought does not form the overall structure. So far as the conduct of the affair is concerned, there is less likely to be real conversational interaction among the participants, and more continuous speech-making and listening. The governing purpose is not to develop a new idea or judgment, but to present ideas or opinions already formulated, seeking understanding or acceptance of them. Many meetings are run according to a planned program, with most of those attending acting as fairly passive observers.

Other parts of this book, therefore, deal sufficiently with your participation in meetings. If you are a part of the program of the meeting, your talk will be a speech of some kind, and you can suitably plan it by referring to Part Four of this book. If you are to be simply an attendee, your major business will be listening, and I refer you to Chapter 5. As an attendee you may have an opportunity to ask questions or to make a short contribution of some kind. In the latter event, you should limit yourself to a single point, developed according to the suggestions in Chapter 13; if you feel the necessity of making more than one point it is usually better to speak briefly several times than to make a single longer talk.

When you are made responsible for a meeting, you must know the type, the specific purpose, and the general form which should be used. Just as there are varieties of conferences, so there are varieties of meetings. After considering these we will finally turn to the matter of planning both conferences and meetings.

Meetings serve specific purposes

Each meeting is generally called to meet a specific communication need within an organization or between members representing two or more organizations. It may be called to create a decision or policy when that outcome cannot be obtained by people cooperating to seek a common goal. For example, a meeting might bring together representatives of a railroad and those of a city administration, both seeking to determine the responsibility for building a new bridge over the railroad tracks but neither willing to accept the financial burden.

Those who speak at meetings usually seek understanding or appreciation from their listeners, or hope to persuade their listeners to accept a given point of view. When a conflict of opinion occurs, speakers may attempt to persuade an uncommitted "third party" (an audience, a judge, an umpire, or an arbitrator), or they may hope to persuade their opponents into a change of view.

Regardless of the character of any given meeting, however, those who go to speak will have a prepared stand or message to which they are committed, and which they expect to communicate. The nature of the message will depend upon the nature of the meeting. Because of this, we must next examine the major kinds of meetings and their functions.

THE INFORMATIONAL MEETING. As one of the Goodyear Tire and Rubber Company's training handbooks points out, there are two major kinds of meetings involving public speaking, the "tell" meeting and the "sell" meeting. The first of these is devoted to the communication of information. While most common is undoubtedly the meeting at which a specialist or a superior officer presents information to colleagues or subordinates, many companies also use meetings to allow an upward flow of information, encouraging various levels of employees to meet with superiors to keep the latter aware of problems, attitudes, organizational or production difficulties, or suggested improvements. A meeting can be one of the best ways to promote face to face two-way communication throughout an organization, and increasingly it is used to promote efficiency and increased morale. Following a meeting of non-academic personnel with the President of my own institution, the latter reported, "There was agreement that general information meetings periodically would be desirable."

There are three general types of informational presentations for which a meeting is ordinarily called, and for each of these the suggestions in part four of this text are appropriate. The speaker should keep in mind, however, the necessity of adapting his presentation to the readiness to respond and to the resources of the audience.

Oral Reports. An oral report summarizes in orderly fashion a body of information, usually assembled by the person making the report. Those listening may be expected to need the information as part of their general background, as the basis of their work, or to assist in making judgments and decisions. A report may cover operations over a period of time, it may deal with observations and evaluations, or it may cover the substance and conclusions of study and research. A small group may bring back to city council a report of its investigation of harbor improvements in other cities, a researcher may report to the vice president and staff the outcome of his search for a more durable plastic, or the camp director may report to the Y.M.C.A. Board of Directors on the summer program just completed.

It is not unusual for a meeting to be devoted to a topic on which several reports will be made; in such situations the individual in charge should see that each speaker dovetails his materials with the others to avoid duplication and to provide proper emphasis and detail.

Briefing. The distinction between reporting and briefing is certainly not exact, but in general the report may be based on a chronological scheme, whereas the brief may be more descriptive or generally informational. As the name implies, such a talk is short, and must be highly understandable. It attempts to convey all the facts necessary to comprehend a given situation. At the same time, it has industrial or business applications such as when a sales staff is briefed on the plan for a new campaign or an office staff is briefed on new procedures. Briefing is often accomplished by teams of speakers, and visual aids, mock-ups, models, charts, and photographs are commonly used to facilitate understanding.

General Information. Except for reports and briefs we may classify all talks at "tell" meetings as general informational. A large number of them are for purposes similar to talks employed by the Employee Information Program of Westinghouse, which are used to develop employee understanding of company plans and policies, to keep employees aware of privileges and benefits, and to cultivate a sense of teamwork and cooperation. This program represents the internal communication system of an institution; general informational talks also implement external communication when facts, policies, and data must be transmitted to groups of buyers, distributors, suppliers, associates, or others who must be informed. Illustrative would be a talk to a Chamber of Commerce Committee outlining the needs of a new industry looking for a location, or one by a school executive explaining policy changes to a meeting of parents.

"Tell" meetings can be highly efficient in presenting a maximum amount of information in the least time, and may provide the benefits of two-way communication by permitting questions and feedback. It must not be assumed, however, that full understanding is always generated, for the common barriers to communication (see Chapter 2) exist and must be coped with. Careful preparation of every phase of such a meeting is necessary to preclude communication failure, including clear establishment of the purpose of the meeting, apt selection of speakers, and thorough consideration of possible barriers. Attention to listener motivation may be particularly important.

THE PERSUASIVE MEETING. The second basic kind of meeting is the "sell" meeting, in which the over-all purpose is to secure a favorable response to whatever is being sold. The purposes and method of planning a speech for such an occasion are described in the final section of this book.

The subjects of persuasion, whether at "sell" meetings or otherwise, may be divided into three categories: ideas, services, or products. Included in the category of ideas would be plans, policies, and principles, the purpose of the speaker being to win approval of or commitment to a proposition or policy. A training director may need to win approval from the members of top management of a proposal to establish a new service, a physician may want to persuade a group of his colleagues that they should join together to support the construction of a new professional building, a supervisor may find it necessary to create enthusiasm for the company campaign to improve product quality, or an executive may wish his board of directors to prefer financial plan A to plan B.

Services to be sold include all functions of assistance and skilled or professional care or advice, while products would include tangible objects of all kinds. The owner of a credit service may want to secure clients among a group of business men, a manager may need to sell employees on the features of a new insurance plan available to them, a school administrator may have to sell his staff on the advantages of recent arrangements to supply them with audio-visual aids, or a representative of an electronics firm may need to sell a bar association on the use of an information retrieval plan to expedite the searching of legal records. All these could be classified as services, while fire fighting equipment, laboratory installations, insecticides, and any other tangible objects represent the product category. While selling is commonly thought of as a person-to-person business, you can quickly see that much salesmanship must be directed at groups gathered at a meeting of some kind.

Some persuasive meetings bring together only persons from within a single organization, while others involve members of a group or class; so far as a given institution is concerned, such a meeting may represent either internal or external communication.

In all persuasive meetings the speaker must take special care to understand his listeners as individuals and as a group, so that he may present his proposal in terms of their wants and interests, showing how it will provide a benefit. A common mistake is to emphasize the good features of a proposal without translating the features into personal benefits. The high speed of a new drill may not interest a dentist in itself, but he may be favorably moved by the fact that the speed makes it possible for him to reduce measurably the time he must work on a patient's tooth, minimizing his own effort as well as any discomfort to the patient. The dentist, like all human beings, is not personally interested in the feature, in this case speed, but he may be interested in the benefits provided by the feature. Thus all selling should be done in terms of the benefits provided the listeners, the benefits in turn satisfying a felt need. The listener reaction may be summed up in "What will it do for me?" The question must be answered in term of the listener's experience and expectation.

THE DELIBERATIVE MEETING. The business or professional man often finds himself participating in a meeting managed under the common rules of parliamentary procedure. This is apt to be true in meetings of business and professional organizations, service clubs, scientific or technical societies, in formal committee actions whose proceedings must go on record, in boards of directors or trustees, or in formal staff action. In every case the conventions which govern all meetings of freely associating people apply, even though specific variations may be necessary.

The purpose of parliamentary order in a deliberative meeting is to conduct the business of the group in a rational and efficient manner to arrive at the judgments and decisions for which the group is responsible. Such a meeting should not be confused with a decision-making, problem-solving conference, for the two are unlike in form and rationale. The conference is creative, the end product emerging from the process of cooperative thinking, the members being uncommitted at the outset. The regulations of parliamentary action do not apply. In contrast, many attending a deliberative meeting are committed at the very beginning to some plan or policy, the proposed action is introduced by its adherents in the form of a motion, the motion is argued, and the decision is made according to parliamentary law. If those at a deliberative meeting wish to use creative conference methods, they must turn the affair into a committee of the whole by appropriate action, thus removing the strictures of formal procedure.

It follows that the kinds of speaking at a deliberative meeting are likely to be planned statements, extempore support of established positions, and frequent impromptu attack or defense of a specific point. This creates a form of debate, the immediate purpose of each speaker being to convince the uncommitted members of the group or to persuade those initially opposed into changing their position. It is the kind of speaking characteristic of legislative bodies at their best, and needs be both tactful and persuasive. There should be no room for personal attacks, those in opposition should refrain from addressing their remarks directly at one another, and the greatest stress should be placed upon the logical elements of decision making. The purpose of the whole process should be to make the wisest decision possible through the testing of ideas by exposing them to the criticism of their opponents.

The basic issue to be decided at any given moment in a deliberative meeting is the motion then on the floor, and all parliamentary law stems from the possible actions on the motion, and from the rules and regulations which apply to the conduct of the meeting. It is not within the scope of this book to present a detailed treatment of parliamentary procedure, nor to outline the theory and technique of debating, there being many excellent texts in these special fields. It should be noted that every organization has the right to determine its own rules of procedure, Robert's *Rules of Order* and Sturgis' *Standard Code of Parliamentary Procedure* being the two most widely used codes.

We should note that in general, however, the rules are to be used for the sake of expediting business, and should not be allowed to interfere with its transaction. Under some circumstances a chairman is justified in relaxing the strict enforcement of regulations; sometimes parliamentary procedure becomes a ritualistic formality, both unnecessary and meaningless. On the other hand, when the decision of the group may have a far-reaching effect, or when there is even a remote possibility of legal involvement, the regulations should be strictly observed, following both the letter and spirit of parliamentary law.

In arguing a question of policy, certain "stock" issues tend to appear, which can be useful to you in planning defense or attack for a deliberative meeting. If you favor a given policy you may build your case around the following points:

1. A problem or difficulty exists which must be overcome.
2. The proposed policy is practical and beneficial.
3. The proposed policy will solve the problem.
4. No serious objections to the policy exist.

If, on the other hand, you will be in opposition, a case can be created from among these stock arguments:

1. No problem or difficulty serious enough to warrant action now exist.
2. The proposed policy is impractical.
3. The proposed policy will not solve the problem.
4. The policy will create new and serious evil consequences.
5. If the problem must be solved, there is a better policy available.

While arguing in terms of the best interests of the group as a whole, you will want also to make special effort to show that your stand will serve the wants and needs of individual listeners—in short, you should hope to blend logical argument with good persuasive psychology.

NEGOTIATION. Although deliberation brings together people who may have conflicting opinions, it provides a means of resolving that conflict by majority vote in an organization having jurisdiction over the conflict. Negotiation, on the other hand, brings into confrontation individuals or teams which may likewise hold preconceived and conflicting ideas, but it provides no system for the resolution of conflict. Consequently, if they hope to avoid the consequences of failure, the negotiators must somehow find a way of solving their differences by mutual adjustment. The pattern of talk may range from cooperative problem-solving through persuasion to cajolery and threats.

The most publicized form of negotiation is undoubtedly collective bargaining, since the confrontation of labor and management frequently appears in dramatic headlines. However, negotiation often takes place when contracts are written, during the process of making sales leases or mergers, whenever legal problems are settled out of court, or, in fact, at any time when differences are settled by barter or bargain. Negotiation is also vital in international relations. Here, although the stakes may be higher and the setting more formal than elsewhere, the behavior of negotiators is unchanged.

At its best negotiation results in fair and amicable adjustment, at its worst it ends in stalemate, and too often the conflict is carried into combat. Negotiators have five recognized methods of effecting a settlement by talk.

1. *The Threat of Force or Violence.* This is an undesirable way of concluding negotiation, since it denies the American belief in settling differences by agreement freely arrived at through talk. Yet there are undoubtedly times when the pressure of threat is preferable to strikes, lockouts, or physical conflict.

2. *Invoking the Assistance of a Third Party.* Conciliation, mediation, or arbitration are often used when negotiators reach an impasse. The first two forms seek to aid the negotiators in finding a satisfactory way of reconciling their differences, while arbitration independently weighs the merits of the two positions and renders a verdict which the negotiators may or may not have agreed to abide by. In some instances the matter is taken to a court of law and a decision rendered by a judge or jury. Both arbitration and legal action turn the process of negotiation into one of argument or deliberation.

3. *Persuasion.* When one party to negotiation is able to get his opponent to see the justice, fairness, or value of his position and thereby win a modification of the opponent's stand, the outcome has been determined by persuasion. This can occur when men of integrity who hold some common ground of understanding truly seek agreement.

4. *Compromise.* Agreement by compromise takes place when each side gives something to the other after a period of bargaining and adjustment. Compromise usually means that neither side has gained all its purposes, but that each is willing to give something in order to gain something else.

5. *Integration.* Sometimes a solution to conflicting positions can be discovered or created which bears little or no resemblance to the original demands of either side but which offers both a way to

find satisfaction. Such a creative solution integrates conflicting desires into an unforeseen pattern permitting both sides to accomplish their essential goals. For example, a company negotiating the purchase of a small manufacturing plant could not meet the owner's price, but was able to solve its needs by an exchange of stock, giving the owner a sense of continuing interest in both concerns and the opportunity to see his assets grow with the company.

If, within specific negotiation, it can be assumed that both sides are dealing in good faith, there may remain the possibility that members of one side or both perceive their opposites as threats. If the perception of threat can be removed, it is then possible to open the way to constructive understanding, and in consequence a method of opening minds and correcting perceptions can be useful. The following steps may promote this end.

First, a negotiator must use every opportunity to make his opponent realize that the latter is being heard and understood. This necessitates continuous and careful listening and frequent restatement of the opponent's position to the latter's satisfaction. Second, the negotiator must search for mutual ground, and must be alert to point out the areas or conditions of validity in the opponent's stand. If these steps are successful, the establishment of full and honest communication may be possible. The negotiator must then, as a third step, reinforce every sign that his opponent is likewise listening and understanding his position. This third step cannot be advanced too openly or too obviously, for it could defeat its own ends by reawakening a sense of threat. If it is successful, however, the result can be a two-way flow of understanding, opening the way toward agreement.

In negotiation, it may often be vital to maintain a way for an opposing negotiator to modify his position without losing face, especially since a negotiator commonly represents a constituency of some kind to whom he must explain his words and actions. Union spokesmen must report to their rank and file, management to boards and stockholders, legal representatives to their clients, and diplomats to their respective nations. For this reason there is a place in negotiation for ambiguity of claim and statement which may be highly undesirable in ordinary communication. Ambiguous statements can be explained or redefined according to a change of circumstance, providing room for maneuver, changed position, and the saving of face when necessary. There is a wide difference between private negotiation between individuals who have authority to make decisions and public negotiation between representatives of interested groups.

ALL CONFERENCES AND MEETINGS SHOULD BE CAREFULLY PLANNED

Conferences and meetings of any kind do not just happen. They must be conscientiously planned, inasmuch as the successful outcome may hinge on advance preparation. Many, of course, are routine in the sense that any particular gathering is but one in a continuing series, but even so, adequate plans should be made for each. Routine itself can encourage carelessness about planning, lessening the value of the meetings.

Determine the nature and purpose

Of first importance is a clear understanding of the purpose of the gathering. If it is to be a decision-making conference, what specific problem or problems is the group to attack? If a meeting, will it be "tell" or "sell"? And what exact understanding, belief, attitude, or action will be expected from the attendees as a result of the meeting? Once the purpose has been determined, the agenda or program can be made up to structure and organize the affair in the most productive fashion.

Involved with the determination of purpose is also the selection of the participants whenever participation is not automatically determined. How many should attend? What divisions or departments should be represented? Who should the representatives be? Should any "outsiders" be invited? What persons possessing special knowledge or experience should attend? Should any "courtesy" invitations be issued to persons whose responsibility touches on the subject of the meeting? Once the list of participants has been made, invitations or notices should be sent as far in advance as possible, very often with a request for a reply indicating whether the person will attend or not.

Notices should obviously include details about the time, place, and date of the meeting, together with a statement of why it is being called. Depending upon the degree of advance understanding or preparation required of the participants, the notices should also include an indication of the agenda or program, together with any special instructions which are necessary. The latter might include requests to bring such things as operating reports, experimental data, special photographs, or cost analyses, or to be prepared to speak on a given item or to defend a salient viewpoint.

If the gathering is to be a conference, the number attending will be limited and the agenda will be flexibly structured so that all can freely participate. Conversely, if it is to be a meeting, the number attending will vary with the purpose and the program will probably be more rigidly prepared. In this event, the number and order of speakers, the assignment of their topics, and the nature of any other features of the program will have to be settled. If a question period or some other form of audience participation will be included, arrangements for this will be built into the program, as will arrangements for motion pictures, exhibits, or visual aids of any kind.

Beyond deciding who should attend the function, those in charge should also analyze the roster of attendees to assess attitudes, opinions, or group forces which might affect the outcome. Each speaker should understand his audience, as pointed out in Chapter 11, but in addition, those responsible for a meeting should likewise be aware of possible factors which might facilitate or inhibit its success. Especially for a meeting at which resistance to the purpose or a division of attitude and opinion among the participants might be expected, the planner needs to take such things into account and to devise strategy to deal with them constructively. Arrangements to encourage listening as a door to understanding, for the introduction of information when it may be desirable, for persuasion, for the clarification of issues or for the capitalization of favorable responses may be necessary.

Planners should determine whether the attendees should be furnished with materials of any kind such as handouts, samples, printed materials, or equipment. They may likewise need to make plans for a follow-up of the meeting, considering whether the attendees will be asked to return a response of some nature, make a report, or do anything else after the meeting has closed.

Plan the physical setting

It is true that people can talk together productively under almost any kind of circumstance, yet it is equally true that the most productive conferences and meetings are those which are held in comfortable and efficient surroundings. For this reason thoughtful attention to physical planning is important.

The room itself should suit the number of attendees, so that a small number will not feel lost in a vast arena or a large number squeezed uncomfortably into a small box. Seats should provide for comfort and working ease, with tablet arms if the members will not be seated at tables. Good heating or air conditioning and ventilation are important, for people cannot work well in hot, stuffy, smoke-filled rooms. The room should be neat and clean, with decoration appropriate to the purpose of the meeting, and with full and glareless illumination.

Equipment should likewise consist not only of that which will be needed for the program, but also that which will make for comfort. Adequate electrical outlets will be necessary for projection machines or for special lighting or other equipment. Blackboards or easels, a speakers stand, a public address system, a wall clock, bulletin boards, or similar items may be needed. Ash trays, drinking water, a convenient location for coats and hats, and perhaps provision for coffee or lunch can be among the necessities. Pencils and paper are commonly provided for every participant.

The seating arrangement itself can make for a smooth working gathering, promoting cooperation and the interchange of ideas, and facilitating understanding of differing options. Conversely, an ill-conceived arrangement can produce cliques, enhance conflict, or make good communication difficult. At a large meeting, conventional seating in straight rows may make for stiffness and formality, whereas rows slanted toward a center aisle can make it easier for people to see each other, stimulating a greater amount of talk. At a small meeting or a conference, one large table or a circle or T-arrangement of small tables is apt to facilitate the exchange of talk. In any event, the leader should be placed so that he can easily see and be seen by all participants, having an effective control of the situation.

It is possible to plan exact seating by having name cards at every place or chair. This enables the planner to separate members of a group or department, preventing cliques, or to keep those who are known to have conflicting ideas from facing each other, in which position they can too easily join battle. It enables him, too, to place strategically those upon whom he can count to provide the needed constructive emphasis and teamwork. Name cards also break down the barrier of strangeness when those around a table are not previously acquainted.

Establish a time schedule

How long should the meeting last? With one voice, every weary meeting-goer will join to shout, "Keep it short!" The maximum limit for an effective meeting seems to be an hour and a half. After that, attention lapses, fatigue sets in, and the mind begins to grow cloudy. Experience has shown that a good problem-solving conference should be kept within this time limit, and that both "tell" and "sell" meetings lose effectiveness if they run beyond. Even collective bargaining has been known to yield to a time limit; indeed, some negotiators insist that unless a deadline has been set real bargaining does not occur.

Accordingly, a planner must deal realistically with the time factor for his meeting. The leader of a conference should make a rough calculation of how much time may be allotted to each step of the problem-solving pattern. If he later finds he has miscalculated, he may be wise to adjourn the conference and to resume the matter at another sitting. Speakers at a meeting should be given specific time limits, and the chairman should insist that these limits be rigidly observed, even if it means interrupting a speaker to bring his presentation to a close. A series of overtime speakers can squeeze out entirely the last one on a program and send the attendees away in disgust. In planning, it is better to allow some leeway in the time schedule than to pack every minute full, even if this means scheduling fewer speakers.

Beginning and ending times should be precisely observed. Start the business at the time announced, regardless of whether every expected person is present or not. End at the time promised for adjournment. Training sessions and convention programs which run all day should be broken into small time-segments with intervals for coffee and relaxation. "Breaks" in the program provide moments for private small talk which often may advance the purpose of the meeting more effectively than if it had not been interrupted.

Plan to avoid fruitless use of time. Keep opening remarks to a minimum, and encourage every person to get to the heart of his message swiftly. Speakers can be introduced briefly and brightly. Transitions between speakers or between items on the program can be kept to a minimum if planning has been effective and if the chairman is alert. Provide a program with enough variety and see that it moves.

All parts of a program, including the timing, should be set up with the purpose clearly in mind. Each speaker, each segment, should fit into a pattern designed to advance the desired outcome.

Anticipate a follow-through

For many conferences and meetings, the moment when the participants rise and start for the door does not so much mark an ending as a beginning. Whatever has been accomplished may be important only as the results are firmly pursued. The least follow-up is for the planners to assess the degree of success or failure of the event, determining its strengths and weaknesses relative to the outcome to guide further gatherings. Beyond this the policies or decisions resulting from conferences will presumably have to be reported or translated into action. Perhaps memoranda will have to be issued to each participant, not only summarizing the conference but suggesting individual responsibility for future action. The new ideas, the fresh enthusiasm, the productive attitudes which develop in meetings will dissipate with time unless positive follow-up is made. Sometimes the post-meeting action is outlined before the meeting itself adjourns, sometimes it is a matter of circulating printed matter afterward, sometimes a matter of seeing that reports are made to members' sub-groups or to local affiliations, and sometimes the members report back to the officials in charge of the meeting on what appropriate action they have taken. Regardless of the specific form of the follow-up, often nothing happens after a meeting unless the need has been foreseen and steps taken as part of the initial planning.

At the outset of your business or professional career you are less likely to be a planner or leader than a participant. Your responsibility, though more limited, is not less vital. Every person

305

attending a conference or meeting should be a fully functioning part of the group rather than a spectator, for it is the process of interaction among people which establishes the relationships, exchanges the ideas, and creates the decisions necessary to the work of any institution. This is the purpose of both talking and listening.

Part Four

SPEAKING TO GROUPS

Chapter 10

The Why of Public
Speaking

*In these days of public relations and image consciousness, the
executive who is not behind his desk is most likely to be found in the
speaker's dais. From the chairman of the board to the assistant
manager of the most obscure department, nearly everyone in
business speaks in public or makes a speech at some time or
other. Executives appear at university commencements, civic organizations, legislative committees—or before the nation's 4,500 Rotary
clubs, whose members listen to an overpowering quarter of a
million speeches a year.[1]*

Dunn's Review and Modern Industry

YOU MAY HAVE STARTED READING THIS BOOK WITH ONE OF TWO
widely-held ideas about the function of public speaking in the business and industrial world. The first of these is that improvement in
public speaking is the only type of training a business or professional person need, and perhaps the only kind of speech education
available. The second is that public speaking is an old-fashioned
art which has little place amid the electronic gear of a technological
age, and that time can be better spent than in learning platform
skills.

By this time you have discovered that neither of these positions
is exclusively valid. It is true that a business or professional person

[1] "The Science of Speechmaking," Vol. 80, No. 6 (Dec., 1962), p. 32.

309

must learn to talk in a variety of situations other than from a speaker's platform. But is it also true that the ability to speak "in public" is increasingly a necessary part of the equipment of a responsible individual. As *Time* magazine observed, "One of the biggest booms in the nation comes from all those businessmen who are getting up to speak."[2]

The facts are that public speaking is a common and widespread necessity in business, professional, and industrial spheres, and that almost anyone may be called on, sometimes with very little advance notice, to make a speech. Sometimes this necessity cannot be avoided, but even when it can, there are benefits for the person who is willing to undertake the assignment and can do the job. The person who has something to say and can say it well often finds that he has enhanced his reputation and his career. He has shown a willingness to meet responsibility which may lead to greater and more challenging responsibilities. He becomes more valuable to his employer, he aids associates and customers, he promotes good will for his business or profession, and he makes a positive contribution to his community. All this has led the editors of *Dunn's Review and Modern Industry* to write:[3]

> The speech of today is every bit as much a tool of business as the conveyer belt or the calculating machine. It is so important, in fact, that the sophisticated corporation no longer passively waits for an invitation to speak. It actively seeks out groups to hear its message—and then makes behind-the-scenes arrangements to speak to them.

Big business and big industry are not alone in their use of the speaker's platform, for small enterprises, groups and associations, individual owners, all branches of government, and various public organizations find public speaking an indispensable skill. Retired general Alfred M. Gruenther, for instance, in four years as president of the American National Red Cross, traveled 422,000 miles to make 540 speeches in America, Europe, South America, and the Far East. During a year as president of American Trucking Associations, Inc., Clarence A. Kelley, president of Dixie Ohio Express, made 70 major addresses, many of them to meet the challenge of the trucking industry's greatest competitor, the railroads.

And so, whatever your vocational plans may be, you will be

[2] "Boom in Speechmaking," *Time*, LXXV, No. 6 (Feb. 8, 1960), p. 84.
[3] "The Science of Speechmaking," p. 32.

better prepared if you, too, are able to speak in public. It is to this part of your preparation that the rest of this book is dedicated.

PUBLIC SPEAKING IS PLANNED CONVERSATION WITH A GROUP OF LISTENERS

Let's start by getting rid of any lingering misconceptions. When we talk about public speaking, we are not talking about high-flung arm-waving oratory. We are not interested in bombastic spellbinding on the one hand, nor in the dull reading of a "paper" on the other. We are not thinking about an address which is transferred from the speaker's manuscript to the listener's notes without going through anyone's mind. Nor are we thinking of "the speech" as an imperishable composition, ready to go down in history.

"Public speaking," said Victor Alvin Ketcham, a master teacher of the art, "is dignified, amplified conversation." It is in this sense that we shall consider it.

A classic explanation of public speaking as conversation must be credited to James A. Winans, writing a half-century ago. Imagine yourself walking down the street, highly excited about some recent event or over a current issue. You meet a friend and engage him in animated conversation, pouring out your experience or opinion. As you talk other friends come by, and then passers-by stop to listen. The listening group grows from two or three to ten, twenty, or more. At some point one of the listeners moves forward a box, and you climb upon it, the better to carry your words to all about you.[4]

At what point does conversation stop and public speaking begin? When the size of the group increases from nine to ten? Or from nineteen to twenty? Obviously there is no identifiable point at which we can say, "You are now making a speech." As the crowd grew you may have spoken more loudly, you may have worked harder to invoke understanding in all your listeners, and you may have gestured more actively, but at all times you were conversing with those who attended you.

[4] See James Albert Winans, *Public Speaking*, Revised Edition (New York: The Century Co., 1923), p. 20.

To be conversational in public speaking, then, means that the speaker has the same attitude in speaking to a group that he would have in talking to one or two friends. He thinks and understands his words as he utters them, fully aware of the idea he is trying to evoke and of the way in which his message is being received. At the moment of delivery he creates or recreates the thought, fully realizing the content of his message as he delivers it.

But public speaking is conversation at its best. This means that the speaker is not satisfied with commonplace ideas or mediocre utterance. His presentation is the finest of which he is capable, both in content and delivery. He avoids carelessness, apathy, slovenliness, and indifference. His conversation is therefore dignified in that it is worthy of both speaker and listener, and the degree of dignity is that which is appropriate to the subject, the place, and the occasion.

Furthermore, the conversation of public speaking is planned. It starts at a definite and prepared beginning, moves through a carefully thought-out development of the message, and ends crisply and with satisfaction to the listeners. This kind of conversation *goes* somewhere because it has been planned that way to evoke a desired response from the listeners. This response can rarely be secured without great care in planning. The speaker who delights listeners by his ability to think on his feet can do so only because he has "thought on his seat" long before he rose to speak.

Finally, this conversation is with a *group* of listeners. It is not directed at a dimly-seen "audience" as a whole, because an audience is not a whole or a unit, but rather a *collection* of people. The listeners hear you individually, and they react individually. True, they sometimes do stimulate one another—when one laughs he arouses laughter in those about him, and when one unconsciously nods his head in agreement he encourages others to agree. But even this is an individual response to the situation as a whole. Therefore the knowledgeable speaker holds his conversation with a group of listening individuals, and to the best of his ability he directs his remarks to those he sees before him as discrete and particular persons.

Next, let's examine some typical situations and kinds of speeches you may find yourself involved with.

GOOD PUBLIC SPEAKING IS VITAL IN A VARIETY OF BUSINESS, PROFESSIONAL, AND INDUSTRIAL SITUATIONS

The kinds of speeches called for, and the range of situations in which speeches are necessary, are so diverse that precise and exact classification is virtually impossible. Yet diligent examination of business and professional needs suggests that we can list five major speaking situations, with a minimum amount of overlapping among the categories.

1. Informal meetings

These are the occasions which do not shout "you've got to make a speech," and which are apt to fail precisely because the person in charge did not sense the challenge and make preparation adequate to the needs of the situation. They are the meetings to which someone is casually invited to "talk to the boys," or at which the departmental manager makes some "off the cuff" remarks which are poorly planned, tedious, and ineffective.

For instance, here is part of a letter sent to all retread shop managers of a major tire and rubber company. The subject is the current year's shop safety contest. "Hold your meeting immediately with all employees assembled," it says. "Enthusiastically inform all employees that your shop is having another big, year-long safety contest. . . . Explain the contest and contest rules. . . . Point out. . . . Stress . . . Review . . . After all questions . . . have been answered . . . conclude your meeting."

The success of the safety campaign may well depend on the ability of every manager to get it started in his shop with a rousing speech. But how many managers will awaken to the challenge, and have the ability to rise to it? This is the sort of situation in which public speaking is apt to be poorest, and yet in which productive speech is highly necessary to the success of the well-laid plans of the company.

At informal meetings of this kind the speaker will have little or

313

no introduction. Indeed, the speaker, as in the case of the retread shop safety contest, may well be the manager, the foreman, the section leader, or the supervisor, and will have to run the meeting as well as make the speech. There will be no set program, nor will there be much formality. Indeed, the audience will not expect a formal address, but it will highly appreciate and favorably respond to a well-planned, well-organized and purposive talk.

Informal meetings can include those in which a supervisor talks to his workers, a small plant manager to his assembled personnel, a sales manager to his staff, a salesman to a purchasing group, or a departmental manager to a meeting of other managers. When such meetings are well done, and the talks are presented with conscientious attention to the need for effectiveness, they can be highly productive. The Timken Roller Bearing Company uses small meetings to make all foremen and supervisors acquainted with the provisions of every new union contract, Republic Steel holds safety meetings to keep employees safety conscious the year around, and General Electric's Missile and Space Vehicle Department has 16 members of management ready to talk to employees on any company topic of interest to them. You can undoubtedly add other examples from your own experience or from the area of your vocational interest.

2. Semi-formal meetings

We can make a very broad distinction between informal and semi-formal meetings by saying that in the latter the speaker is a part of a planned program and is introduced. A semi-formal meeting is less apt to be held on company time, and quite likely a given speech may be a part of a larger program which includes more than one speaker.

Included in this category are "tell" or "sell" meetings of various sorts, the appearance of manufacturers' representatives before a sales staff, medical symposia, panels of technical or scientific men, special training sessions, and short course meetings designed to bring workers or specialists up to date in their fields.

Many a sales presentation assumes semi-formal status, as when a Chamber of Commerce representative speaks to a management group considering locating in his area, a manufacturer's man discusses new fire hose before city council, a flooring salesman meets with the local school board to promote his product in the new building, or a team of industrial products salesmen outline the uses of a new plastic to an automotive manufacturer's planning board. The word "presentation" itself has come to mean a semi-formal speech accompanied by visual aids of various descriptions, and this kind of address has become so widely used that William H. Whyte, Jr. of *Fortune* magazine has written with a tongue-in-cheek attitude:[5]

> The presentation is becoming so vital to corporate life, indeed, that some corporations regularly stage presentations to middle management on how to give presentations. Scientists, instead of merely reading technical "papers," are also turning to the flip-flop chart, and entertaining professional meetings with full-scale presentations.

The semi-formal meeting has become, whatever its variations, an indispensable tool in business and industry, and merits a very carefully prepared talk.

3. Formal meetings

Although some formal meetings may be characterized by black-tie attire and a high degree of pomp, the true mark of such meetings is an established pattern of behavior. The speaker is expected to give an address, and he will be introduced by the chairman, often with a flourish. Formal meetings include those involving dinner, a banquet, or some other ceremonial affair, at which a speech or speeches are traditional.

Speeches of welcome or farewell, those marking an anniversary of the plant, organization, or chapter, those of presentation or acceptance, or those formalizing an opening or ribbon-cutting ceremony may be classed as formal addresses, even though in most instances the talk may be short.

Every town has its quota of service clubs—Rotary, Kiwanis, Lion, Optimist—meeting weekly, with special semi-annual or annual occasions. The larger cities have other organizations, like the Economic Club, the Athletic Club, The City Club, or the Press Club, many of which meet on a regular basis for dinner and a program. In

[5] William H. Whyte, Jr., "The Art of the Presentation," *Fortune*, LV, No. 3 (March, 1957), p. 130.

addition there are the industrial organizations, the technical and scientific groups, the trade associations, and the professional societies, all of which gather for local and regional meetings and business. Every one of these meetings may be an occasion for an address.

All these, and similar meetings we may characterize as formal, which means that the speaker must not only plan what he has to say with extra care, but must as well make sure that his whole effort will be in keeping with the form and atmosphere of the gathering.

4. Conventions

Overlapping somewhat in nature with the semi-formal and formal meetings, yet sufficiently unique to provide a separate category, are the thousands of conventions which are held each year in the nation. It has been estimated that six million persons attend the 75,000 conventions which mark each calendar year. Twelve thousand of these meetings are those of industrial associations, trade shows, and technical and professional societies. More than sixty thousand are company conventions. Each runs for several days as a rule, with a program crammed with speeches, papers, seminars, symposia, and panel discussions, as well as other events. Some companies find it necessary to be represented at so many conventions that they employ full-time conventioneers.

In a single day 29 conventions in Chicago attracted 55,000 delegates. Included were representatives to the District Superintendents Conference of the Methodist Church, the Music Teachers National Association, the U.S. Chamber of Commerce, the American Association of Colleges for Teacher Education, the American Management Association, the Mason Contractors Association, and the National Retail Grocers Secretaries Association.

Popular gossip has it that most people attend conventions to get away from home, have a vacation, and "live it up" for a few days. It must be admitted that the sideshows of each convention do hold an attraction, but nevertheless thousands of business and professional men and women attend in order to improve their vocational competence, promote their joint interests, or enhance the competitive position of the enterprise for which they work. According to *Fortune* magazine[6]

[6] Daniel Seligman, "Are Business Conventions Worth It?" *Fortune*, L, No. 2 (Aug., 1954), p. 100.

J. Gordon Roberts, president of the Roberts Dairy Co., in Omaha is typical of businessmen who aim to squeeze the last ounce of usefulness out of the conventions they attend. Before each of the twenty or so conventions he and his associates attend every year, he studies the program and the list of delegates. His own company's delegates are then given specific assignments—information to procure, people to meet, convention sessions to attend—so that their time is accounted for pretty much down to the minute.

It is for representatives of this kind that the convention speaker must prepare. Whether his presentation be major or minor, semi-formal or formal, feature address or panel contribution, there will be in the listening group those who have come to benefit, and who have invested a great deal of time and effort as well as money.

5. Good will or public relations speeches

Our final category is less characterized by the situation or by the degree of formality required than it is by the basic purpose of the speaker. The good will or public relations speech exists for the purpose of making friends, for developing positive attitudes toward the speaker, his company, or his business, profession or industry.

To this end the good will or public relations talk is not unlike any other instrument used for the same purpose. Almost all significant enterprises have a public relations department or office whose function is to communicate outside the organization to segments of the public, using advertising, press releases, institutional publications, and special events such as open houses, special showings, or sponsored tours to cultivate understanding and good will. Among public relations instruments, public speaking can be one of the most effective. The task is to demonstrate an attitude of cooperation with the community, to cultivate an informed public, to offer an organizational service, or to create public appreciation of good work and service. As Lionel Crocker has written in an American Bankers Association manual,[7]

Why is public speaking by bankers so important? It is the alert, dedicated bankers who, in their relations with the public, convince their customers and neighbors that

[7] Lionel Crocker, *The Banker Speaks* (New York: American Bankers Association, 1955), p. 44.

banks are friendly, helpful places. One of the ways this is done is by speaking to the public, again and again, at meetings of its own groups.

The good will talk may be one of a carefully planned and programmed series based on a definite corporate strategy, it may be an address arranged by a speakers bureau attached to the company or other enterprise, or it may be an incidental appearance of some individual.

Effective use of the planned public relations talks may be illustrated by the Ohio Bell Telephone Company or by the Smith, Kline, French Laboratories, pharmaceutical manufacturers. In the best practice, public attitudes of importance to the company are discovered by opinion surveys, after which a speech or speeches are built to alter unfavorable attitudes and heighted favorable ones. In one year Ohio Bell speakers, who are volunteers from any department and trained by the company, delivered 3744 talks to audiences totalling 214,000 listeners. SKF speakers, who are volunteers from the sales staff, delivered one master speech 2100 times in 21 months, the audiences amounting to 90,000 people. In five years the SKF speaking staff has grown from 12 to 400 men, who have appeared before audiences totalling more than 5 million.

That these public relations talks are effective is attested by James Cline, Public Activities Supervisor of the Ohio Bell Telephone Company. Speaking of one talk designed to improve public attitudes toward the profit system, he said, "We measured audience attitude immediately before and immediately after the presentation of these talks. And the results were astounding in the marked shifts of attitude toward greater approval of the profit system as a result of exposure to the talk."[8]

While these two organizations are among the leaders in the use of speakers to deal with measurable public attitudes, many others, such as the B.F. Goodrich Company and the Dow Chemical Company, operate a speakers bureau for the purpose of getting their men into the public eye. Without attempting to cope with identified public attitudes, the B. F. Goodrich Company booked speakers from its nine corporations before 768 audiences in one year. Nor are large organizations like Goodrich alone in using a regular bureau to book

---

[8] Address, "Purposive Public Speaking," Tenth Annual Conference on Communication in Business and Industry, Kent State University, April 27, 1961.

speakers, for local bar associations, mental health associations, the Girl Scouts, theatre guilds, utilities companies, welfare and philanthropic organizations, and hosts of others constantly organize and operate speakers bureaus. In Cleveland the Public Library centralizes information on available speakers, and reports that the city has 150 separate speakers bureaus, offering 2000 speakers on almost as wide a range of subjects.

Even a small businessman or lone professional person can use the good will speech to develop positive attitudes toward, and a favorable image of himself and his business. When Jim Purdy of the local men's clothing store talks to the high school assembly on selecting clothes, he is building good will. When Carl English, county judge, speaks to one of the town's service clubs on inheritance taxes, he may be opening his campaign for re-election. And when Ralph Fertig, who runs a camera shop, speaks on "Snapshot Magic," he is building understanding of and good will toward his business.

Regardless of speaker or subject, all public relations talks have one thing in common. They offer worthwhile and interesting information to an audience. They are seldom argumentative and never undertake any kind of a sales appeal. In a public relations talk to attempt direct selling in any form would destroy the very good will being sought, since the speaker would trespass upon the time of the audience for his own purposes, not those of the listeners. Good will must come as a by-product of reliable, useful, and entertaining information presented by one who is an authority on the subject.

These five major kinds of talks do not exhaust the variety of demands made upon business and professional people. As responsible citizens and community, state, and national leaders, these men and women must frequently appear in symposiums and panels, talk at public and private hearings, engage in debates, testify at legislative inquiries, or participate in civic and political meetings. As Brigance has noted, "Effective speech is a national necessity among free men," and speech leadership cannot be restricted to any one select or elite group if we wish to maintain our democratic institutions. Business is keenly sensitive to its reponsibility in giving direction to the American destiny, and must have highly articulate spokesmen.

We are quite aware that in all this speaking many of the best known and most responsible businessmen and industrialists have assistants who help in the preparation of their speeches. We know, too, that there are some who give addresses which have been completely ghost-written. Some companies, like Republic Steel, hire teachers of speech on a full or part time basis to train their platform representatives. But you, at this moment, at least, will not have this assistance, and you will be the better for it, since you must learn to develop your own powers, to stand on your own feet, and to express your own thinking. For this reason we must next examine your responsibilities.

YOUR LISTENERS HAVE RIGHTS; YOU HAVE OBLIGATIONS

You noted earlier that business and professional people attending conventions look forward to definite benefits from their experience. We also observed that listeners to a good will speech resent a speaker who uses their time to sell something instead of giving them the new ideas and information they were expecting. A crew of workers expects its foreman to have something to say when he calls them together, and many salesmen would be less apathetic about the weekly sales meeting if they could look forward to a productive investment of their time. All listeners, as a matter of fact, invest valuable time in a speaker. For this investment they have a right to expect certain returns. It is your obligation as a speaker to make sure the listener receives useful goods. Your obligation is four-fold.

Listeners have a right to a message worth the time and effort invested in listening

If you talk to thirty people for twenty minutes, the audience has collectively given you 10 hours of time. And while the value of no speech can be measured purely in dollars and cents, we can reach an approximation of value by supposing that this time represents a full eight-hour day, with two hours of overtime. Multiply this time by the hourly income of your average listener, and you will arrive at a figure which stands for their minimum investment. In addition, many may have traveled a distance to hear you, may have altered the day's schedule at some inconvenience, or otherwise made arrangements to be present. It is your obligation to see that what they hear from you is worthwhile.

Furthermore, these are people with business and professional problems. They may hope to learn something which will help them made a difficult decision, they may want technical or engineering information, they may need encouragement or hope, or they may simply be wishing for new insights into time-worn topics. At any rate, they look to you with an anticipation you cannot disappoint. Even a sales message must be presented for the benefit of the listener, for if a salesman cannot benefit his customers he should shut up shop. The listener is eager for an idea that will make a difference in his affairs.

Beyond these considerations is the fact that you or your company have something at stake in your talk. Your reputation may be increased or diminished. Future business may depend on the address. The efficiency of production, the safety of a group of workers, the cooperation of other organizations, the success of a new policy, or some other outcome may hinge on your ability to present a worthy message clearly and effectively.

All this means that your first obligation is to have a message for your listeners. You must give them some new ideas or must present a fresh approach to old ideas, for they will have a right to complain if they hear the same old message in the same old words. The audience, as a general rule, is eager to learn from *you;* it is not interested in the second-hand material you have appropriated from somebody else. This is not to say you shouldn't do research on your subject—you should. But the research should be to develop and to round out your own thinking, since the integrity of your message depends on its being essentially your own. This is the only way public address attains its best, and the only way you can give your listeners what they have a right to expect.

Listeners have a right to an orderly presentation of material

Even an important message can become almost repulsive to an audience if it is not presented in a clear and easy-to-follow way. When the listener is forced to submit to a confused jumble of words and ideas, when he would like to understand the speaker but is frustrated by hearing a hodge-podge of unassorted thoughts which do not merge into a clean-cut development of theme, the speaker has failed to meet his second basic obligation.

Your listeners have a right to expect that you will have taken the time and effort to plan what you have to say so they can follow you without trouble. They have a right to expect that you will be able to give them a complete message within the time limits which have been set for your talk, or within a reasonable length of time if no limit has been set. Your obligation, then, consists in so arranging your material, in so planning the order or sequence of your remarks, that your audience will be able to think with you without effort, from a specific conversational opening to an ending which wraps up the speech with satisfaction and completeness. And you are obliged to make certain that you do not overstep the bounds of courtesy and common sense by talking longer than you should.

Listeners have a right to direct communication, sparked with enthusiasm

Your listeners are not at all unreasonable to insist that you talk *with* them. They have a right to sense that you seek mental and emotional rapport and that you do so because you have a high desire to communicate something of importance. As Louis Nizer, famous for his speaking both inside and outside the courtroom, has observed, "Is there anything more discouraging to an audience than to be virtually ignored by the speaker whose head and often astigmatic eyes are buried in papers before him? . . . If a speaker can throw off the shackles of his script, he can face his audience a free man."[9] You may want notes at times, and rarely a manuscript, but under no conditions will your audience become a part of the communicative process with you if you are not free from all encumbrance and able to converse with directness.

Furthermore, your audience expects, and you have an obligation, to talk with verve, enthusiasm, and physical animation. This does not mean that you must be a table-thumping rabble-rouser, but that you must be alive with the excitement of your message and the opportunity to do something for the audience. As G. P. Meredith, respected British scholar, thought back over all the lectures he had ever heard, he identified the one quality which marked the memorable ones:[10]

[9] Louis Nizer, *Thinking on Your Feet* (New York: Pyramid Publications, Inc., 1963), p. 34.
[10] Quoted in T. M. Higham, "Basic Psychological Factors in Communication," *Occupational Psychology*, XXXI, No. 1 (Jan., 1957), p. 9.

You can wander about, you can indulge in irritating mannerisms, you can hum and haw, you can remain glued to a desk, you can twiddle your fingers, you can commit all the crimes in the statute book, . . . and you can get away with all of them if only you have the one supreme virtue. What is that virtue? The name I would give it is *vitality*. This was the common quality in all my remembered lectures.

And while I cannot recommend that you commit all the speaking crimes in the statute book, I can insist, as will your audiences, that you add vitality to your conversation.

Listeners have a right to material which is specific and factual and therefore interesting

Unless your audience is captive, it will walk out on you if you insist on talking in generalities and abstractions. And if it is captive, it may sit before you but won't listen. It will go to sleep—and audiences can easily sleep with eyes wide open! You will have to pin your ideas down with illustrations, examples, instances, facts, and figures. You will have to express your thinking in specific words—in words which sparkle because they have meaning in the everyday life of the listener.

A quip on a five-cent card reads, "Your argument is sound. All sound." Unless you want the audience to make remarks like this about your speech, you must substitute facts for sound. You cannot interest or impress business and professional audiences with noise and fireworks, but you can do so with specific materials which show that you know what you're talking about and which make sense to the listener. This is your obligation.

If you can give your audiences these four things which they have a right to expect, they will appreciate you as a speaker, and you can reasonably anticipate success in achieving the results you are after. A solid message, clear arrangement of material, enthusiastic delivery, and specific content are the minimum satisfactory requirements. This is not to say that you should not aspire for greater virtues as a speaker, but that you cannot get by with less. The minimum requirements are based on the rights of the listeners.

As for the results you are after, we must next recognize that speeches are known for the purposes they serve, and must therefore examine the kinds of purposes.

YOUR TALK MUST SEEK A CHOSEN RESPONSE FROM YOUR LISTENERS

In Chapter 2 we examined the various elements of behavior and noted that the purpose of speech was to evoke a desired kind of behavior from others. As we turned to listening in Chapter 5 and to the basic forms of speech communication in subsequent chapters, we continued to see that in every case communication is governed by the purpose sought by the speaker or listener. The principle applies equally to public speaking, for the speech is planned and presented with one overriding consideration in mind, and that is the response sought by the speaker. In each situation it is the purpose of the speaker rather than the nature of the gathering which determines the character of the speech, although the gathering will, of course, influence the choice of purpose.

It should be clear that at any given moment while you speak you must be achieving one or a combination of responses from your listeners.

You must be interesting, so they will pay close attention.

You must be clear, so they will understand.

You must be vivid, so they will be impressed.

You must be convincing, so they will believe.

Ordinarily you will not have to succeed continuously in producing all four of these responses, but as a rule you must be constantly successful in two or three. Prerequisite to obtaining any other response, you must keep attention and therefore you must be fundamentally concerned with making yourself interesting.

Often, however, responses such as these must be considered no more than way stations en route to your ultimate goal. If you will refer back to the behavioral pyramid in Chapter 3, you will note that we have termed some of the elements *terminal behavior*, to signify that any one of them may be the desired result of a specific communication. To obtain such a result it may be necessary to obtain other responses as means to your ultimate end. Indeed, the purpose of the behavioral pyramid is to make graphic this concept.

In planning and delivering a speech, therefore, you must select one final response to which all other forms of responding behavior must contribute. Perhaps this can be illustrated by supposing that you would like to travel. In order to avoid wasting time and money by traveling aimlessly, you decide to visit the famed Taj Mahal. To get there you choose to go by train to New York, fly to Bombay, and secure the best local transportation to Agra, the site of the great mausoleum. New York and Bombay become steps toward your destination; they are not the end, but are stages on the way.

So it is with a talk. The speech must not wander, or it will waste time and money. Therefore you must select a destination. All audience responses short of that destination become stages on the way to your ultimate goal. You will not have succeeded if you stop in Bombay when your purpose is to visit the Taj Mahal. Neither have you succeeded if you want to convince your audience of something, but are able only to interest them. Your final goal designates the nature of your talk, enabling you to classify it by kind in terms of the behavior you intend to elicit.

In this light, people have generally come to recognize five kinds of speeches, each known by the nature of the ultimate response sought by the speaker. It will be useful to consider each.

The speech to entertain seeks to hold favorable attention only

In many situations it is legitimate for a speaker to desire no more than to be interesting, and therefore only to hold the attention of his listeners. However, it is highly unusual for a business or professional person to undertake such a talk. When a business, industrial, or professional group wants entertainment it generally secures the services of a professional who is experienced in providing light entertainment, high humor, or unrestrained laughter, and the results are certain. A few business people have become noted for their ability to entertain, but they usually weave at least a faint message into their remarks. Unless you are unusually gifted you are not likely to have to deliver a talk for its entertainment value, and therefore we shall not consider this a vital skill for you.

The speech to inform seeks to develop understanding

In Chapter 9 we saw that briefings, reports, and presentations of various sorts were common and appropriate at meetings. Earlier in this chapter we likewise saw that many semi-formal meetings and convention sessions were given over to informative speaking. When your speech, like these, can be classed as informative, the response you seek from your listeners is understanding, and your success will not be measured by the well organized accumulation of facts and ideas you may present, but solely by what your listeners comprehend.

The classroom lecture and the professional or industrial presentation, then, are alike in the response sought. Technical, research, and operating reports, the exposition of new ideas, approaches, and developments, the explanation of new programs or projects, or talks to develop greater understanding of old ideas, such as the values of the American business system to employees, all call for a talk whose purpose is to get listeners to understand something they have not known before. This means that the material must be brought within the framework of the audience's experience. The significance of this principle was discussed in Chapter 3, parts of which you should review in connection with informative speaking. You should also note the importance of motivating your listeners by creating a need for the ideas and information you want them to understand.

The informative speaker cannot be satisfied merely by knowing that he wants people to understand. He must know *what* they are to understand, and must specify at least to himself, the exact nature of the desired response. The first of these necessities calls for the speech to be organized around a central idea or thesis; the second for a precise determination of the expected response to the speech. Does the speaker simply desire that his central idea become more significant and meaningful to his listeners? Does he want them to remember and be able later to recall certain items or parts? Does he want to awaken a deeper appreciation of his subject? Does he want the new understanding to influence the behavior of his audience as they see things in a fresh light? Does he want them to use or apply the information whenever that information is relevant to their problems? Or does he want to alter certain of their attitudes as a result of the information he presents? (This last objective is the purpose of the good will or public relations speech.)

In brief, then, the informative speech deals with motivation in order to affect the understandings and attitudes of listeners.

The speech to stimulate seeks to intensify old beliefs

From this point we are dealing with the so-called persuasive purposes of speaking, in which information may be presented but is
used as a means of guiding or regulating the beliefs and behavior of
listeners.

We have seen that not infrequently a speaker must address an
audience which already believes as he does, and that consequently he
will not have to win them to a new idea, opinion, or line of action.
Therefore his purpose must be to touch the feelings of his listeners,
to arouse their emotions, to inspire, to awaken, or to animate them.
They may believe with him, and yet their belief is feeble, so that the
speaker's persuasive problem is to intensify, to vitalize, or to energize it. A speech of this nature is commonly called a speech to
stimulate.

The effect of a speech to stimulate may be seen by supposing
that Randy has been bitten by a dog suspected of having rabies. The
doctor tells Randy that he should have a shot of anti-toxin to
prevent serious consequences, but Randy protests. He and the doctor
are both of the opinion that such shots are medically desirable, but
the vitality of Randy's opinion is low. It cannot overcome his fear of
the needle, hence his objection. Then the doctor paints a vivid word
picture, describing the horrors of death from rabies—the choking,
the convulsions, the agony. The picture energizes Randy's belief in
anti-toxin by creating a fear greater than his dread of the needle,
and he consents to the treatment. The doctor has stimulated him to
act upon his verbalized belief.

A speech to stimulate, like the doctor's statement, is one which
increases the emotional power of an idea, but unlike the doctor's,
most such speeches dwell on positive emotions. Occasions calling for
speeches of this kind are not as numerous as occasions for informative speaking, but nevertheless are common enough in business,
professional, or industrial situations. The sales manager wants to
arouse his staff to greater enthusiasm, the minister needs to increase the dedication of his parishioners, the foreman must renew
his workers' desire to observe safety regulations, the president must
restore loyalty to the traditions of the firm, the athletic coach faces
the necessity of increasing his team's desire to win, or the chairman
of the board must make the "kick-off" address at the start of the

United Fund campaign. Each situation calls for an address on an idea to which the listener is but weakly dedicated, and through which he should be stimulated to positive behavior. This is the sort of speech which is appropriate to the ceremonial occasions of business life—the presentation of an award, the introduction of a new chief, the acceptance of a going-away gift, or the remarks in tribute for services unselfishly given. New ideas and new themes are less called for than a heightened appreciation of old ones at new levels of warmth and inspiration.

The speech to convince seeks decisions or commitment to new ideas

Unlike the talk to stimulate, that to convince presents new ideas to an audience. Its purpose is to gain acceptance of opinions, ideas, or policies which the listeners have not yet considered, which they have doubted, or may have rejected. Frequently it seeks a decision or a specific choice among alternatives.

The reponse desired by the speaker is purely verbal or symbolic. As pointed out in Chapter 3, when one believes he accepts an idea as true, he dismisses all doubts or inhibiting thoughts, and honestly consents to the validity of the proposition being presented. There was a day when people had to be convinced of the proposition that, "The world is round." That day is past, for the idea has been accepted, and no educated person would refuse his assent. The speech to convince, then, is always on the advancing edge of time— its purpose is often to secure assent to propositions which are disputed or disputable, and its frequent haunts are situations which are deliberative in nature.

Will the corporation benefit by merging? Should the new product be put into production? Is the new curriculum feasible? Should the price of fuel or steel or milk be raised? Questions like these call for a speech to convince, either to persuade the listeners to accept a decision already made, or to deliberate a proposed decision.

The speaker must adapt himself and his address to the audience and situation. There are times when assent or a decision will be won on an essentially emotional appeal, and there are times when success depends largely upon the logic of the presentation. There are times when any opposition to the proposal exists only in the doubts or fears of the listeners, and there are occasions when a speaker must contend against a vigorous opponent, when a conflict of opinion occurs and issues must be resolved. Nevertheless, these are only variations, however significant they may be, for always the rooted persuasive problem is to win the assent of the audience. The speaker must move people to his point of view.

The speech to actuate seeks specific action

The reasons for placing the speech to gain action in a separate category are based on the principle that a speaker must make known the precise response he seeks, and that when he wants a definite action unless he specifies it he will not get results. If you are serious in wanting people to act, you cannot be content with merely convincing them that they *ought* to act, for they can agree with you that they should and still fail to perform. You must impel them to the deed or deeds you propose.

The act may be of various sorts, but it entails physical behavior which can be observed. The speaker wants his listeners to *do* something. He wants them to go to the polls on election day, to fasten their seat belts without fail, to send a telegram to their Senator, to read a given book, to review their insurance coverage, to sign for blood donation, to give to the cause, to mail a coupon, to sign a petition, or to study an added half-hour each day.

Because a listener may have to be convinced or stimulated before he can be expected to act, this kind of speech must deal with wants, reasons, or satisfactions, but these considerations must lead toward and culminate in an overt response. The speech, therefore, suggests, induces, directs, or commands the listeners to commit a described action. It is different from other persuasive speeches only in the demand for a specific kind of response.

From the foregoing, you can see that any speech you are called upon to make may be classed as belonging to one of five general kinds, and that it will take its character from the sort of response you seek. This determines what you will say and how you will say it, and therefore in deciding what *kind* of speech you will make you are often taking the first step in planning it. In the next chapter we will take up in detail the specific factors you must consider in preparing the speech.

329

Chapter 11

Planning Your Talk

The late Marshal Foch said once: "The best inspiration is preparation." *At least 90 per cent of the success of a talk before any audience depends upon proper preparation. Here a great many people have difficulty. First, they procrastinate before starting to marshal their facts and organize their thinking. The result—the date and the hour of the talk bear down upon them, and they start scrambling around to develop something to get them off the spot.*[1]

GRANVILLE B. JACOBS
General Foods Corporation

SOME TIME AFTER HE HAD MADE HIS NOW-FAMOUS REPLY TO SENATOR Hayne in the critical debate of 1830, Daniel Webster was stopped by a friend. "Tell me, Senator," asked the friend, "how long did it take you to prepare that speech?" Webster's reply was sharp and saturated with meaning. "All my life, sir, all my life."

Webster's answer only emphasizes the fact we considered in Chapter 4, that the measure of the speech is the measure of the man. It similarly emphasizes that a few hours work over a desk does not make up the whole of speech preparation, for the work of creating a speech of high merit is never a matter of hours, and may be a matter of years. The significant preparation of the speech is the

---

[1] "When You Have To Make a Speech," in *Effective Communication on the Job*, ed. M. Joseph Dooher and Vivienne Marquis (New York: American Management Association, 1956), p. 283.

preparation of the speaker. "How did I do that speech?" said a student speaker. "I lived it."

Recognizing this truth, you are nevertheless looking for a workable method by which you can lay hold of the things life has given you to say. Having determined the basic nature and function of a given speech, you need a system which will enable you to shape the raw material into the finished product. This is a task that cannot be handled all at once, but must be attacked in manageable chunks, and in some practical order of procedure. All experienced speakers work by some scheme of operations, and you can save time and effort by taking advantage of their experience.

What follows in this and subsequent chapters is a plan of procedure by which, starting from scratch, you can develop a speech. You may be disappointed to know that it cannot guarantee you instant success, or that by using it you will wake up some morning to find yourself famous. But you may be encouraged by the fact that it has evolved from the experience of hundreds of people over many years.

In this chapter we consider the five steps necessary to the fundamental planning of your talk, ending with a statement of the central idea, which is the heart of your message. You must understand, however, that you will not necessarily accomplish the first three steps, choosing a subject, understanding your audience, and specifying an exact purpose, in this order. The order in which we take them up is the ordinary sequence of operations, but for various reasons there will be times when you cannot follow it. On some occasions you will have to decide on your purpose before selecting a subject, while on others your first challenge will be to diagnose and understand the audience you will face. On still others you will have to weigh subject, purpose, and audience concurrently and in relation to one another before you can move ahead. You must be practical enough to recognize the best sequence for planning a particular talk. With this in mind, let us turn to your planning.

CHOOSE A SUBJECT THAT WILL PRO-
VIDE YOU WITH A SIGNIFICANT
MESSAGE AND PREPARE TO BE
MASTER OF THAT SUBJECT

Albert J. Beveridge, noted Senator from Indiana, made his first rule of successful public address, "Speak only when you have something to say." In this one significant sentence may lie the key to your own success or failure, for when you discover that you are a man with a message it will be difficult for you to fail. Conversely, if you are a man without a message, it will be equally hard for you to succeed.

It has been wisely observed that people face the challenge of a speech under one of two conditions. The first is when they *have to say something,* and the second is when they *have something to say.* This observation may describe your immediate problem in a nut-shell, for if you are studying speech in a class you are subject to the first condition. You *have* to say something. But even later there will be times, too, when you will be expected to talk, and you will rise knowing that you have to say something. It's a common problem. "What can I talk about?" you ask yourself.

Those with experience have come to know that success lies in converting the first condition into the second. When you have to say something, the secret to making a talk of which you can be proud is to *discover that you have something to say.* You must become a man with a message. The principle is simple, but there may be times when you have to search your soul to bring out your message. Be not dismayed, though—that's a good place to find it! Oscar Hammerstein is said to have once remarked, "You have to have a soul to a show to have it remembered." The same is true with a speech, which, as Ruskin wrote of art, "is that in which the hand, the head, and the heart of man go together."

Explore yourself! What notable experiences have you had which may provide the kernel? From which of them have you learned lessons you should share with others? What has life taught you? What of your triumphs and your failures? Like Daniel Webster, you have been living all your life with speech material, and now you have an opportunity to look back and rediscover it for the benefit of others.

Men whose experiences have given them something to say are those who are sought by audiences. This is what happened to Herman D. Sahagian, a businessman of Belgrade Lakes, Maine. After a trip into the Middle East, he spoke to the Rotary Club of Rumford, Maine, using his experience abroad as the topic of his speech. Later his address was published in *Vital Speeches*, a magazine devoted to the significant speeches of the day.[2]

Of course, you may earn the right to talk about a subject in ways other than direct experience. You may become an authority by studying the subject, by spending time investigating it, by reading about it, and by thinking about it. This is the way many writers make themselves capable of turning out stories, books, or articles. Kenneth Roberts, for instance, declared that in writing his famous novel, *Northwest Passage,* he studied enough history, politics, economics, and biography to equal three college educations put together.

Drawing your subject from your personal experiences, either direct or vicarious, will give you the initial power necessary to a good speech, for as the great Frenchman, Francois Fenelon, observed in *Dialogues on Eloquence,* "One speaks easily of things when he fully knows and loves them." Yet the subject alone is not enough. You must have, as we said at the beginning, a *message,* and a significant one at that. The message is why Mr. Sahagian's speech at the Rumford Rotary Club was worth publishing. He was not content to describe his journey through Damascus and Jerusalem, which would have been interesting but not truly significant. Instead he told the Rotarians, "Gentlemen, I am here . . . to utter a warning. I think it is time the American people established methods of funneling money directly into the hands of those who need help the most in the Middle East. . . . I think . . . swift action on our part as private citizens is of essence." He had something to say which was significant both to him and to his listeners.

As in this instance, the message is the lesson derived from experience or study, the essence of the subject distilled into meaningful form, the principle derived from the facts and data, the thesis which you wish to present, the theme you intend to develop, the advice you hope will benefit others, or the conclusion you offer

[2] *Vital Speeches,* XXVII (June 15, 1961), pp. 526–7.

for acceptance. It must be one for which you feel an enthusiasm and which you can make of consequence to your auditors.

Having selected a subject and from it distilled the idea of a message, your next step is to see that you are master of that subject, for a major share of your power in presenting the talk depends on mastery of subject and message. You must have an intimate and detailed acquaintance with its ins and outs, with its ramifications and implications, and with its relationships in every direction. You must know at least ten times more about it than you can possibly use in the time allowed you to talk. This is the only way to assure yourself of reserve power, of ability to modify and adapt your remarks to the responses of your audience, and of freedom from involved and encumbering notes and papers. Later in this chapter we will come to ways of analyzing your subject which will be useful in helping master it.

Thorough knowledge and full command of the subject, together with a feeling for the importance of your message will give you a capability lacking in most speakers who depend heavily on ghost-writers or assistants to prepare their addresses. When the message is *yours* from beginning to end you will have an inner compulsion which is notably lacking in second-hand speeches a compulsion to communicate ideas. Booker T. Washington, outstanding negro leader of the last century, wrote, "I do not believe that one should speak unless, deep down in his heart, he feels convinced that he has a message to deliver." It is this feeling which lends force and urgency to your speech, generating the enthusiasm which, as Bulwer-Lytton observed, "is the genius of sincerity."

With your message clearly in mind, then, you are ready for the next step, which is knowing the people to whom it must be presented and adapted, for the speaker's task is to make *his* subject interesting and important to others.

UNDERSTAND THE PEOPLE YOU WILL BE TALKING TO AND THE CIRCUMSTANCES OF THE MEETING

Unlike a written message, which in most instances will be read individually and in a variety of times and situations, your speech will be presented to win an immediate response from a group of

334

people gathered at a particular time and place. As we have seen, each listener brings to an occasion his own feelings, his own past experiences, his own conviction, his own desires, and his own expectancies. To the extent that any speaker is aware of what his audience brings to their meeting, he fits himself for effective communication. The speech, then, must be adapted to fit the unique combination of audience and occasion and speaker which will happen only once. You and your message have full and complete meaning only *in relation to* the audience and the occasion. What you say must be tailored to fit, and in order to do the tailoring you must understand the elements to which you must make the fit. You can best base this understanding on a consideration of your listeners as individuals, on the audience as a group, and on the specifications of the occasion.

Understand your listeners as individuals

What kind of persons will you be talking to? The more fully you know and understand them as individuals, the more effectively will you be able to "talk their language"—that is, to speak in terms of their interests, desires, capacities, and daily life. Who are they? What is the vocation, niche, job, or calling in life of each? How old are they? Will you face men, or women, or both? What triumphs or defeats has life meted out to them? You may be able to determine partial answers to questions like these if you inquire into their background and general affiliations. Where do they live? What is their creed? What social, political, business, professional, or fraternal organizations do they belong to? Do they have strong family ties? What do they do with their spare time or on vacation? Recognizing that it will undoubtedly be impossible to secure all the information you would like, and that you will know or understand some listeners more fully than others, you must nevertheless try to know your audience as completely as possible.

Even more specifically, you will want to ask yourself, "What do they want?" This question will direct you toward the motivations with which you must deal. In general, what goals in life do they have? What broad aspirations move them, what ambitions drive them? What problems or frustrations do they face? What barriers must they surmount to reach their goals? And, in terms of the moment you speak to them, what are their immediate wants and expectations? What present desires or hopes may you be able to help fulfill? What do they lack at the moment? What problems, difficulties, fears, or discouragements exist that can be related to your message? The answers to some of these questions will provide you with the key which opens the way to their attention, their interest, and their motives.

In addition to these things, you must also try to assess the possible attitudes of your auditors. What attitudes toward you as a person will they likely possess? Will they be hostile toward or suspicious of you? Will their attitude be positive and friendly, disposing them to an open mind? Or will they more likely be neutral or passive in attitude? And what attitudes may govern their reception of your subject? Are they concerned with it, indifferent to it, or averse to hearing about it? Further, what of their attitudes toward your purpose? Will their predisposition to respond be negative, positive, or neutral? Each listener will have a complex of attitudes toward you, your subject, and your purpose. With these you must deal to attain success.

Another item of pertinent information may be the answer to the question, "Why haven't they already responded as I hope they will to my speech?" If you intend a talk to inform, why haven't they known before what you intend them to understand? If your talk is to convince, why have they not already accepted the position or made the decision you propose? If you want to actuate them why haven't they already done what you would have them do? And if you plan to stimulate, why do they not *now* feel as strongly about your message as you think they should? If you can discover what has prevented your listeners from behaving as you want them to, you will have an immediate clue to a way of achieving the desired response.

Finally, you must assess the resources possessed by your listeners. What amount of intelligence, knowledge, background, and experience relative to your topic can you draw upon? Everything you say will be absorbed, understood, and responded to only as the listener has personal resources which can be brought to bear upon your words. Unless you plan to give your listener an entirely new experience which will provide its own meaning, you must create meaning out of what he has and is. Either way you cannot proceed until you are aware of the resources available for you to work with.

If you can find answers at least to the most significant of the questions here suggested, you will be in a position to begin understanding your listeners.

Understand the audience as a group

It will be necessary, however, to understand your audience as a group as well as a collection of individuals. For one thing, you must consider what characteristics the members have in *common* so you may adapt your remarks to wants and interests shared by most or all. And for another thing, you need to take into account the degree to which the members identify themselves as members of a gathered group and subject to group norms and patterns of behavior.

To begin with, you will want to assess the degree of homogeneity of the people who will listen to you. Considering the various items already listed, in what ways are these people alike and in what ways are they different? Are they similar in age and outlook? In attitudes toward you and your speech? In wants and desires? In readiness and ability to respond as you wish? If you can discover a *common denominator*, it may provide you with a way of framing your speech which will involve and interest all the listeners. Otherwise you may find it difficult if not impossible to speak with equal success to every auditor. Obviously, whatever common denominator you do find must be significant, or capable of being made significant. If you were speaking on factory maintenance it would hardly be pertinent to know that all your listeners owned portable radios. (Although some speaker would find a way to capitalize even on that bit of irrelevant common identification!) At any rate, you should try to find out ways in which your listeners are alike or things they have in common. By knowing these things you may be able to address yourself to most or all at once.

You may next be aided by seeking to know the extent to which your audience can be considered a true *group*. A group is distinguished from a collection of individuals in that its members are aware of a common motive or goal, they possess a set of habits or ways of behaving to which all conform, they like or accept one another, they recognize and interact among themselves, and they tend to cohere through interpersonal attraction, each possessing a role in relation to the others. A sidewalk or store demonstrator may induce an aggregation of people to stop and listen to his presentation, but his audience will not possess group characteristics. In contrast, a professor of medicine lecturing to a class of hospital interns will face an audience with strong group characteristics. Your own speaking task will be more clearly defined when you ascertain the extent to which your audience may have the character of a group.

The store demonstrator collects an audience of passers-by, which has been aptly termed a *pedestrian* audience, whereas a military officer before his command faces what has been called an *organized* audience, since a single order will evoke the wanted behavior. The pedestrian and the organized audiences establish the extremes of group character, with most audiences falling somewhere between these extremes. You may wish to establish at what point between the extremes your particular audience can be placed, to assess how ready they may be as a group to respond to your message, and how that message must be presented to secure a favorable response. A general audience, such as that at a popular lecture or many a stockholders' meeting, will be more like a pedestrian gathering, whereas a select audience, such as a Rotary Club or a meeting of Y.M.C.A. secretaries will tend toward more of the characteristics of an organized group.

Occasionally there may be among your listeners a very few individuals whom the others recognize, formally or informally, as leaders. It can be useful to you to identify these leaders and to direct a portion of your message specifically at them, even though you do so unobtrusively. If you can evoke favorable response from a group's leadership, it will be easier to win the remainder of the group.

Understanding the degree of group identification possessed by members of your audience, then, is the second step in knowing those to whom you will speak. By understanding this you may be able to predict their possible response to what you want to say, and how you may best present your message.

Understand the specifications of the occasion

Remembering that you will be talking to your audience at a given time and place, you must finally examine these circumstances as they may affect what you will say and how you will say it. You should not miss significant elements either in the meeting itself or in the physical setting.

As to the meeting, you might begin by asking why it is being held. Is it a regular and periodic meeting of an organization, or a special convocation of people for a particular reason? Will there be a theme or topic, or some specific business at hand? What about the time? Is there something special about the hour of the day or the day of the month which must be recognized or might be capitalized upon? What *kind* of meeting will it be? Will it be largely business, largely social, or a combination? Will anything happen in addition to your speech? A dinner? Regular business? Other speeches, some ceremony, or entertainment? What degree of formality or informality will be appropriate?

As you consider these aspects of the occasion, consider also the effect they may have on your listeners *at the time of your talk*. Will they have been stimulated toward and focused on your appearance, so that you will be the climax or major event? Or will you have to combat the effects of a tedious business session or of a succession of other speakers before you? Will a generous dinner have made your listeners dull, or will the anticipation of adjournment make them eager to escape? Many a "company dinner" for a group of employees is prefaced by a session at the restaurant bar, which can give you an entirely unpredictable audience. In answering questions like the foregoing, you can estimate the probable physical and mental activity level of your listeners when you rise to speak, and the degree to which they may or may not be ready to give you undivided attention.

You must not overlook the physical circumstances of your talk, either. Will you be speaking to a big audience in a small room, a small audience in a large hall? What kind of room indeed? Will the acoustics make you easily heard, or will you have to project your voice strongly? Will there be other meetings nearby, the sounds from which might be annoying? Will you have a speaker's stand, or must you handle yourself and any notes without such benefit? What of a public address system? Much of this information you cannot learn until you actually arrive at the place, which means that you should try to anticipate every contingency. As a matter of fact, it is wise to arrive early enough that you can explore the setting before the meeting begins, not to be caught off balance by something completely unexpected, or by some arrangement to which you are unaccustomed. Do not find yourself in the position of a speaker at a Christmas Eve meeting who arrived to find the hall illuminated by candles and so dim he couldn't see his notes.

If you plan to use visual helps, it is especially vital not only to visit the place of your speech, but to try a run-through with some of your material. Don't let yourself be caught at the last minute without the screen promised by the chairman's assistant, or with a dead electric outlet for your opaque projector!

How can you find out all the things you should know about the audience and the occasion? If you have no prior information, the most obvious source is the person who invited you to speak, who will probably be able to supply many of the answers. If you are speaking to an organization which meets regularly, you may be able to find someone who has spoken to the group before and who can be helpful. The nature of the organization itself, or of the meeting, can supply you with clues. A meeting of United Rubber Workers will have characteristics unlike a meeting of the P.T.A., the Monday Morning Quarterback Club, the Future Teachers of America, or a unit of the National Association of Training Directors. From whatever source, however, you must assemble as much information as you can which will enable you to understand the individuals to whom you will talk, the audience as a group, and the specifications of the occasion. Armed with as much understanding as possible, you can then take the next step in planning.

WRITE DOWN A STATEMENT OF YOUR EXACT PURPOSE

Having determined your subject or message and having arrived at some understanding of your audience and the occasion for the speech, you must next further clarify your own intentions (if you have not been doing this concurrently with the other steps). Your task is to arrive at a clear understanding with yourself of the *exact* response you mean to evoke in your listeners.

In the preceeding chapter we considered the general kinds of speeches, and saw that a determination of the nature of the desired response is often a first step in planning a talk. The kind of speech to be given may sometimes be decided by the speaker's own desires, but it is more probably dictated by the nature or function of the meeting or by the needs and characteristics of the audience. At a convention, for instance, business sessions are likely to demand deliberative speeches seeking conviction on proposed policy or informational reports from committees, whereas "conference" sessions are more apt to be given over to speeches explaining new developments, or reporting recent trends. A ceremonial occasion usually requires a speech to stimulate or inspire.

Knowing the general kind of speech, however, is not enough, and the speaker must narrow and define his purpose, and must do so in the light of the things we have taken up so far in this chapter. He must make himself consciously aware of his precise aim, for otherwise his purpose may be so general and diffused that real success would be impossible. He must know that he intends to get the audience to approve of Program A, to switch to Brand X, to understand that academic grades are an important index to job performance, or to deeply respect the retiring company president for his courageous leadership. These purposes are specific aims for speeches to convince, to actuate, to gain understanding, or to stimulate.

In deciding his specific purpose, the speaker must be careful to select a response which he can actually get from his listeners, for it would be folly to hope otherwise. There are responses impossible to achieve because the audience is powerless to respond, such as asking a group of college students to vote for a local candidate or issue when they do not have voting privileges. There are responses impossible to achieve because the goal is too remote, such as urging the adoption of world federal government upon people not yet fully committed to the United Nations. And there are responses impossible to achieve because they are inconsistent with strong beliefs or imbedded cultural patterns, such as arguing for medicare to a county medical association. In instances like these, the speaker must select an attainable specific purpose by asking *Why haven't these people already done what I would like? How far toward my goal will it be possible to take them in one speech?* Answers to these questions will help to discover a realistic and attainable purpose.

Once you have identified the specific response you will seek, you should write it down as a declaration of purpose, naming the exact behavior you hope to evoke. The act of writing it forces you to think clearly, accomplishing a fineness of aim too easily glossed over at this stage of preparation. Unless you rigorously put down your thoughts so that you may examine them more objectively and refer to them in later stages of preparation, you may too easily satisfy yourself that your planning is adequate when in fact it is not. Francis Bacon made the point centuries ago when he declared, "Writing maketh an exact man."

We must here make a distinction between your purpose statement and the statement which will be the central idea or message of your speech, for the two are not identical. It is true that when you write out your specific purpose, you *may* include in it the exact

341

message you wish to deliver, but this will not always be so. Your purpose statement declares what you want to *accomplish.* Your central idea declares what you want to *say.* The latter telescopes your entire message into a sentence. The central idea is that which, *if understood and accepted as true,* should produce the response you are after. It is the means to the end, and the end is response. If your specific purpose, for instance, were to "develop more favorable positive attitudes toward real estate brokers," your central idea might be, "Real estate brokers protect both buyers and sellers of property from hidden hazards."

Suppose we take a definite instance, and see how a statement of specific purpose might issue in a given topic for each of the general ends. We will suppose that you are speaking on behalf of the Poison Control Center of an urban hospital, your topic being poisons in the home. Statements of specific purpose for each of the general ends could be:

To inform: I want my audience to understand the danger of poisons in the home.

To stimulate: I want my listeners to become vividly aware of the poisons commonly found at home.

To convince: I want my audience to believe that the home is more dangerous than the highway.

To actuate: I want my listeners to inventory their homes and place all poisonous articles out of the reach of children.

Once you have written it and determined that the specific purpose statement represents a response which you want to achieve, one which you can achieve, and one which is appropriate to the speaking situation, you have taken careful aim. You are then ready for the next step in the planning of your talk.

EXPLORE AND ANALYZE YOUR SUBJECT TO DECIDE WHAT SHOULD BE SAID

What possibly can be said on the subject you have chosen? If you pursued every facet and every implication to the utmost limits, can you imagine a definite ending? Yet if you are to be master of your subject, and you must be, yours is the obligation to trace the myriad of facts, ideas, causes, consequences, relations, and applications which may concern your message and the response you hope to evoke from it.

Your primary task, then, is to see your subject in its entirety, to so master it that you understand the relationship of each part to the whole. Only then can you achieve your subsequent aim, that of determining what must be said in the amount of time given you to speak. To know everything about your subject is clearly an impossible task, yet your talk will not be worthy if you neglect to try.

You can begin by seating yourself with a sheet or two of blank paper and jotting down everything you can think of relating to your subject. Let your mind run free, allowing each fact or idea to suggest others in a chain reaction. Do not be concerned with organization or neatness, but simply pile up your thinking, recording every fact and every idea that occurs to you. In time you will discover patterns and relationships emerging, you will discover the areas with which you are most acquainted, and you will find the gaps in your knowledge which must be filled by research.

To aid yourself at this stage of preparation, try a *forecast* of what you think can and might be said on the subject, using some device or form to stimulate your thinking. A glance at the next chapter will show you a speech formula which provides a psychological structure for your talk, the main phases of which can help you forecast what might be said. Examine carefully the "want" and the "satisfaction" phases to discover relationships which will be fruitful.

If your talk is to be deliberative in nature, that is, if you expect your audience to make a decision, it will help you to discover the possible *issues* involved. The issues are the subordinate or minor decisions upon which the final decision can hinge. What are they? Does a problem exist which demands a decision? Will your proposal solve that problem? Is your proposal superior to any other? Is the decision you advocate a practical one? What values or benefits are involved? Will your proposal create undesirable side effects or other unwanted consequences? Asking and answering questions like these can provide you a forecast on an argumentative subject.

If your talk will be informative in kind, make a forecast by partitioning the general subject. What can be said of its past, present, and future? Can it be divided into causes and effects? How about the social, moral, and legal aspects? Or political, economic, psychological, and cultural divisions? The general heads of theory

343

and application might be useful. You can try Kipling's "six honest serving men" by asking *Who? What? Where? Why? How?* After subdividing your subject in various ways, examine the relationships and patterns which may appear and which may stimulate your thinking in new directions.

For a forecast on any kind of speech, investigate the elements of the total speaking situation: speaker, subject, audience, occasion, and purpose. Each may suggest something to be said, and the inter-relationships can be additionally revealing. What do you, the speaker, have in common with your audience, either as individuals or as a group? What unites, touches, or perplexes you in common? What is the relationship of you or of your listeners to the subject or occasion? What do the circumstances suggest should be said? Handling your subject in terms of the recent and the immediate can make it highly relevant, and therefore interesting and perhaps significant.

Not until you have exhausted your own thinking by putting it on paper, and not until you have looked for ideas and directions by making a detailed forecast, should you begin research for facts and materials. By that time you will have an understanding of your own knowledge, and of its strengths and weaknesses, and you will be better able to search intelligently to plug gaps, diminish weakness, and add breadth to your command of the subject.

Your research can be advanced along two lines. The first is to talk with friends and colleagues, seeking new information and ideas and subjecting your own to examination. You may also want to arrange interviews with experts, since by this time you may have specific questions which require authoritative answers. The second line of research is, of course, to read. Go to the library—your college library, the city library, or the library of your firm or organization—and collect the data, thought, and opinion of the best writers and investigators. Clifford Massoth, writing in the *Public Relations Journal*, declared that, "To end up with something worthwhile to say, the speech writer often has to do considerable research. The library, trade journals, company files, back issues of company magazines, trade association files, government publications, industrial yearbooks, and, of course newspapers, general interest magazines and broadcast programs are all sources of material."[3] From

---

[3] Clifford G. Massoth, "That Speech-Writing Chore," Reprinted from the Public Relations Journal, by permission, copyright April, 1960.

whatever source, you will want to use the method of the professional and investigate your subject fully before deciding what you will have to say. It is not the purpose of this book to tell you how to use the library, but if you are unfamiliar with its resources or procedures, the professional librarian is there to help you.

With a mass of material ten times greater than you can possibly use, you are finally ready to select that which will go into the talk. Now your task is to narrow your subject, to set apart only that which *must* and *can* be said in the time alloted you to speak. You will therefore limit your material to what is strictly relevant to your message and your purpose, and to what will be appropriate to the audience and occasion. No doubt you will have to exclude some things you would like to say, but you must remember that *everything cannot be said in one speech*. In making your final determination, you should be guided, not only by the considerations we have examined in this chapter, but also by the nature or structure of the speech organization (see Chapter 12).

As you work over your material, strive always for simplicity. It is better and more effective to say less and say it well than to attempt to say too much and risk failing your purpose. Remember that you must always be interesting and clear, and that sometimes you must be impressive and convincing. These consequences depend upon the reception by your listeners of what you say, and therefore possible listener response at every stage of the speech is the ultimate factor determining the speech content.

When you have explored and analyzed your subject, you are ready to take the first real step toward getting its structure on paper.

WRITE DOWN YOUR CENTRAL IDEA

"As to the preparation of a speech," wrote Grove Patterson, noted newspaper editor who for forty years was in wide demand as a speaker, "write down exactly what you want to say in one sentence. Make up your mind: This is it. This is the idea I want to sell."[4]

[4] *I Like People; the Autobiography of Grove Patterson* (New York: Random House, 1945), p. 241.

The final step in planning your talk, and the first in organizing it is to follow Mr. Patterson's advice. Take a piece of paper and on it write one sentence which will capture your entire speech. This is your message. It is the central idea, the thesis, or the proposition of the talk. It may have been in your mind throughout the entire planning process, in keeping with the principle that you must choose a subject which will provide a significant message. If so, you are ready to test the adequacy and accuracy of the message-statemeunt by reducing it to writing. If you have not yet crystallized your message into a simple, declarative statement of your central idea, now is the time. You cannot move ahead until you have done so.

Therefore, write down the message in one sentence. Are you satisfied with it? Does it say exactly what you want to say—no more and no less? Does it express your point in the best possible words? Is it clear, forceful, and simple? Will it make sense to your listeners? If they understand and accept it, will they respond as you want?

You may not be satisfied with your statement of the central idea on the first try, and quite probably you will not. That is one reason for putting it on paper, for thereby you can look at it carefully, and then go to work on it if it does not satisfy. How can you say it better? Try changing the order of words or replacing some of them with more vigorous, more exact, or more colorful ones. Make the verbs active. Get rid of useless adjectives. If there is a subordinate clause, see if you can eliminate it, for you would like a simple sentence. Keep at it until that one sentence asserts your message as well as that message can be said.

To illustrate, let us return to the speech on poisons in the home for which we listed four diverse statements of purpose. Suppose we now put down in order four statements of central idea, one for each of the purposes, remembering that these are not the only possible ones, but simply samples.

To inform: Familiar home products are deadly killers.
To stimulate: Tragedy can begin at the kitchen sink.
To convince: The home is more dangerous than the highway.
To actuate: Keep your children alive by searching out and putting all poisonous home products beyond their reach.

When you have arrived at a satisfactory and workable statement of your central idea, the planning part of your preparation is completed, and you are ready to begin arranging and outlining your talk. You are ready to place the central idea into the outline *exactly as you have written it*. If you use the persuasive pattern explained in the next chapter, your central idea will become the statement of the satisfaction phase. If you do not use this pattern, the central idea will become the thesis which governs the body of the speech.

As we leave this discussion of the five steps in planning your talk, we need to remind ourselves of two things about them. First, although they have been listed in a given order, you will not always be able to complete them in that order. If you start with a clearly crystallized message in mind, you may have accomplished the last step first and you must then go back to a consideration of the audience and occasion to which you must adapt the message. Or if you began with a purpose which was imperative, you will find it necessary to select a topic and central idea to support that purpose. The five steps of planning offer you a method instead of a rigid sequence, and must be used with that in mind.

Second, at any moment as you plan and develop your talk, you cannot consider that any part of it is irrevocably fixed. You could be deep in the outline and discover that your central idea is not worded to suit you. Change it. The entire process of conceiving and developing a talk is an exercise in clear and mature thinking, and subject to change and improvement up to and including the instant you utter each word to your listeners.

The planning and development of a speech is not an easy process. Grove Patterson, whose advice you read earlier in the chapter, wrote, "I think few men and women who are not accustomed to making public addresses realize just how much hard work is required."[5] Channing Pollock, one of America's great preachers, remarked that he spent a month or six weeks to prepare a lecture, and that no preacher could prepare a worthy sermon in less than a week. A New York trial lawyer declared, "An important part of the trial is the work of preparation. Not the science, not the art, but the *work* of preparation."[6]

George Leisure, a young lawyer associated with the great Clarence Darrow in the Massie case, was eager to find the secret of

<hr/>

[5] Patterson, pp. 233–4.
[6] Franklin R. Weiss, "How the Lawyer Uses Rhetoric," *Today's Speech*, VII, No. 3 (Sept., 1959), p. 7.

Mr. Darrow's magnificent summations. During the course of the trial Leisure studied his colleague thoroughly, and came to this conclusion :[7]

> Mr. Darrow was an insatiable reader. It was almost impossible to mention any book that he had not read and with which he was not thoroughly familiar. . . . He knew all the facts of the case thoroughly when he started to sum up, and with his knowledge of those facts he drew upon his tremendous store of knowledge and gave his address just as the atmosphere and character of the courtroom demanded.

The lesson we can take from Darrow is the same taught by Webster. The significant preparation of the speech is the preparation of the speaker, and great speeches are the result of years of sensitive and meaningful living adapted to the necessity of obtaining a response from an audience. Life itself is the best general preparation for any speech you will ever give, particularly if that life is enriched by wide and continual reading.

To make general preparation most useful, however, a method of specific planning is necessary, and that method in five flexible steps we have considered in this chapter. We are now ready to take up the way in which you can organize your talk for maximum effectiveness.

[7] From *Clarence Darrow for the Defense* by Irving Stone. Copyright 1941 by Irving Stone. Reprinted by permission of Doubleday & Company, Inc., p. 166.

Chapter 12

Arranging Your
Talk

First of all, we must remember that a speaker cannot cram things down people's throats. He must lead the thoughts of his audience naturally. The structure of a speech, then, must not be planned with no thought of the audience and then brought out and displayed before them. Rather, the speech must be built with the specific audience always in mind, and the structure of the speech must conform to the thinking process of the listener. To do otherwise is as foolish as trying to make a man fit a suit.[1]

ALAN H. MONROE
Purdue University

AS A RESULT OF PLANNING, YOU HAVE CRYSTALLIZED THE CENTRAL idea of your speech into a single sentence, and you have an assortment of related and subsidiary ideas which go along with it. You are now faced with the fact emphasized in Chapter 10, that listeners have a right to an orderly presentation of material. You must therefore avoid at all costs the kind of speech described by Shakespeare as "a tangled chain; nothing impaired, but all disordered." In contrast, your aim will be to produce a talk which is "completely organized from beginning to end; it must go from nowhere to somewhere and sit down when it arrives."[2]

---

[1] By permission of Scott, Foresman and Company from *Principles and Types of Speech*, Fifth Edition, Copyright © 1962 by Scott, Foresman, and Company, Chicago, Illinois.
[2] "The Story of an Experiment," *Time, Inc.*, 1948, n.p.

The task, then, to which we will devote this chapter is that kind of arrangement—the task of synthesizing your ideas into some kind of structural form. And since those ideas must "march single file into the consciousness of your hearers," your structure will take its nature from the order or sequence in which you present them. You must decide what to say first, and then second, and so on, and this decision will be made in consideration of the response you seek to the central idea. You will want to lay out your task in the order best calculated to achieve your purpose.

As you can see, arranging your talk is an assignment in clear thinking, for it is axiomatic that you will be unable to take another along a path of thought which you have not thoroughly developed first in your own mind. Actually, the process of arrangement can be divided into three particulars. The first takes place in your mind as you marshal your thoughts, mentally sorting and placing them, clarifying as you go. The second may also be mental, but you can help yourself by putting your ideas on paper. During this time you arrange your thoughts into a consecutive development which creates unity, while putting each into proper relationship to the central idea. The third and final act is the creation of an outline which commits to paper the final skeletonic plan of the speech.

If you mull over your ideas long enough, sorting and arranging them in various combinations, you are very likely to find a pattern of some sort emerging. Such a pattern might very well provide the basis for your speech structure, yet there is a very real danger that such a structure would not be well adapted to the interests and wants of the audience. Since the time of the ancient Greeks, speakers and theorists alike have suggested standard outline forms, the most common today being that which divides the talk into three major parts, the "introduction," "body," and "conclusion." The difficulty with all such formulas is that they tend to be subject-centered rather than audience-centered. They thereby tend to violate the principle that good public speaking is characterized by careful adaptation to the audience.

What we want, therefore, is a formula which will allow us to structure or arrange a speech in the way best suited to the listener. Variations of such a formula have been available for many years, all based on some kind of problem-solution sequence. When such a sequence is used, the listeners are presented with a problem, the solution to which is the central idea of the speaker. We shall call our variation of the problem-solution sequence the *persuasive pattern*, since it provides a pattern by which we can arrange the ideas for almost any speech, and since, as we have seen, almost all speaking situations involve persuasion to some degree.

THE PERSUASIVE PATTERN AFFORDS A PSYCHOLOGICALLY FUNCTIONAL SPEECH ARRANGEMENT

To win understanding, acceptance, and perhaps overt action, the speech content must be brought to the listener, rather than requiring the listener to come to the content. Therefore the order or pattern of the speech must conform to the behavioral tendencies of the listeners; it must be created to follow what we know of human motivation and response. Typically, a cycle of human behavior seems to move through five phases, and it is these five phases which offer the basis for arranging a talk according to the *functions* of the parts.

Imagine that it is five o'clock in the city, and a driving rain is drenching everything. From a towering office building workers begin to emerge who have been inside and cut off from the weather since early morning, when a few clouds were all that foreshadowed the coming storm. They stop under the marquee of the building, staring in consternation at the sheets of rain. *Phase one: the workers have had their attention taken from the thoughts which occupied them as they left the building, and abruptly focused on the rain.*

Let us now watch Emily, a secretary who works on the twelfth floor. She stands under the marquee, with growing awareness that she is not prepared to battle the rain. In a thin dress and light coat she will be drenched in no time. Thus she faces a problem which to her is a threat. There is anxiety in her face. *Phase two: attention has been concentrated on a situation which is, to say the least, unpleasant.* Emily begins to *want* to overcome her difficulty.

Rapidly she begins mentally to canvass possible ways out of the situation. She could return to the twelfth floor and get an umbrella, but that would involve unwelcome time and effort. She could try to get a ride with one of her fellow workers. But who? At that moment one of her co-workers says, "Let's share a cab. We can split the cost, and we're going in the same direction." *Phase three: the idea of a solution which will get Emily out of her predicament has been offered and made practical.*

Speedily Emily considers the alternatives. She visualizes the annoying return trip on the elevator and the possibility of not finding an umbrella. She sees herself searching for a ride in vain. She feels the dry comfort of the cab, and the companionship of her friend. She chooses the cab, accepting her colleague's offer. *Phase four: the consequences of the proposed action have become more desirable than any alternative.*

Together the two now move toward the curb and signal a cab from a near-by rank. *Phase five: the idea has produced response.*

With this pattern of behavior as an example, we can apply the several phases to the arrangement of a speech, deriving the following formula:

Phase one: ATTENTION. Begin your plan of conversation by saying something which will immediately take the attention of your listeners from whatever was occupying their minds and will concentrate it on the continuing development of your message.

Phase two: WANT. Name, explain, or describe a situation which involves the listeners and creates dissatisfaction. Make them want to escape, avoid, or overcome the difficulty.

Phase three: SATISFACTION. Present your central idea as the solution to the difficulty, the goal which will satisfy the want you have created. Demonstrate that your idea can and will provide satisfaction.

Phase four: DESIRE. Portray the benefits which will be enjoyed once your proposal has been adopted, your idea accepted. Picture these benefits as preferable to any alternative.

Phase five: ACTION. Ask the listeners to respond in the way you planned when you wrote the specific purpose of your talk.

By examining advertisements in any major magazine you can find additional examples of the use of this sequence. For instance, in one of the women's magazines this appeared:[3]

(*Attention*) (In headlines) RING TWIST? KNUCKLE PROBLEM?

(*Want*) Tired of rings twisting around on your fingers? Or being so tight you have to tug them off?

---

[3] Used by permission of the Finger Fit Company, Royal Oak, Michigan.

(*Satisfaction*) Just have your jeweler attach Finger-Fit to any ring—one you have or a new one. You'll end ring problems for keeps.

Finger-Fit opens up three sizes to easily slip over your knuckles. And once on, it snaps closed to your exact finger size.

(*Desire*) Always keep your ring displayed at its loveliest —with the setting perfectly positioned on your finger.

(*Action*) Ask your jeweler to show you Finger-Fit and tell you about its surprisingly modest cost. In yellow or white gold or platinum.

Advertisers may, of course, use pictures, color, or unusual layouts to gain attention, whereas a speaker's resources are more limited. Advertisers, furthermore, may not always separate the five phases into distinct units—indeed, the advertisement may combine two of the phases in a single paragraph. Still, a speaker may also do this, for each phase must not always be a discrete speech unit. The observed phases of human behavior, however, provide a rationale and a structure for the ad or for the speech, and to organize your speech in step with these phases provides four advantages:

1. It gives direction to your thinking as you assemble and analyze your ideas.
2. It concentrates your preparation on the desired response.
3. It provides for adaptation of your speech structure to the nature of your audience.
4. It offers your central idea as the satisfaction of a felt need, and therefore impels the audience toward the desired response.

Before we proceed, let it be understood that it is the *sequence* of these phases which is important, and not the relative duration of each. Each phase should be developed only sufficiently to accomplish its mission, and on occasion one phase, or even two, may be omitted or telescoped into another if that will satisfy its purpose. You will learn to adapt and modify the persuasive pattern only after you have first firmly mastered the fundamental sequence, and so our next step is to examine each phase in greater detail.

EACH PHASE OF THE PERSUASIVE PATTERN ADVANCES YOU TOWARD YOUR GOAL

In this section we shall examine, not only the functions of the several phases, but also some methods of fulfilling those functions. In so doing, we shall notice some basic principles which apply in places other than the phase in which the principle is introduced.

The first phase attracts the attention of the listeners and directs it toward that which is to come

"What we attend to controls our behavior. What we can get others to attend to controls their behavior."[4] With these words Harry A. Overstreet sets forth the speaker's initial duty and his continuing fundamental responsibility as well, for the speaker must begin by attracting the full attention of his listeners, and he must maintain that attention throughout his talk. Furthermore, through this attention the hearers must be influenced to perceive both speaker and subject with respect or good will. Your concern is with ways of accomplishing this task.

You may be introduced to your audience by someone who is a skilled speaker, in which case you begin under favorable circumstances. But you cannot rely on this to happen, and there may be times when you will not be introduced at all. The minds of your listeners may be concentrated on their own private thoughts. Perhaps one has dropped a pencil, another is uncomfortable in his seat, two are whispering, and several are daydreaming. How can you arouse attention and focus it favorably upon the developing theme of your talk?

An examination of the most widely-used textbooks on public speaking shows that the authors recommend a total of at least twenty-six ways of opening a talk. We shall be concerned with only six.

[4] *Influencing Human Behavior* (New York: W. W. Norton & Co., Inc., 1925), p. 9.

YOU MAY BEGIN WITH A STORY. From Aesop to James Thur-
ber, speakers and writers have proved that human beings never
outgrow the desire to hear a well-told tale. Begin with, "On a cold
December day in 1960 three men stood on a bleak hilltop in Alaska,"
and your audience will want to find out what happened. You have
attracted their attention and caused them to anticipate what comes
next. You are in motion.

When Dr. Marvin A. Rapp, Vice President of Nassau Community College, spoke to the Rotary Club of Albany, he began:[5]

> I looked down into his face, now so still. He had a fine
> Biblical name. It was Peter. Peter means rock. He was
> only 18 years of age. What age has more life than 18? Now
> Peter was dead. To mark the barren spot where he died
> was only a black and white picture–a picture of Peter
> dying. I looked long and longingly at the picture. About it
> were banks of fresh flowers; behind them a cross gar-
> landed in black; and behind the cross, the wall, where
> Peter died only a few feet from freedom.

You would find, were you to read the whole speech, that Dr.
Rapp's moving story leads directly into the development of his
message. When you open your talk with a story, be sure that it does
the same.

YOU MAY BEGIN WITH AN ARRESTING STATEMENT. Say something in your first sentence which is unusual, unexpected, dramatic,
or magnetic. A paradoxical assertion will do, or an account of some
unusual fact or statistic which is meaningful to your listeners,
being sure, of course, that it gains you favorable attention and is
related to your message. For example, "It's hard to realize today
that the best educated and most affluent societies lead the world in
delinquency, divorce, alcoholism, insanity, crime, and suicide,"
might be an effective opener to a talk on one of our social problems.

Speaking in Munich, Germany, Isaac Auerbach began by
saying:[6]

> During the past ten years of your lifetime, the num-
> ber of computers in the world has grown from a few to
> over 12,000 systems. In this short time you have seen

[5] *Vital Speeches*, XXIX (Aug. 15, 1963), p. 665.
[6] *Vital Speeches*, XXVIII (Sept. 15, 1962), p. 729.

information processing become one of the fastest growing scientific activities in our contemporary civilization.

As you have probably noted, such an opening does not have to be shocking, and indeed, it should not be. But it must be interesting to those who hear it.

YOU MAY BEGIN WITH A THOUGHT-PROVOKING QUESTION. A good question always makes an appropriate beginning for a talk, but not all questions are good ones. The effective question makes the audience want an answer. It creates a degree of suspense. Perhaps it forecasts the direction the talk will take, but its answer is never obvious. To the contrary, the best question is one which makes the audience think. A speaker who wanted to present the advantages of home ownership to an audience of young married people began appropriately by asking, "Where will you be living sixteen years from tonight?" He gained attention by posing a question which deeply involved his listeners, and for which they wanted an answer.

Paul Findley, Congressman from Illinois, began a breakfast address with a series of questions. He said:[7]

> Have you ever considered this question: What was America's greatest invention? Was it Alexander Graham Bell's telephone, which opened a new era in communications? Was it Thomas A. Edison's electric light, which turned a world of flickering night time into one in which night can be as brilliant as day? . . . Each has a claim to greatness. Each is uniquely American. Each has contributed greatly to progress. Which would you choose?

An opening as well planned as this is almost certain to get your talk off to an interesting start, but it is not as simple to invent as might appear. Try it for your next speech.

YOU MAY BEGIN WITH AN INTERESTING QUOTATION. One speaker began conversing with an audience by saying, "More than one hundred years ago Thoreau wrote, 'We are living in an age of improved means and unimproved ends.' How much more true that is today!" You will notice that Thoreau's words are not the first the audience hears, but have become a part of the conversation of the speaker. Often an otherwise good quotation loses some of its impact

[7] *Vital Speeches*, XXIX (Oct. 15, 1962), p. 26.

because it is unexpected—the audience is prepared for the speaker's own words, and fails to comprehend the significance of a quotation which has not been identified as such. Dr. Robert T. Oliver of the Pennsylvania State University was careful to avoid confusing his listeners in this way as he started to speak to the Tennessee Speech Association:[8]

> Oliver Wendell Holmes, the Supreme Court Justice, not his father the poet, once defined truth as, "the majority vote of the nation that can lick all the others." Sometimes we in our profession feel that way when we attend a faculty meeting, or a session of a School Board, in which a majority of traditionalists votes against introducing a course in speech.

When a quotation is presented to an audience ready to understand it, and when it immediately becomes a springboard into the speech, it makes an effective attention getter.

YOU MAY BEGIN WITH A COMPLIMENTARY OR CHALLENGING REFERENCE TO YOUR LISTENERS, TO THE OCCASION, TO YOUR SUBJECT, OR BY A MODEST REFERENCE TO YOURSELF. This can be an effective opening, but it is used so often that it has become trite. If you will take the trouble to examine the printed record of a hundred speeches delivered before business or professional audiences, you will discover that nearly three of every four begin with some kind of an expression of how pleased or complimented the speaker is to be there! This is very appropriate, but it is also extremely commonplace.

Chauncey Depew, noted speaker of another generation, is reported to have remarked that a good way to begin a talk is to tell the audience something nice about themselves they didn't think you knew. The significance of this statement is that it shows a willingness to think and plan, and to do some research. So if you want to begin with a reference to your listeners, the occasion, or even to yourself, make the effort to find something new and specific. If you want to say that you are glad to talk, at least have a specific reason for being glad!

Harlee Branch, Jr., President of the Southern Company of Atlanta, began with a reference to himself and his audience when

[8] *Vital Speeches*, XXIX (May 15, 1963), p. 459.

he spoke to the Indiana State Chamber of Commerce, but he took the trouble to use a light and original touch:[9]

> I am grateful to you and your Program Committee for this opportunity to visit again the Hoosier haunts of Penrod Schofield, Willie Baxter, Little Orphan Annie and the Raggedy Man—all of the beloved, if vicarious, companions of my boyhood.
>
> I am also pleased to revisit the state which nurtured the late, great Claude G. Bowers, author of *The Tragic Era*, one of my favorite historical works. . . .

And Clarence B. Randall, then President of Inland Steel Company, made effective use of personal reference when he addressed the National Press Club on April 25, 1952:

> No man could have a more deeply moving experience than that which came to me on the evening of Wednesday, April 9. Facing the largest audience which any private citizen had ever addressed, and looking straight into the eyes of the millions who were watching television, I was determined to speak the truth as I saw it. Every word was my own, every phrase forced out by deep conviction.

This opening statement unites the best qualities of personal reference and arresting statement, as you may have noted, and shows that two methods of beginning a talk may be effectively combined.

YOU MAY BEGIN WITH A BIT OF SHOWMANSHIP. With a keen sense of good taste and of the appropriate, you may find it possible to create an unusual and dramatic opening which does not smack of the sideshow, and yet which will seize the attention and interest of an audience. Former President Dr. Henry N. Wriston of Brown University actually began one speech by singing a few bars of a popular song and then converting the words into an approach to his central idea. Donald E. Kramer, Vice President of the Tectum Corporation, began a speech in this manner:[10]

> Ladies and gentlemen and distinguished guests of the Ninth Annual Middle Atlantic Public Relations Conference. Buenos Tardes, Senors y Senoras! *in Spanish;* Kock-

[9] *Vital Speeches*, XXVIII (April 15, 1962), p. 392.
[10] *Vital Speeches*, XXIX (Oct. 15, 1962), p. 17.

Pah-Jah-Yeh-Tee! *in Russian;* Wie Befenden Sie Sicht! *in German;* Ohio Go-Sah-Ee-Mash-Ta! *in Japanese;* Ahn-Yngee Hah-Simneekah! *in Korean.*

I have greeted you in several different languages for a specific purpose. It is not my feeling that the business executive of the future must be totally multi-lingual. But it is my firm conviction that by 1970 the successful industrialist and corporation executive will have to have some foreign language at his command. . . .

As noted earlier, these six methods do not exhaust the number of ways to open a speech effectively, but they do give you a useful selection. Regardless of your method, however, the attention phase of the talk must perform three indispensable services. It must:

1. Gain the attention and arouse the interest of your hearers.

2. Secure respect and good will for you and your message.

3. Lead to or blend into the succeeding want phase.

Although your entire talk should abound in material possessing the "factors of attention," the first phase should be especially rich in these qualities. The factors of attention are the attributes of discourse which command the involuntary attention of listeners. Their use is one of the principles of productive speaking which I earlier indicated we would notice from time to time. You should develop your speech so that what you have to say is expressed through the use of the following factors.

1. REALITY invites attention by presenting things in the concrete or specific. The concrete deals in word pictures or in material which arouses the memory of physical sensations, while the specific refers to particulars rather than generalizations. The speech beginnings of Marvin Rapp and Harlee Branch, Jr., cited a few pages back, are strong in concreteness and specificity. Both depend upon reality to help get the listeners' attention.

2. PROXIMITY arouses attention by referring to something present in the room or something fresh in the listeners' memories. Things commonly known and recent are proximate in time, things visible or close at hand are proximate in space. Reference to either can assist you in holding an audience, as it did Clarence Randall in his speech to the National Press Club. At that moment he was referring to a speech he had delivered nationally by television just

two weeks before, which most of his listeners had undoubtedly heard, or at least were keenly aware of.

3. NOVELTY is the characteristic of material which is unusual and generally vivid. Since we are all impelled to attend to things which are unusual in size, color, shape, arrangement, or are otherwise out of the ordinary, speech material with this quality can gain a hearing. Newspaper men are eager to fill their pages with material which is unusual, for in a sense this is the definition of news, and the speaker may well learn one of his lessons from them. Donald Kramer's attention phase in six languages was good showmanship because of its novelty.

4. ACTIVITY attracts attention. We are always more interested in things which move than in those which are still, as attested by the flashing, moving electric signs that compete for attention along the streets and highways. A speaker who is in meaningful motion will have more attention than one who is still, and a speaker whose material has motion or activity will also more easily invite attention. That is why many speakers are lavish in their use of stories and illustrations, especially ones in which the characters are busy *doing* something. Notice the action in this paragraph from a speech by Dr. Max Rafferty, California's Superintendent of Public Instruction:[11]

> I'm reminded of the time I was in a motorcade in San Francisco at the mid-point of the campaign. I don't know whether any of you have been in a motorcade or not, but it's sort of the closest thing politicians have to a serpentine, homecoming night. Everybody gets in cars, decorates them with banners, sends balloons out the windows; boys proceed down the street, trying to attract votes. And on this particular motorcade they stuck me in the lead car and I felt pretty foolish, as you can imagine.

5. SUSPENSE invites attention by arousing curiosity or by creating uncertainty, provided the matter is important enough to be worthy of attention and provided there is reasonable expectation by the hearer of having his suspense resolved. Dr. Edward Teller, noted scientist, used the element of suspense briefly as he began a

---

[11] *Vital Speeches*, XXIX (May 15, 1963), p. 450.

talk to the Economic Club of Detroit, "I should like to start by telling you something which you already must know, but since it happened today I think it is almost necessary to mention it." Suspense can be created by *revealing* part of a story or point, and *concealing* the remainder until the moment of climax.

6. CONFLICT, involving the opposition of two forces of some kind, invites attention partly because an element of suspense may be present, and partly because of sheer dramatic impact. Conflict may involve a man against himself, teams or groups against each other, man against the world or against nature, or two ideas in issue. It is dramatized in games, novels, plays, law courts, or wherever man must wage a struggle against competition. When the audience itself becomes involved in the conflict, a *challenge* is imposed which may be motivating as well as attention-demanding, as illustrated in this part of a talk by James N. Patterson, Director of Public Relations of the American Oil Company, speaking to an Illinois School Public Relations Conference:[12]

> The responsibility, as I see it, belongs primarily in one place: right at home. It belongs with the parents and the taxpayers in our local communities. And if they don't accept and discharge that responsibility, if they don't provide the number and quality of schools that are needed in their local areas, there are others outside the community who are ready—in some cases eager—to assume the job.
> If that happens, you and I—the home folks—are going to lose a substantial measure of our control and supervision of our local schools—their policies, methods, and curricula.

7. THE VITAL, finally, commands attention by dealing with things which are close to the hearts of listeners—their children, their homes, their jobs, their futures and all its hopes and fears. When you talk with people about things that make a difference to them and to their lives, you will have their undivided attention. Charles M. Sligh, Jr., former President of the National Association of Manufacturers, used this fact when he began a speech to a group of furniture makers meeting in New York:[13]

[12] *Vital Speeches*, XXIX (May 15, 1963), p. 463.
[13] *Vital Speeches*, XXX (Nov. 1, 1963), p. 51.

Today, each of us is only a minority partner in his own business. Our senior partner takes from 50 to 52 per cent of the profits, he determines what the cost of doing business will be, how our products will be advertised, how they will be priced, to whom they will be sold. He tells us who we may hire or fire, and determines what we will pay them.

If you can be sure that your opening has one or more of these seven attention-getting qualities, you will have your speech off to a good start, and if you can fill the remainder of the talk with material of similar quality, your listeners are likely to be keenly willing to listen from beginning to end.

Perhaps, however, you have wondered why I have said nothing about putting humor into your speech. Surely humor is an attention-getter, you think, and has been successfully employed by many speakers. This is true, but the question is, can *you* use it? Not all speakers can inject humor into a talk and make it tell; sometimes, in fact, it can boomerang. Nothing is worse than a would-be "funny" story that falls flat. For this reason you will be better off without humor than to try it and fail.

As a matter of fact, the funny-story speech beginning is the first kind you should be warned against. Too often it is hazardous, and when the story has nothing to do with the theme of the speech, it is inappropriate. If you must begin with this kind of an opening, be sure the story makes a point which is necessary to the speech. Then if it does not prove to be funny, you are at least saved by the fact that you have illustrated your point.

There are other things to avoid at the beginning of a talk, one of which is the trite, "I'm glad to be with you tonight," which has already been commented upon. Neither should you begin with an apology unless you have done or said something to which offense could be taken, and which would normally require a statement of regret. But the old, "I don't really have a regular speech tonight," or "I'm sorry I couldn't get all the exhibits I wanted to bring," or "I was asked to speak on this subject, although I'm not really an expert" will repel listeners, not win them. Neither should you begin with a broad general statement, no matter how true it may be. "We stand today at the beginning of the space age," will put your listeners to sleep. So will a label, such as, "My subject this morning is. . . ." And although it is possible to awaken an audience with a sensational beginning, you should avoid this variety too, because it

362

may not always win favorable attention, and because too frequently it is followed by a let-down when the speaker cannot maintain the level of excitement with which he began. Finally, do not let your beginning dawdle or be tedious; for many talks the quickest improvement would be to cut out the first paragraph!

But if you can stand quietly until your audience looks at you, and then catch their attention with an opening statement that makes them want to hear more, you have successfully accomplished the first phase of your talk.

The second phase disturbs the equilibrium of the listeners by arousing a want

Whereas the first phase of your talk is concerned with attention, the second is usually devoted to motivation. It can be conceived as a phase of preparation essential to the presentation of your central idea or message, predisposing the listeners so that they are ready to accept the central idea when it is revealed. Its effect is to open their minds and hearts in readiness to receive what you want to tell them, or, to use the terms of Chapter 3, to create a homeostatic imbalance which can be restored to equilibrium by accepting the message of the satisfaction phase.

Let us return for a moment to Emily, the secretary who emerged from her office building to find herself in a pouring rain. As she rode the elevator down she had no thought or intention of sharing a taxi home, yet when the suggestion was made, she accepted the idea. What prepared her for the proposition? What motivated her to accept? *She found herself in a situation which was disturbing.* She was moved to seek some kind of satisfaction for the feeling of distress created by the rain.

An amusing but preceptive example of the want phase of a speech can be found in a song from the recent Broadway musical, *The Music Man.* "Professor" Harold Hill, an itinerant salesman of musical instruments, addresses a group of citizens of River City, Iowa, opening in song and patter with the theme:[14]

[14] "Ya Got Trouble" by Meredith Wilson. © Copyright 1957 by Frank Music Corp. and Rinimer Corporation, 119 West 57th Street, New York, N.Y. 10019. All rights Reserved. Used by Permission.

Ya got trouble—lots and lots of trouble—
Trouble, right here in River City.

After thus arousing and motivating his audience, Harold Hill reveals his proposal, one which he predicts will alleviate the trouble of the River City folks:

I can deal with trouble.
I'm here to organize a River City Boys' Band!

Since the "trouble" described by Hill is the concern of parents for the behavior of their youngsters, a boys' band offers a way of removing that concern while giving him a market for his instruments. From the example we may conclude that the function of the want phase is to demonstrate to the listeners that "they got trouble." Although this is obviously a broad generalization, it does explain the essence of what you should try to accomplish in the second phase of your speech. More specifically, we may say that the want phase intends to arouse unrest in the listeners by demonstrating that they are or may be involved in a situation which unsettles, disturbs, or threatens them in some way.

Note that in both instances motivation is secured from *the situation as perceived*. This suggests that the speaker must get his listeners to perceive a situation as disturbing. They will be less apt to be aroused by generalities than by concrete circumstances, less by abstract appeals than by specific conditions. This leads to the question, "What kinds of situations are listeners likely to perceive as arousing wants?"

For simplicity, we can classify the kinds of situations as two: 1) a problem situation, which is perceived as threatening or disturbing to the listener, or 2) an unfulfilled-goal situation, which is perceived as lacking benefits or satisfactions which are attainable. In theory, listeners can be motivated by perceiving themselves involved in one of these situations, or by *identifying with other people who are so involved*.

The description, explanation, or portrayal of the situation should establish clearly the ways in which that situation affects the listeners, for it must be related to their wants or needs. In the publication "Talking Safety to Your Workers," Marsh and Mc-Lennan, Inc. stress the point as it applies to motivating employees to follow safety regulations:[15]

[15] Marsh & McLennan, Inc., "Talking Safety to Your Workers," in *Effective Communication on the Job*, ed. M. Joseph Dooher and Vivienne Marquis (New York: American Management Association, 1956), p. 111.

Point out what the individual stands to lose in event of serious injury and explain the effects of non-compliance on production, even where no injury results. Anticipate that employees may not be too interested in the adverse effect upon production and be prepared to point out to them what they personally stand to lose if they should be injured. For example: (a) compensation never equals full earnings; (b) other expenses are often incurred which are not covered by compensation; and, (c) the probable loss of opportunity for advancement. All this is in addition to the physical pain, the shock and emotional upset to himself and his family, and the interference with his own plans, and with his outside life.

When he spoke to the Family Service Association of America, Ralph Lazarus, President of Federated Department Stores, Inc., suggested the way in which the situation he was discussing affected both his listeners and the people they serve. Note, too, that he presented an unfulfilled-goal situation and one with which the members of the audience could identify themselves.[16]

I shall begin with a proposition. Let us suppose, as many well-informed people believe, that the most important product of what is now being called the Second Industrial Revolution will turn out to be time—oceans of it. You may call it leisure time, idle time, unwanted time, or free time, depending on your personal outlook on life. In any case, it is a commodity we are not presently prepared to consume in the bounteous quantities in which it is going to be presented to us by the new factory and office systems that are now being dreamed up in our automation laboratories. . . .

If we are to work with known facts, we need make only a few fairly conservative assumptions, in my opinion, to reach the conclusions that our economy is going to provide us with substantial blocks of spare time in the next 15 or 20 years. . . . I want to focus your attention on the goal ahead—the society of fulfillment that I believe is within the grasp of our children. If we think now, we can create that society so that they can live it later. If we know what our goal is, we can wend our way far more successfully through the problems that lie between us and it.

If we can fairly assume that the members of the Family Service Association are moved by desires to attain a satisfying life

16 *Vital Speeches*, XXX (Mar. 1, 1964), pp. 301–2.

of independence, of creative fulfillment, and of human dignity for themselves, their children, and those whom they serve, then this want phase is directed at the wants and needs of the listeners and is consistent with the classification of wants suggested in Chapter 3. It portrays a reasonably specific situation which arouses wants by revealing potential and unfulfilled goals. Although abstract, it moves the listeners to desire a way to satisfy the wants which have been aroused.

In showing how a situation relates to the needs and wants of listeners, the speaker must take into account and adapt to their attitudes and to the degree of sensitivity to that situation they possess at the time he speaks. In some cases the audience may be so aware of the situation that he need do little more than mention it, whereas in others he may have to spend a major part of his speaking time developing this phase of the talk. As a rule you will find that an audience can be identified as possessing one of four degrees of sensitivity to a situation, and you must adapt your presentation to its consequent readiness to accept and respond.

THE AUDIENCE KEENLY FEELS THE SITUATION, OR IS FULLY AROUSED BY IT. If your hearers are already disturbed by the state of affairs you intend to deal with, if they are aroused or concerned, there is little need for you to expand on the subject. They are motivated to seek a satisfaction, and the function of the want phase is largely accomplished. Emily was quite aware of her predicament the moment she walked out of her office building, and it needed no long discourse on the discomfort of getting soaked to make her ready for a remedy. In most talks, however, even when the audience is already aroused, it is desirable to make an explicit reference to the conditions in order to establish the point of departure of your thinking and to identify yourself with your listeners.

When the audience is aroused, an initial statement referring to the disturbing condition can accomplish the functions of both the attention and want phases, and you can proceed quickly to the satisfaction.

THE AUDIENCE IS AWARE OF THE PROBLEM, BUT NOT AROUSED BY IT. If the listeners know that the problem or difficulty exists but are not moved by it, then the want phase must excite them about it. It must stimulate and arouse. It must impress them so deeply that they will feel impelled toward actively seeking a way out of their predicament. You may achieve this result partly by a dynamic and enthusiastic presentation based on your own depth of feeling, but much will depend upon the kind of material you use to present the point. Be sure that you set forth the situation concretely and specifically. Use facts and illustrations that are clearly meaningful in terms of the daily life of your hearers, creating vivid word pictures. Choose words which will stir the wants you intend to excite. For an audience which acknowledges the situation but remains unmoved, the want phase must take on the character of a speech to stimulate.

THE AUDIENCE IS UNAWARE OF THE SITUATION. When the situation you intend to present will be news to your listeners, you will have the double task of both explaining it and evoking excitement about it. Under such conditions you may find it helpful to: 1) state and explain the situation, 2) illustrate it vividly, using one or more examples, 3) present additional factual information, perhaps in statistical form, to show the extent and significance of the difficulty, and 4) demonstrate that vital interests of the listeners are involved, pointing out what they personally stand to gain or lose. Do not reveal the satisfaction phase until you are reasonably certain that your hearers are keenly alive to the disturbing situation.

THE AUDIENCE DOUBTS THAT THE SITUATION EXISTS, OR THAT IT THREATENS THEM. In the face of an unbelieving group of listeners, you must begin on common ground and with acceptable facts and proceed inductively toward the conclusions you want accepted. Use the testimony of authorities respected by your hearers to establish or reinforce your point. Develop the idea with illustrations or examples, but be sure that they are consistent with the experience and predispositions of your audience. Be sure, too, that the emotional response of the audience to your facts and illustrations will move them to see the situation as you do. Your attitude should be reasonable, avoiding any hint of dogmatism. Show how, from the listeners' point of view, a careful consideration of all facts and evidence makes your conclusion inevitable, and how the interests of the hearers are at stake. Make each step of your development meaningful to avoid the impression that you are overwhelming the audience with a confusing and massive barrage of material.

Two questions remain to be answered concerning the adaptation of the want phase to specific conditions. The first is, "How is adaptation accomplished to a hostile audience?" The answer lies in the fact that an audience will rarely be hostile *to the idea of the existence of a threatening situation.* If you are called upon to face an unfriendly audience, their dislike is more apt to be directed toward what you will present as a solution to the problem than to the problem itself. Therefore your persuasive task lies in showing that your proposal is preferable to any other, and the adaptation in this phase must be made by describing the situation in such a way that your proposal will become the best way to satisfy their wants. Facing a hostile group of listeners, you must also consider the possibility that their ill will is directed toward you or toward the movement or organization you represent rather than toward the situation you propose to discuss. In this case, you must gain respect and good will before you can successfully present your message.

The second question is, "Is the want phase necessary in an informative speech?" The answer is "Yes." *Information may have to be sold, just as any other commodity.* The listeners must *want* to understand before you can hope that they *will* understand, for they will tend to resist information for which they feel no need. Therefore, the kind of want phase you should use in a particular informative talk depends upon the active eagerness of your listeners for the material. It depends upon the attitude of the listeners, as already discussed.

Technical presentations, business or operating reports, or research reports are likely to be made for audiences which have a use or need for the information, and are therefore pre-motivated to listen. For these people, the want may merely be mentioned. Other informational speeches, orders, explanations, instructions, and lectures should usually include a developed want phase which will create a need for the information about to be presented. In all cases the material to be understood constitutes that which will satisfy a need felt by the listener.

In all speeches, you cannot safely proceed until the hearers are aware of an unsatisfied want or need. The want phase should create or magnify such an awareness.

The third phase presents that which will satisfy the aroused want

This part of your talk is dedicated to the presentation and development of your central idea. As a matter of fact, the term "central idea" is used to denote the proposition of the talk because *every-thing else revolves about it.* The portions of the speech which precede the satisfaction phase are designed to prepare the audience to accept the central idea, while the portions which follow are designed to intensify the motivation and to secure the response you are after. The satisfaction phase in most instances represents the basic substance of your message.

It follows that the central idea should precisely satisfy the want or wants which have been aroused in the listeners. If you are selling typewriters to a group of college students, and have developed the theme that college students are concerned with better grades, you must then show how your typewriter will make possible the better grades they want. If you are trying to arouse more wholehearted compliance with safety regulations in a shop and have vividly shown that shop accidents drain the purse, ruin health, and undermine family security, you must show that following regulations guards the purse, protects health, and promotes the security of the family. It will not do to create wants which you do not satisfy.

Since it contains the heart of your message, the satisfaction phase, more often than any other part of your talk, is likely to be sub-divided into component parts which of necessity must be arranged according to some *internal order.* In this chapter we have been considering the over-all arrangement of the speech as a whole, dividing it into five major phases. Each of these phases, however, may require an arrangement of ideas *within itself.* What we say of such arrangement for the satisfaction phase can be applied to the other phases, and constitutes another principle which for convenience we consider here.

The four most common methods of arranging material for internal order are according to *topic,* according to *time,* according to *space,* and according to *cause.*

When you arrange sub-ideas according to topic, you simply sub-divide your central idea into from two to four convenient parts which can be understood easily by your hearers, and treat each part in succession. If you were speaking on competition in the container industry, for instance, you might sub-divide your material into competition among *metal* containers, *paper* containers, *plastic* containers, and *glass* containers. Or you could sub-divide by supporting the central idea with *reasons,* usually from one to four. There is no inherent or natural sequence among sub-divisions of this nature, and therefore the order is purely arbitrary. This means that you

369

must be especially careful to make the audience understand what the subordinate sections are, and the way in which you progress from one to the other.

When your internal arrangement is based on a time order the sequence is natural and relatively easy for the audience to grasp. You proceed from yesterday, through today, and into tomorrow, or through morning, noon, and night. If you were discussing the process by which your listeners received their daily newspaper, for example, you could divide the main idea chronologically into 1) getting the news, 2) editing the news, 3) printing the news, and 4) distributing the news.

When you lay out an internal arrangement by space, you consider parts in their physical relation to one another, again moving naturally. You may go from north to south, from here to there, from top to bottom, and so on, being sure that you use a small but definite number of stopping points. Discussion of facilities in a summer camp or a new office building, or of the market potential for a new product could easily be based on a space sequence.

Arrangement by cause is similar to that of time, except that the relationships among the parts is more than a simple sequence in order of occurrence. It is based on the creative or causative relations among events, and may move forward in time from cause to effect, or backward from effect to cause. Thus if you were talking about automation, you might take up in turn the factors which have brought about the present use of automation, and then the effects of automation in the foreseeable future. Or you could begin by viewing automated production in the years to come, and then taking up present facts upon which your forecast is based.

It is entirely possible to combine some of these four systems of arrangement into a complex structure or pattern, but for your ideas to be understood, experience shows that simplicity is important. It is easy to lose listeners when you try to take them through a complicated pattern of thought, just as it is to lose them when you have no pattern at all.

Regardless of the kind or degree of internal structure, however, the satisfaction phase should gain understanding and acceptance of your central idea. In an informative speech it should clearly outline and explain the ideas and information for which you have created a need. In a persuasive speech it should present a way to escape from the unpleasant situation posed in the want phase, or to achieve one or more desirable but unattained goals. In either case it should show

370

that the central idea is theoretically and practically sound. If the audience should be hostile toward the central idea, or if for any other reason the speaker must establish preference for his proposal in comparison with another, he should use the satisfaction phase to win the desired decision, preferably developing his material inductively as described in the next chapter.

The fourth phase intensifies the desire of the listeners

The desire phase of a talk acts as a booster to the motivation already secured by offering the central idea as the satisfaction of a want. It magnifies the desirability of the central idea, thereby tending to overcome any lingering resistance to the desired decision or response. Since the phase is purely motivational, it may be omitted from a talk to inform when there is no apparent necessity to increase the desire of the listeners to understand or to apply their new knowledge. Even if brief, however, it should be included in every persuasive speech.

This phase intensifies motivation by enlisting the feeling and imagination of the hearers on behalf of the central idea. To accomplish this, it does three things:

1. It projects the listeners into the future.
2. It portrays the benefits they will enjoy from believing, feeling, understanding, or acting as you would have them.
3. It visualizes their enjoyment by creating word pictures in which they see themselves.

The dynamics of the phase can be illustrated by an incident which took place in the showroom of a major urban automobile dealer. The salesmen noticed that any car located in a particular spot on their showroom floor sold more quickly than a car in any other place in the room. The location seemed to have a magic sales quality regardless of the style of the car placed there, and therefore the salesmen set out to discover the secret. After carefully watching prospective buyers in the showroom over a period of time, they discovered an explanation of why that one place seemed to be magic. They discovered that the secret lay in a huge mirror on the wall next to the spot. Prospective buyers would climb into the car, relax in the comfort of the interior, and then turn to see their image in the mirror. *And they wanted what they saw!* The mirror magnified desire—it made the difference. As a consequence of this discovery,

371

the manufacturer the following year adopted the advertising theme, "Picture Yourself Here!"

The above three words sum up the desire phase. The listeners must be taken, in their imagination, into the future where they will see themselves enjoying the benefits of accepting or acting on the central idea. This may not always take long, but the words should be carefully chosen to create a word picture which will act as the mirror on the wall. Usually the picture is positive, portraying the future as it will be if your idea is accepted. But you can also paint a negative word picture which will act as did Scrooge's Ghost of Christmas Future—a dismal forecast of things to come if your idea is rejected. If you would like to give the phase heightened force through contrast, both the positive and negative forms can be used.

The following example is a desire phase for a speech urging the adoption of measures to control urban air pollution. The speaker has sought contrast by using both negative and positive pictures:

The choice is up to us. We can go on living as we have, rising in the morning, dull from sleeping in closed rooms to keep out the oily smell of trucks and busses. We can look out through soot-covered windows to see a tarnished place in the smog where the sun should be. We can cough our way downtown through traffic which fills our lungs with the odorless death of carbon monoxide, and we can park our cars where industrial fumes cut into the metal—the same fumes which rot the nylon in our wives' hosiery. Or by controlling the pollution in our air, we can sleep with our windows open to the soft night breezes, wake to the sparkle of sunshine, ride to work through sweet-smelling air, and park our cars in contentment, knowing that they won't be gnawed by air-born acid. Which do you prefer?

And here is the desire phase of a speech given to the Rotary Club of Cleveland by Ralph M. Besse, President of the Cleveland Electric Illuminating Company. His central idea had been that the city must make increased effort to solve the problems of its Negro citizens. Note the use of contrast and the topical internal development.[17]

What are the benefits?
First. A higher economic level among our Negro people. More jobs and upgrading of jobs mean more buying power and a healthier economic climate for the entire city.

[17] *Vital Speeches*, XXVIII (April 1, 1962), p. 381.

The present buying income of the Negro market in Cleveland is $300 million a year. The potential is double.

Second. It would result in a sharply reduced tax budget for health, welfare, and police protection.

Third. It would result in a more vigorous, more progressive city as a whole. The Reeducation in blight areas, and solutions of environmental problems break down the walls of ghettos, create happier indigenous communities and release untapped human energies for creative activities.

And finally it would move toward the treatment of Negroes as human beings.

These are the benefits we may expect if we make an honest, individual effort to eliminate the problems rising out of racial discrimination here in Cleveland.

If we fail to make the effort, we will in time pay the penalty in our own environments for the want, the misery, the tensions and bitter frustrations we have turned our backs on in the Negro environment.

We will pay it here in Cleveland, even as the so-called white nations of the world have paid it in India, Africa, the Near East and China.

The desire phase should heighten the motivation of your listeners to respond favorably to your central idea. If you are successful, you are ready to move to the final phase of your talk.

The fifth phase rounds out the speech and animates response

The final phase of your talk should end it on a high note, leaving the audience with a sense of satisfaction and the conviction that the listening time has been wisely invested. It should summarize or recapitulate your message, finishing the thought with a sense of fulfillment for the audience. Above all it should name or otherwise indicate the response sought.

You can command, advise, request, inspire, suggest, ask, direct, outline, challenge, or urge your listeners to respond, and you can find in textbooks at least fifteen ways of doing it. As with the attention phase, however, we shall be content with six good ways to end the talk and to encourage the response you seek.

You May Close by Telling the Audience What You Want Them to Remember, Believe, or Do. There is nothing more natural and generally more effective than a statement which knits together your central idea and what you want the audience to do with it. It may range from a single sentence, as "Let's remember this one thing: without research there is no progress," to a full recapitulation.

If your speech is informative, you will want your audience either to remember the significant ideas or to apply their new knowledge at some appropriate future time. If the former is your purpose, you must realize that within two weeks your listeners will have forgotten half of what you have said. Therefore the action phase should select and emphasize the ideas or data you want retained. If the latter is your purpose, you must suggest how and when to apply what they have learned, and perhaps indicate how they will benefit from using their new learning.

If the speech is persuasive, the action phase should assert or reaffirm what you wish the audience to feel, believe, or do. This may be a pure and unadorned repetition of your central idea, or it may employ a more varied way of saying the same thing in fresh or colorful language.

J. Peter Grace, President of W. R. Grace and Co. of New York, speaking at the World Trade Dinner of the Dallas Chamber of Commerce, used a simple summary to reaffirm his message and suggest the response:[18]

> In summary, ladies and gentlemen, I am urging an immediate and substantial increase in the use of our financial and human resources all across the board, from government on down to the private individual. The Great Challenge of Latin America cannot be won by government working alone, nor by private individuals engaged in their own pursuits. The Great Challenge can be won—and I am confident it will be won, by the total effort of governments and private organizations and individuals, each acting in his own specialized sphere, but all engaged in a common massive program to achieve a better life for the Latin American people in a free and democratic society.

Examination of the texts of many business speeches shows the summary to be one of the most commonly used forms of ending; perhaps its very appropriateness leads to overuse.

YOU MAY CLOSE BY REPEATING THE OPENING OF YOUR TALK IN CAPSULE FORM. To tie the ending of a talk back into the beginning

[18] *Vital Speeches*, XXIX (Aug. 1, 1963), p. 616.

lends a sense of completeness and fulfillment which audiences find satisfying, especially if they see how the connection emphasizes the central idea. For instance, "As I said at the beginning, there are more telephones than automobiles in the United States, and because of this fact the world is at your elbow," is an ending statement which rounds out a speech and at the same time reaffirms a message.

Speaking at the annual dinner of the New York Group of the Investment Bankers of America, Eugene R. Black, President of the International Bank for Reconstruction and Development, tied his conclusion to the opening theme, adding specific detail to inspire the appropriate response.[19]

But let me say again in conclusion, as I said at the start, that your support will be effective only if and to the extent that you emphasize the right issues.

We must stop asking whether foreign aid is really winning us popularity and ask whether it's really buying us development.

We must stop worrying every time the Soviets extend development assistance to one of the underdeveloped countries and concentrate instead on whether our own programs are being effectively carried out. For this development business is *our* game and our heritage, and not Khrushchev's or that of the Soviets.

It is *our* heritage which has demonstrated to the peoples of the underdeveloped world that there is an alternative to abject poverty.

It is *our* heritage which introduced the radical idea of self-determination and national independence.

It is *our* heritage which has shown the way to mass consumption and to the widest participation in the fruits of economic progress.

It is *our* heritage which, by giving impetus to this whole revolutionary business of development, has carried a message of hope to human beings the world over.

So let's play the game with good heart and cool head. Let's play it with vigor but without panic. Surely, we need not fear to lose if only we play it well.

Not only does this action phase end by repeating the opening, but by the use of repetition and by the request for response, it gives force and direction to the message.

[19] *Vital Speeches*, XXVIII (Dec. 1, 1961), p. 113.

You May Close by Presenting a Simple Plan to Accomplish Something. This kind of action phase may range from a single sentence suggesting the application of a new understanding, to a lengthy summation of steps necessary to accomplish the object of the speech. It has the advantage of giving the listeners something definite and specific to take home, answering their invariable and unvoiced question at the end of a talk—"So what?" Edward Hegarty, formerly of Westinghouse, said in his book, *Showmanship in Public Speaking*, "The formula ending is one of the most popular. I like the one, two, three type ending: first, do this; second, do this; third, do this."[20] It is Mr. Hegarty's contention that to give the audience more than three items in the formula or plan is confusing. He illustrates the formula with this conclusion to a hypothetical talk:[21]

> If you want these streets repaired, here is a plan. Tonight, when you go home, sit down and write a letter to your councilman. Better still, tomorrow, telephone him. Then get the first two men you meet tomorrow to do the same. Get enough telephone calls made and letters written, and we'll get those streets fixed. All you do is these two things:
> First, write or telephone your councilman.
> Second, get two of your friends to do the same.

An action step of this kind can be developed for almost any talk.

You May End with a Bit of Poetry or an Appropriate Quotation. You may use someone else's words, whether poetry or not, to achieve one or more of three things in your action phase. The words may (1) summarize your talk by stating the central idea in a new way and in the words of another, lending it greater dramatic power, (2) add an aura of emotion or feeling to the ending which you might not be able to secure in any other way, and (3) signal graciously that your talk is concluded. If you were finishing a talk on the importance of education, for instance, you could say, "I can do no more than remind you of the words of Wendell Phillips, who declared, 'Education is the only interest worthy of the deep anxiety of thoughtful men.' "

[20] Edward J. Hegarty, *Showmanship in Public Speaking* (New York: McGraw-Hill Book Company, Inc., 1952), p. 137.
[21] Hegarty, p. 138.

Ralph Eubanks, professor, writer, and lecturer, combined a personal declaration with quotation as he ended an address before the Annual Leadership Conference of the Arkansas Federation of Business and Professional Women's Clubs. Said he:[22]

My own conviction is that we shall have no bright image of the good leader until we fully recover our lost faith in true greatness, in heroism. One of the sad effects of our abandonment of the ancient search for wisdom is our contempt for heroism. We have celebrated the "common man"; we have treated the exceptional man meanly. Yet I believe we are beginning at last to sense the folly of our lotus-feast. Robert Oppenheimer spoke for many of us when he said in an AP interview recently: "We hunger for nobility; the rare words and acts that harmonize simplicity and truth." It matters very much that we kindle the three kinds of consciousness we have described today. For these are the very stuff of nobility and, at last, of cultural sanity. And if I may put it, in this three-fold consciousness is contained the spirit of the West—the very spirit that enabled Western man to form an image of himself as "Man the Wise." Suburbia must find ways to reanimate this heroic image of man. For as Arthur M. Schlesinger, Jr., has put the issue: "If our society has lost its wish for heroes and its ability to produce them, it may well turn out to have lost everything else as well."

An action phase of this nature can rarely be improvised. This fact simply emphasizes that your conclusion must be thought out thoroughly.

You May End with a Story Which Illustrates Your Message. This is one of the best methods of suggesting to your listeners that they apply the knowledge you have given them, or that they behave in the way you would like. There are times when a direct command or request for action would not be tactful, and in these times a story or illustration which whispers, "Emulate this" can be effective.

The Illinois State Chamber of Commerce heard Gaylord A. Freeman, Jr., President of the First National Bank of Chicago, speak on the theme that American businessmen are avoiding difficult decisions. He concluded by saying:[23]

[22] *Vital Speeches*, XXIX (May 15, 1963), p. 480.
[23] *Vital Speeches*, XXVIII (Jan. 15, 1962), pp. 204–5.

There is the story of a boy who was faced with a very
unpleasant duty which he had to perform within the
day. As he rose in the morning and looked at his watch,
it said seven. Postponing his unwelcome duty, he played
through the morning and when the sun reached the zenith
he looked again. The watch still said seven. He knew it had
stopped but it provided the support he needed to avoid his
task. The afternoon wore on, the sun set. The day was over
and the sounds of night were all about him. He had failed
in his duty.

So may we.

The comfort of the status quo is the clock that has run
down. We've avoided our decision until the night is all
around.

It is late.

Notice how Mr. Freeman used two short sentences, emphatic by
contrast with those surrounding them, to give force to the emotional
overtones and the suggestion implicit in the story.

YOU MAY END WITH AN AFFIRMATION OF YOUR OWN BELIEFS
AND FEELINGS.   In this kind of action phase there can be strong
suggestion impelling an audience toward the desired response. It is
the same principle that gave force to Patrick Henry's famous, "I
know not how others may feel, but as for me, give me liberty or
give me death!" If your message is one that you feel strongly, there
can be an imperative urge in ending a speech in this manner.

In 1952 Benjamin Fairless, then Chairman of the Board of
United States Steel Corporation, concluded an address at the fall
meeting of the Georgia State Chamber of Commerce with a personal
affirmation.

So in this non-partisan spirit, I want to conclude these
remarks by congratulating the Democrats on the title of
the campaign song which they are using this year, and by
commending it most favorably to your consideration.

The title, as you know, of course, is:

"Don't Let Them Take It Away!"

I can think of no sentiment which should appeal more
strongly to the heart of every American taxpayer, and I
know of no motto which might be adopted more appropriately by American business and enterprise.

Just as Mr. Fairless combined personal affirmation with a
quotation, you can often combine some of the six methods of ending
a speech. You need only to keep in mind that in ending your talk,

378

your main function is to secure the response you are after. Use the method or combination of methods most likely to bring you success.

Before leaving our consideration of the final phase of your talk, we should notice some things to avoid. For one thing, do not applogize in the conclusion any more than you would at the beginning. Don't say, "Well, I haven't told you all about it, but my time is up . . ." Similarly, avoid adding an after-thought: "And I did want to say just one thing more . . ." It is also desirable to omit the too-familiar, "And in conclusion . . ." Nor should you just fade out with a statement like, "You see, we've covered a lot of territory, and it's very interesting, and . . ." Finally, do NOT add, "Thank you," after your concluding words. If you have made the kind of talk you should make, the audience ought to thank *you*. You have spent a great deal of time, research, and effort in preparing a worthy message and the listeners should feel in your debt.

Having seen that the persuasive pattern provides you with a functional method of arranging your talk, enabling you to present what you have to say so that it fits the normal motivational cycle of your listeners, let's look briefly at the most useful method of building your speech outline. It will be the skeleton framework of your points or ideas.

THE ORDER IN WHICH YOU BUILD A TALK IS NOT THE ORDER IN WHICH YOU GIVE IT

The most natural thing in the world is to sit down and outline the points of your talk in exactly the same sequence in which you will later deliver it. The most natural thing, however, is the wrong thing. You should build the outline, not in the order in which you will present your ideas to your listeners, but starting with the satisfaction phase and central idea, you should work in the sequence which follows.

Create the satisfaction phase first

The sentence declaring your message or central idea was, as you recall, created as the last step in planning your talk, as discussed in Chapter 11. Now write down this statement. The development of

379

your outline following the persuasive pattern begins with it. Add beneath it any sub-points, their order depending on some plan of internal arrangement.

Let us suppose you are to make a speech, for which we will develop an outline in the following pages. After considerable thought you have decided that you will tell the audience that reading is one major avenue to a full and successful life. This is something experience has taught you, and you will make it your message. Having determined this, you write a simple statement of your central idea, "We ought to read more."

You then decide that you can best adapt your message to your audience, a group of young businessmen, by sub-dividing it into three topics, each of which you think will be important to them. The skeleton outline for the satisfaction phase of your talk will then look like this:

(*Satisfaction*) We ought to read more.
1. Reading provides know-how for business advancement,
2. Reading provides breadth to understand the world we live in.
3. Reading provides the experience which makes life meaningful.

In wording the central idea, you have said "we" instead of "you" to avoid appearing didactic and to identify yourself more closely with your listeners. You have used parallel wording in the statement of your sub-points to secure emphasis and cumulative impact, and the order of the points is topical. Your basic plan for the satisfaction phase is now done.

Next, create the statement of the want phase

Having begun the outline with the statement of your message, you must now discover what situation or what conditions will arouse an eager want which can be satisfied by your central idea. Since determining the motivation will be a pivotal stage of your preparation, take time to consider carefully both the audience and the message. The want phase is pivotal because it establishes the relation between the message and the audience, answering in effect the

380

question of each of your listeners, "Why should this message be important to me?"

Remember that as a rule, your speech will be stronger if you *do not forecast your central idea in the want phase,* but develop for your listeners an idea which, if accepted, will lead them to feel a need for it. Thus, if you wanted to convince a group of airport managers that they should install auxiliary electrical generating equipment, your want phase should not be, "You need stand-by generators to maintain operations," but, "When your power source fails, operations stop and passenger lives are endangered." If the listeners accept this proposition, they will sense a need for what you will present.

For the hypothetical talk you are planning, how shall we set up a need to read more? Under what conditions will your listeners *want* to increase their reading? What happens to people who do not or cannot read widely? In the world of today they are left behind, like high school dropouts. They forego the opportunity to grow through the experience of others, brought to them in books and magazines. They stunt their lives by cutting themselves off from the accumulated knowledge of mankind. They limit the growing circle of opportunity which could be opened to them. This line of thinking can provide a key to your want phase, and so we place in the outline a statement encompassing it:

> (*Want*) The man who fails to tap the experience of others limits his powers.

If you can make your listeners feel the truth of this statement, they should be eager to escape the limitations and be ready for your central idea. You can arouse their needs for self-respect and human dignity, for independence, for opportunity, for security, and perhaps for the esteem of others. It could be possible to appeal to these needs in a series of topical sub-points, but for the moment you decide against sub-division.

Third develop the action phase

What can you reasonably expect from your audience? How can you elicit the response you are after? What sort of close will be most effective for your talk? You are now setting up the ending of the speech, and want it to be strong and appealing.

381

For your talk on reading you decide that you will make a direct request for action, and that you will use the formula for accomplishing something as your technique. So you place this in your outline:

(*Action*)   Resolve to increase your reading experience.
1. Join a good book club.
2. Subscribe to the best periodical in your business.
3. Get acquainted with your librarian.

You are now ready for the desire phase

You must now create the desire phase. Although its effectiveness will depend in large measure on the word pictures you present, you will need a key sentence in the outline to crystallize the mood and theme of the phase. What sentence can express this mood and theme, within which your hearers will be able to picture themselves?

For the speech you are working on, you decide that the theme will portray the sense of personal power which can be derived from reading. You then write this part of your outline as:

(*Desire*)   The man who reads is the man who knows.

The last step is to determine the attention phase

Now that you have the principal parts of the talk in outline form, you are ready to find out what you can say to get attention and to lead that attention into the conditions of the want phase. The attention phase is developed last because you must know to what the listeners must give attention before you can satisfactorily decide on the techniques for getting it.

You now cast around for an attention-demanding idea for the beginning of your talk on reading, considering the six methods of opening explained earlier in this chapter. Finally, taking your cue from the word "experience" in your statement of the want phase, you look up that word in Bartlett's *Familiar Quotations*. In that book you find testimony which seems to have the potential you are after, a comment made by one of England's foremost statesmen.

For your outline you have an attention phase based on a quotation from William Pitt:

(*Attention*) In 1741 William Pitt told the English Parliament that he wished he were "not of that number who are ignorant in spite of experience."

With the key statements of your talk prepared, you are now ready to put them together as an outline in the order in which you will deliver them.

MAKE AN OUTLINE OF ALL KEY IDEAS IN THE ORDER OF PRESENTATION

Your outline is the skeletonic structure of the thought to be communicated by your talk. It represents the ideas you want the audience to understand, accept, and respond to, and is written in the order in which you will present and develop those ideas. It relates to the speech you will make as the steel skeleton of a building relates to the whole building. After the skeleton is erected the job remaining is to fill it out with useful materials and perhaps to add some decorations to make it more pleasing.

In the outline every significant idea is put down in the form of a complete sentence because in no other way can you guarantee to yourself that you have thought out the essence of your speech thoroughly and with precision. You cannot communicate an idea you do not yourself possess, and the outline is your visible evidence that you know what you want to say.

The final step of arranging your talk, therefore, is to assemble into an outline the ideas you have worked out, using any conventional system of symbols and indentation to indicate the sequence and relationship of those ideas. The basic outline for any speech will look very much like the outline for your hypothetical speech on reading. Here it is, in order and ready to be developed for use:

(*Attention*) I. In 1741 William Pitt told the English Parliament that he wished he were "not of that number who are ignorant in spite of experience."

(*Want*) II. The man who fails to tap the experience of others limits his powers.

(*Satisfaction*)   III. We ought to read more.
  1. Reading provides know-how for business advancement.
  2. Reading provides breadth to understand the world we live in.
  3. Reading provides the experience which makes life meaningful.

(*Desire*)   IV. The man who reads is the man who knows.

(*Action*)   V. Resolve to increase your reading experience.
  1. Join a good book club.
  2. Subscribe to the best periodical in your business.
  3. Get acquainted with your librarian.

As a basic outline, this could be adequate for a 30-minute talk. The length, of course, could vary, depending on the amount of elaboration you expend on each of the phases—it could be condensed to fifteen minutes or expanded to forty-five or fifty.

In this chapter we have seen the way to plan and arrange a talk which will be adapted to your listeners, and have examined the steps to be taken in building a simple, useful outline. We must recognize again that there are other forms of arrangement which are common in speechmaking, but in the persuasive pattern we have a formula which can be applied to almost any kind of speech and which constitutes a most serviceable sequence and method.

In the next chapter we will deal with the way you develop the framework of ideas into a complete discourse.

Chapter 13

Developing Your
Talk

If, then, the coming into the life of the listener is a means to successful speaking, it logically follows that the more closely the reference touches the life, the greater the effectiveness, or, to state it formally as a working principal:

The more the speaker brings his idea within the vivid experience of the listener, the more likely will he attain his end, *and, obversely:*

The less the speaker brings his idea within the vivid experience of the listener, the less likely will he attain his end.[1]

ARTHUR EDWARD PHILLIPS
Theological Seminary,
Evangelical Lutheran Church,
Chicago
Effective Speaking

AT THIS POINT YOU HAVE ARRANGED THE IDEAS FOR YOUR SPEECH AND placed them in an outline showing their sequence and relationship. You must now develop these ideas so that they become meaningful to your listeners. The process of developing your talk is therefore not only one of filling out the skeleton, of elaborating and amplifying the thought, but also one of adapting to each listener's world-as-he-sees-it, bringing your ideas into his realm of experience and making them congruent with his beliefs and expectations.

In arranging your speech according to the persuasive pattern you adapted it as a whole to the wants and interests of the audience.

[1] Arthur Edward Phillips, *Effective Speaking* (Chicago: The Newton Company, 1929), p. 33.

The development of the speech now involves both establishing your relationship to the audience as you deliver the speech, and the finer adaptation of its parts to the attitudes and background of the hearers. In this chapter we shall be concerned with the methods of securing this adaptive development, beginning with the establishment of a sound relationship between yourself and your audience.

ESTABLISH CREDIBILITY AND CREATE GOOD WILL THROUGH WHAT YOU SAY

In Chapter 4 I pointed out that a major part of your effectiveness as a communicator depends upon the kind of person you are, indicating that the most effective speaker has always been Quintilian's "good man skilled in speaking." In addition, Chapter 6 stressed the fact that mutual respect and friendship are necessary for the most productive communication.

As you develop and present your talk, you should not leave to chance the establishment of a productive rapport between yourself and your listeners based on these things. You must, of course, be a person of integrity with an intimate knowledge of what you are talking about, and must have a sincere concern for the wants and interests of those with whom you speak. Still, these indispensable qualities may not be enough, for you may have to give what Emerson called "the authentic sign" that you are worthy of confidence. In the preface to Fiorello LaGuardia's autobiography, M. R. Werner wrote, "What made LaGuardia such a good public speaker was that he was deeply sincere about whatever he was discussing and a great actor in his ability to make that sincerity felt."[2] What LaGuardia revealed through his ability as an actor, most speakers more easily accomplish through what they say. This means that as you develop your speech you should plan to say that which will establish your credibility and create rapport.

This problem has been faced by speakers since rhetoric was first studied as an art, and has been embodied in the classic doctrine of ethos. According to this doctrine, a speaker can heighten his persuasive impact when his words reveal, first, a thorough knowl-

[2] Fiorello H. LaGuardia, *The Making of an Insurgent* (New York: The J. B. Lippincott Company, 1948), p. 11.

386

edge of his subject, second, sincerity toward his listeners, and third, friendliness and good will. Your own authority, sincerity, and good will should preferably be made manifest in the opening or early stages of the speech, so that the effect of what you say later may be conditioned by the way you have gotten your hearers to perceive you. As we examine the three elements, however, keep in mind the desirability of continuing to build ethical power throughout the speech.

Reveal your qualifications to speak on the subject

How did you accumulate the store of facts and knowledge from which to draw as you address your audience? How did you achieve some degree of authority to make the statements you will make? What right do you have to talk to these people on the topic you have chosen? Not depending on having the answers to these questions made known before you speak, either by a reputation which precedes you or by a fitting introduction, you should firmly but modestly indicate your qualifications as you talk.

Have you had significant experience with the topic? Do you know it first hand? Mention some of your experience. Perhaps a personal illustration or example will at once support a point and affirm your authority. Have you done study and research? Quote from or refer to your sources, allude to your study. Are you acquainted with outstanding figures in the field? Without becoming a "name-dropper," indicate that some of your knowledge is derived from knowing and talking with experts of recognized standing.

Notice now how David Rockefeller, President of Chase Manhattan Bank, suggested both the travel experience and the personal reflection which qualified him to speak on American business in Latin America. In Los Angeles, he told an Institute on Finance, "An area that has long engaged my attention, both personally and professionally, is Latin America. Since returning from Moscow, I have reflected a great deal on the mounting Communist pressures on our southern neighbors. . . . The challenge to U.S. businessmen to tell their story effectively is so compelling, in my judgment, that it is worth making an attempt to give shape to the problems we face and to indicate some possible approaches to the solution."[3]

[3] *Vital Speeches*, XXXI (Oct. 15, 1964), p. 8.

Peter Howard, world leader of Moral Re-Armament, in an address to Town Hall, also in Los Angeles, carefully indicated some of the personal background which supported his authority to speak. Here are some of his phrases: "A Russian diplomat, believed by the F.B.I. to be one of the most skilled Communizers in this country, said to me. . . ." "I was listening a few days ago to an influential American discussing De Gaulle on a national program. . . ." "On my recent journey through Asia. . . ." "I read a book called 'The Ugly American.' I did not like it because some of it was true." "I read in the *New York Times*. . . ."[4]

With modesty you can and should establish your qualifications to speak within the context of what you say.

Reveal the ethical motives which prompt you to speak

If you will read again the words of David Rockefeller in the preceding section, you will see that in addition to indicating some of his qualifications for speaking he also disclosed his concern at the Communist pressures in Latin America and his conviction that American businessmen must grapple with the problem. In declaring his concern he made known to his listeners the basic motives which impelled him to speak.

Hearers will tend to assess the motives of those to whom they listen, sometimes deliberately, sometimes unconsciously, but always with a view to weighing the credibility of the speaker. If they become convinced that the speaker is addressing them with selfish or ulterior purposes they will discount what they hear, but if they hold the speaker to be impelled by unselfish motives they give greater credence to his words. The Rockefeller statement should heighten the respect of his audience for what he has to say.

Similarly, you will find that indicating to your listeners the sincere and ethical motives which prompt you to speak will add to your own credibility. Do you have their best interests at heart? Make sure that they know this from what you say. Are you impelled by a sense of duty, of urgency, of fair play, of search for truth? Reveal the fact. Are you dedicated to a cause? Announce it. Was the invitation to speak a challenge or a high compliment which you could not ignore? Show that your address is a response in a noble

---

[4] *Vital Speeches*, XXX (Mar. 15, 1964), p. 339 ff.

key. Ask yourself the question *Why should I speak to these people on this subject?* If you cannot honestly answer that your motives are highly ethical, decline to speak; if your answer establishes a sincere motive for speaking, then you can and should make that known in the context of what you say.

Notice how Senator Wayne Morse suggested his own dedication to truth and to the public interest in a talk to the Portland City Club in his own state. After referring to Senator Gruening of Alaska, he went on to say:[5]

> I have shared his views not only in respect to U.S.-Latin American Relations, but also in reference to our foreign policies in Asia. He, too, believes as I do, that the primary obligation a Senator owes to the people of his state and nation is to find out, as best he can, what the facts are in connection with an issue, and to follow where those facts lead in respect to promoting the public interest.
>
> Sincere and honest men can disagree as to what is the best public policy to follow in light of a given set of facts, but under our system of government it is important that they have an abiding faith in the ultimate judgment of the people of our country once they have been given an opportunity to consider a full disclosure of the facts.
>
> It is so important in this turbulent period of our nation's history that politicians do not sweep facts under the political rug, so to speak, for purposes of political advantage, or out of fear of public disapproval.

With these words, Morse disavows speaking for political gain and declares that he is motivated by concern for the public welfare. In so doing, he can hope for a fair and full hearing of his message. And with sincere words akin to these, you can help create for yourself an ethical credibility.

Reveal good will toward your listeners

An adage advises, "Never stand begging for something which you can earn for yourself." We can apply this adage to the task of gaining good will and therefore a fair hearing from your listeners.

[5] *Vital Speeches*, XXX (Sept. 1, 1964), p. 678–9.

You cannot ask for or command good will; it must be earned, and the best way to receive it is to give it.

In order to be persuasive, you want the respect, the esteem, and the friendship of those to whom you speak. Therefore you must communicate these attitudes to them, something which you can do only if you truly possess such attitudes. If you have a genuine interest in your hearers, if you respect them, the attitudes will reveal themselves and cultivate a return in kind.

What specifically, can you include in your speech that indicates your respect for and interest in your hearers? Look for the opportunity. Have you taken the trouble to learn something about the organization to which you are speaking which is complimentary? Mention it. Do you know personally some of the people to whom you are talking? Refer to them by name. Avoid talking in the third person, but use direct address, preferring "we" to "you." Show appreciation of the achievements of others, and of the help you have received from others. Identify yourself with those who hear you.

The following paragraph shows how Leo Rosten, social scientist and author, cultivated good will toward himself and his subject as he spoke on "The Myths by Which We Live" to the 20th National Conference on Higher Education in Chicago. Notice that he compliments his audience, establishes an identification with its members, and reveals an attitude of humble self-respect as well as one of respect for both the achievements and weaknesses of others.[6]

> I was struck by a feeling of inadequacy when I was asked to address this elite group. My daughter said to me, "Daddy, what can you tell college presidents and deans that they don't already know?" I took thought and remembered that I had once committed pedagogy, and that there was plenty, and is plenty, that you can tell me, if only by the way in which you react to what I say. I also remembered that for a year and a half I worked at the Rand Corporation, which was then a hush-hush collection of advanced figures working on problems of security, and that I worked with some of the most brilliant mathematicians and physicists and electronicists and chemists in our land, and I still remember the shock to my nervous system when it dawned upon me that, with rarest exception, they could not pass an elementary examination in economics or history, or political theory or social science or even philoso-

[6] *Vital Speeches*, XXXI (April 15, 1965), p. 410.

phy, for they had never been taught how to think about certain kinds of questions.

CHOOSE APPROPRIATE SUPPORTING DETAIL

Each idea in your speech outline is an abstract statement, and often a broad generalization. It represents the nucleus of what we shall call a *speech unit*, each unit being made up of the one idea and the material we shall call *supporting detail* used to reinforce, amplify, or support that idea. Thus you may think of your speech as a series of units, each consisting of an idea and its supporting detail, which must be made to march in sequence into the consciousness of the hearers.

The only exception to the principle that each speech idea must be directly amplified or developed will occur when you have a major idea supported by one or more sub-points. In this case, each of the sub-points becomes the nucleus of a speech unit and is substantiated by appropriate supporting detail. Every idea in your speech therefore is ultimately grounded in supporting detail. If we apply this principle to the outline of the satisfaction phase for the speech developed in the last chapter, we will have:

We ought to read more, (because)
> (*This major idea is supported by three sub-ideas. It therefore has little or no primary supporting detail.*)

1. Reading provides know-how for business advancement.
   (*This sub-point is the nucleus of a speech unit, and is developed with supporting detail.*)
2. Reading provides breadth to understand the world we live in.
   (*This sub-point is the nucleus of a speech unit, and is developed with supporting detail.*)
3. Reading provides experience which makes life meaningful.
   (*This sub-point is the nucleus of a speech unit, and is developed with supporting detail.*)

The reason for this principle should have been made clear as you read earlier chapters of this book. Your ideas are perfectly understandable to you, but *they may be neither clear nor acceptable to your listeners.* Since your job as a communicator is to make your ideas both meaningful and acceptable in terms of the listeners' experience, you must amplify, support, or develop each idea with material which will cause the listener to supply the intended interpretation of the statement of your ideas. You must help him to decode your message as accurately as possible.

You secure audience adaptation, therefore, as you select and use supporting detail which is appropriate to the particular audience and to the immediate response to each point you want from your hearers. Detail which might be appropriate to make a point clear to a group of factory workers might be inappropriate to make the same point acceptable to an audience of professional women.

A further reason for the use of supporting detail was suggested in Chapter 10. There I pointed out that, although your speech is intended to achieve one ultimate response, you will have to be consistently interesting, clear, vivid, and convincing. You must always be interesting to hold attention, and clear to be understood. At any given moment you may also have to be vivid or convincing or both. The use of well selected supporting detail is your method of accomplishing these results.

The following guides have been used successfully over the years by many speakers to help select necessary supporting detail. You, too, may find them helpful.

1. Define technical, unfamiliar, or ambiguous words in understandable language or by illustration.
2. Illustrate each idea from the everyday life of your listeners.
3. Reduce all abstractions to concrete particulars.
4. Bring distant scenes into the daily environment of your hearers.

A speech unit, then, is created by presenting your idea and reinforcing, amplifying, or developing it with an appropriate variety of supporting detail. Detail for any idea may be selected from among the following nine kinds.

Explanation, definition

The first and most obvious way of getting listeners to grasp your meaning is to explain or define the statement of your idea, or of key words, especially those which may be unusual, technical, ambiguous, or foreign.

You may support an idea by definition in a number of ways. You may use simple exposition or explanation which clarifies an idea by relating that idea, or the important terms of it, to the experience of your listeners. You may use a dictionary definition, either from a standard dictionary or from a specialized one, such as a *Dictionary of the Social Sciences*. You may use the words of some authority to tell what you mean, or you may outline what you do NOT mean, thus defining by exclusion or negation. Or you can give an example illustrating the word or concept you wish understood.

In the following excerpt, note how Charles F. Moore, Jr., Vice President–Public Relations of the Ford Motor Company, defines what he means by *professional* as he talks about excellence.[7]

One course that the pursuit of excellence takes is a professional approach to the job at hand. I am sure you have heard many discussions of the professional versus the amateur, and of what constitutes a professional. I do not intend to throw any more fuel on those fires.

But I do believe that, when we speak of a professional job, or the professional touch, we are conveying a fairly clear and acceptable concept. It does not mean merely a sophisticated as opposed to a naive approach, nor slick work as opposed to clumsy work. It does mean that there is present a considerable degree of craftsmanship, attention to all the details and a fundamental integrity in the work itself. It means that the work gives evidence that the workman knew what he was doing and carefully brought his skill to bear on the task. The workman who does that consistently is a professional, whether he gets paid or not. He could even be a student.

Or again, note the method of Allan R. Broadhurst of the Department of Speech of the University of Connecticut. In the first sentence of the following paragraph he states his *idea*, developing it with detailed explanation. His audience comprised members of Kappa Delta Pi, an education honorary fraternity, to whom the material would have meaning in terms of contemporary experience and interest.[8]

This impersonal approach is evidenced on the college campus today. No faculty member (with rare exceptions)

[7] *Vital Speeches*, XXIX (Jan. 15, 1963), p. 223.
[8] *Vital Speeches*, XXXI (April 1, 1965), p. 361.

is rewarded by administration if he shows a personal concern for his students; nor is he punished if he doesn't. All the incentives, to the contrary, seem to be rigged to divert him away from such a personal concern, and to penalize him if he wastes too much time on mere students. Bypassing the traditional concept of teacher-student, each inspiring the other through an exchange of personalities, we now have administration rewarding and punishing teachers on the coldly impersonal basis of research and publication. The number of column-inches in learned journals, the pounds of books published, the foundation grants awarded, the prizes won, these become the goals of the struggling teacher who wishes to "get ahead."

You will agree that explanation and definition tend to be abstract, that the method attempts to make one group of words clear by using other words. Because of this fact, the method may be less interesting than other ways of developing an idea, and most useful with audiences having a good educational background.

Restatement, repetition, or detail

Advertisers drive home a theme or idea by repeating it, sometimes in identical word patterns and sometimes with enough variety to revive lagging attention. Speakers may do the same thing to help the audience secure a grasp of what they are saying.

In the following example, Joseph Mitchell, City Manager of Newburgh, New York, emphasizes by repetition the magnitude of the challenge his administration hurled against what he considered entrenched and vested welfare interests. The Economic Club of Detroit listened.[9]

> We challenged the welfare state and everything it stood for.
> We challenged the minority voting bloc racket. We challenged the right of the state to interfere in local affairs. We seized the reins of home rule. . . . We challenged the right of social parasites to breed illegitimate children at the taxpayer's expense. We challenged the right of moral chiselers and loafers to squat on the relief rolls forever. We challenged the right of cheaters to make

9 *Vital Speeches*, XXVIII (Jan. 15, 1962), pp. 214–15.

more on relief than when working. We challenged the right of those on relief to loaf by State and Federal edict. We challenged the right of people to quit jobs at will and go on relief like spoiled children. We challenged the right of citizens to migrate for the purpose of becoming or continuing as public charges. . . . We challenged the right of welfare programs to contribute to the rise of slums, to the rise of illegitimacy, to the rise of social disease among children and adults, to the losses of assessed evaluation, to the wreckage of a business and residential district, to overcrowding, to fire and fire hazards, to sanitation hazards, to school problems, to emptying the city of responsible, taxpaying citizens, and filling it with those who create crime and violence. . . . We challenged all those who would prevent the City Council from governing the city's economic social future.

While Mr. Mitchell employed repetition of a given phrase to secure emphasis, William I. Nichols, publisher of *This Week Magazine,* used restatement to make the increasing influence of youth in today's world vivid before another meeting of the Economic Club of Detroit. Notice the way in which he makes a transition from the preceding idea to the one he is about to develop.[10]

But beyond that, beyond the sheer numbers, is a second fact: *Youth's increase in influence.* Today the "Cult of Youth" is on the way to dominate our *total* society. On every side *Youth is King.* And whatever our actual age, we all seem to be engaged in a headlong, intoxicating race to see who can look, who can act and who can be the swingingest—who can live the youngest.

We see this urge in the cars we buy. (Here Come the Mustangs!) We see it in the clothes we wear—or don't wear. (Up with Chanel and off with the Bikinis!) We see it—God help us—in the books and magazines we read, the plays and the movies (The "Lolitas," the "Kittens" and the "Candys").

In short, the Youth Cult is everywhere. The moment a teen-age fad is launched, the adults adopt it. Whenever a discotheque is opened, the grown-ups start pouring in. The sports cars, originally designed for kids, are now for everybody. As Art Buchwald said recently, "The automobile has now become the *No. 1 Virility Symbol* in the

[10] *Vital Speeches,* XXXI (June 15, 1965), p. 525.

United States." . . . We are being exhorted to *Go Young, Think Young, Dress Young, Live Young, Smoke Young, Cook Young*—and with fantastic practical results. Youth is the subject which is on everybody's mind. And so, regardless of when you were born, we are *all* part of the Youth Explosion.

In a similar manner, by repeating a key phrase or sentence, by saying the same thing in different forms, or by adding details to the idea you wish to develop, you can make yourself more interesting, clear, vivid, and convincing.

Illustration

Better than any other method for developing an idea is the use of illustration. From the beginning of time, speakers have used illustrations to drive home their messages, for an illustration can hold attention and make an idea live as can nothing else. Russel Conwell, whose celebrated message, *Acres of Diamonds,* is a classic in the history of public speaking (he delivered it 6000 times, earning approximately $3 million, with which he founded Temple University), used a simple theme as a thread upon which he strung story after story. Abraham Lincoln was known for his ability to influence people by his use of anecdotes. Their success derived from the fact that an illustration is entertaining, for it satisfies mankind's enduring desire to listen to a story, but in being entertaining it also makes clear and convincing the thought or principle which the story illustrates.

An illustration, then, is a narrative involving a setting, a few characters, and action which is told as vividly and as concretely as possible. It should be fully relevant to the point being illustrated, long enough to develop emphasis but not so long that listeners remember the story but not the point, and as specific as you can make it. Such an illustration was used by Charles F. Kettering of General Motors as he made the point that too many people limit their achievement by closing their minds.[11]

As I said before, my home is in Dayton, and we have had our laboratories for years in Detroit, which is several

---

[11] "Get Off Route 25, Young Man," *Collier's,* Vol. 124 (Dec. 3, 1949), pp. 13–15.

hundred miles away. I keep my home in Ohio and drive back and forth on week ends.

Some of the people who work with me also drive between Dayton and Detroit. One said, "I understand you drive from here to Dayton in four and one-half hours."

I said, "I can do that once in a while, depending on traffic."

He said, "I don't believe it."

I said, "But I do."

He said, "I'm a much better driver than you are, and I can't do it."

I said, "I'm going down Friday. Why don't you ride along with me?"

So we rode into Dayton in about four and one-half hours, or a little more, and he said, "Hell, no wonder you can do it. You didn't stay on Route 25!"

Now, Route 25 is the red line that is marked on all the maps between Detroit and Dayton. If you are a stranger, that's the road you should take. It never occurred to my colleague that you could take any other road on either side of Route 25. There's a lot of country on either side of it; in fact, half the earth is on each side of it.

While the best illustrations are apt to be true incidents, speakers can sometimes make very effective use of invented or hypothetical illustrations, as did G. Keith Funston, President of the New York Stock Exchange, lecturing on corporate finance at Trinity College.[12]

We would undoubtedly all agree that the basic function of finance—whether personal or corporate—is to facilitate paying for the things that people and corporations want to do. . . . Take, for example, the company which has a brilliant new idea. The company may have a plan for converting that idea into a marketable product. It may have access to both the manpower and the materials needed to make the product. And it may have the necessary management ability to insure efficient production. But if the company cannot raise the money needed to put all these things in motion, nothing of very much consequence is going to happen.

If you want to hold an audience and make your point clear, adopt the method of these men. Use illustrations frequently.

[12] *Vital Speeches*, XXXI (May 15, 1965), pp. 467–8.

Example

Examples are abbreviated versions of illustrations. Sometimes called specific instances, they do not tell a story about an event, but simply cite the event. While the illustration is effective because it is a "chunk of life" which provides a new and meaningful experience for the listener, the example is effective because it recalls for him some experience from his past. For this reason you should use examples which you have reason to know are familiar to your hearers. And because examples are so brief, they are generally presented in groups, a speaker using from three to ten to develop his point.

While the illustration is effective in making an idea clear and vivid, examples often have the effect of demonstrating that the point refers to a frequent situation. Arnold Maremont, President of the Maremont Corporation, made an idea impressive in this manner when he spoke to the American Association of Industrial Editors:[13]

> Ironically, every time business deliberately tries to go into politics, it ends by paying a heavy price for its activities. Business literally brought the roof down on its head when the Jay Goulds, the Jim Fiskes and other manipulators not only controlled railroads but extended their political influence into the White House itself. Their tactics resulted in the Stockyards Act, the Interstate Commerce Act, the Pujo investigations of the "money trust," the Sherman Act, the Clayton Anti-Trust Law and Federal Reserve regulation of banking and credit.
>
> At a later period, business excesses under President Harding's "return to normalcy" brought into being SEC and the Public Utilities Holding Company Act; it forced additional strengthening of interstate commerce laws and rewriting of the Railroad Act. As for the much-maligned New Deal regulations—I think the reasons for them are by now self-evident.

Bernard F. Hillenbrand, Executive Director of the National Association of Counties, at a gathering paying tribute to Thomas Jefferson, aptly led from that topic into the first point of his speech

---

[13] *Vital Speeches*, XXVIII (May 15, 1962), p. 461.

by extending a principle through a series of examples. Note both the way in which he emphatically specified the point, and his use of repetition.[14]

> We often hear the lament that we have no modern-day Thomas Jeffersons. We are not sure that this is true. Perhaps Thomas Jefferson, in addition to his own phenomenal capacity, towered over his contemporaries because the great mass of men in Jefferson's time had very little education. Remember that Thomas Jefferson's contemporaries still believed in slavery and had recently been burning witches in Salem.
>
> The modern-day Thomas Jefferson is not one man, thinking and working alone, but rather, he is a composite man working in close fellowship with other men of superior mind.
>
> The modern Thomas Jefferson is a research team at the Mayo Clinic, trying to find a cure for cancer. The modern Thomas Jefferson is the President's Task Force on Poverty. The modern Thomas Jefferson is the Project Apollo staff at the National Aeronautics and Space Administration.
>
> *In other words, the first point we would like to make in discussion of administrators in the county of tomorrow is that, increasingly, the modern administrator will be called upon to direct and give life to programs that involve whole teams of people, wide ranges of varying talents, and which will involve participation by private agencies, as well as every level of government.*

Examples make excellent supporting detail, especially when coupled with an illustration, or as in the preceding paragraphs, with explanation.

Factual information

In Chapter 10 the point was made that your listeners have a right to expect material which is specific and factual, and therefore interesting. It follows that factual information will provide effective supporting detail, and that it should be not only interesting but convincing.

[14] *Vital Speeches*, XXXI (Feb. 1, 1965), p. 243.

By factual information is meant any observed, reported, or recorded event, phenomenon, or relationship which can be used to explain, clarify, or prove your idea. Examples and illustrations are also factual information; but examples have rhetorical character-istics which make it desirable to classify them separately. Within the category of factual information we may therefore include *single facts or events* (Babe Ruth holds the record for strike-outs as well as home runs. The net cost of absenteeism in this country is estimated at $13 billion a year.), *collected facts* (In the War Between the States, the Union lost 110,000 men in action, the Confederacy 75,000. American wheat exports vary from 4 million to 300 million bushels a year.), and *statistics* (In 1960 women com-prised 27.5 percent of the total working population. Passenger deaths average 2.2 per 100 million miles of travel by auto, but 1.01 per 100 million miles by air.). Statistics are collected facts, usually the product of mathematical treatment, and frequently expressed in terms of averages, percentages, comparisons, and ratios.

Dale D. McConkey, Vice President of the United Fruit Com-pany, employed a combination of facts and statistics as he discussed American investment in South America:[15]

> No matter what one's political orientation is, it is im-possible to ignore the stake of free enterprise in Latin America. An estimated seventy to eighty per cent of eco-nomic activity there rests in private hands. And while some ninety per cent of this activity is controlled locally, the remaining ten per cent in foreign hands exerts huge leverage on the economy. U.S. investment alone totals some 8½ billion—about the same amount as in all Western Europe, and exceeded only by Canada. American invest-ment south of the border:
>
> > Accounts for one-third of Latin America's industrial and mineral production;
> >
> > Directly employs about 2,000,000;
> >
> > Produces one-third of the continent's exports;
> >
> > Pays one-fifth of her taxes;
> >
> > Contributes a whopping $6.1 billion *annually* in wages, expenditures on local materials and serv-ices, and taxes to Latin America's economy (as against a projected U.S. Government aid contribu-

[15] *Vital Speeches*, XXX (Jan. 15, 1964), p. 209.

tion to the area of an average of $1.1 billion a
year);

Retains and reinvests in these countries $3 out of
every $5 of net profits after paying Latin Ameri-
can taxes.

Note that figures and statistics can be confusing and difficult
for a hearer to understand. Therefore when you use them in a
speech, make every effort to keep them simple, and if possible to
reduce them to terms which come within the every-day experience of
the listeners. To say that the liner *Queen Mary* is 1018 feet long is
not likely to produce a vivid impression on most hearers, but to say
that it is longer than three football fields will bring the dimension
within the experience of most people.

Analogy

Analogy describes or portrays a likeness or comparison between two
objects or situations, making the unfamiliar clear in terms of the
familiar. You will find it one of your most effective tools in making
your points or arguments understandable and acceptable to listeners. Analogy may be *literal* when the objects or situations being
compared are actually similar, belonging in the same class of
things, or it may be figurative when in reality the things being
compared are of dissimilar or unrelated classes. An example of the
latter kind is a classic analogy used frequently to explain the difference between a democracy and a dictatorship: "The difference is
that between a yacht and a raft. On the yacht you are safe if you
have a good captain for dictator, while on the raft your feet are
wet all the time but you never sink."

In the following example of literal analogy, note how John L.
Snyder, Jr., President of U.S. Industries, Inc., makes use of a quotation to establish the basis of his analogy:[16]

The paradoxical age we live in is well illustrated by
the opening of Dickens' *Tale of Two Cities:*
It was the best of times, it was the worst of times
[Dickens wrote]; it was the age of wisdom, it was the

---

[16] "The Total Challenge of Automation," *Representative American
Speeches: 1963–64*, The Reference Shelf, Vol. 36, No. 4 (New York: The H. W.
Wilson Company, 1964), pp. 157–8.

age of foolishness; it was the epoch of belief, it was the epoch of incredulity; it was the spring of hope, it was the winter of despair.

Dickens, of course, was writing about the time of the French Revolution but he could have been setting the stage for a thesis on the automation revolution.

On the one hand, Americans are earning more, spending more, and enjoying more material wealth than any other peoples in the history of the world. In these respects we are living in "the best of times . . . the season of light . . . the spring of hope."

On the other hand, as you've been hearing all week, more than 4 million of our people—or more than 5 per cent of our labor force—are without jobs, and more than 2½ million have completely exhausted all of their unemployment benefits. For these people, it is "the worst of times . . . the age of foolishness . . . the epoch of incredulity . . . the season of darkness . . . the winter of despair."

Testimony, quotation

A common way of supporting a speech idea is to use the words of someone else as John Snyder, Jr. used the words of Charles Dickens in the preceding section. Quotation, or the citation of testimony, can be employed for one of two purposes: (1) to make the idea convincing by supporting it with the statement of someone whom the audience respects and will believe, or (2) to make the idea clear and vivid by using words which express it more strikingly than the speaker is able to. Quotation of familiar passages also helps bring the thought into the experience of the listener, and it can be used for emphasis by repetition.

Ralph T. Eubanks aptly used a variety of quotations to emphasize and illuminate his point when he spoke to the Louisiana Speech Association:[17]

The so-called "crisis of modern man" is a crisis of value. Abraham Maslow, the American psychologist, put the matter well. "The ultimate disease of our time," he says, "is *valuelessness.*" Various terms are used to describe our cultural state—hopelessness, amorality, rootlessness, emptiness, etc. The modern West has cast aside such a

[17] *Vital Speeches*, XXXI (Feb. 1, 1965), p. 242.

great part of the cultural meaning that sustains man's dignity. As one character in Steinbeck's *The Winter of Our Discontent* puts it : "So many old and lovely things are stored in the world's attic." In short, modern man has progressively "denatured" himself. Robert Oppenheimer has described more accurately than any other modern critic the plight of "denatured man." "We hunger for nobility," he said, "the rare words and acts that harmonize simplicity and truth."

Many speakers use poetry as a kind of supporting detail, for poetry is apt to kindle the hearers' imaginations and blend thinking with feeling.

Demonstration, exhibits, visual aids

The seven kinds of supporting detail we have so far considered provide amplification of an idea only through what a speaker may say. It is obvious that a speaker may also reinforce or clarify his verbal message with visual materials, and in so doing open up a second channel of communication by appealing to the eyes of his listeners. Sometimes a visual presentation can produce responses which are beyond the power of words to effect, and often it can gain results more quickly and effectively than words, demonstrating that there is some truth in the saying, "One picture is worth a thousand words."

Many kinds of visual aids are commonly available to you, and need only be thoughtfully used. First, of course, is the blackboard on the wall of any classroom. Failing this, you will find portable blackboards or large easel-mounted pads of paper almost as useful and frequently supplied as standard equipment in meeting rooms. You can take with you demonstration pieces, samples, models, maps, charts, and graphs. Normally you can use any of these without special or technical assistance, and each may be effective in making some point clear or impressive.

More sophisticated visual presentations are apt to involve equipment of various kinds, including motion picture, opaque, or overhead projectors, tape recorders, and flannel boards or hook boards. For presentations using this sort of visual support you are quite likely to need special or technical help in producing the material, and often will require someone to operate the equipment while you concentrate on your speaking. Often visual presentations are so imaginatively designed and so skillfully executed that the speaker in fact becomes only an accessory, somewhat dehumanizing the communication process.

One of the most important principles in using visual aids is that *words and display should be integrated into a unified presentation*. What the audience *sees* should at that moment be related to what it *hears*. The speaker should guide the attention of the hearer, indicating both what to look at and the significance of what is seen. If you will examine the following segment from a speech by J. Carlton Ward, Jr., President of Vitro Corporation, to the Economic Club of Detroit, you will see how he coordinated what he said with the chart he displayed:

"I will have to explain Chart No. 3 (*page 405*) which covers a period of 100 years, from 1850 to 1950. This chart shows the percentages of different fuels which have furnished the motivating power energy sources that determine economy. At the top the area shaded with horizontal lines (9) represents the contribution of human energy, the chopping of wood, the hauling of water, the following of the plow, anything that is muscularly generated as energy sources. You will notice in the Civil War this was about 12% of the total energy used. Below it is the horse or the draft animal, (8), and you will notice that between man and the horse, two-thirds of all the energy that ran civilization was furnished by animal power and their food. And you will notice that today they are almost extinct. In fact, I made a prediction one day in philosophical discourse that this question of the mechanization of the home and the office and the factory had gone to such an extent with automation that we have only one unsolved power problem—motor driven zippers.

The checked area (6), underneath that particular group is water power and this is, as you see, about 8% of our total power resource and has been developed lately under the guise of irrigation for farm purposes, regulation of flood waters and the like.

Below that you find natural gas, (5), the black area, and then you find the vertical striped area (4)—oil—and then you find the large dotted area, (3), which is John L. Lewis's domain, and you will see that those three today are about as equal one to the other, and that the three together concentrate a fuel energy supply source in the

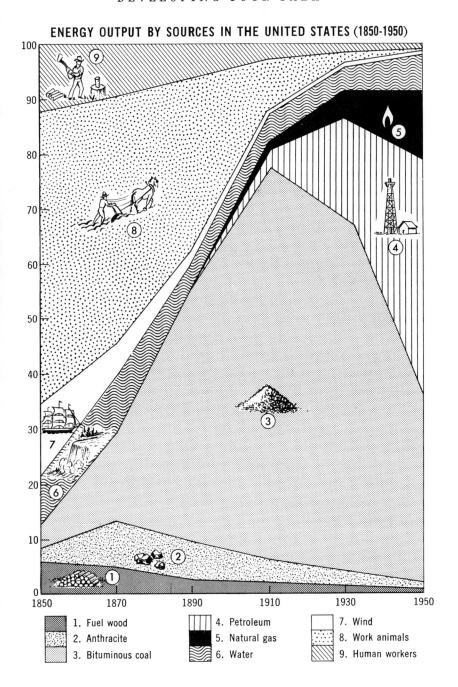

ENERGY OUTPUT BY SOURCES IN THE UNITED STATES (1850-1950)

1. Fuel wood
2. Anthracite
3. Bituminous coal
4. Petroleum
5. Natural gas
6. Water
7. Wind
8. Work animals
9. Human workers

United States of 90 percent of all the energy that runs our civilization.

At the bottom is hard coal, (2), and wood, (1), which were factors during the days of the Civil War with its woodburning locomotives and steamboats, but are today no more."

Obviously, a speaker must be familiar with whatever visual aid he plans to employ, should know precisely what he intends it to prove or explain, and should have reviewed or practiced its presentation. When you use visual aids you should observe these suggestions:

Keep the display simple, do not allow its significance to be obscured by non-essential details.

Be certain that it can be seen easily by everyone. Do not stand in front of it. Make certain that it is large enough for the expected viewing distance and for the number of people in the audience.

While using the display, talk to the audience and not to the visual aid.

Keep displays out of sight until you are ready to use them; get them out of sight again when you are through. Do not allow a visual aid to compete with you for the attention of your auditors.

If a visual is too small to be seen, do not use it. Never pass one through the audience where it will distract your listeners from what you are saying.

If you use pass-outs to your listeners, do not try to talk until they have been distributed.

Remember that visual aids should be used to explain or prove a point; they are not a substitute for an idea or for skill in speaking.

Showmanship

Showmanship can be defined as the method of supporting or developing an idea by *dramatizing* it. In a sense, visual aids are a form of dramatization, yet some speakers make highly effective use of *persons* and *properties* to make an idea attractive and vivid. They may themselves act out a thought, they may involve members of the audience in the dramatization, or they may use dramatic aids of various kinds, being limited only by the scope of their own imaginations.

Will a bit of showmanship be inconsistent with the dignity necessary for some speeches? Not at all, for an idea can be dramatized in any degree of dignity. I have already noted that former President Wriston of Brown University once began an address by singing several bars of a song. That was showmanship. So too was the method of Robert St. John, noted foreign correspondent and author. He wanted an audience to be impressed by the successive partitions of Israel through which that nation had lost much of the territory originally granted it by the League of Nations and the United Nations. Whipping from his pockets a pair of scissors and a huge piece of paper previously shaped to represent the original territory of Palestine, he snipped away as he described each partition. Quickly the floor was littered with paper, Palestine was cut to a fraction of its former size, and the audience clearly understood an important part of the history of Israel. If it was impressed by what Mr. St. John said, it was more impressed by what he did.

Dr. Lionel Crocker, former President of the Speech Association of America, knows that showmanship can make a lasting impression, for he has written:[18]

> I shall never forget a returned missionary's illustration on the number of Christians there were in all India. He took from his pocket a tape many yards long. On it he had indicated in different colors the various sects. He asked a member of the audience to run the tape to the back of the auditorium. Then with his fingers he pointed out the small section of the tape that represented how many Christians there were in comparison with the other religions. Was that audience impressed!

Showmanship should never be so dramatic that the listeners remember the stunt but forget the point. However, with a little thought you can learn to use the technique to make your own ideas come alive before an audience.

From the foregoing nine kinds of supporting detail you should select for each speech unit the number and variety you think adequate to accomplish your purposes. Use illustrations generously, for they hold attention and make your ideas clear and convincing. Explanation and detail are satisfactory when you must be clear, but they are not usually interesting. To achieve clarity, use analogy,

[18] Lionel Crocker, "Make the Illustration Linger," *Today's Speech*, IV, No. 1 (Jan., 1956), p. 4.

examples, and visual aids. To gain impressiveness, use apt quotation, illustration, and showmanship. To win belief, use repetition, facts, figures, and specific detail. Remember that if you fail to develop your ideas with specific supporting detail you will not have a speech, but an essay. And essays are meant to be read, not heard.

ORGANIZE EACH SPEECH UNIT TO SUIT THE LISTENERS' ATTITUDES

Not only should you select supporting detail which will be appropriate to the specific audience and which is best calculated to win the response you are after, but you should also organize each speech unit to meet the attitudes you expect the listeners to hold. There are three basic methods of organizing a unit, (1) the deductive, (2) the inductive, and (3) the combined. Although it may make little difference which you choose for many audiences, there will be times when audience attitudes will strongly suggest that one is preferable.

When your audience is interested in what you have to say and is likely to respond favorably to you and your purpose, the deductive method will serve you well, since its structure is clear and forthright. For many ordinary situations this method has general utility. However, when you must cultivate audience interest or when you must overcome negative attitudes or antagonism, you will probably find the inductive method preferable, since it delays revealing your point until you have developed interest and have effected some common ground with your listeners. For many speeches, the combined method has advantages, especially in maintaining attention and interest. In any speech you may, of course, use a variety of methods if that seems best.

The deductive method consists of stating your point first, then presenting the supporting detail, and finally restating the point, usually in the identical words you used at the outset. The structure of the unit would be something like this:

1. State your idea.
2. Make it clear with explanation, illustration, or analogy.
3. Support it further with examples, statistics, or quotation.
4. Restate the idea.

You are probably more familiar with the deductive method than with the others, since it follows the usual form of an outline in which the statement of the point precedes the detail. In fact, many people do not realize that a speech unit can be developed in any other way; since detail is written *below* the point in an amplified outline, they always offer support *after* stating the point. You can increase your skill by learning to use the inductive and combined patterns.

The inductive method simply dispenses with the opening statement of point and starts with supporting detail which arouses interest and implies the point. After presenting enough supporting material to lead the audience to infer the conclusion, the speaker finishes by stating the point clearly. The structure might be thus:

1. Present an illustration which contains the idea you plan to make.
2. Amplify the illustration with additional examples, analogies, figures, or testimony which imply the idea without stating it.
3. Use explanation or definition to show how this supporting detail leads inescapably to your conclusion.
4. State your idea.

The combined method of building a speech unit is a combination of deductive and inductive pattern put together to gain some of the most effective features of each. It begins interestingly with detail, leads into the point, which is stated, and then followed by additional supporting detail. At the end the point is restated. The following suggests the method:

1. Present an analogy or illustration involving the idea.
2. State the idea, showing that it derives from the analogy or illustration.
3. Present examples, facts, testimony, or statistics to enlarge or prove the idea.
4. Restate the idea as your conclusion.

You will find it worth while to practice using these three methods of building a speech unit until you develop high proficiency, for the unit is the basic communicative pattern. Once you have mastered its structure, you can easily apply your skill to the various situations in which it functions, adapting the organization of each speech unit to your audience. Remember that a speech can

409

be understood as a sequence of units integrated into a larger pattern which has unity, coherence, and emphasis.

MAKE YOUR LANGUAGE SPARKLE

Rhetorician I. A. Richards, among others, has pointed out that there are two fundamental functions of language. The first of these is the symbolic function in which language is used to make factual or referential statements. The second has been termed the emotive function, in which language is used to express or to excite feelings and attitudes, the purpose being less to point to a definite and objective referent than to reveal subjective moods or to arouse emotions.

Throughout this book we have given our attention almost exclusively to the first or symbolic function as we considered the language of communication. This is as it should be, for speech in the business and industrial world must first of all convey a clear idea and must do so without unnecessarily evidencing or arousing emotions which might interfere with full understanding. Yet one of the continuing complaints about the public speaking of business and professional people is that the speeches are drab and colorless, dull and uninspiring. In his book, *The Ethics of Rhetoric*, Richard M. Weaver suggests that there is indeed a long-standing feud between the businessman and the poet or rhetorician over the use of language, adding, "It is the historic tendency of the tradesman . . . to confine passion to quite narrow channels so that it will not upset the decent business arrangements of the world."[19]

All this suggests that if you would have your speaking more attractive and more inspiring than the average business talk, you should look to the style of your spoken expression, you should seek ways of "firing up" what you have to say. This is not to suggest that words alone will do the job, for you will never make an exciting speech if you yourself are unexcited. As Robert I. Fulton, beloved teacher of speech to an earlier generation observed, "Art cannot take the place of truth, nor form the place of substance." Yet it is to stress that the style of the spoken word does make a difference, and that you should seek a speaking style which has some color.

[19] Richard M. Weaver, *The Ethics of Rhetoric* (Chicago: Henry N. Regnery Company, 1953), p. 14.

Consider an example provided by Marie Hochmuth Nichols of the University of Illinois. A given idea is expressed in three contrasting statements :[20]

> Winston Churchill is eighty-three years old.
>
> The grand old man who occupied 10 Downing Street during the Second World War is eighty-three years old.
>
> Four-score and three he counts his years, proud England's mighty son.

The first of these is plainly symbolic in its language. It states a fact. The third does not state a fact, although in the proper context it implies one. It is almost completely emotive and is the stuff of which poetry is made. The second should be our main concern, for it reasonably balances the qualities of symbolic and emotive language and represents a style which escapes much of the dullness of routine business speaking.

Are there ways in which you can improve your style without undue involvement in the technicalities of the English language? Yes, there are some which will help you add sparkle to what you have to say and which you can put to immediate use if you will. It is those to which we turn.

Use imagery

One of the ways of making your ideas vivid is to evoke the sensory memories of your hearers, thereby causing them to flood your words with the most vigorous experience possible, the experience of direct, personal impression. To do this you must make use of the principle of imagery by choosing concrete words which present your ideas in terms of the original sense impressions of the listeners.

Stored in the nervous systems of those to whom you speak are thousands of impressions of sights, sounds, odors, and indeed of all the stimuli of direct sensual experience. Well chosen words which recall these impressions can make your speech as vividly intense as it is possible to make it. We have only to recall Winston Churchill's famous "blood, toil, sweat, and tears" to recognize the power of

[20] Marie Hochmuth, "I. A. Richards and the 'New Rhetoric'," *The Quarterly Journal of Speech*, XLIV, No. 1 (Feb., 1958), p. 4.

carefully selected concrete words. And without entering into a discussion of the exact number of the human senses, we can conveniently classify the impressions of our listeners into six categories: visual, auditory, gustatory, olfactory, tactile, and motor. These are the kinds of sense experience which your words must evoke.

Visual, of course, is the memory of things seen, and is probably the most fruitful source of effective imagery. Use words which will recall exact pictures if you want your audience to "see" the point you are making. The more precise the word, the more effective the image. Wordsworth's "host of golden daffodils" creates a picture which "I saw a bank of flowers" does not. Don't say "automobile" or "car" when "red VW" or "Ford convertible" will do the job better.

Auditory imagery recalls the experience of things heard—the squeak of dry hinges on a door, the hum of an electric fan, or the soft breathing of wind through pine trees. Gustatory is the memory of things tasted, the tang of mustard, the saltiness of sea spray, the acid pucker of lemon juice. Although most people are visual minded, many receive vital impressions through their ears and mouths, and imagery of these kinds can add dimensions to your style of expression.

The memory of what we smell constitutes olfactory imagery, and is evoked by words referring to exact odors. The mingled odors of bacon over an open fire may recall pleasant experiences, while reference to exhaust fumes in crowded traffic may recall unpleasant ones.

By tactile imagery I refer to memories of things touched or felt—the softness of velvet, the cold of an ice cube, a fly on your arm. Motor imagery refers to memories of muscle effort or internal sensation. Illustrative of the latter might be the stubborn refusal of a door knob to turn, the dreaminess of complete exhaustion, or the feeling of lightness when the express elevator swings up to stop at the twentieth floor.

These are the six useful kinds of imagery, the six pathways to the original experience of your audience. How can you use them? Your illustrations should abound in imagery. Facts and statistics should be presented in terms of sense experience. The want phase of the persuasive pattern can be explained by imagery if you will picture the difficulty or the unsatisfactory condition as it would be perceived by one who has experienced it. The desire phase offers additional opportunity for imagery, since you want your hearers to picture themselves enjoying the satisfaction or benefit of accepting your ideas.

The following excerpt is from a speech by Kenneth I. Brown, retired Director of the Danforth Foundation, delivered at Bluefield State College, West Virginia. Notice the way in which the speaker has carefully used image-evoking words to make his idea vivid.[21]

> Charles—let's give him a name—was a victim of family poverty, who had been robbed by circumstances of so many of the riches of life—riches which so often seem unevenly distributed. His family was without much faith in education; his home was without books or magazines, or good music, or art-prints: a home of cultural bareness. . . . I am certain that when we first met he didn't know himself to be a victim of two-dimensional living that he was.
>
> . . . As a student in a freshman course of music appreciation, [he] had been *urged* to attend the concert. . . . The next morning he came to my office. "Were you there?"
>
> "Where?", for I was not at that moment thinking of Mr. Bach or St. John.
>
> "At the church, the big church, the cathedral. I never knew there was anything like that—so big, so beautiful. Our church back home is tiny and ugly. . . . And did you hear the music? I didn't know there was such music in the world, never before. . . . Where have I been all these years? Why didn't someone tell me? You know yesterday I turned my eyes on and looked around. I turned my ears on and listened hard, all through. . . ." Then slowly, "Until yesterday I never knew how much I've missed all these years." The words came pouring out like hot lava. All I could find to say was, "Lucky man, Charles. Now you know some things you've missed and knowing, you can search for them, and you'll recognize them, when you find them."

Whenever possible, *translate your abstract statements into concrete ones which open as many doors to memory as you can.* For instance, in each of the following pairs of statements, the first is highly abstract, the second concrete. Each of the pair expresses a similar idea, but the second utilizes imagery, and achieves greater sparkle.

21 *Vital Speeches*, XXXI (July 1, 1965), pp. 567–8.

Atomic warfare threatens mankind.
A mushroom cloud blots out the sunshine of peace.

The individual must strive to understand other cultures.
He who drinks Coke must strive to understand those who chew betelnuts.

The measure of democracy is not the number of people able to move, but the number able to think.
Democracy can better be measured by libraries than by automobiles.

Capital is the raw material for progress.
Dollars are the raw materials from which come new classrooms for the young, new medicines for the ill, new roads into pockets of poverty, and new paths to the stars.

The use of imagery is not hard to achieve, if you will consciously practice it as a technique of style.

Use rhetorical questions

Another device useful to give liveliness to your speech is the rhetorical question. This is one put to the audience without expecting a reply, its purpose being either to evoke a desired answer by suggestion or to forecast one, causing the listeners to anticipate it. For either purpose, the rhetorical question provides a variety of style, breaking the monotony of a single sentence form.

Aptly used, the rhetorical question can imply a conclusion or implant a suggestion in the manner of Patrick Henry's famous, "Why stand we here idle when our brethren are already in the field? Is life so dear, or peace so sweet, as to be purchased at the price of chains and slavery?"

As a forecast of what is to come, the rhetorical question supplies emphasis or marks a transition from one idea to another. For example, "What is the first step? I suggest that we. . . ." "Why does this situation exist? Field studies show that. . . ."

You will not find it difficult to make rhetorical questions work for you, sharpening the impact of your speech.

Use direct quotation

If you will refer back to the excerpt from the speech by Kenneth I. Brown you will notice that not only did he use imagery to achieve sparkle, but he also employed direct quotation to add life to his message. This kind of quotation is not used as testimony for supporting detail, but is a technique for bringing alive a portion of an illustration. It permits the listeners to hear the actual words of those in the story, thus enhancing the crispness and vigor of the style. You have enjoyed novels and short stories written in brisk dialogue; the same technique will serve to make your own speaking brighter.

In an address at Wartburg College, Eldon F. Scoutten, Vice President of the Maytag Company, employed direct quotation to make more pungent a point about modern art:[22]

> This sort of thing is alleged to be self-expression. In reality, it is a retreat from standards of excellence and it is, in fact, a fraud and a delusion. If there are no standards, then truly anyone can paint; but the sad part of this is that it is accepted by many gullible citizens as being a new kind of art. As my friend Jenkins Jones says, "When somebody welds together some old gears, some corset stays and a piece of sheet metal, and says it is art, we may conceivably ignore him; but when he contends that it is more beautiful than Michelangelo's 'David,' then we should say 'It looks like junk, and it probably is.' "

Use figures of speech

For centuries writers and speakers alike have recognized that vividness of style can be heightened by the use of figurative language. Although the varieties of figures are many, the most common and immediately useful are the simile and the metaphor, for these help to turn abstract ideas into concrete realities, invoking imagery to create pictures. Both the simile and the metaphor are capsuled analogies which pithily draw a comparison between the idea to be

[22] *Vital Speeches*, XXX (Feb. 15, 1964), p. 272.

understood and some experience of the listener. The simile makes the comparison explicit by using the word *like* or *as:*

His mind was so vacant that ideas flowed through it like breezes across an empty attic.

The gang boss gave orders like a bull elephant sounding the charge.

She was as relentless as the winds of a hurricane.

In contrast to the simile, the metaphor makes a comparison implicit by declaring that one thing *is* another:

History is a tired old man with a long beard.

Youth is a fire and the years are a pack of wolves who grow bolder as the fire dies down.

His face was a page on which were written a thousand stubborn opinions.

Both kinds of comparison can be made even more effective by careful choice of verbs, for verbs can enliven style by suggesting vividness of action:

An army of clouds charged down the valley.

He insisted on bypassing every new thought.

April was whispering in the fields.

MAKE CLEAR THE SEQUENCE AND RELATIONSHIP OF YOUR IDEAS

In Chapter 10 I pointed out that your listeners have a right to an orderly presentation of material. This means that you must not only think carefully to arrange your ideas in a purposive and meaningful order, but that as you speak you must with equal care make certain that your hearers understand that order. You must first arrange your ideas clearly in your own mind, after which you must make certain that your listeners understand that arrangement. This may sometimes be done by giving them a skeletonic preview of your ideas, but it always requires effective introductions, transitions, and summaries.

In many speeches you will find that an introductory summary or *partition* of your subject will be useful in making clear what is to come. This means that you should present a terse preview of the major structure of your speech or should preview the subdivisions of a specific phase. The effect is to provide a road map of what you intend to say, permitting the listeners to relate details to the basic ideas as you take them up.

A clear example of such an introductory summary was furnished by Guilford Dudley, Jr., President of the Life and Casualty Insurance Company, when he spoke to the National Society of the Sons of the American Revolution:[23]

> I would like to touch briefly on three of these symptoms clearly visible in our nation today, characteristics that are fostered and fed by a slowly-developing welfare state, signs of national weakness that grow more prevalent as each day goes by.
>
> They are:
>
> THE GROWING TREND TOWARD PERSONAL NON-INVOLVEMENT.
>
> THE RISING TIDE OF MEDIOCRITY.
>
> THE CHOICE OF SECURITY OVER OPPORTUNITY.

Having indicated in these words the three major areas of his address, Mr. Dudley then proceeded to consider each in turn. Such a preview gives the listener some familiarity with the terrain to be covered before he is forced to attend to the detailed supporting material, and assists him to see the speech in its larger dimensions. Full understanding is enhanced by a realization of structure, for a pattern in itself is meaningful.

Regardless of whether or not you use an introductory summary, you should usually give some sign to indicate the moment you embark on the development of a speech unit. The sign may be the introductory *statement of the idea* if the unit is organized deductively, it may be a rhetorical question, or it may be some less obvious phrase or statement, such as, "Let's begin by looking at . . ." or "At the outset. . . ."

Often when a speaker uses a rhetorical question to introduce a given unit, he follows that question with a succinct answer to make certain his hearers grasp the idea he is about to develop. The following suggest ways in which a given unit might be introduced:

23 *Vital Speeches*, XXXI (Aug. 1, 1965), p. 632.

An introductory statement: "The first prerequisite to successful business is a philosophy."

A rhetorical question: "What is the first prerequisite to a successful business? A philosophy."

In this pair you will notice the use of the word "first" in each case, indicating the number of the point. The device of enumeration is commonly employed where a series of ideas is to be presented in sequence. If such skeletonic bluntness seems painfully obvious, remember that it is better to be obvious than to be confusing.

Just as you should give the audience some indication of the beginning of a speech unit, you should also make clear the ending of that unit, usually by a summary or conclusion to stress the idea you would have understood or accepted. Such a summary may take the form of an exact restatement of the idea as it was introduced, or it could be a paraphrase or an elaboration of that statement. Regardless of the form, however, the audience must know when a given segment of a talk is finished, and should grasp the point or idea.

At the conclusion of a part of the speech which has contained more than one sub-point, particularly if an introductory summary has been used, a concluding summary should be used to review and re-emphasize the important ideas. Such a summary is often effective in the action phase of the talk (see Chapter 12), and is particularly appropriate when the audience is expected to remember major areas of information or be impressed by certain arguments.

Introductions and summaries or conclusions are necessary not only to help the audience fully grasp the ideas and their sequence in the talk, but also to help the listeners understand the relationships among those ideas. To this latter end, *transitional* elements are often required in addition to the other signposts. Such elements may be words, phrases, statements, or questions, but regardless of their form, they indicate the ways in which the successive ideas are related. They help the hearers see the connection among the parts, thus enhancing the coherence of the speech.

The wording of transitional or connective elements depends upon the nature of the relationship being explained, which means that you must understand thoroughly those relationships. The following selected list of possible relationships and common connectives illustrates the kinds of devices you will find helpful in making yourself clear:

Relationship	Connective
Addition	In addition to . . .
	Besides this . . .
	Not only . . . but also . . .
	Moreover . . .
Contrast	However . . .
	In contrast to . . .
	Looking from a different viewpoint . . .
Choice	Either . . . or . . .
	Otherwise . . .
Result	From all this . . .
	Therefore . . .
	Consequently . . .
	Because of these facts . . .
Time	Before all this . . .
	Later . . .
	Until . . .
Space	Beyond this . . .
	Looking ahead . . .
Cause	Since this . . .
	Creating this situation . . .
Condition	Provided . . .
	In spite of this . . .

In consequence of the suggestions in this chapter, you may have raised the question, *Should I write out my speech?* Usually you should not, but under one or two conditions you will want to do so. The first is, of course, when you think it desirable to read the speech. When this is true, you will write the entire address and work it into the form of a reading copy. The second condition is when you hope to make the most polished presentation possible without reading from manuscript. If this happens, you should write out your material only for the discipline and clarity that writing imposes, and then make your presentation from notes without attempting to recall the precise wording of the manuscript. Writing a speech is excellent practice in composition and wording, and a useful way of learning to develop expression, but if you insist on trying to present a talk exactly as you remember having written it, the process is liable to inhibit your spontaneity and freedom in delivery. For this reason, unless you feel you must read the talk, you should look upon writing a speech only as an exercise to develop your skill.

YOU MAY USE SPEECH-UNIT METHODS IN ALL SPEAKING SITUATIONS

The basic methods of organizing a single speech unit as part of an address, of making each succeeding idea interesting, clear, vivid, and convincing, can also be used in almost any speaking situation. They are especially useful to meet three specific situations.

To make a brief "one-point" speech

There are many occasions when you may be called upon to speak briefly, at ceremonial meetings, at dinners, at business meetings, or at other events. On such occasions a long talk may be inappropriate, even though you are expected to have "a few words" for the group. Under these conditions the presentation of a single well-chosen idea will allow you to make a succinct contribution to the affair, especially if you develop your idea as a single speech unit. The following is an example of such a one-point speech appropriate for a meeting of teachers:

> Not long ago many of us sat by our television sets to attend, at a distance, the funeral services for Sir Winston Churchill. The final homage to Britain's hero was made even more impressive by its surroundings, especially the magnificent beauty of St. Paul's Cathedral, one of London's inspiring landmarks.
>
> When this "parish church of the British Empire" was under construction during the 17th Century, according to an ancient tale, the architect, Sir Christopher Wren, was accustomed to visit the site and talk to the workmen. On a certain day, he put a question to those with whom he talked, receiving answers which even today have significance for us.
>
> "What are you doing?" he asked a workman. "Pounding stone," was the reply.
>
> "What are you doing?" he asked a second. "Earning sixpence a day," said the worker.
>
> "What are you doing?" he asked again, and was

touched by the answer. "Sir," said the workman, "I am building a great cathedral."

I am sure that many of us who teach often get so close to our work that we cannot see it in perspective. We are like those workmen of the 17th Century. We see ourselves only as pounding stone or earning money. Tonight I should like to suggest that we inspire ourselves with the larger view, that we are building something of consequence. And in truth we are—we are builders of something more magnificent than any cathedral, for we teachers are builders of human lives. Only as we see ourselves in this light can we know the reward of our labors.

If you will examine this brief speech analytically, you will see that as a single unit it is composed of the following technical elements:

First, an introduction designed to bring the distant scene into the experience of at least some of the hearers.

Second, the anecdote with its conversation.

Third, the application of the anecdote, creating an analogy, ending the unit with a statement of the idea and purpose.

The introduction, anecdote, and application make up the supporting detail, while the central idea is contained in the words, "we teachers are builders of human lives." Together these components form a complete one-point speech, organized inductively.

To make a contribution in a conference

I warned in Chapter 9 that a conference was not an appropriate place for a speech. Nevertheless, a conferee may often find himself obligated to make an idea clear or convincing. To do so, he utilizes the basic speech unit technique of stating and supporting his idea. In the following excerpt, notice how two participants in a radio discussion work together to develop an idea. The discussion was about implications of the study of human growth.[24]

Mr. Weiss: Is there a particular size trend in the human race, Washburn?

[24] "The Study of Growth and Its Meaning: II," *The University of Chicago Round Table,* No. 765 (Nov. 23, 1952), pp. 2–3.

Mr. Washburn: If we go back to the fossils of many thousands of years ago, we find big ones and little ones. The statures for Cro-Magnon men range from a little over five feet to around six—not too different from the sizes of the people now around this table. But in relatively recent time there seems to be a definite tendency to increase in stature. Several studies made at Smith College and at Harvard and at other places in Europe and even in Japan have shown a general tendency for fairly rapid increase in size in the last few years. So that children tend to be taller than their parents.

Mr. Havighurst: Particularly have children increased their size. The difference seems to be much greater among children than among adults. For an example of this we might compare two studies of the sizes of fourteen-year-old boys of north European stock. One study was made in 1877; and another was made almost sixty years later in 1936. Between these dates the fourteen-year-old boys had gained six inches in height. By this, I mean that a group of fourteen-year-old boys in 1877 compared with a group of fourteen-year-old boys in 1936 showed a gain of six inches in height and fourteen pounds in weight.

As you participate in business or professional conferences, you may find the one-point technique useful to you in a way similar to that employed by the above participants.

To make a contribution in an interview

An interview, like a conference, is no place to give speeches. Yet, like a conference, it frequently requires that a participant make a single point clear and acceptable, either as an idea he had planned to present to his respondent, or in response to a question.

In the following single unit, J. Edgar Hoover, Director of the Federal Bureau of Investigation, replies to the question of a journalist, "Have any studies of the FBI been made by foreign governments?"[25]

Yes. Almost monthly some representative of a foreign agency—intelligence or criminal investigative agency

[25] Interview with J. Edgar Hoover, *U.S. News & World Report*, LVII, No. 25 (Dec. 21, 1964), p. 40.

—visits this country. They will usually come to FBI head-quarters. They will sometimes spend days studying our procedures, our techniques, and exchanging information with us. This procedure has been beneficial to them and to us.

A typical example is the assistance we have rendered to French intelligence and criminal-investigative officials. I was asked by the head of the Sureté Nationale whether the FBI would be willing to give one of their men the FBI firearms training. All of our men have to be expert in the handling of firearms. They have to qualify once each month. I assured the head of the Sureté that we would be glad indeed to provide this training.

This organization sent over one of its men, who stayed at our training base at Quantico, Va. We gave him a complete course of firearms training. He has gone back to France, where he is now training members of the Sureté, using exactly the same techniques that we use to train our men here.

Regardless of the type of interview, the statement of an idea together with appropriate supporting detail can make an effective communicative unit.

In this chapter we have examined the most important princi-ples and methods of developing the outline of a speech from a skeleton arrangement of essential ideas into a complete talk, and have noted that the techniques of developing a speech unit can be applied to speech forms other than a public address. With the sub-stance of your speech prepared, you are now ready to look into the question of delivery.

Chapter 14

Delivering Your
Talk

*What a speaker says is mental—how he says it is physical. It is
frequently not only so much what is said as how you say it—the
way the message is put across.*

*Regardless of the speech content, even though well prepared
and well organized and of the utmost importance, the speech can fall
short of the mark in the event that it is delivered in a fashion that
is lifeless and lacks "punch."*

*Delivery implies a mastery of animation and a display of emo-
tion. It means telling the story most graphically which, of course,
means more convincingly. Delivery is dramatization of the speech
content.*[1]

NATIONAL ASSOCIATION OF MANUFACTURERS
Education Department

YOUR MESSAGE IS FULLY PREPARED AND YOU ARE ABOUT TO MEET
your audience.

You face one final question. "Can I deliver the goods?" Your
whole concern now is with the "getting across" of your message.

If delivery seems to be a problem, it is time to pause and
review. It is time to recall that speech is the total act of communication, and that you cannot really "deliver" a speech. You can, and
you are about to, converse with a group of listeners, speaking with a

---

[1] National Association of Manufacturers, Education Department, *Helpful
Suggestions for Industrial Speakers Appearing Before College and School
Audiences* (with the cooperation of Dr. Neal Bowman, 1952), p. 10.

greater degree of amplification and with more dignity than you would were you lounging over a cup of coffee, but still conversing. This will not be the moment for you to repeat a prepared monologue; it will be the moment for you to talk with a number of people as naturally as you would with a single person. The "delivery" of your speech is the act of communicating what you have so carefully planned to tell these people.

Of course the manner of your speaking is of vital importance. Dull, listless speaking can turn an important message into a recital of relatively meaningless words, while vigorous and animated speaking can add color and persuasiveness, enriching and amplifying the meaning. As I have insisted throughout this book, the meaning stirred up in the listener is always the result of the total impact of the speaker—what he is, what he says, and how he says it. Yet before an audience, much of both what you are and what you say can be interpreted by your listeners only in terms of what they see and hear.

Make no mistake about one thing, however. Good delivery cannot be put on from outside, it cannot be applied as a veneer to the exterior of an address. To the contrary, good delivery arises from within, from the motivating forces which make you a man with a message, from your eagerness to communicate, from your willingness to let yourself go, forgetting yourself in your desire to get people to understand and believe. You should concern yourself, not with the *mechanics* of delivery, but with the things which *cause* it. The thesis of this chapter is that *how you say it* depends to a great extent upon *what you are* and *how you feel* about your message. From that viewpoint, let us examine some principles of delivery.

PUT YOURSELF IN THE RIGHT FRAME OF MIND

Good conversation begins as an attitude. It begins when one is interested in other people, when he is willing to listen to or attend to them, and when he has something to say which he thinks is worth their hearing. Unless a speaker possesses such a frame of mind, his speaking is likely to be listless and apathetic. Good conversation is characterized by naturalness and sparkle when the speaker has established rapport with his respondents, when he recognizes the impact his words are having, and when he unconsciously modifies his manner of speaking to suit both the significance of what he says and the circumstance of the occasion. You can lay the foundations for this kind of speaking by doing those things which will help you establish an affirmative and creative attitude.

Remind yourself that you have an important message

From Chapter 11 you will recall that to make a successful speech you must have something to say, something which you want to talk about and which you think will be of importance to your hearers. Preferably it should arise from whatever life has taught you.

Now is the time to remind yourself of these facts. Recall that you DO have a message for these people. Remind yourself of how important it is for them to have it. Remember that you know more about the subject than they do, or you wouldn't have the opportunity to speak to them. Review the experiences which have provided you with ideas and illustrations. Tell yourself that this is an exciting and vital topic, one which concerns you deeply. Emphasize that you have earned the right to speak about it.

By doing these things, and doing them just before you speak, you can help build the kind of affirmative attitude which will enhance the directness and conversationality of your speaking. The presence of such thoughts in mind will tend to give you confidence.

Keep your purpose uppermost in mind

Many speakers fail to generate force and directness because they seem to be concerned only with voicing so many words before an audience. They are consuming a given amount of time rather than energetically trying to secure a planned response from their listeners. Enthusiastic purpose is a necessary prerequisite to animated presentation.

In both Chapters 10 and 11 the importance of the speech purpose in governing the building of your talk was stressed. That purpose also governs to a great extent the manner in which you talk with your hearers. If you are unconcerned with the way in which your listeners respond to what you say, you will speak in a desultory

426

manner, but if you are keenly aware of the effect you want to produce, you will unconsciously use every ability you possess to secure the desired response. When you WANT people to understand or believe, when you WANT to communicate, you will speak at your natural best. Your face will come alive. You will use action to describe or emphasize the things you are saying. Your voice will respond to the urgency of your purpose. You will talk with the vigor and directness of resolution.

Sometimes it takes a direct challenge to arouse a speaker to full power. This happened one day to Joe Robinson, then Senator from Arkansas. The incident was recalled by Josh Lee, former Senator from Oklahoma, who is also a powerful speaker:[2]

> One time he [Senator Robinson] was speaking to the Senate in a rather humdrum fashion when an opposing senator interrupted to ask if he implied so and so. Senator Robinson came alive like a tolerant, easy-going giant who at last has been thoroughly angered. He shot back, "I don't imply anything. I say what I mean!" This was the spur he needed, because the rest of the speech was delivered with energy.

You, however, should not depend upon another to bring you alive. Remember that you have a purpose in speaking, and direct all your energies toward securing it. Let controlled enthusiasm for your central idea and dedication to your purpose stoke the fires of delivery.

Remember that your listeners are probably on your side

You may from time to time face an audience in some degree hostile to you, but this is likely to be a rare occasion. Most of your public speaking will undoubtedly be done before a group of people at worst indifferent, and more probably friendly toward you. From such knowledge you can take encouragement.

Put yourself in the place of your listener. Either you have come with a genuine desire to hear what the speaker has to say, or you are a member of a "captive" audience, unable to escape after dinner or directed by your superior (or teacher) to listen. In either event, do

---

[2] Josh Lee, *How to Hold an Audience Without a Rope*, Second edition, (Chicago: Ziff-Davis Publishing Company, 1949), p. 128.

you hope that the speaker will be a failure? Do you want him to stumble through his address, vacant-eyed and trembling? Never! You earnestly hope that he will prove to be interesting and alive, that he will have something worthwhile to say, and that you will be able to take a profitable idea away with you. If he fidgets, you fidget. If he is tense and nervous, you are tense and nervous. If he is uncomfortable, you are uncomfortable with him. Therefore, you want him to be purposive, commanding, and to enjoy speaking to you.

This is the kind of listener you are likely to meet in your audience. He is hoping that you will succeed, for your success is also his success. He is hopeful of the best, and willing to tolerate the human difficulties that he himself would have were he speaking in your place. He is able to recognize the problems you face, and is willing for you to meet them in a natural and agreeable way. He wants you to converse with him as you would if you were speaking privately and personally, but loudly enough so he can hear you without effort.

Therefore, meet your listeners with an affirmative frame of mind. Remember that they are hoping for the best, and are anxious for you to succeed. If you want to be interesting, have interest in the people you face. On almost all occasions they are your friends.

Know that "stage fright" is normal, and may be an asset

Sweating palms, a dry mouth, shaking knees, a knot in the pit of the stomach, and a rapidly beating heart are some of the symptoms of the malady commonly called stage fright. The symptoms vary from person to person, and the intensity of the onset likewise is felt differently by different people. Regardless of its severity, the problem is a very real and a very disconcerting thing, having both physiological and psychological elements.

Studies confirm what we might expect, that stage fright tends to disappear as an individual gains experience in public speaking. This may, indeed, be one of the reasons you should deliberately seek experience in talking to groups, and why a course in speaking can be extremely beneficial. As you gain seasoning you tend to develop confidence and the ability to use your full mental and physical powers before an audience. Meanwhile you should find the following

428

principles helpful in creating the frame of mind needed to successfully overcome the degree of concern which may beset you.

1. Know that stage fright is as common as the ordinary cold. It
attacks the famous and the professional as well as the unknown and
the inexperienced, so that you are far from abnormal if you feel its
symptoms. In various surveys and studies, fully 90 percent of the
respondents affirmed that they suffered stage fright when facing an
audience. Clarence B. Randall, former Chairman of Inland Steel,
wrote that he always had a "gone" feeling in the pit of his stomach
before he made an address. Harry Emerson Fosdick, one of
America's recent great ministers, fought to overcome platform fear
when a student. Clinton Giddings Brown, an outstanding Texan
trial lawyer, actually found it necessary on some occasions to have
his stomach pumped before appearing in court! Having stage fright
does not mean that you have less courage than other people; it
simply means that you are a very normal individual.

2. Know that the symptoms you feel are the typical responses
of someone facing a situation which seems to him a threat. You are
anxious to succeed, yet you are uncertain of your reception. You
want to make a good impression, yet you are afraid that you may
not. You are fearful that you may make yourself look foolish in
public. Your nerves become high strung, your muscles tense. Your
reactions are precisely those of an athlete before an important
contest: you are keyed up for success.

This is why experience will help you. You will learn that
feelings of *fear* can be overcome, but that feelings of *concern* can
help you to be a better speaker. *Unless you are aroused you will not
do your best.* "When I am on my feet I am always afraid till my
knees shake under the table," said Rufus Choats, brilliant lawyer of
the last century. "When they knock together, then I know I am
going to make a good speech." As you yourself become seasoned you
will discover that the process of becoming physically and mentally
keyed up is as necessary to the best public speaking as it is to the
best of any effort. As one person put it, "I'd never bet money on a
horse that stood at the barrier with his feet crossed!"

3. Know that there are ways of minimizing fear and taking
advantage of constructive concern. The most important of these, of
course, is to have adequate preparation and clear purpose. If you
have already heeded these matters, you are well on the way toward
making a productive speech.

Beyond these things, which have already been emphasized, you can follow the Shakespearian advice which Lily Pons used to help conquer her nervousness. "Assume a virtue, if you have it not," said Shakespeare's Hamlet, thereby suggesting to Miss Pons and to you that adopting the virtues of calmness and poise will help to meet the situation. Specifically:

> Command yourself to relax. Is your jaw tight, are your hands clenched? Deliberately allow your head to sag forward, and your jaw to drop, as if to yawn. Drop your hands limply. Assume a calm exterior, which is the first step to a calm interior.
>
> Breathe deeply and regularly. As you advance to your speaking position, take at least one deep breath and allow the air to escape slowly and fully. It is hard to feel tense when breathing is deep and regular.
>
> Pause before you speak. Do not hurry your opening remarks, thereby increasing tension, but *look at* and *see* your listeners, waiting until you have complete attention before beginning. Then start speaking at a deliberate rate.
>
> Do something purposive. The nervous energy built up within you and which may make you uncomfortable can be dissipated by physical activity. This fact can drive you to see-sawing on your heels or to unconsciously pacing the floor to the distraction of your listeners. Resist the temptation and channel your energy into action which seems purposive to the audience. Reposition the speaking stand. If you have notes, stack them. Take a drink of water. Use your accumulated energy for purposive or communicative physical action and you will gain an increased sense of control and well being.
>
> Be honest with your hearers. Many a speaker has instantly dissipated all tension by saying something like, "Right at this moment I'm scared to death!" If you forget a point, tell your listeners. Better to say, "The next point was a priceless pearl of wisdom which you may never know because I can't remember it," than to freeze up to both your discomfort and your hearers'. Do not forget that you are CONVERSING, and usually with friends.

"Do the thing you fear to do, and the death of fear is certain," wrote Emerson. If you are plagued by the symptoms of stage fright, the best known cure is to refuse to be afraid of fear and to adopt the virtue of courage. "Courage is not the absence of fear, but the mastery of it."

Familiarize yourself with the physical setting beforehand

Elsewhere I have suggested that knowledge of the physical conditions under which you will speak can sometimes be helpful in planning your address. Such knowledge can also aid in creating the confident attitude necessary to effective delivery. Therefore arrive at the meeting place well ahead of time and get acquainted with it. How will the audience be arranged? Are there acoustic problems? Will you speak from a raised platform? Is there any way you would like the arrangements changed to make you more comfortable? You may want to get acquainted with the person who will introduce you, or you may want to deposit notes or equipment where they will be handy when needed. You may even want to try speaking in the room before the audience has arrived. Familiarizing yourself with the conditions under which you will speak can do much to give you a sense of confidence when you speak.

Since the *causes* of effective delivery lie within yourself, ounces of effort in putting yourself in the right frame of mind are worth pounds of concern about voice and gesture. Nevertheless, we do need to pay some attention to the basic mechanics of presentation.

USE THE MOST SUITABLE METHOD OF PRESENTATION

There are a number of methods you can employ to deliver a speech, each of which has variations. You should select the method which gives promise of most effectively meeting your own capabilities, but even more importantly of meeting the requirements of the particular speaking occasion. Among the latter must be reckoned the length of the speech, the degree of formality of the occasion, the necessity of strict accuracy in text, and the response desired from the audience.

The extempore method is generally preferable

The most widely used and generally effective method of presentation is extempore. This means that the speech is thoroughly prepared, usually in outline form. The ideas, the structure, and even the supporting detail are carefully put together, precisely as described in the preceding chapters. The actual choice of words, however, is left to the moment of speaking. Using this method, you would be highly conversational, leading your listeners along a path of planned and purposive thinking in a highly spontaneous manner.

One who speaks extemporaneously may or may not use notes. He may, and probably most speakers do, take with him to the platform a brief set of speaking notes which act as reminders of the ideas he wants to discuss, and of the order in which he wants to present them. Such notes may also include reminders of the chief items of supporting detail, occasionally augmented with some facts or figures or with the exact words of authorities the speaker wants to quote verbatim. Speaking notes are *not* the full outline which was made during preparation, but *reminders* of that outline.

The only difference between the speaker who uses notes and the one who does not, is that the latter depends upon his memory for full recall of his original speech plan, whereas the former uses a "road map." As you gain experience you will find that *you need notes much less than you think you do,* and that the supposed disadvantage of not having them is usually more than offset by the increased directness of presentation and the more sustained conversational contact you have with your listeners.

When you do use notes, do so openly and frankly. The audience will not resent your having notes; it will resent only your speaking *to those notes,* or your attempt to conceal them. Make your notes large enough to see easily, and do not try to talk while you consult them. Pause while you check your notes, and then resume the conversation.

Under usual conditions, you will be most effective with an extempore delivery. If you are master of your topic, if you have thoroughly planned the order of your thinking, and if you are possessed by a clear purpose, you can converse animatedly with an audience, noting and responding to their reactions. As Lionel Crocker has put it, you can "collaborate with the occasion."

Some talks are read from manuscript

There are times when reading a speech from manuscript is necessary or even desirable, but you should be certain of the necessity or desirability before deciding to deliver a talk in this manner. Statesmen and high ranking business executives read from manuscript when it is necessary that their words be carefully weighed and accurately stated to avoid the unfortunate consequences which could follow a "slip of the tongue" or thoughtless "off-the-cuff" statement. Scholarly papers and technical reports are read when accuracy of detail or clarity of complicated reasoning are involved. Some speeches are also read when the address will become part of a permanent record, or when adherence to a strict time limit is necessary, as in a broadcast.

I must grant that many speeches are read because they have been ghostwritten and do not truly represent the mind and personality of the individual who delivers them. In some cases there are legitimate reasons for the practice (the pressure of time on a political candidate, for instance, may not allow him to prepare every speech he is forced to make), but too often speeches are ghostwritten because the speaker lacks the ability or the ideas necessary to a good address. The line between the integrity of a speaker who seeks help to meet an important situation and the dishonesty of one who represents another's writing as his own is, unfortunately, not always immediately evident.

If you find that reading your speech seems the most appropriate method, the following suggestions will be useful:

Write the speech out completely, and then edit it at least twice to achieve a smooth oral style. Read it out loud as you do the editing, making sure that the words and sentence structure have the feeling and rhythm of natural conversational expression. Avoid long or involved sentences.

Create a reading copy for your presentation, preferably typed in triple space, and on only one side of the paper.

Practice out loud, marking your reading copy by underlining or in any other way that will help you grasp the *ideas* as you read them. Too elaborate marking is apt to confuse you, however.

Master your manuscript so that you will not bury yourself in it as you read. Remember that reading is communication, and that you must read *to people*. Vocalizing words is not enough. See your hearers as you read.

If you plan to read, READ! Do not preface your address with an impromptu irrelevance, nor insert side remarks as you go along. The contrast between these and your prepared material can blemish what otherwise could be a well-formed address.

Do not depend on your voice alone. To enliven your delivery use gestures or bodily action in response to the thought. Even radio broadcasters frequently gesture, knowing that although they cannot be seen, physical action helps to produce vocal vigor.

Speakers rarely memorize an address

In the past there have been speakers who wrote and memorized their material for delivery. Many of the ancient Greek and Roman orators did this, and on occasion did such men as James A. Garfield and William Jennings Bryan closer to our own time. Today, outside of some interscholastic speaking contests, it is rare to find one who follows the practice.

While there are some benefits of personal discipline to be gained from writing and memorizing a speech, unless you are peculiarly suited to the form, you will probably find one of the other methods of delivery better for you.

We have, at the other extreme the *impromptu* talk, which is fully created at the moment of delivery and without any prior planning. Few people can be effective in impromptu; many who seem superbly able to deliver, on occasion, "just a few words" have secretly prepared against a possible opportunity to speak.

WHAT THE AUDIENCE SEES SHOULD BE PART OF YOUR MESSAGE

"Here was a man who could not 'make' a speech," said Emerson of his "almost perfect orator." "He WAS a speech." The observation suggests the necessary blending of mind, voice, and body into total communicative behavior, the kind of speaking which is most effective because it is a unified message. It emphasizes that bodily action should be as much a part of the speech as the language which symbolizes the idea of the moment.

There are in truth two good reasons for encouraging full bodily vigor while speaking. The first is, of course, that such action com-municates—it strengthens and enriches the impressions being formed by the listeners, for whom the visible code takes precedence over the visual. They are impressed more quickly and more thoroughly by what they *see* than by what they *hear*. The second is that bodily action is reflexive. A speaker in action tends to stimulate himself. And since the mind is a function of what the body is doing, the speaker who is physically alive tends also to be mentally alive. He is more alert, more sensitive, and more responsive.

Therefore, you should work toward a speech delivery which is physically animated. And just what rules or principles should govern your bodily activity? The pages of detailed advice to be found in many of the textbooks can be summarized in one basic principle: *Everything the audience sees should contribute to your message.* Conversely, whatever the audience sees which is not a part of the message is distracting. Irrelevant physical behavior competes for the attention of the listener with whatever the speaker is saying —and sometimes the irrelevant behavior wins!

With the idea in mind of working for purposive animation, then, let us turn to a few more specific principles.

Visible action should suggest spontaneous vitality

Have you ever tried to direct a stranger to a location in your town, and found yourself pointing out the course he should follow? Have you ever told stories to little tots, and found yourself augmenting the words with gestures? (Try explaining how Santa Claus gets into the house!) Have you ever tried to gain the attention of some-one a block away, and found yourself waving or jumping up and down? If you can recall experiences such as these, you will realize that communicating by physical action is natural and spontaneous. It issues impulsively as a consequence of the strong desire to communicate.

When two conditions exist, then, you will find yourself in purposive action on the speaking platform. First, you must have a strong desire to communicate, and, second, you must free yourself from the inhibitions which restrain your natural impulse to com-municate physically. If you are average, your essential problem is not to assume a new set of speaking characteristics, but to remove the restrictions which hamper response to your inner communicative impulses. You must succeed in getting yourself to "speak like a human being," and at your natural best.

At first this may not be easy, for the inhibitions are born of self-consciousness. You may hesitate to "let yourself go" for fear of appearing foolish before an audience. Many speakers are stiff and stilted because they insist on acting out the "image" they think other people have of them. They try to act as they think bankers, or industrialists, or physicians, or professors are supposed to act. As a result they hide themselves within a shell of artificiality, never letting the real person come through.

Assume the virtue of eagerness to communicate. Advance to your speaking position briskly but not hurriedly. Stand squarely on both feet. Look at your listeners. Actually see them as individuals—some of them, at least. One professional speaker insists that he always smiles at this moment of contact. Relax momentarily, as a diver does at the end of his board. Then, as the diver, gather your whole body to serve your purpose and begin speaking. From this moment on, let yourself go in response to an unqualified desire to be heard, understood, and believed.

Posture should be alert

You have been speaking all your life, yet now you are reading this book and probably taking a formal course in speech in order to improve yourself. Similarly, you have been sitting or standing all your life, yet now you need give some deliberate thought to the manner of your sitting and standing as part of your speech delivery.

As a rule, your posture should neither be rigid nor limp, for rigidity prevents both you and your listeners from participating comfortably in the communicative process, while limpness leads you to slouch on the lectern, suggesting to your hearers that you have little of importance to tell them. The best term to describe a desirable posture is alertness.

The alert speaker sits erectly but comfortably in his chair, knowing that there will be those who will "size him up" before he rises to speak. He walks to the speaker's stand with every visible sign of self respect and purposive confidence. Knowing that the entire carriage of his body depends on the foundation, he avoids standing with his weight on one foot or shifting his weight uneasily at periodic intervals. He may move about the platform as he feels necessary to emphasize a point, to work with visual aids, to draw closer to a segment of his audience, or to glance at notes, but he does not walk aimlessly back and forth nor shuttle uselessly between the lectern and a chalk board.

Good posture may be thought of as the visible expression of an inner poise, which in turn consists of mental and emotional balance and stability. Not only does alert posture communicate a sense of the speaker's poise to the audience, it also, as an assumed virtue, tends to foster the very feeling of purpose and confidence desired by the speaker. If you will control the behavior of your body, you have taken an important step toward controlling your mental and emotional behavior.

Gesture should be purposively communicative

While it is undoubtedly true that some people by nature "talk with their hands," more freely than others, and are therefore physically more fluent, facility in gesture can and should be cultivated by even the most restrained. While we often think of gesture only as communicative hand and arm movement, in truth it includes any significant action. Franklin Roosevelt was prevented from using his hands and arms at the speaker's stand, but communicated magnificently with his face, head, and torso.

Gestures, defined as any significant movement, may be divided into four categories. The first of these includes all *descriptive* gestures which signal such things as size, shape, or direction. A nod of the head, a meaningful glance, or a pointed finger may all indicate, "That way." *Emphatic* gestures are used to give stress to words and ideas, and may range from a fist banged against the table to a horizontal sweep of the finger or an affirmative motion of the head. *Suggestive* gestures are those which reveal feeling or atttiude, adding color to the uttered words. A scowl may suggest irritation or anger, a shrug of shoulders may indicate uncertainty or indifference, while a clenched fist can mean intensity of feeling. Finally, *symbolic* gestures are those which signal a specific meaning, some of which may be nearly as conventionalized as language. A raised palm held vertically means "stop," a thumb turned down is a sign of rejection. A shake of the head means negation. Many will recall that Casey at the plate silenced the crowd with a raised hand, while during World War II Churchill's famous two-fingered V for victory produced encouragement everywhere he went.

How much gesture should you use? It is, of course, possible for you to distract an audience by constant or exaggerated movement; as with language, restraint is often more effective than exaggeration. Yet if your gesture is honestly motivated and an integral part of your communicative behavior, and if it is appropriate to the audience and the occasion, you need not be concerned.

Visual aids should be integrated into the verbal context

Specific suggestions for the use of visual aids were made in the preceding chapter, necessitating at this point only a re-emphasis of the fact that they should be only a part of the total presentation. The speaker himself should dominate, *using* the aids rather than allowing them to replace him as the center of attention. Drawings, graphs, slides, and the like should not become a substitute for the speaker, but should be used to reinforce his message, adding to his words and actions their unique ability to dramatize and visualize an idea.

In using visual aids you will find that directing the attention of your hearers to the specific part of the display to be noticed is often vital. For instance, if you were showing the construction of an industrial hose having three plies, you would want to point out each ply with your finger or a pointer. Simply exhibiting a cross-section of the hose would not assure that the listeners had actually seen the several plies. You will want to indicate clearly exactly *what* is to be seen, and to discuss its significance as you go along.

Similarly, you will want to be sure to talk to your hearers rather than to the display, as some speakers do. Admittedly you must look at your exhibit to locate the sections you wish to emphasize and to help guide the attention of your listeners to it. But having oriented yourself, and perhaps having placed a pointer on the spot to be noticed, look at your hearers and direct your remarks to them, thereby continuing to maintain control of the situation. The speaker who breaks contact with his listeners has lost a vital part of his speaking power.

The only way you can get the most from visual helps is by rehearsing with them until you can use them effectively. Like any tool, the use of an exhibit demands skill gained from practice.

438

THE FARTHEST PERSON VISIBLE
SHOULD HEAR AND UNDERSTAND
YOU EASILY

It is clearly impossible for a man speaking to be *only* a voice or *only* a performing person. Voice and visible action are not separable, but are part of an organic whole, manifestations of a single personality which produce a total effect upon an audience. What has been said so far about physical action in speech delivery, therefore, cannot be divorced from consideration of voice and diction. Nor can what is to follow about your vocal delivery ignore physical activity.

The first and indispensable test of your utterance is whether it can be easily heard and understood, and without calling unfavorable attention to itself. If people cannot understand what you are saying, or if your utterance takes attention from your message, your speech communication suffers. Voice and diction should stir up desired meanings and not compete with communication by drawing attention to themselves.

The second test of your utterance is whether it adds depth of meaning and emotional color to the language you use. Powerful words spoken in feeble tones lose much of their force; ordinary thoughts may be adequately expressed in a pedestrian voice, but thoughts fraught with feeling must have appropriate expression if they are to be sensitively perceived.

It is not the province of this book to deal with matters of voice improvement or with articulatory problems. A pleasantly modulated and resonant voice is indeed an asset, as is clear and attractive diction. Yet most of us can speak to reasonably good effect with our normal voices, provided we take care to meet the demands of the larger communicative situation. If you have a speech problem, or if you are one who must have an excellent voice for professional reasons, you should talk with your instructor or consult one of the books recommended in the list of readings.

With these observations, let us take up some fundamental matters about vocal delivery, remembering that your voice reflects what you are.

Talk to people

Do not make the mistake of talking *at* an audience or *toward* an audience as if it were a mysterious being somehow independent of the individuals who comprise it. True, there is often a social facilitation of response as listeners affect one another, and you may find it possible to use such interaction to help achieve the response you seek. However, you are always conversing with individuals who have gathered to hear you, and the focus of your attention should be on those people. Only in this way will you naturally achieve the unaffected voice of good conversation rather than the stilted tones of some political orators.

Talking with people requires that you see them; your voice is quite likely to follow your gaze. Therefore, in the pause just before you begin speaking, look to your audience and *see somebody*. Let your gaze go to others, mentally noting what kinds of people they seem to be and whether they are attentive and ready to hear you. When both you and they are ready, you may begin. Start deliberately, as a rule speaking more slowly than normal, so that your opening words will not be lost while the hearers get accustomed to your unique speaking characteristics. You will quicken your pace as you warm to the occasion.

As you talk, or even during your initial scanning of the audience, locate those on the far fringes of the group. They are the ones most likely to have difficulty hearing and understanding you, and you must therefore devote special attention to reaching them. Note if they seem to be getting your message, and adjust your volume and projection as necessary—do not assume that a public address system automatically makes you understandable. If those along the outer edges can understand you comfortably, your speaking is probably satisfactory.

Your goal should be to speak conversationally with a relaxed voice, even though you will have to use more power than you would over a luncheon table. If you give the effect of shouting or straining you are not conversational. And if you speak with tension, your voice will tire easily. Tension and power are not synonymous, for tension strikes the throat and jaws, while power generates at the abdomen. You can best converse with greater volume than normal

440

by keeping your jaws relaxed and bringing your tones from your abdomen.

Speak with energy

Good conversation is not flat and colorless, but quite the opposite. When persons with zest and enthusiasm exchange ideas the speaking is vital, alive, and stimulating. Voices rise with excitement, or ebb with thoughtfulness; there are flashes of hurried fluency and moments of deliberate pause. People talking about things which interest them easily forget themselves and speak with spirit.

The best of these conversational qualities should be carried over into the delivery of a speech. To do so means that you must have enthusiasm, that you must be vitally interested, not only in the people to whom you are speaking, but in what you have to say. Enthusiasm will lead you to speak with vitality. It will color what you have to say. Every speech which makes a deep impression upon the hearers is a product of enthusiasm, not in the sense that the speaker is a table-thumper, but in the sense that he is aroused by ardent concern for what he is saying.

Enthusiasm, however, must be projected to the audience. This means that you must speak with force. Practiced speakers testify that they are often physically tired after a speech because they have expended a tremendous amount of energy in the very act of presenting their ideas. They are not necessarily loud, but they are forceful, intense, and animated.

You will find it helpful, therefore, to support your words with an amount of physical energy greater than you would normally use, and probably greater than you think is sufficient. You must translate your enthusiasm into audible signs that will carry it to your listeners. You must increase its physical magnitude. And if you do not *feel* enthusiasm, speaking with spirit will help you generate it, for the visible sign can be an important part of assuming the virtue.

Articulate clearly

Too many speakers tend toward fuzziness in their speech. They mismanage vowels, slur consonants, omit important word-endings, and often substitute one sound for another. "Pen" becomes "pin," "government" becomes "govement," "this" becomes "dis," and "for instance" comes out like "frinstance." Such speech is usually the product of either an inability to hear and understand the sounds of spoken English or sheer laziness, for the number of people who have speech disorders is but a small fraction of the whole.

The results, however, can be unfortunate. Listeners often fail to catch and understand parts of what is said; gaps, so far as they are concerned, therefore exist in the content. Even when no great loss in communication occurs, an unfavorable impression of the speaker develops because attention is drawn from what he is saying to the careless way in which he says it. To avoid these consequences, you should make it a point to be especially careful with the mechanics of your speaking before an audience. If your daily speaking is below an acceptable public standard, the need for diligent practice to improve is indicated, for daily habits cannot easily be put aside the moment one finds himself before an audience.

Listen to your own speaking—you can do it if you attend to the sounds you utter. Or use a tape recorder, transcribing your speaking not only at times of careful practice but in moments of ordinary and unconscious utterance as well. Listen objectively, determining the sounds you must improve, and then set about a discipline of improvement. Your instructor or a close friend can help you.

Listen to your vowels. Does "any" sound like "inny"? Listen to word endings. Does "going" sound like "goin"? Listen especially to key consonants, for they often are the sounds which identify words. Take the vowels from the word "consonant" itself—o, o, a—and you have a series of meaningless sounds. The consonants must be added if the word is to have sense as a significant language symbol. Can your listeners hear the difference between "goal" and "gold" *as you say the words?* Or between "debt" and "death"? Or "glow" and "grow"?

Distinctions between words like these must be clearly heard and understood by the last person visible in your audience. Therefore must you articulate clearly.

Achieve color and variety

Much of what you have already read in this chapter has stressed the importance of variety and color in the vocal delivery of your speech. Still, the topic deserves special attention, since it is entirely possible

442

for you to speak with some energy but without much variety. For this reason, you should identify the elements of speech which together create variety and color.

The *quality* of your voice is its timbre, the unique combination of fundamental tones and overtones which makes it different from most other voices. Your physical and emotional state can produce change in your vocal quality, for your voice is apt to be husky or thin in illness, strident or harsh under strain or tension, or hollow with fatigue. A person is normally at his vocal best when refreshed and relaxed. The average person has little voluntary control over the quality of his voice; it will communicate much of his feeling and intention unconsciously.

Time in speech refers to a combination of three variables which you can learn to use for communicative effect. *Rate* is the tempo of your speaking, whether it be fast or slow. *Duration* is the amount of time used to utter a tone, normally a vowel or vowel equivalent. Some things are uttered in a staccato, others demand that tones be held. *Pause* is the interval between words, phrases, or sentences. A common sin of inexperienced speakers is that they do not change these variables, but plod along with the monotony of a drum-beat. With a little practice you can learn to h-o-l-d your t-o-n-e-s for deliberate emphasis, to slow down or speed up according to the way your meaning should be stressed, and to pause without fearing silence. Varying the time of your utterance is one of the basic ways of achieving variety in speaking.

Together *intensity* and *loudness* make up the *force* of your speaking, although either element may be varied alone. Sometimes meaning is best expressed when a word is "squeezed" out, sometimes when it is allowed to roll off the tip of your tongue. Intensity refers to the pressure behind your speech; loudness indicates the volume. Some speakers can boom out to fill an auditorium with sound, having volume without energy; others can fire a whisper like an arrow. It is a mistake to assume that emphasis demands loudness or high intensity, for deliberate use of a faint voice or moderate power can often do better. Force sustained too long will tire an audience; seek variety.

Melody is the musical pattern of your voice, the rise and fall of pitch according to meaning intended. This rise and fall occur as either a *step*, when a word or phrase succeeds another on a different pitch, or as a *slide*, when a sound changes pitch during utterance. As with other vocal qualities, monotony of pitch is deadening. Some

443

speakers, however, fall into a patterned variety which is in itself objectionable, usually beginning each sentence on a high note and allowing the pitch to drop with tedious regularity. The melody of a conversational voice achieves meaningful variety without premeditation, but in public address the normal changes must sometimes be exaggerated. Changes which may seem normal to the speaker may be so faint at fifty feet as to be nearly imperceptible. Under such conditions, your conversational voice must be enlarged.

Although you should seek variety in utterance, it should not be forced or mechanical, but should come as the outer expression of inner feeling and intent. If you are mentally and emotionally prepared to speak, and if you will let yourself respond to thought and feeling, the probability is great that you will meet the demands of the occasion.

MAKE ANY QUESTION PERIOD AN INTEGRAL PART OF YOUR PRESENTATION

A question and answer period following either an informative or persuasive speech is becoming increasingly common, since it provides the audience with an opportunity to clear up any uncertainties concerning information covered or to raise doubts or objections which a persuasive speaker has not satisfactorily answered. The question and answer period can make for fuller understanding by the listeners.

Unfortunately the speaker too often sees the period only as an ordeal to be survived after he has successfully delivered his prepared speech. In consequence he fails to meet his questioners with the directness and purpose of the address, he allows the questions and answers to wander in any and all directions, and the period ends in a feeble last question to which is given a lame reply. It can be a disappointing anti-climax to an otherwise good talk. The original purpose of the speech has been forgotten by both speaker and listeners.

To avoid dissipating the effect of his speech, the speaker should take the question and answer period exactly for what it is, an added length of time for him to accomplish the purpose of his speaking. In answering questions he should aim for the same response which he sought in the speech proper. If his speech purpose was to get his listeners to understand the photographic process used to take pictures of the moon from a space craft, his answers should help achieve that purpose. If his purpose was to get his listeners to approve an amendment to the constitution of their professional society, his responses should provide additional persuasion to that end. And if his speech purpose was to create good will for his corporation, his answers should promote good will in line with the theme of his speech.

You will find that a question and answer period will help you accomplish the final principle of good communication listed at the end of Chapter 2. To a significant degree you will be able to verify the success of your speech and perhaps increase that success by dealing with the questions of your listeners, for the prior provides you with valuable feedback. This is the reason successful salesmen often welcome a prospect's objections—objections are not only a sign of interest but they provide the salesman a means of helping the prospect come to a favorable decision. You should deal with a question period in the same way.

A major element in answering questions successfully, therefore, lies in your skill in providing answers which relate to what you said in the speech, and which re-emphasize your purpose. In the following suggested sequence for answering a question, note that the final step calls for you to tie your reply to the speech purpose.

1. Listen carefully to the question, making every effort to understand the intent of the questioner. Many answers go wide of the mark, leaving dissatisfaction among the listeners, because the speaker has replied to what he *thinks* was asked instead of to the real question. If you are in doubt about the question, repeat it in your own words for verification. If it is complex or confused, elect to answer one part at a time or have it simplified. But listen before you speak.

2. Make sure the entire audience hears and understands the question. If the questioner has not been heard by everyone, have him repeat the question so all can hear it, or repeat it yourself. Everyone should understand what you are replying to, for your answer will not make good sense to those who have not heard the question. In repeating a question, never belittle either the question or the questioner unless you are certain the intent is to heckle you.

3. Evaluate the question quickly. Elsewhere I have indicated that not all questions are motivated by a genuine desire for in-

formation. Some may reflect an attempt by the questioner to gain recognition from others, some to cover up a failure to listen carefully, some to heckle you, and so on. You will find it useful to make a quick appraisal of the character of the question to guide the nature of your reply. Sincere questions merit honest answers; troublesome questioners may be skillfully ignored or tactfully criticized. Whenever you are not sure, the question should be handled as honest. Many questions designed to embarrass you are also best given a straightforward reply. When the questioner's intention is obviously unfriendly, however, a rebuff skillfully delivered may be called for. At a mid-Western college public health symposium a Dr. Brown appeared as one of the speakers. Afterward a young questioner scornfully inquired, "Isn't it true that you are a veterinarian?" The doctor replied winningly, "Yes. Are you ill?"

4. Answer the question directly and to the point. Not often will it be desirable to return an ironic or evasive reply, and under most circumstances your listeners will appreciate a forthright answer. *Each answer is a brief one-point speech*, and may be handled as such, the amount of development depending upon the importance of the matter. If you do not know the answer, say so, but if possible try to arrange to furnish an answer later.

Answers to questions, like the speech as a whole, should be directed to all the members of the audience. You should never allow a dialogue to develop between you and a questioner, for you will quickly lose the interest and attention of every other listener, and thus lose control of the situation. To maintain control and keep sustained attention, it is often advisable to receive the questions yourself, rather than allowing the chairman of the meeting preside over the question and answer period.

5. Relate your answer to the response you seek. Only by doing this can you bring a sense of organization to the question period and utilize it to advance your purpose. You must show that your answer relates to one of your speech points or otherwise provides additional reason for responding in the desired way.

Suppose a speaker has been talking to a group of civic leaders interested in attracting new industry to the community. His purpose is to get his hearers to understand that a company looks for a healthy and balanced business climate when seeking a location for a new plant. Afterward he responds to questions, one of which is:

Q: "How much is a company impressed by the vigor with which a local community seeks new enterprises?"

The speaker must answer the question, and then relate his answer to the central idea and purpose of his speech. His reply might be this:

A: "Any company looking for a new plant location will be impressed by the initiative and vigor of community leaders in selling their community. But such vigor may come from desperation as well as foresight. A company is more apt to be favorably impressed by the way in which the community has treated the industries already located there. The existing industries are the best indication of a healthy and balanced business climate, and I would like you to remember that the total climate is what an expanding corporation wants to examine."

The following example represents a type of question and answer frequently heard after a persuasive talk.

Q: "What colors does the product come in?"

A: "It comes in red, blue, and green. (The speaker has answered the question, but if he stops he has not related his reply to his purpose, so he continues.) One of these shades will blend well with your present decorative scheme, and all of them are fade-proof, so it simply is a matter of choosing the one you like best." (The speaker has related the reply to his purpose, hoping for a favorable decision.)

During a long question and answer period, to take every answer back to the point and purpose of the talk may become tedious. Under such conditions the speaker will employ the technique as part of every second or third answer, trying also to avoid monotony by varying the length of his replies.

6. At the end of the question period, make a final summary. When questions begin to come slowly the time to end the period is at hand. Rather than letting the event run down, it is better to announce, "We'll have time for one more question," and let the reply be your last. However, do not stop with that answer, but end the whole presentation with a final summary. You may summarize by bringing together the gist of the questions and answers in a final wrap-up, or you may in effect repeat what you said at the conclusion of your speech. Either way, your purpose is to round out both the speech and the question period as a single unit, leaving your central idea with the listeners and encouraging the response you set out to achieve.

One final word. During your speech everything will not happen exactly as you had foreseen or planned, and you must learn to

447

expect the unexpected. During the 1960 Presidential campaign, Richard Nixon had to be pulled from beneath a set of floodlights which had started to fall. L. S. Buckmaster, former President of the United Rubber Workers had one speech interrupted by an earthquake, another by an explosion in a near-by power plant. Such events are unlikely to happen to you, but you may be startled to see the little old lady in the front row turn off her hearing aid and pull it from her ear! Even more likely, you may have a sudden draft blow your notes from the speaker's stand. When the unexpected happens, your audience expects you to behave like a normal human being and do whatever seems most appropriate at the moment. You are not on exhibition, but are conversing with a group, and behavior which would be reasonable in an analogous conversational situation would likely be appropriate on the platform.

Suggested Readings

Here is a list of readings which will add depth to the principles and ideas treated in this book. In some cases I have suggested an entire volume whose contents are relevant, in others I have simply indicated a chapter or chapters. A few books appear in the readings for several chapters, different sections being cited in each case. And although the journals and periodicals furnish much which is worth reading, I have not attempted to include such material because the list would be too long for even a representative sampling. Here, then, are some places to look if you wish to study further.

Chapter I

Marting, Elizabeth, Robert E. Findley, and Ann Ward, editors, *Effective Communication on the Job,* revised ed. New York: American Management Association, 1963.

Newcomb, Robert and Marg Sammons, *Employee Communications in Action.* New York: Harper & Row, Publishers, 1961.

Peters, R. W., *Communication Within Industry.* New York: Harper & Row, Publishers, 1950.

Pigors, Paul, *Effective Communication in Industry.* New York: National Association of Manufacturers, 1949.

Redding, W. Charles and George A. Sanborn, *Business and Industrial Communication: A Source Book.* New York: Harper & Row, Publishers, 1964. Valuable not only for the selected journal articles, but for the excellent sections written especially for the book.

Redfield, Charles E., *Communication in Management.* Chicago: University of Chicago Press, 1958.

Roethlisberger, F. J., *Management and Morale,* especially Chapter 6,

"Of Words and Men," on the verbal environment of managers. Cambridge: Harvard University Press, 1943.

Thayer, Lee O., *Administrative Communication*. Homewood, Ill.: Richard D. Irwin, Inc., 1961.

Chapter II

Berlo, David K., *The Process of Communication*. New York: Holt, Rinehart and Winston, Inc., 1960.

Harnack, R. Victor and Thorrel B. Fest, *Group Discussion: Theory and Practice*, Chapter 1, "The Individual vs. the Group: A Conflict in Communications," Chapter 15, "Communication Principles." New York: Appleton-Century-Crofts, 1964.

Leavitt, Harold J., *Managerial Psychology*, revised edition. Chicago: The University of Chicago Press, 1964.

Miller, Gerald R., *Speech Communication: A Behavioral Approach*. Indianapolis: The Bobbs-Merrill Company, Inc., 1966.

Zelko, Harold P. and Harold J. O'Brien, *Management-Employee Communication in Action*. Cleveland: Howard Allen, Inc., 1957.

Chapter III

Bass, Bernard M., *Organizational Psychology*. Boston: Allyn and Bacon, Inc., 1965.

Brembeck, Winston L. and William S. Howell, *Persuasion*, Chapter 6, "The Social Basis of Persuasion." New York: Prentice-Hall, Inc., 1952.

Maslow, A. H., *Motivation and Personality*, Chapter 5, "A Theory of Human Motivation." New York; Harper & Row, Publishers, 1954.

Minnick, Wayne C., *The Art of Persuasion*, Chapter 8, "Winning Belief and Action Through Wants and Values." Boston: Houghton Mifflin Company, 1957.

Oliver, Robert T., *The Psychology of Persuasive Speech*, Chapter 3, "Human Motivation." and Chapter 8, "Identification." New York: Longmans, Green and Company, 1957.

Shaw, Steven J. and Joseph W. Thompson, eds., *Salesmanship: Modern Viewpoints on Personal Communication*. New York: Henry Holt and Company, Inc., 1960.

Chapter IV

Brigance, William Norwood, *Speech: Its Techniques and Disciplines in a Free Society*, second ed., Foreword, "Why Speak? Who Listens?" New York: Appleton-Century-Crofts, Inc., 1961.

450

Brown, Charles T. and Charles Van Riper, *Speech and Man*, Englewood Cliffs, N.J.: Prentice-Hall, Inc., 1966.

Haiman, Franklin S., *Group Leadership and Democratic Action*, Chapter 5, "The Group Leader as a Person." Boston: Houghton Mifflin Company, 1951.

Minnick, Wayne C., *The Art of Persuasion*, Chapter 12, "The Ethics of Persuasion." Boston: Houghton Mifflin Company, 1957.

Nilson, Thomas R., *The Ethics of Communication*. Indianapolis: The Bobbs-Merrill Company, Inc., 1966.

Oliver, Robert T. and Dominick A. Barbara, *The Healthy Mind in Communion and Communication*. Springfield, Ill.: Charles C. Thomas, Publisher, 1962.

Rogers, Carl, *On Becoming a Person*. Boston: Houghton Mifflin Company, 1960.

Sarett, Alma Johnson, Lew Sarett and William Trufant Foster, *Basic Principles of Speech*, fourth ed., Chapter 3, "The Person Who Speaks," Boston: Houghton Mifflin Company, 1966.

Chapter V

Nichols, Ralph G. and Thomas R. Lewis, *Listening and Speaking*. Dubuque, Iowa: William C. Brown Company, 1954.

——— and Leonard A. Stevens, *Are You Listening?* New York: McGraw-Hill Book Company, Inc., 1957.

Walter, Otis M. and Robert L. Scott, *Thinking and Speaking*, Chapter 7, "Listening Analytically." New York: The Macmillan Company, 1962.

Chapter VI

Bonner, Hubert, *Group Dynamics*, Chapter 9, "Human Relations in Industry." New York: The Ronald Press Company, 1959.

Chase, Stuart, *Roads to Agreement*. New York: Harper & Row, Publishers, 1951.

Conway, Lawrence V., *Customer Relations*. Chicago: American Savings and Loan Institute Press, 1962. Although written for savings and loan people, much of the material is applicable elsewhere.

Maier, Norman R. F., *Principles of Human Relations*. New York: John Wiley & Sons, Inc., 1952. The scope of this book is broader than the title would indicate. It centers on human relations training, but extends to group decision-making and non-directive counseling.

Reilly, William J., *Successful Human Relations*. New York: Harper & Row, Publishers, 1952. Recognizes the use of force in human affairs, unlike most treatments of human relations. Nevertheless, it presents a useful formula for persuasion.

Chapter VII

Bois, J. Samuel, *Explorations in Awareness*. New York: Harper & Row, Publishers, 1957.

Chase, Stuart, *Power of Words*. New York: Harcourt, Brace and Company, 1954.

Haney, William V., *Communication: Patterns and Incidents*. Homewood, Ill.: Richard D. Irwin, Inc., 1960. Rich in illustrative material.

Hayakawa, S. I., *Language in Thought and Action*. New York: Harcourt, Brace and Company, 1949.

Lee, Irving J., *How to Talk With People*. New York: Harper & Row, Publishers, 1952.

——— and Laura Lee, *Handling Barriers in Communication*. New York: Harper & Row, Publishers, 1957. A teaching handbook which applies language principles to specific industrial communication problems.

Chapter VIII

Bingham, Walter and Bruce Moore, *How to Interview*. New York: Harper & Row, Publishers, 1941.

Fear, Richard A., *The Evaluation Interview*. New York: McGraw-Hill Book Company, Inc., 1958. Especially useful in its treatment of the interpretation of data.

Fenlason, Ann, *Essentials in Interviewing*, revised edition. New York: Harper & Row, Publishers, 1962.

Harral, Stewart, *Keys to Successful Interviewing*. Norman, Okla.: University of Oklahoma Press, 1954.

Kahn, Robert L. and Charles F. Cannell, *The Dynamics of Interviewing*. New York: John Wiley & Sons, Inc., 1957. Strong on motivation and communicative interaction.

Maier, Norman R. F., *The Appraisal Interview*. New York: John Wiley & Sons, Inc., 1958.

Richardson, Stephen A., Barbara Snell Dohrenwend and David Klein, *Interviewing: Its Forms and Functions*. New York: Basic Books, Inc., 1965. Concerned with interviewing in the social sciences.

Sullivan, Harry Stack, *The Psychiatric Interview*, ed. Helen Swich Perry and Mary Ladd Gawel. New York: W. W. Norton & Company, Inc., 1954.

Weinland, James D. and Margaret V. Gross, *Personnel Interviewing*. New York: The Ronald Press Company, 1952.

Chapter IX

Braden, Waldo and Earnest Brandenburg, *Oral Decision-Making.* New York: Harper & Row, Publishers, 1955.

Clark, Charles H., *Brainstorming.* New York: Doubleday and Company, 1958.

Cortright, Rupert L. and George L. Hinds, *Creative Discussion.* New York: The Macmillan Company, 1959.

Haiman, Franklin S., *Group Leadership and Democratic Action.* Boston: Houghton Mifflin Company, 1951.

Harnack, R. Victor and Thorrel B. Fest, *Group Discussion: Theory and Practice.* New York: Appleton-Century-Crofts, 1964.

Keltner, John W., *Group Discussion Processes.* New York: Longmans, Green and Company, 1957.

Maier, Norman R. F., *Problem-Solving Discussions and Conferences.* New York: McGraw-Hill Book Company, Inc., 1963.

—— and John T. Hayes, *Creative Management.* New York: John Wiley & Sons, Inc., 1962. Useful on the place of the conference in organizational management.

Phillips, Gerald M., *Communication and the Small Group.* Indianapolis: The Bobbs-Merrill Company, Inc., 1966.

Rapoport, Anatol, *Fights, Games, and Debates.* Ann Arbor: University of Michigan Press, 1960.

Sattler, William M. and N. Edd Miller, *Discussion and Conference.* New York: Prentice-Hall, Inc., 1954.

Snell, Frank, *How to Hold a Better Meeting.* New York: Harper & Row, Publishers, 1958.

Chapter X

Brigance, William Norwood, *Speech Composition,* second ed., Chapter 3, "The Speech Purpose." New York: Appleton-Century-Crofts, Inc., 1953.

——, *Speech: Its Techniques and Disciplines in a Free Society,* second ed., Chapter 24, "Dynamic Persuasion in an Industrial Society." New York: Appleton-Century-Crofts, Inc., 1961.

Phillips, David C. and Jack Hall Lamb, *Speech as Communication.* Boston: Allyn and Bacon, Inc., 1966.

Walter, Otis M., *Speaking to Inform and Persuade.* New York: The Macmillan Company, 1966.

Chapter XI

Clevenger, Jr., Theodore, *Audience Analysis.* Indianapolis: The Bobbs-Merrill Company, Inc., 1966.

Hegarty, Edward J., *How to Write a Speech*. New York: McGraw-Hill Book Company, Inc., 1951. Practical advice based on industrial experience.

McFarland, Kenneth, *Eloquence in Public Speaking*. Englewood Cliffs, N.J.: Prentice-Hall, Inc., 1961.

Zelko, Harold P., *How to Become a Successful Speaker*. New London, Conn.: National Foremen's Institute, 1950.

Chapter XII

Borden, Richard C., *Public Speaking as Listeners Like It*. New York: Harper & Row, Publishers, 1935. An early and popular approach to functional public speaking.

Monroe, Alan H., *Principles and Types of Speech*, fifth ed., Chapters 14–17. Chicago: Scott, Foresman and Company, 1962.

Chapter XIII

Braden, Waldo W., *Public Speaking: The Essentials*, Chapter 5, "Selling Yourself to Your Listeners," and Chapter 8, "How to Be Interesting," New York: Harper & Row, Publishers, 1966.

Loney, Glenn M., *Briefing and Conference Techniques*, Section 7, "Audio-Visual Aids for Speakers." New York: McGraw-Hill Book Company, Inc., 1959.

Monroe, Alan H., *Principles and Types of Speech*, fifth ed., Chapter 12, "Supporting Main Points." Chapter 18, "Wording the Speech," Chicago: Scott, Foresman and Company, 1962.

Chapter XIV

Braden, Waldo W., *Public Speaking: The Essentials*, Chapter 6, "Effective Delivery." New York: Harper & Row, Publishers, 1966.

Casey, Robert S., *Oral Communication of Technical Information*. New York: Reinhold Book Division, 1958.

King, Robert and Eleanor DiMichael, *Improving Articulation and Voice*. New York: The Macmillan Company, 1966.

Ross, Raymond S., *Speech Communication*, Chapter 11, "Questions and Interruptions." Englewood Cliffs, N.J.: Prentice-Hall, Inc., 1965.

Wilson, John F. and Carroll C. Arnold, *Public Speaking as a Liberal Art*, Chapter 11, "Delivery." Boston: Allyn and Bacon, Inc., 1964. Excellent treatment of the delivery of a speech.

INDEX

455

Index

Index

Index

Index

Index

Index

Index

Index

Repetition, of detail, in speeches, 394-396

and understanding, 209

Reports, and evaluations, 203-205

Reputation, 180

and communication, 71

Research, speech, 344-345

Resistance, in interviewing, 230-232, 242-243

Respect, 170-171

of rights and opinions, 181

Respondents, understanding of, 49-50

Responsibility, acceptance of, 127-128

and communication, 11

Restatement, 394-396

Revenge, 97

Reviewing remarks, 150, 151

Rhetoric, 410-416

Rhetorical questions, 414

Richards, I. A., 410

Richardson, Stephen, 452

Right, sense of being, 171-172

Rights, respect for, 181

Rockefeller, David, 337

Roethlisberger, F. J., 157, 449

Rogers, Carl, 153, 451

Role, importance of, and human relations, 162

Ross, Raymond S., 454

Rosten, Leo, 390

Rules, exceptions to, 110

Rules of Order (Roberts), 297

Rumors, combating, untrue, 13

Sahagian, Herman D., 333

St. John, Seymour, 111

Sales interview, 219-220

Sammons, Marg, 33, 449

Sanborn, George A., 449

Sarett, Alma Johnson, 104, 451

Sarett, Lew, 104, 451

Satisfaction, demonstrating, 352

Satisfaction phase, 379-380

Sattler, William M., 149, 453

Saturday Review, 56, 116

Schein, Edgar H., 163

Scott, Robert J., 451

Scoutten, Eldon F., 415

Security, 76

Self-appraisal, 105-108

Self-preservation, 76

Self-respect, 75

Seligman, Daniel, 316

"Sell" meeting, 293, 295, 314

Semantics, 200-209

Semi-formal meetings, 313-314

Sender, role of, in communicative process, 20-22, 24

Sensation, 66-67

Sensory pleasure, 74

Sequence, relationship with idea, 416-419

Service clubs, speaking at, 315-316

Shaw, Steven J., 450

Showmanship, use of, 358-359, 406-408

Silence, and listening, 135

Simplicity, 345

Situation(s), analyzing, in interviews, 226-228

arousing audience to, 366-367

an awareness of, 367

behavior in, 60-61

doubt in, 367-368

perception in, 364

Sligh, Charles M., Jr., 361

"Small talk," 157

Smile, effect of, 176-177

Smith, Gordon, 175

Snell, Frank, 453

Snobbishness, 140

Snyder, John L., Jr., 401-402

Social groups, participation in, 36-37

Social matrix, and communication process, 36-48

Social needs, 77-93

Society, defined, 77

growth and progress, 112

Solution(s), criteria for, 276

effecting, 278

to problems, 183-184, 352

Sound decision, 115-120

Sound judgment, 115-120

Spare time, use of, 149-151

Speaker, audience, adaptation to, 328-329

development of, 103-105

obligation of, 320-323

qualifications of, revealing, 387-388

quality of, 119-120

responsibilities of, 58-59, 103-131

seeks excellence, 114-131

sympathy of audience with, 427-428

464

Index

Index